NATIONAL ACADEMY PRESS

Publisher for The National Academies

National Academy of Sciences ◆ National Academy of Engineering ◆ Institute of Medicine ◆ National Research Council

Leading the World in Science, Technology, and Health

Visit our web site at

www.nap.edu

Use the form on the reverse of this card to order additional copies, or order online and receive a 20% discount.

Working Families and Growing Kids: Caring for Children and Adolescents

ORDER CARD
(Customers in North America Only)

Use this card to order additional copies of **Working Families and Growing Kids**. All orders must be prepaid. Please add $4.50 for shipping and handling for the first copy ordered and $0.95 for each additional copy. If you live in CA, DC, FL, MD, MO, TX, or Canada, add applicable sales tax or GST. Prices apply only in the United States, Canada, and Mexico and are subject to change without notice.

____ I am enclosing a U.S. check or money order.

____ Please charge my VISA/MasterCard/American Express account.

Number: _____

Expiration date: _____

Signature: _____

FOUR EASY WAYS TO ORDER

- **Electronically:** Order from our secure website at: www.nap.edu
- **By phone:** Call toll-free 1-888-624-8422 or (202) 334-3313 or call your favorite bookstore.
- **By fax:** Copy the order card and fax to (202) 334-2451.
- **By mail:** Return this card with your payment to NATIONAL ACADEMIES PRESS, 500 Fifth Street NW, Washington, DC 20001.

All international customers please contact National Academies Press for export prices and ordering information.

PLEASE SEND ME:

Qty.	Code	Title	Price
____	FAMPRE	Working Families and Growing Kids	$59.00

Subtotal	____
Shipping	____
Tax	____
Total	____

Please print.

Name _____

Address _____

City _____ State _____ Zip Code _____

8958

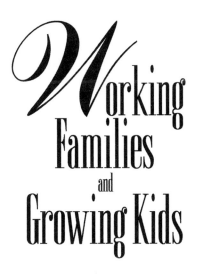

Working Families and Growing Kids

Caring for Children and Adolescents

Committee on Family and Work Policies

Eugene Smolensky and Jennifer Appleton Gootman, *editors*

Board on Children, Youth, and Families
Division of Behavioral and Social Sciences and Education

NATIONAL RESEARCH COUNCIL
INSTITUTE OF MEDICINE
OF THE NATIONAL ACADEMIES

THE NATIONAL ACADEMIES PRESS
Washington, D.C.
www.nap.edu

THE NATIONAL ACADEMIES PRESS • 500 Fifth Street, N.W. • Washington, DC 20001

NOTICE: The project that is the subject of this report was approved by the Governing Board of the National Research Council, whose members are drawn from the councils of the National Academy of Sciences, the National Academy of Engineering, and the Institute of Medicine. The members of the committee responsible for the report were chosen for their special competences and with regard for appropriate balance.

This study was supported by the Foundation for Child Development, the Ford Foundation, and the David and Lucile Packard Foundation. Any opinions, findings, conclusions, or recommendations expressed in this publication are those of the author(s) and do not necessarily reflect the views of the organizations or agencies that provided support for the project.

Library of Congress Cataloging-in-Publication Data

Workshop on Caring for Infants and Toddlers (2001 : Washington, D.C.)
  Working families and growing kids : caring for children and adolescents / Committee on Family and Work Policies ; Eugene Smolensky and Jennifer Appleton Gootman, editors.
    p. cm.
  "Board on Children, Youth, and Families, Division of Behavioral and Social Sciences and Education." "This study was supported by Contract/Grant No. XXX between the National Academy of Sciences and the Foundation for Child Development, the Ford Foundation, and the David and Lucile Packard Foundation." "This report is a product of the Committee on Family and Work Policies, a project of the National Research Council (NRC) and the Institute of Medicine (IOM)"—P. .
  A report based on presentations from a one-day October 2001 Workshop on Caring for Infants and Toddlers convened by the Committee, with additional data from other researchers and consultants. Includes bibliographical references and index.
  ISBN 0-309-08703-1 (hardcover) — ISBN 0-309-52587-X (PDF)
  1. Child welfare—United States—Congresses. 2. Children of working parents—Care—United States. 3. School-age child care—United States—Congresses. 4. Child development—United States—Congresses. 5. Work and family—Government policy—United States—Congresses. I. Smolensky, Eugene. II. Gootman, Jennifer Appleton. III. Committee on Family and Work Policies (U.S.) IV. National Research Council (U.S.). Board on Children, Youth, and Families. V. National Research Council (U.S.). Division of Behavioral and Social Sciences and Education. VI. Title.
  HV741.W69 2001
  362.7'0973—dc22
                                            2003015125

Additional copies of this report are available from the National Academies Press, 500 Fifth Street, N.W., Lockbox 285, Washington, DC 20055; (800) 624-6242 or (202) 334-3313 (in the Washington metropolitan area); Internet, http://www.nap.edu

Suggested citation: National Research Council and Institute of Medicine. (2003). *Working Families and Growing Kids: Caring for Children and Adolescents*. Committee on Family and Work Policies. Eugene Smolensky and Jennifer A. Gootman, eds. Board on Children, Youth, and Families, Division of Behavioral and Social Sciences and Education. Washington, DC: The National Academies Press.

THE NATIONAL ACADEMIES
Advisers to the Nation on Science, Engineering, and Medicine

The **National Academy of Sciences** is a private, nonprofit, self-perpetuating society of distinguished scholars engaged in scientific and engineering research, dedicated to the furtherance of science and technology and to their use for the general welfare. Upon the authority of the charter granted to it by the Congress in 1863, the Academy has a mandate that requires it to advise the federal government on scientific and technical matters. Dr. Bruce M. Alberts is president of the National Academy of Sciences.

The **National Academy of Engineering** was established in 1964, under the charter of the National Academy of Sciences, as a parallel organization of outstanding engineers. It is autonomous in its administration and in the selection of its members, sharing with the National Academy of Sciences the responsibility for advising the federal government. The National Academy of Engineering also sponsors engineering programs aimed at meeting national needs, encourages education and research, and recognizes the superior achievements of engineers. Dr. Wm. A. Wulf is president of the National Academy of Engineering.

The **Institute of Medicine** was established in 1970 by the National Academy of Sciences to secure the services of eminent members of appropriate professions in the examination of policy matters pertaining to the health of the public. The Institute acts under the responsibility given to the National Academy of Sciences by its congressional charter to be an adviser to the federal government and, upon its own initiative, to identify issues of medical care, research, and education. Dr. Harvey V. Fineberg is president of the Institute of Medicine.

The **National Research Council** was organized by the National Academy of Sciences in 1916 to associate the broad community of science and technology with the Academy's purposes of furthering knowledge and advising the federal government. Functioning in accordance with general policies determined by the Academy, the Council has become the principal operating agency of both the National Academy of Sciences and the National Academy of Engineering in providing services to the government, the public, and the scientific and engineering communities. The Council is administered jointly by both Academies and the Institute of Medicine. Dr. Bruce M. Alberts and Dr. Wm. A. Wulf are chair and vice chair, respectively, of the National Research Council.

www.national-academies.org

vi

Acknowledgments

This report is a product of the Committee on Family and Work Policies, a project of the National Research Council (NRC) and the Institute of Medicine (IOM). The 15-member committee met over an 18-month period to review and evaluate the science of early child and adolescent development and its application to policies and benefits that encourage, support, or require parents to participate in the paid labor force. The funding for this project was provided by the Foundation for Child Development, the Ford Foundation, the David and Lucile Packard Foundation, and NRC internal funds.

Beyond the expertise and hard work of the committee, we were fortunate to have many leaders in the field enthusiastically participate in this project. These individuals shared their knowledge and years of experience as researchers, evaluators, practitioners, policy makers, and funders. We are thankful for their time and their intellectual insights.

In October 2001 the committee convened a one-day Workshop on Caring for Infants and Toddlers. Participants included leading social scientists, researchers, economists, business leaders, policy makers, and funders: Sanders Korenman, Baruch College; Ann Segal, David and Lucile Packard Foundation; Suzanne Bianchi, University of Maryland, College Park; Harriet Presser, University of Maryland, College Park; Jody Heymann, Harvard University; Ross Thompson, University of Nebraska; Gina Adams, The Urban Institute; Ann Collins, National Center for Children and Poverty; Toni Porter, Bank Street College of Education; Jane Waldfogel, Columbia University; Donna Klein, Marriott International, Inc.; Ellen Bravo, 9to5; and Joan Lombardi, The Children's Project.

In addition to these formal presentations, a number of individuals were consulted in the development of this report, and we also wish to acknowledge their support and assistance. They include: Greg Duncan, Northwestern University; Jean Flor, University of Wisconsin; Dana Friedman, Bright Horizons Family Solutions; Ellen Galinsky, Families and Work Institute; Michael Grapkowski, New York University; Virginia Knox, Manpower Demonstration Research Corporation; Andrew London, Syracuse University; Heather Lord, University of Wisconsin, Madison; Ann Meier, University of Wisconsin, Madison; Lana Nenide, Wisconsin Center for Education Research; Connie Nickels, University of Wisconsin; Jacob Strand, University of Wisconsin, Madison; and Thomas Weisner, University of California, Los Angeles.

The committee worked with a number of consultants who helped prepare background material or data that was incorporated into this report: Jay Bainbridge, Columbia University School of Public Health; Dan Blanchette, University of North Carolina, Chapel Hill; Wen-Jui Han, Columbia University; JoAnn Hsueh, New York University; Angela Odoms-Young, University of Illinois, Urbana Champaign; and Margery Leveen Sher, Caliber Associates, Inc. and Fred & Sher.

This report has been reviewed in draft form by individuals chosen for their diverse perspectives and technical expertise, in accordance with procedures approved by the Report Review Committee of the NRC. The purpose of this independent review is to provide candid and critical comments that will assist the institution in making the published report as sound as possible and to ensure that the report meets institutional standards for objectivity, evidence, and responsiveness to the study charge. The review comments and draft manuscript remain confidential to protect the integrity of the deliberative process.

We thank the following individuals for their participation in the review of this report: Gina Adams, The Urban Institute, Washington, DC; Elizabeth K. Briody, General Motors, Troy, Michigan; Laurie T. Charest, Human Resources, University of North Carolina, Chapel Hill; Janet Currie, Department of Economics, University of California, Los Angeles; Mark Greenberg, Center for Law and Social Policy, Washington, DC; Aletha C. Huston, Department of Human Ecology, University of Texas at Austin; R. Duncan Luce, School of Social Sciences, University of California, Irvine; and Barbara (Bobbi) Wolfe, School of Public Affairs, University of Wisconsin-Madison.

Although the reviewers listed above have provided many constructive comments and suggestions, they were not asked to endorse the conclusions or recommendations, nor did they see the final draft of the report before its release. The review of this report was overseen by Timothy M. Smeeding, Center for Policy Research, University of Syracuse and Lyle V. Jones, L.L. Thurstone Psychometric Laboratory, University of North Carolina, Chapel Hill. Appointed by the National Research Council, they were responsible for making certain that an independent examination of this report was carried out in accordance with institutional procedures and that all review comments were carefully considered. Responsibility for the final content of this report rests entirely with the authoring committee and the institution.

The committee wishes to recognize the important contributions and support provided by several individuals connected to the NRC and the IOM. We thank the members of the Board on Children, Youth, and Families, under the leadership of Michael Cohen, and the Committee on Adolescent Health and Development, under the leadership of Robert Blum. We also thank Harvey Fineburg, IOM president; Susanne Stoiber, IOM executive officer; Michael Feuer, executive director of the NRC's Division of Behavioral and Social Sciences and Education; Jane Ross, director of the Center for Economic and Social Sciences; and Susan Cummins, director of the Board on Children, Youth, and Families, for their steadfast support of the project and their critical review of drafts of the report. Also, we appreciate the support of Michele Kipke, former director of the Board on Children, Youth, and Families for helping develop this project.

We appreciate Eugenia Grohman, associate director for reports of DBASSE, Christine McShane, editor, and Kirsten Sampson Snyder, reports officer, who patiently worked with us through several revisions and who provided superb editorial assistance. Vanee Vines of the National Academies' Office of News and Public Information provided advice and assistance with report dissemination.

Finally, it is important to acknowledge the contributions of the committee staff who worked on this report. Amy Gawad, research associate, played an invaluable role in helping manage the committee process and collecting, summarizing, and organizing background materials. Elizabeth Townsend (from July 2002) and Meredith Madden (until June 2002), senior project assistants, did a superb job of managing the numerous and often complicated administrative and research responsibilities.

Eugene Smolensky, *Chair*
Jennifer A. Gootman, *Study Director*
Committee on Family and Work Policies

Contents

EXECUTIVE SUMMARY   1
1   Setting the Stage   11

PART I: WORK, FAMILY, AND CHILD CARE TRENDS   21
2   Work and Family Trends   23
3   Trends in the Care of Children   42

PART II: IMPLICATIONS FOR THE DEVELOPMENT
         OF CHILDREN AND ADOLESCENTS   65
4   Maternal Employment and the Family Environment   67
5   Effects of Child Care   99
6   Parental Employment and Adolescent Development   178
7   Effects of Welfare Reform   199

PART III: SUPPORTS FOR WORKING FAMILIES   227
8   Public Policies to Support Working Families   229
9   Findings and Next Steps   260

REFERENCES   281

BIOGRAPHICAL SKETCHES   327

INDEX   335

xi

Executive Summary

hanging parental work patterns are transforming family life. Among the many transformations that have occurred in the American family over the past 30 years, few are as dramatic as the increased rates of paid employment among mothers with children. From 1970 to 2000, the overall maternal labor force participation rate rose from 38 to 68 percent; for mothers with the youngest children, birth to age 3, this rate rose from 24 to 57 percent. This trend has held for mothers in a wide variety of circumstances—first-time mothers and never-married mothers, for example—and for all groups, regardless of family income, education, race and ethnicity, or place of residence.

During this same period, use of nonparental child care also increased dramatically, taking place in a variety of child care arrangements, including child care centers, family child care, care by family members, neighbors and friends, and other organized activities. Many more children and adolescents are spending much more of their time in the care of adults other than their parents than did young people in the past.

This dramatic transformation of work and family life in the United States has brought many benefits to society, but a significant challenge remains: a large percentage of the 35 million children and adolescents ages birth to age 14 with working mothers are in a child care arrangement with someone other than their parents for an average of 22 to 40 hours a week—amounting to nearly 1 billion hours these children spend in out-of-home care each week.

Substantial progress has been made in the past 15 years in determining

1

the effects of child care on children's cognitive and social functioning. If children and adolescents are exposed to high-quality care, their development can be significantly enhanced, benefiting them and society as well. The benefits of early childhood educational interventions and of after-school programs for early adolescents, particularly for children and young people from low-income families, have helped persuade municipal governments, state legislatures, and the federal government to invest more in these programs. However, society has not taken full advantage of the opportunities child care provides. Many children and adolescents spend long hours, often at early ages, away from their parents in unstimulating, mediocre care.

COMMITTEE CHARGE AND SCOPE

The Committee on Family and Work Policies was established by the Board on Children, Youth, and Families with support from the Foundation for Child Development, the Ford Foundation, and the David and Lucile Packard Foundation to consider the implications of work trends for child and adolescent well-being and development. The committee was asked to synthesize the research regarding work and family trends; to integrate the scientific, theoretical, and policy literature on the implications these trends have for the well-being and development of children and adolescents; and to explore the range of policies and programs that might support the development and well-being of the children and adolescents in working families.

The committee's primary focus was the area of overlap among four areas of research: (1) work patterns and experiences of working parents; (2) developmental needs of children and adolescents; (3) support available to families; and (4) the roles of parents and caregivers. The committee's foremost priority was to understand the implications of work on the well-being of the children and adolescents in working families. While we considered the experiences of working families across economic, cultural, and social contexts, we looked most particularly at the challenges of families with low incomes in meeting demands of work and parenting. These families face particular challenges in managing these two spheres of their lives.

The committee looked specifically at the effects of two laws on families' work patterns: the Family and Medical Leave Act (FMLA) of 1993, which established the rights of certain workers to 12 weeks of unpaid, job-protected leave to care for a newborn or newly adopted child or for ill or disabled family members; and the Personal Responsibility and Work Opportunities Act of 1996, which made cash assistance for poor families contingent on employment or participation in activities to prepare parents for work.

We also reviewed information on the ways in which supports for working families have been integrated into employment policies of private sector companies. The data that do exist suggest that access to corporate policies and benefits is uneven, with lower-income workers less likely to be covered. However, overall, the committee found that the scientific data in this area are limited and do not provide a comprehensive understanding of who these policies affect and the extent to which they support the well-being of children in working families. The committee's findings are therefore focused on public policies.

FINDINGS

Employment Trends

- **More children have employed parents.**

  The number of working mothers has increased. From 1970 to 2000, overall maternal labor force participation rates rose from 38 to 68 percent and paternal labor force participation remained high and stable. The result of this labor force change is that a larger fraction of children live in families in which all available parents are in the labor force—either they live with a single parent who is employed or they live with two parents, both of whom work at least some hours for pay each week.

- **Access to parental leave is limited.**

  Only 45 percent of parents working in the private sector have guaranteed unpaid parental leave through the 1993 Family and Medical Leave Act. Less than 5 percent have access to paid parental leave. Many parents do not have the right to more than the 12 weeks of leave mandated by the FMLA.

Child and Adolescent Care

- **Children and adolescents spend significant time in nonparental care.**

  Children and adolescents are spending many hours in the care of someone other than their parents. Approximately 80 percent of children ages 5 and younger with employed mothers are in a child care arrangement for an average of almost 40 hours a week with someone other than a parent, and 63 percent of these children ages 6 to 14 spend an average of 21 hours per week in the care of someone other than a parent before and after school.

- **Opportunities for care for adolescents are limited.**

Opportunities are limited for school-age children and adolescents, particularly those from low-income families, to engage in meaningful and enriching activities during nonschool hours. Since the workdays of most parents often do not fully coincide with the school days of older children and adolescents, many adolescents—as many as 40 percent of 14-year-olds with working mothers—care for themselves without adult supervision during nonschool hours.

- **Quality of care matters.**

The quality of child care has implications for children's development. The relation between participation in child care and children's development depends on such variables as the activities children experience in care, the quality of their interactions with their caregivers, the type of setting (e.g., day care center, family day care home, relative care), and amount of time in care. The quality of care does not only matter in early childhood. The characteristics of care and activities for school age children and adolescents are also linked with developmental outcomes. For example, structured, supervised, and skill-focused activities for adolescents show favorable outcomes, while unstructured programs may not only fail to offer benefits, they may also amplify existing problems or encourage the development of new problems.

- **Much child care is not of high quality or developmentally beneficial.**

There is a wide range in the quality of care that is available for young children in the United States, but the evidence indicates that much of the child care is mediocre or worse. Children in lower-income families often receive lower quality care than children in higher income families. Publicly funded early care and education programs which are intended to provide developmentally beneficial nonparental care for young children, such as Head Start and Early Head Start, reach only about 40 percent of those who are eligible. Although efforts are being made at better integration, at present programs to provide care for children of working parents are often not integrated with programs to provide developmentally beneficial care.

Implications of Work and Care Trends

In some circumstances, employment of both parents in a two-parent family or employment of the only resident parent in a single-parent family can be beneficial for children. Work can result in additional income, provide a positive role model for children, and expose children to stimulating and supportive care environments—if the child is being cared for in a quality setting—and, for adolescents, can result in increased autonomy and responsibility. But if a consequence of employment is the use of poor-quality child care, lack of supervision of children and adolescents before and after school, increased parental stress because of time demands, or a stressful or low-paying job, then the implications for children and adolescents can be negative.

Some young children are particularly affected by maternal employment. For newborns, outcomes for mothers and children are better when mothers are able to take longer periods of leave. Outcomes for children may be better when mothers are able to return to work part time or to delay returning to work full time until after the first year of a child's life.

Adolescents whose parents work and who do not have an adult-supervised arrangement after school may experience social and academic problems as a result of time spent in self-care.

Benefits for children and adolescents may be generated when employment increases a family's economic resources. Family income influences the adequacy of food, clothing, and housing, safety from injury and from dangerous elements in the physical environment, availability of health care services, and access to a variety of toys, books, and stimulating outings and opportunities. A family's income also appears to affect material well-being, which in turn affects children and adolescents.

Current Public Policy Response

The public sector has responded to the challenges facing working families in caring for their children by providing them with greater resources. Many new public programs for children and adolescents have developed in the past 25 to 30 years in response to the increasing movement of mothers into the labor force. There has also been an expansion of social welfare programs to cover such services as early childhood education and medical care for low-income children. However, many of these programs are still not specifically designed to enhance the cognitive, social, and behavioral development of children. Those that do are not available to all children and adolescents. Fundamentally, policies and programs for working families and their children often focus on only half of the equation—either the employment of the parent or the well-being of the child—without taking into consideration the simultaneous and interactive needs of both.

POLICY OPTIONS

A primary goal for public policy should be to improve the quality of care for children and adolescents in working families.

The committee identified *policy options* in the areas of child and adolescent care and family leave that could assist in meeting this goal. Whenever possible, the committee developed rough cost estimates of these policy options, as well as some of the likely benefits, but the information needed for a complete cost-benefit analysis of all of the policies discussed here is not available. The committee is also sensitive to the reality that additional funds will be required to improve care for children and that budgets are constrained. The policy options presented have implications for state as well as federal decision making. The recent devolution of much public responsibility for child and family well-being from the federal government to the states presents opportunities to develop innovative strategies that respond to local employment and demographic conditions.

Child Care

• **Policy Option: Expand and increase access to Head Start and Early Head Start.**

Expand the hours of Head Start, increase access to serve more children who are not currently eligible, including children under age 3, or provide full-day, year-round care. Head Start and Early Head Start are currently limited to children whose families have incomes below the poverty line (or whose child has a disability). Head Start targets children ages 3 and 4; Early Head Start targets children under age 3. The results of the Early Head Start Evaluation, as well as the National Head Start Impact Study currently under way, will provide guidance for program improvement, as the program expands to serve more children from birth to age 5 for more hours and ensures that the program meets the full-day, full-year needs of working families.

• **Policy Option: Expand prekindergarten and other early education programs delivered in community-based child care programs.**

Provide state prekindergarten dollars directly into full-day, community-based child care programs and tie prekindergarten funding to higher standards, teacher qualifications, and curriculum requirements. These approaches would allow parents to choose providers that meet their full-day needs but also allow programs to improve quality.

• **Policy Option: Expand child care subsidies through quality-related vouchers.**

Provide vouchers with a reimbursement rate that increases with the developmental quality of child care purchased from accredited child care centers or family day care homes for children from birth to age 12. These vouchers would give parents an affordable incentive to seek child care of high quality and would give providers an incentive to improve quality in order to attract consumers with the greater purchasing power.

Cost information for these child care policy options is summarized in Box ES-1 and discussed in more detail in the full report. Fully implemented, these policy options could cost as much as an extra $25.2 billion for Head Start and Early Head Start, as much as $35 billion for prekindergarten and early education, or as much as $54 billion for quality vouchers. Costs could be reduced through partial implementation of these options. The implementation of one or more options could also make the expansion of the other options unnecessary, given the overlap in the populations they serve.

Adolescent Care

• **Policy Option: Increase the availability, hours, and quality of after-school programs.**

Expand after-school program coverage and the provision of after-school enrichment activities for children and adolescents from low-income families through multiple settings, including schools, faith-based organizations, community centers, and programs such as the 21st Century Community Learning Centers.

Family Leave

• **Policy Option: Improve parents' ability to take leave after the birth of a child, especially among low-income parents.**

BOX ES-1
Cost Estimates for Child Care Policy Options*

Policy Option: Expand and increase access to Head Start and Early Head Start.

Per child cost estimate (in 2001)
Part-day, part-year Head Start: approximately $5,021 per child.
Full-day, full-year Head Start: approximately $9,811 per child.

Current spending
$6.67 billion

Cost estimate for this policy option
The costs in addition to the current budget to expand or enhance services would vary depending upon who is served and by what level of services:

*   Full-day, full-year services provided to all eligible children ages birth to 5 years not currently served: $25.2 billion.
*   Part-day, part-year services provided to all eligible children ages birth to 5 years not currently served: $14.0 billion.
*   Year-round, full-day services extended to all children ages 3 to 4 years currently served only part-day, part-year: $2.5 billion.
*   Year-round, full-day services extended to all eligible children ages 3 to 4 years who currently are not served at all or are served only part-day, part-year: $7.8 billion.

It should be noted that some of the eligible children not currently served by Head Start might be enrolled in similar programs funded by Title I-A or by state prekindergarten initiatives. Thus, these figures may overestimate the cost of expanding Head Start, but insufficient information is available to estimate by how much.

Policy Option: Expand prekindergarten and other early education programs delivered in community-based child care programs.

Per child cost estimate
Part-day, part-year prekindergarten program: $4,000 to $5,000 per child.

Current spending
States are currently spending a little over $2 billion on prekindergarten initiatives for children at risk of school failure; at the federal level, $500 million is spent on prekindergarten through Title I (the education program for disadvantaged students); $6.67 billion is spent on the federal Head Start program. These expenditures do not take into account the amount spent on child care and prekindergarten by private paying parents with children ages 3 and 4.

---

*The details of cost estimates included in this chapter can be found in Chapter 9 of the full report.

Cost estimate for this policy option
It is estimated that publicly funded prekindergarten for all would cost an additional $25 to $35 billion annually.

Policy Option: Expand child care subsidies through quality-related vouchers.

Per child cost estimate
The estimated cost of a voucher for full-day year round high-quality child care for a child aged 0-5 in a family with income below the poverty line is $6,000, with lower estimates for older children, lower-quality care, and children in higher-income families.

Current spending
Approximately $21 billion

Cost estimate for this policy option
It is estimated that the program would cost an additional $54 billion.

There is evidence that taking family leave benefits parents and children, and that the right to do so is available to some but not others. However, unless there is some provision for earnings replacement while on leave, many low-income workers will likely forego the opportunity to take unpaid leave.

- **Policy Option: Discourage the practice of requiring mothers on welfare to return to work full time during the child's first year.**

    Given the negative effects on child outcomes when a mother returns to work full time in her child's first year of life for some groups of families, policies that would allow new mothers to delay returning to full-time employment until after the first three months of a child's life, and possibly until after the child's first birthday deserve attention.

- **Policy Option: Expand coverage of the Family and Medical Leave Act.**

    Cover activities and individuals not currently eligible (for example, attending meetings at children's schools, taking children to routine medical or dental visits), to provide options for working part time or with flexible hours, and to cover other family members (such as grandparents).

Research

The committee notes throughout the report areas in need of further research. The most recent nationally representative data on the structural measures of child care quality (group sizes, caregiver to child ratios, provider education and training, provider turnover rates) are from 1990. No nationally representative data are available on the process measures (the experiences that children have with their caregivers, with other children, and with age-appropriate activities and materials). No national surveys of child care collect information on quality, and process quality data are currently available from only a few state-specific surveys. In the committee's view, the highest research priority should therefore be the collection of national data on process quality through the institution of a new nationally representative survey of child care arrangements with a focus on the quality of care.

CONCLUSION

This report identifies important opportunities that have the potential to improve the quality of child and adolescent development in this country through new or expanded public policies. Children are spending vast numbers of hours in child care that fails to add as much to their social and cognitive skills as we know can be provided. Recent research has convinced the committee that the nation is not doing nearly enough as a society to help families, particularly low-income families, with the difficult task of providing for the material and the developmental needs of their children. The committee has identified some promising policy options for action by policy makers. These policies should receive serious consideration.

1

Setting the Stage

mong the many transformations that have occurred in the American family over the past 30 years, few are as dramatic as the increased rates of paid employment and changing patterns of work among mothers with children. From 1970 to 2000, overall maternal labor force participation rates rose 79 percent (from 38 to 68 percent); for mothers with the youngest children, birth to age 3, this rate more than doubled (from 24 to 58 percent). This trend has held for mothers in a wide variety of circumstances—first-time mothers and never-married mothers, for example—and across demographic categories, including family income, education, race and ethnicity, and place of residence.

During this same period, the availability and use of nonparental child care also has increased, both in response to trends in parental employment and as a result of growing public confidence in a variety of care arrangements. Research documenting the benefits of early childhood educational interventions and of after-school programs for early adolescents, particularly for those from low-income families, has helped persuade municipal governments, state legislatures, and the federal government to invest more in these programs. Public policies that support parental employment are a diverse lot. Some reduce the tax burden or increase the tax credit for certain working families (for example, the federal earned income tax credit). Others subsidize child care or improve its quality. As well as responding to employment trends, a number of these policies are likely also to encourage parents who were not working to enter the labor force; policies that help parents find and pay for child care are an example. The recent devolution of certain public responsibilities for child and family well-being from the federal government to the states also has created opportunities to develop innovative strategies that respond to local employment conditions.

Although states and localities have increasingly become engaged in supporting working families, many consider two pieces of federal legislation, in addition to the expansion of the earned income tax credit noted above, as pivotal in this regard. The Family and Medical Leave Act (FMLA) of 1993 established, for the first time, the rights of certain workers to 12 weeks of unpaid, job-protected leave to care for a newborn or a newly adopted child, or for ill or disabled family members. Enacted in 1996, the Temporary Assistance for Needy Families (TANF) provisions in the Personal Responsibility and Work Opportunities Reconciliation Act (PRWORA) made cash assistance for poor families, for the first time, contingent on employment or participation in activities to prepare single mothers for work. These policies have helped bring the domains of work, family life, and child well-being into unavoidably close contact.

These are dramatic societal changes in parental employment, particularly of mothers, in the range of options available to them to care for their children while they are at work, in public sentiment about the advisability of these arrangements, in policies that support working families, and in the knowledge base about environmental factors that promote child and adolescent development. They raise questions about the effects of parent employment and employment-related policies on the well-being of children and adolescents.

In November 2001, the National Academies, with support from a consortium of private foundations, established the Committee on Family and Work Policies to address these questions.

COMMITTEE CHARGE

The Committee on Family and Work Policies is comprised of an interdisciplinary group of individuals with expertise in several relevant fields, including sociology, economics, public policy, business, early child development and care, adolescent development and care, demography, psychology, and anthropology. It was asked to review, synthesize, and characterize available research on the roles of working parents, other caregivers, and caregiving arrangements in promoting the health and development of children and adolescents. The committee explored the range of policies and benefits that support working families and their implications for child and adolescent well-being. Of particular interest were policies of four types: policies that impose work requirements on parents (such as TANF), policies that require work as a condition of receiving benefits (such as the earned income tax credit), policies that support care arrangements for the children of working parents, and policies that grant job-protected family and medical leave to employees.

In order to address these issues, the committee relied on recent advances in research on child care and development; adolescent care and development; effects of employment on parents and on child and adolescent development; research on current programmatic supports for child and adolescent development; and ethnographic research on working families.

SCOPE OF THE STUDY

The committee's primary focus is the area of overlap among four spheres of interest (see Figure 1-1): work patterns and experiences of working parents; developmental needs of children and adolescents; support available to families; and the roles of parents and caregivers. Our foremost priority is to understand the implications of work on the well-being of children and adolescents in working families.

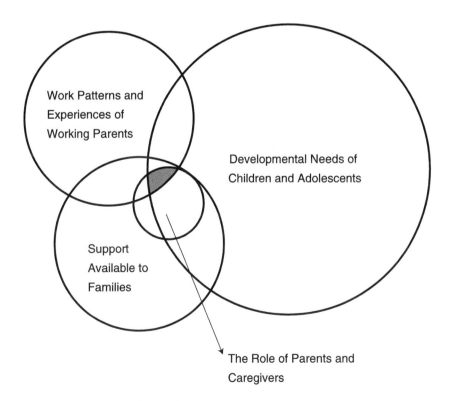

Work Patterns and Experiences of Working Parents

Developmental Needs of Children and Adolescents

Support Available to Families

The Role of Parents and Caregivers

FIGURE 1-1   Four spheres of interest.

Population of Concern

The committee considered the experiences of working families across economic, cultural, and social contexts, given that all families face challenges in meeting the demands of work and parenting. But early on, committee members acknowledged that families with low incomes face particular challenges in managing these two spheres of their lives; this may be especially true for families in which the parents have been obliged to enter the labor force because of policies such as TANF. It also often appears to be the case that children in low-income families have the most to gain from high-quality care arrangements, both in preschool and school-age settings. We therefore chose to pay special attention to this subgroup, as researchers continue to debate the implications of welfare reform, a strong economy, and such policies as the earned income tax credit for the well-being of families and their children (Joint Center for Poverty Research, 2000).

Poverty in single-mother families has fallen dramatically in the period after the passage of welfare reform, and many poor families on welfare have shown that they are capable of supporting themselves by working (Haskins, 2001). But that does not mean the end of hardship. Even though poverty rates and the number of children in poverty declined, there is some evidence that rates of extreme poverty did not decline as fast as the overall poverty rate, and there are many challenges for those who manage to escape poverty and leave welfare through work.

The committee sought to develop a comprehensive and representative description of the experience of these families. Recent qualitative investigations, especially those that have collected data from TANF participants, help to contextualize the findings on the experience of low-income families reported later in this report.

Not surprisingly, the qualitative evidence indicates that jobs held by low-income workers often pay among the lowest wages allowable by law. Furthermore, adults who earn low wages report difficulties making ends meet (Nicolas and Baptiste, 2001; Lengyel and Campbell, 2002). Research further reveals that for women moving from welfare to work, employment can actually worsen their financial position, given the added costs of transportation (car, insurance, gas, bus fare), work clothes, and child care (Edin and Lein, 1997; Hicks-Bartlett, 2000; Jarrett, 1994; Rosier, 2000). Although evidence shows that the wages of those leaving welfare rise with time on the job at about the same rate as other workers, opportunities to increase wages are sometimes limited, given that these workers largely hold unskilled and semiskilled jobs, such as cashiers at car washes (Rank, 1994), fast food attendants (Newman, 1999; Shook, 1999), nursing and home care attendants (Hicks-Bartlett, 2000; Oliker, 1995), circuit board testers, clerical workers (Puntenney, 1999), laborers at recycling centers, and part-time

A New Jersey mother of two who is working in a temporary job details a common plight (Amstutz, 2002:67):

Now I'm getting Medicaid. I'm going to get taken off in February and then I will have to get New Jersey Kids Care but I won't have any benefits. I feel they should have something for parents too. You know, for working parents everybody needs health benefits.

janitors (Reaves, 2000). These workers take on multiple low-paid or temporary jobs, sometimes combining formal and informal employment or work in the underground economy (Edin and Lein, 1997; Newman, 1999).

Low-wage and part-time employment often lacks health benefits. The absence of critical benefits means that parents must pay out-of-pocket costs for attention to their own or their children's health (Jarrett, 1994; Newman, 1999) unless a source of free care is available. Others may forego medical treatment for short-term and chronic illnesses for themselves or their children (Amstutz, 2002; Edin and Lein, 1997).

Rigid work schedules that fail to accommodate family and personal needs (such as unexpected illnesses, gaps in child care arrangements, parental illnesses, long distance travel, disruptions in transportation) may further undermine job stability (Harris and Lengyel, 2002; Iversen, 2002). Workers may have limited flexibility to respond to family emergencies, such as a sick child or an appointment at school (Johnson, 2002).

Jobs that require physical stamina characterize the work experience of some poor adults. These included ditch digging, construction, nursing, and home care assistance that requires heavy lifting (Hamer, 2001; Hicks-Bartlett, 2000). Long-term employment of this nature may compromise their health and future economic prospects.

Poor adults may need to travel to employment in distant suburban areas that lack easily accessible public transportation. When public transportation is available, it can require several hours of travel. Moreover, poor adults rarely have reliable cars (Cook and Fine, 1995; Jarrett, 1994; Reaves, 2000; Thomlinson and Burrows, 2002; Young, 2000). The challenges related to low-income work affect children and adolescents in numerous ways. Children lose time with their parents if their parents must hold multiple jobs or commute long distances (Cook and Fine, 1995; Edin and Lein, 1997).

Employment may make it more difficult to ensure the safety of children on their way to or from school or on other excursions in their neighborhoods, and it may make protecting young children from violence, gangs, and drugs more of a challenge (Fordham, 1996; Hicks-Bartlett, 2000;

Oliker, 1995; Puntenney, 1999). With parents absent during daytime hours, children may become involved in risky behaviors, such as sexual activity, drugs, and gangs (Anderson, 1999; Cook and Fine, 1995; Hicks-Bartlett, 2000).

These difficulties in the workplace and at home make obtaining and maintaining employment particularly challenging for low-income workers. They also make it hard to ensure the well-being of children and adolescents in these families. This disconnect is a fundamental challenge working families face as they attempt to simultaneously work and care for their children and adolescents (Adams and Rohacek, 2002; Adams et al., 2002a).

Research Context

During the past several decades, research in the neurobiological, behavioral, and social sciences has also dramatically altered the landscape for early childhood policy, service delivery, and childrearing in the United States. This research has led to major advances in understanding the many factors that influence child health and development. These scientific gains have generated a much deeper appreciation of the importance of early life experiences on the development of the brain and the unfolding of human behavior, and of the central role of early relationships as a source of either support and adaptation or risk and dysfunction (National Research Council and Institute of Medicine, 2000). There has also been an increased understanding of adolescent development and functioning, and as a result, a greater understanding of the opportunities and challenges associated with parental employment during adolescence (National Research Council and Institute of Medicine, 2002).

This report builds on a foundation of work from the National Academies on issues related to children, youth, and families. More than a decade ago, a report of the National Research Council—*Work and Family: Policies for a Changing Work Force*—examined changes in the composition of American families and the increased participation of women in the workforce (National Research Council, 1991). The report assessed the major areas of conflict between work and family responsibilities and possible ways of easing them. It offered an ambitious agenda for employers and suggested the need for additional public policies.

At about the same time, another report, called *Who Cares for America's Children* (National Research Council, 1990), considered the effects of nonmaternal care on children's development and recommended major changes to improve the quality, affordability, and accessibility of child care in the United States. It called for substantial increases in public funding for subsidies to support the use of quality child care by low-income families, expansion of Head Start and other compensatory preschool programs, and strengthening of the infrastructure of the child care system through expanded resource and referral services and other programs.

A decade later, *From Neurons to Neighborhoods* (National Research Council and Institute of Medicine, 2000) summarized a large body of literature on the scientific knowledge about the nature of early development and the role of early experiences. It made a series of recommendations for how public policies and childhood interventions could be brought into closer alignment with what science has to say about the essential needs of children and families. This current report brought together the findings of these three reports by urging federal policy makers to recognize the importance of strong, early relationships between young children and their parents and other caregivers.

From Neurons to Neighborhoods also recommended supporting working parents by expanding coverage of the Family and Medical Leave Act to ensure that all working mothers and fathers have equal access to this benefit. The study committee that authored that report found that the then-current law, which provided three months of unpaid leave, was insufficient and recommended that paid family leave benefits be available for all families. Furthermore, the committee recommended that policy makers explore financial supports for low-income parents who meet the eligibility requirements but do not take unpaid leave because they cannot afford to forego pay, even on a temporary basis. In keeping with its emphasis on supporting early family relationships, the committee also recommended that government leaders extend the amount of time that welfare recipients with very young children are excused from meeting the work requirements of recent welfare reform policies.

In 2001 the National Academies published *Community Programs to Promote Youth Development* (National Research Council and Institute of Medicine, 2002). This report evaluated and integrated the science of adolescent health and development and made recommendations for design, implementation, and evaluation of community programs for youth. It identified a set of personal and social assets that increase the healthy development and well-being of adolescents and facilitate a successful transition from childhood, through adolescence, and into adulthood. The study committee concluded that continued exposure to positive experiences, settings, and people, as well as opportunities to gain and refine life skills (in families, community programs, schools, etc.) helps young people acquire these assets.

Taken together, this group of reports reflects advances in theory, research, and practice in understanding how children and adolescents develop and the effects of everyday contexts on their development and well-being. They also focus needed attention on specific programs and policies, in both the public and private sectors, which influence parental behavior and well-being, including the extent to which parents are able to fulfill their childrearing responsibilities. And each report, in its own way, insisted on enlarging the scope of investigation to include environments outside the family—workplaces, child care and after-school programs, neighborhoods, and communities. This present report has profited from these previous efforts.

GUIDE TO THE REPORT

This report is organized in three parts. Following this introduction, Part I summarizes trends in the areas of work and family patterns and the care of children and adolescents. Chapter 2 reviews current trends in employment patterns and family functioning among working families—particularly working mothers—in the United States. It highlights various dimensions of work and family trends, including work schedules, parenting patterns, and family management. Chapter 3 describes the diverse patterns of child care use and details family expenditures on child care, the child care supply, and child care quality.

Part II considers the effects of the trends described in Part I. Chapter 4 reviews the research on maternal employment and its effect on the family environment. Chapter 5 looks at early child care and child care settings during middle childhood and considers the effects of care on these children. Chapter 6 reviews the evidence on the effects of parental employment on a particular group of children—adolescents ages 12 to 18. And Chapter 7 reviews evidence on the effects of welfare reform on the family, with particular attention to employment, earnings, poverty, fertility, and marriage, as well as their effects on children and adolescents.

Part III highlights current public supports available to working families and describes possible next steps for promoting the positive development of care for children and adolescents in working families. Chapter 8 considers the public policies, including leave policies, tax policies, and education programs, as well as programs to assist families in paying for child care and their implications for child and adolescent well-being. Finally, Chapter 9 summarizes the committee's findings and presents possible options for public policy and research. For reference throughout the report, a list of acronyms is provided in Box 1-1.

BOX 1-1

Acronym	Full Title
ACF	Administration for Children and Families
AFDC	Aid to Families with Dependent Children
CACFP	Child and Adult Care Food Program
CCDBG	Child Care Development Block Grant
CCDF	Child Care and Development Fund
CCLC	21st Century Community Learning Centers
CDA	Child Development Associate
CDC	Centers for Disease Control and Prevention
CDCTC	Child and Dependent Care Tax Credit
CE	Consumer Expenditure Survey
CED	Committeee for Economic Development
CF	The Children's Foundation
CPC	Chicago Child-Parent Centers
CPS	Current Population Survey
CQO	The Cost, Quality, and Outcomes Study
CTC	Child Tax Credit
DCAP	Dependent Care Assistance Program
DHHS	Department of Health and Human Services
ECERS	Early Childhood Environment Rating Scale
EHS	Early Head Start
EITC	Earned Income Tax Credit
FDCH	Family Day Care Home
FDCRS	Family Day Care Rating Scale
FMLA	The Family and Medical Leave Act
GAO	General Accounting Office
GED	Graduate Equivalency Degree
ITERS	Infant Toddler Envirnoment Rating Scale
MDRC	Manpower Demonstration Research Corporation
MFIP	Minnesota Family Investment Program
MOE	Maintenance of Effort
NAEYC	National Association for the Education of Young Children
NASF	National Survey of Families
NCCS	The National Child Care Survey
NCCSS	National Child Care Staffing Study
NICHD	National Institute of Child Health and Human Development
NLSY	National Longitudinal Survey of Youth

(continued)

BOX 1-1 Continued

Acronym	Full Title
NSFH	National Survey of Families and Households
NYCAP	New York State's Child Assistance Program
OBRA	Omnibus Budget Reconciliation Act
ORCE	Observational Record of the Caregiving Environment
PCS	Profile of Child Care Settings
PDA	Pregnancy Disability Act
PLA	Parental Leave Account
PRWORA	Personal Responsibility and Work Opportunity Reconciliation Act
SACERS	School-Aged Environment Rating
SECC	Study of Early Child Care
SEM	Structural Equation Modeling
SES	Socioeconomic Status
SFSP	Summer Food Service Program
SIPP	Survey of Income and Program Participation
SSBG	Social Services Block Grant
SSP	Canada's Self Sufficiency Project
TANF	Temporary Assistance for Needy Families
TASC	The After-School Corporation
TDI	Temporary Disability Insurance
UEP	Urban and Environmental Policy and Planning
UI	Unemployment Insurance
USDA	United States Department of Agriculture
WRP	Vermont's Welfare Restructuring Project
YAA	Younger Americans Act

Part I

Work, Family, and Child Care Trends

Part I reviews evidence concerning rates of employment, family responsibilities, and the care of children and adolescents. Chapter 2 reviews current trends in work patterns and family functioning among working families in the United States. It highlights various dimensions of work and family trends, including work schedules, parenting patterns, and family management. Chapter 3 describes the diverse patterns of child care use, as well as details family expenditures on child care, the child care supply, and child care quality.

2

Work and Family Trends

$\mathscr{T}$he changing context of working families in America includes delayed marriage, more childbearing outside marriage, high levels of
divorce, lengthening life expectancies, and changing work patterns of parents, especially mothers (Casper and Bianchi, 2002). Perhaps
the most profound change, which has influenced the reallocation of time in
working families over the past few decades, is the dramatic rise in the labor
force participation of women—particularly married mothers.

For families, this has meant a shift away from maternal time spent in
housework and other nonmarket activities to paid market work. More
families juggle childrearing with paid market work without benefit of the
services of an adult in the home full-time. Historically, economic need has
compelled single mothers to enter the paid labor force in larger proportions
than married mothers. In recent decades, married mothers—a group traditionally thought to have more freedom to curtail market work to rear
children than single mothers—have become increasingly likely to remain in
the labor force throughout their childrearing years. The change in employment rates has been most dramatic for mothers, while employment of fathers has remained high and stable. Our focus, therefore, is primarily on
the implications of maternal employment on the well-being of children and
adolescents in working families.

In this chapter, we first review evidence on the timing of childbearing
and work patterns of mothers surrounding the first birth. Then we describe
the labor force patterns of women in the most intense years of childbearing
and rearing, ages 25 to 44. We next examine data on mothers' and fathers'

involvement in housework and child care. We conclude with a look at nonstandard work schedules and family functioning.

WORK AND CHILDBEARING PATTERNS

Most women in the United States (more than 80 percent) become mothers by age 40, averaging two children per woman. As shown in Table 2-1, among cohorts of women born in the 1950s who have now completed their childbearing, 83 percent became mothers by age 40, and the cumulative births (per 1,000) of these cohorts were just under two per woman (O'Connell, 2002: Table 3.1). In the 1958 birth cohort, 22 percent had already become mothers by age 20, 50 percent by age 25, and 83 percent by age 40. The percentage of mothers with births by age 20 hover in the range of 20-23 percent for the cohort of women born up through the mid-1970s; the percentage who are mothers by age 25 is a little under 50 percent (47-49 percent) for women born in the mid-1960s to the mid-1970s, women still in their childbearing years and for whom we do not yet know their completed fertility by age 40. Although fertility is being delayed by many women, more than half are likely to become mothers by their early to mid-20s, and another third will enter parenthood between age 25 and age 40.

One significant change has been the increase in the workforce participation of new mothers. Table 2-2 shows the employment patterns before and after a first birth for the 1961-1995 period. In the 1990s, more women

TABLE 2-1 Cumulative Fertility Patterns to Age 20, 25, and 40, by Year of Woman's Birth: 1918 to 1973

	Percentage with a Birth by Age			Cumulative Births per 1,000 Women by Age		
Year	20	25	40	20	25	40
1918	19.6	52.8	83.9	254	939	2,468
1923	21.5	61.0	88.7	287	1,086	2,776
1928	24.8	66.6	88.9	325	1,306	3,024
1933	29.7	73.0	91.3	425	1,591	3,193
1938	32.6	74.3	90.8	476	1,691	2,930
1943	30.1	68.5	88.2	446	1,414	2,438
1948	26.2	62.3	86.2	357	1,126	2,091
1953	24.9	52.6	82.9	322	898	1,948
1958	22.2	50.1	83.2	285	852	1,957
1963	21.0	47.4	X	271	809	X
1968	20.3	47.2	X	266	835	X
1973	23.0	49.7	X	311	874	X

SOURCE: O'Connell (2002). Reprinted with permission.

TABLE 2-2   Employment Before and After First Birth Among Women by Year of First Child's Birth: 1961-1965 to 1991-1995

Child's Birth Year	Worked 6+ Months Continuously Before First Birth	Percent Working During Pregnancy		Percent Employed After First Birth	
		Total	Worked Until Birth	3 Months After First Birth	12 Months After First Birth
1961 to 1965	60.0	44.4	10.1	9.9	16.8
1966 to 1970	66.4	49.4	12.9	12.7	23.9
1971 to 1975	68.9	53.5	14.5	15.6	27.9
1976 to 1980	73.1	61.4	25.1	22.4	38.8
1981 to 1985	73.4	62.0	32.6	35.9	56.2
1986 to 1990	75.5	67.2	36.8	41.5	60.8
1991 to 1995	73.8	66.7	35.1	40.9	60.9

SOURCE: O'Connell (2002). Reprinted with permission.

worked continuously for at least six months before their first birth. In addition, in the 1990s, two-thirds of women worked during their pregnancy compared with 44 percent in the early 1960s. Over one-third of pregnant women at the later time point worked right up to the birth and, by one year after the birth, 61 percent had returned to employment compared with only 17 percent of women who became mothers in the early 1960s. These data suggest a growing demand for infant and toddler care while mothers work.

Shifting attention to slightly older children, children ages 3 to 5, regardless of their mother's employment status, increasingly spend some hours per week in an early education or care setting (e.g., nursery schools, child care centers with an educational curriculum, prekindergartens), as shown in Figure 2-1. Interestingly, although mothers who are in the labor force are more likely to enroll children in preprimary education settings, the increase in the use of nonparental care for at least some hours per week for young children has been as great among mothers not in the labor force as among employed mothers. This suggests that, along with the increase in maternal employment, preferences may be changing more generally toward the desirability of at least some nonparental care and organized educational experiences in early childhood.

TRENDS IN MOTHERS' EMPLOYMENT

Mothers' workforce participation has risen rapidly over the past three decades, as suggested by the statistics on mothers who return to work after

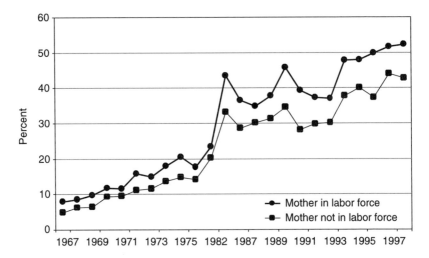

FIGURE 2-1 Preliminary enrollment status and attendance in early education or care settings for children 3 to 5 years old, by labor force status of mother, selected years.
SOURCE: Casper and Biancchi (2002).

the birth of a child. Table 2-3 shows the percentage of mothers employed by age of youngest child. Data are shown for both single and married mothers, ages 25 to 44, for selected years between 1970 and 2001. Given the timing of births, this is the age group of mothers who for the most part have completed schooling but are intensively involved in childrearing. Employment rates for all women of this age group increased over the period, from 43 to 71 percent (first row of the table). The levels of employment showed similar sharp increases for mothers, rising from 38 to 67 percent for all mothers with children under age 18 living in the home.[1] Among those with children under age 3, 24 percent were employed in 1970 compared with 57 percent in 2001 (see Cohen and Bianchi, 1999, for similar findings).

The trends for single mothers and married mothers are distinctive in the following ways. First, single mothers in most years had higher levels of participation than married mothers. The employment gap by marital status shrank between 1970 and 1995, when, in fact, married mothers had slightly higher employment rates than single mothers. Among married mothers, the most rapid increases occurred prior to 1990, and increases were quite modest in the 1990s. For single mothers, in contrast, employment rates

---

[1]During this same period of time, employment of fathers of a comparable age remained high and stable, fluctuating between 86 and 91 percent.

TABLE 2-3 Mothers' Workforce Participation by Age of Youngest Child (percentage employed), 1970-2000

	1970	1975	1980	1985	1990	1995	2000	2001
Total women (ages 25-44)	42.5	47.2	59.3	63.6	68.1	68.9	71.6	71.4
Total mothers (ages 25-44)								
with children ages 0-3	23.8	28.7	40.0	45.9	51.6	55.4	57.5	56.8
with children ages 0-5	27.5	31.8	42.5	48.2	54.0	57.5	60.2	59.3
with children ages 0-17	37.9	41.9	53.7	57.6	62.5	64.6	67.7	67.4
Single mothers (ages 25-44)								
with children ages 0-3	33.0	32.9	44.1	39.4	45.4	48.4	67.0	63.8
with children ages 0-5	41.5	40.9	51.1	44.9	51.0	52.2	69.6	66.8
with children ages 0-17	55.1	54.0	62.9	61.4	64.1	63.2	75.3	74.6
Married mothers (ages 25-44)								
with children ages 0-3	23.2	28.4	39.5	46.7	52.6	56.6	56.1	55.7
with children ages 0-5	26.6	30.7	41.4	48.7	54.6	58.6	58.6	57.9
with children ages 0-17	36.4	40.1	51.9	56.8	62.1	65.0	65.7	65.5

NOTE: All numbers are weighted to correct for differential probabilities of selection into the sample and to adjust for nonresponse.

SOURCE: Casper and Bianchi (2002).

TABLE 2-4   Marital Status of Unmarried Mothers Living with Children
Under Age 18 for 1978, 1988, and 1998

	1978	1988	1998	Percentage Point Change
Total (number)	6,194	8,160	9,845	
Total (percent)	100	100	100	
Never married	22.4	33.2	42.1	19.7
Separated/spouse absent	27.6	21.9	18.7	-8.9
Divorced	39.0	38.3	34.9	-4.1
Widowed	11.0	6.7	4.4	-6.6

NOTE: All numbers are weighted.
SOURCE: Casper and Bianchi (2002).

jumped rather dramatically in the second half of the 1990s, a period of strong economic growth and restructuring of welfare support for single mothers and their children (see Chapter 7 for overview of welfare reform). By 2001, single mothers again had employment levels that were substantially higher than those of married mothers.

Single-mother families increased most rapidly in the latter 1960s and 1970s; the increase then slowed in the 1980s. During the latter half of the 1990s, the percentage of families with a single mother remained steady. The composition of these families shifted over time, with never-married mothers accounting for a growing share of such families. For example, in 1978, 22 percent of single mothers with children under age 18 had never married, whereas this percentage was almost twice as large by the end of the 1990s (see Table 2-4). This compositional shift tended to dampen labor force participation rates of single mothers at the same time that higher average education levels of all women, including single mothers, increased the likelihood of employment. Overall employment rates of single mothers, which did not change greatly during the 1980s or even the early 1990s, did rise considerably after the mid-1990s (Casper and Bianchi, 2002:Table 4.4). Single-father families also increased rapidly after 1970, although they remain a relatively small proportion of all single-parent families (Casper and Bianchi, 2002:Table 1.1; Garasky and Meyer, 1996).

The trend data on marital status of single mothers does not adjust for the fact that the proportion of unmarried mothers who live with a cohabiting partner has been rising. Table 2-5 shows that the proportion of single mothers with children who were living with a cohabiting partner increased from 5 to 13 percent between the late 1970s and late 1990s. The proportion of these mothers who lived with a parent also increased slightly. Due to these trends, the proportion of single mothers who had no other adult present in the household declined.

TABLE 2-5 Living Arrangements of Unmarried Mothers Living with Children Under Age 18 for 1978, 1988, and 1998

	1978	1988	1998	Percentage Point Change
Total (number)	6,194	8,160	9,845	
Total (percent)	100	100	100	
Never married	59.8	56.4	54.0	−5.9
Separated/spouse absent	4.7	9.6	12.7	8.0
Divorced	14.3	15.2	16.7	2.7
Widowed	21.2	18.8	16.6	−4.6

SOURCE: Casper and Bianchi (2002).

With respect to the increase in married women's employment, some argue that the increase has been propelled by the stagnation in men's wages (Jacobs and Gerson, 2001), but market opportunities have also expanded for women. Between 1978 and 1998, increases in annual hours of employment were greatest for highly educated women, but the positive correlation of a husband's earnings with market participation of wives diminished (Cohen and Bianchi, 1999). Hence, although in the aggregate the increase in wives' employment would seem to compensate for the decline in men's earning power, this need-based interpretation is at odds with the fact that labor force gains have been largest for wives married to highly educated, high-earning husbands (Juhn and Murphy, 1997).

The implication of these demographic and labor force changes is that a larger fraction of children live in families in which all available parents are in the labor force—either they live with a single parent who is employed or they live with two parents, both of whom work at least some hours for pay each week. In 1997, 68 percent of children had all parents with whom they lived working for pay, compared with 59 percent of children in the mid-1980s (Bianchi, 2000a).

Work Hours

Table 2-6 shows the average hours of employment per week for working mothers (ages 25 to 44) for the 1970-2001 time period. The most striking feature of these data is that weekly work hours rose only slightly, certainly far less sharply than employment rates, over the period. Employed mothers with children averaged 33 hours of employment per week in 1970, and this rose by 3 hours per week (to 36) hours in 2001. Hence, balancing work with child care is not a new issue for working women. What is new is that the pool of women who work outside the home, who

TABLE 2-6 Employed Mothers' Workforce Participation by Age of Youngest Child (average hours per week), 1970-2001

	1970	1975	1980	1985	1990	1995	2000	2001
Total women (ages 25-44)	34.1	34.4	35.4	36.2	37.1	36.7	37.5	37.7
Total mothers (ages 25-44)								
with children ages 0-3	30.1	30.9	32.0	32.6	33.1	33.4	33.3	34.5
with children ages 0-5	31.1	31.4	32.3	33.0	33.5	33.6	34.1	34.9
with children ages 0-17	32.8	32.9	34.0	34.5	35.1	35.0	35.6	36.0
Single mothers (ages 25-44)								
with children ages 0-3	34.8	34.2	37.3	37.0	36.3	36.4	37.3	37.4
with children ages 0-5	34.8	34.9	37.4	36.7	37.0	36.0	37.5	38.0
Married mothers (ages 25-44)								
with children ages 0-3	29.7	30.6	31.3	32.2	32.7	32.9	32.6	34.0
with children ages 0-5	30.7	30.9	31.4	32.5	33.0	33.2	33.4	34.3
with children ages 0-17	32.3	32.3	33.0	33.6	34.2	34.3	34.9	35.3

NOTE: All numbers are weighted to correct for differential probabilities of selection into the sample and to adjust for nonresponse.

SOURCE: Casper and Bianchi (2002).

face issues of balancing work and family needs when their children are young, has expanded.

More generally, scholars disagree on the extent to which individuals' work hours have actually increased in recent years, if they have at all. Juliet Schor (1992), in *The Overworked American,* argues that work hours have increased, whereas John Robinson and Geoffrey Godbey (1999), using time diary evidence, argue that the trend in leisure activities is not consistent with the notion that work hours are expanding. Leisure time has not decreased. Careful examination of employment data from the Current Population Survey, by Rones et al. (1997), shows that, on average, work hours have not changed much, but the unchanging average disguises the fact that there is increasing heterogeneity among workers, with some unable to work as many hours as they would like and others working very long workweeks. In addition, with the rise in mothers' employment, households as a unit are allocating more of their "available adult time" to paid work and there is evidence that the share of dual-earner couples working very long workweeks (exceeding 100 hours for the couple, husband's and wife's hours combined) has increased over the past three decades (Jacobs and Gerson, 2001).

Wives as Primary Earners

Beyond the increase in the overall time spent in paid work in dual-earner and single-parent households, nontraditional breadwinning patterns in married couple households have increased. Households in which wives earn more than their husbands and are the primary earners have grown from 15.9 percent of married-couple families in 1981 to 22.5 percent in 2000. Not surprisingly, such households are especially common among dual-earner couples with low-wage husbands (Winkler, 1998).

Despite the growth in the number of wives who earn more than their husbands, it remains more common for wives rather than husbands to adjust their labor force attachment downward when children are born. While a majority of married mothers with young children (under age 6) were employed in 1998, only a little over one-third of married mothers of preschoolers were full-time, year-round workers (Cohen and Bianchi, 1999). This suggests that, at least when young children are at home, married mothers continue to reduce their hours of employment or even drop out of the labor force altogether for a short time. In-depth interviews with over 100 middle-class dual-earner couples confirmed that, relative to their husbands, wives disproportionately reduce and restructure their commitment to paid work over the life course to protect the family from work encroachments (Becker and Moen, 1999). In addition, young mothers in America incur a wage penalty for motherhood of approximately 7 percent per child, which is unexplained by measured productivity factors, such as years of past job experience and seniority, and which remains after corrections for unobserved heterogeneity (Budig and England, 2001).

HOUSEWORK AND TIME WITH CHILDREN

Virtually the only data that exist with which to measure trends in nonmarket activities, such as housework and child care, are time diaries that capture all uses of time over a reporting period, typically a 24-hour period. Time diaries have been conducted at roughly 10-year intervals since 1965, using consistent coding categories over time. Labor market surveys, such as the Current Population Survey (CPS), only capture market activities because they are included in the system of national accounts. When respondents are asked direct questions in surveys about how much time they spend on nonmarket activities, such as housework, reports tend to be inflated (Bianchi et al., 2000). Often survey reports of time use sum to more than 24 hours in a day or more than the possible 168 hours in the week (Bianchi et al., in press). Time diaries for which respondents are walked through the previous day's activities have proven to be a more reliable way to obtain estimates of time use, especially in nonmarket domains in which there is no other source of comparable estimates (Juster 1985; Robinson and Godbey 1999).

What effect has the change in market work had on the allocation of time to nonmarket activities? With respect to housework, Table 2-7 shows that mothers have dramatically curtailed the time they spend in housework tasks. Mothers' hours of housework (exclusive of child care) fell from an average of 32 hours per week in the mid-1960s to about 19 hours per week in 2000. Fathers' participation in housework chores increased from 4 to around 10 hours per week. This increase occurred in the 1965-1985 period, with little change afterward. In 2000, mothers of children under age 18 averaged about twice as much time as fathers in household chores.

Time diary evidence on fathers' participation in child care suggests greater change than in housework, at least among married fathers. Such data allow for three measures of father's participation in child care: the time they spend primarily engaged in a direct child care activity, the time they spend either directly focusing on child care or doing a child care activity in conjunction with something else, and finally, the overall time they spend with their children whether engaged in child care or not (the most inclusive category). Figure 2-2 shows estimates of married fathers' hours per day with their children. For comparison purposes, comparable figures for mothers are shown in Figure 2-3 and Figure 2-4 shows the ratio of married fathers' to married mothers' time with children.

On average, mothers' time with children has not decreased and fathers' time, at least among married fathers, has increased appreciably. Whereas

TABLE 2-7 Trends in Housework by Gender of Parent (average hours per week)

	All Mothers					All Fathers					Ratio of Mother's Time to Father's Time				
	1965	1975	1985	1995	2000	1965	1975	1985	1995	2000	1965	1975	1985	1995	2000
Total housework	32.1	23.7	20.5	18.8	18.6	4.4	7.5	10.3	10.8	9.5	7.3	3.1	2.0	1.7	2.0
Core housework	29.2	21.7	17.6	15.0	14.8	1.6	1.8	4.0	3.9	4.4	18.5	12.3	4.4	3.9	3.4
Cooking meals	10.1	8.7	7.5	5.3	5.4	0.7	0.9	1.8	1.5	2.2	13.8	10.0	4.2	3.5	2.5
Meal cleanup	4.8	2.5	1.9	0.8	1.3	0.3	0.2	0.4	0.1	0.3	14.0	11.4	4.6	6.8	4.9
Housecleaning	8.1	7.1	5.5	6.5	4.8	0.4	0.5	1.5	1.6	1.6	23.0	14.8	3.7	4.0	2.9
Laundry and ironing	6.2	3.4	2.7	2.4	3.3	0.2	0.2	0.3	0.6	0.4	34.5	17.6	8.7	3.8	9.4
Other housework	3.0	2.0	2.9	3.8	3.8	2.8	5.8	6.3	6.9	5.1	1.0	0.3	0.5	0.6	0.7
Outdoor chores	0.3	0.4	0.4	0.7	0.7	0.6	1.0	1.3	2.3	2.0	0.5	0.3	0.3	0.3	0.3
Repairs	0.4	0.6	0.5	0.7	1.0	1.3	3.2	2.3	1.9	1.4	0.3	0.2	0.2	0.3	0.7
Garden and animal care	0.5	0.4	0.6	0.5	0.7	0.2	0.4	0.9	1.1	0.4	2.4	1.0	0.7	0.4	1.6
Bills, other financial	1.8	0.7	1.4	2.0	1.5	0.7	1.1	1.8	1.6	1.3	2.4	0.6	0.8	1.2	1.1
Sample size	405	607	913	312	728	337	480	699	181	472					

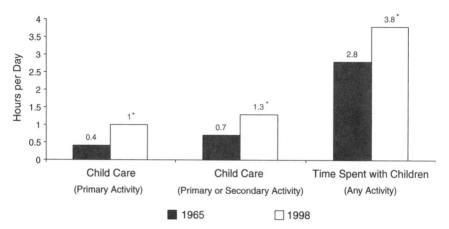

FIGURE 2-2 Change in married fathers' hours of child care and time with children.

NOTES: Estimates based on one-day, "yesterday" time diaries collected from 326 married fathers in 1965-1966, 194 married fathers in 1998-1999, all with children under age 18 at the time of the interview. Child care includes: child and baby care, helping/teaching children, talking/reading to children, indoor/outdoor play with children, medical/travel/other child related care. "*" indicates that test of 1965-1998 difference in means is statistically significant, p < 0.05.
SOURCE: Bianchi (2000a).

in 1965 fathers reported only one quarter of the time mothers reported in direct child care, they reported 55 percent as much time as mothers in the late 1990s. And whereas fathers were only with their children half as much time as mothers were in the 1960s, in the late 1990s they were spending 65 percent as much time with children as were mothers. Note that some of this time is double counted, in that both mother and father can be present. Fathers remain much more likely to have their spouse present when with their children, whereas mothers spend more solo time with children (Sayer et al., 2002).

Other research shows parallel findings of fathers' increased time with children, at least among married fathers, and no substantial decline in mothers' time with children, on average (Sandberg and Hofferth, 2001). While most research shows that employed mothers spend less time with their children relative to nonemployed mothers, the difference is not dramatic, except perhaps for very young children. The differences between employed and nonemployed mothers in time spent with children may be minimized because working mothers curtail work hours when children are young, try to synchronize work hours with children's school schedules when children are older, "tag-team" work hours with a spouse so as to maximize parental availability to children, and curtail time spent in other

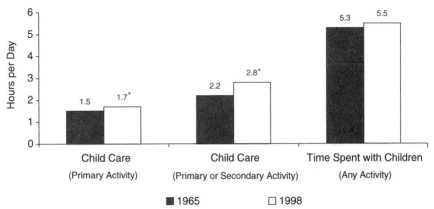

FIGURE 2-3 Change in mothers' hours of child care and time with children. NOTES: Estimates based on one-day, "yesterday" time diaries collected from 417 mothers in 1965-1966, 273 mothers in 1998-1999, all with children under age 18 at the time of the interview. Child care includes: child and baby care, helping/ teaching children, talking/reading to children, indoor/outdoor play with children, medical/travel/other child related care. "*" indicates that test of 1965-1998 difference in means is statistically significant, p < 0.05. SOURCE: Bianchi (2000a).

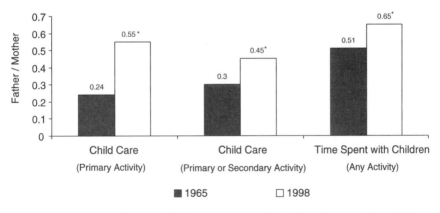

FIGURE 2-4 Ratio of married fathers' to married mothers' hours with children, 1965 and 1998. NOTES: Estimates based on one-day, "yesterday" time diaries collected from 358 married mothers in 1965-1966, 326 married fathers in 1965-1966, 194 married mothers in 1998-1999, 141 married fathers in 1998-1999. Ratios are averages across married men and women with children under age 18, not couples married to each other. "*" indicates that test of 1965-1998 difference in means is statistically significant, p < 0.05. SOURCE: Bianchi (2000a).

activities, such as housework other than child care, volunteer work, personal care, and free-time pursuits (Bianchi, 2000b).

With respect to fathers, one large gap in knowledge is the involvement of nonresidential fathers in their children's lives. For fathers who live with children, there is evidence that stepfathers spend less time with children than biological fathers. A father who cohabits with a partner and her children spends more time with those children than stepfathers, on average, but still less than biological fathers (Hofferth et al., 2002). A stepfather's involvement is greater when he also has a biological child in a remarriage (Hofferth, 2002). Whether this is because biological children enhance the likelihood of a father's involvement or whether more "child-oriented" fathers have children in a second marriage is not clear. The end result, however, is that fathers who are married to a child's mother and biologically related to a child spend more time rearing those children than fathers whose linkages are other than biological. Consequently, some children benefit from much higher involvement, financial and otherwise, from their fathers than other children.

NONSTANDARD WORK SCHEDULES AND FAMILY FUNCTIONING

While the number of hours that people work has not changed much over the past few decades, distribution of these hours has become more diverse (Bureau of Labor Statistics, 2002). The economy in the United States is increasingly operating on a "24/7" basis, with more people working late hours and on weekends. The demand for such around-the-clock employment has been attributed to growth in the service economy, interrelated with demographic and technological changes, including, but not limited to, the growth in women's employment and in dual-earner couples (Presser, 1999). The result appears to be that more workers are employed at nonstandard times—and, indeed, that nonstandard hours are becoming less so. Although good trend data are not available, it is estimated from the May 1997 Current Population Survey (the most recent year of available data) that one-fifth of all employed people in the United States work most of their hours in the evenings, during nights, on weekends, on a rotating schedule, or have highly variable hours (see Box 2-1 for shift definitions). Moreover, one-third of all those employed work weekends (Presser, 1999).

Presser (1999) has estimated that of the 134 million people employed in the United States in 1997, only 29.1 percent worked 35-40 hours a week, Monday through Friday, and during daytime hours. Without the full-time restriction of 35 to 40 hours a week, only 54.4 percent work Monday through Friday and most of their hours during the daytime. One in five people works mostly during the evenings, nights, or on rotating schedules,

---

**BOX 2-1
Shift Definitions**

Fixed day shift: at least half the hours worked during the reference week fall between 8:00 a.m. and 4:00 p.m.

Fixed evening shift: at least half the hours worked during the reference week fall between 4:00 p.m. and midnight.

Fixed night shift: at least half the hours worked during the reference week fall between midnight and 8:00 a.m.

Rotating shift: work hours change periodically (e.g., from daytime to evening to nighttime).

Hours vary: an irregular schedule that cannot be classified in above categories.

SOURCE : Adapted from Presser (1999).

---

and one in three works Saturdays or Sundays or both. Furthermore, it is more common for married couples with at least one spouse working nonstandard hours to have children (see Table 2-8).

There is a large body of literature on the health consequences for individuals who work nights and rotate shifts because of its effect on circa-

TABLE 2-8 Percentage of Married Couples with at Least One Spouse Who Works Nonstandard Hours

At least one earner		23.8
At least one earner and	Child < age 14	25.8
	Child < 5	30.6
Two earners only		27.8
Two earners and	Child < age 14	31.1
	Child < 5	34.7

NOTES: Based on data from the May 1997 Current Population Survey. Nonstandard work hours are work hours most days of reference week being between 4:00 p.m. and 8:00 a.m., rotating hours, and those too variable to classify. Couples with at least one employed spouse on the job during the week, including all rotators. Both spouses age 18 and over. Couples with both spouses on the job during the reference week, including all rotators, both in nonagricultural occupations, and both age 18 and over.

SOURCE: Presser (in press).

A mother living in an inner-city neighborhood in Chicago cares for her children during the day. However, she leaves them on their own during the evening hours as she works the graveyard shift:

Before she left for work at 11 P.M., she made sure the children had completed their homework and gone to bed. The children, ages five and seven, had her work number posted on a telephone between their beds. Because there had been three fires on their block that winter, she and her children would stage a fire drill each night after supper (Edin and Lein, 1997:134-135).

dian rhythms, which in turn affect body temperature, hormone levels, and sleep. Behaviorally, there is evidence of greater gastrointestinal disorders, higher rates of cardiovascular disease, preterm births, and low birthweight (U.S. Congress, Office of Technological Assessment, 1991; Boggild and Knutsson, 1999; Wedderburn, 2000; Schernhammer et al., 2001).

While employment at nonstandard hours is widespread among all those employed, it is disproportionately found among those with low incomes. For example, the top five occupations of nonday workers are cashiers, truck drivers, waiters and waitresses, cooks, and janitors/cleaners (Presser, in press); these jobs are often low paying. Until recently there has been limited research on how low-income working families cope with work responsibilities while caring for their children (Bogen and Joshi, 2002). Data from the 1997 Current Population Survey on reasons for working such hours indicate that most employees do so for job-related reasons (e.g., because it is a requirement of their job or they cannot find another job) rather than for personal reasons (e.g., child care or other family reasons), even when looking specifically at parents with young children (Presser, in press). Thus, while some parents may prefer such schedules, employment at nonstandard times is driven by demand and those with limited job possibilities are generally recruited. This includes mothers who move from welfare to work, who often experience a lack of correspondence between their required hours and days of employment and the availability of formal child care arrangements (Presser and Cox, 1997).

The limited data available indicate that working nonstandard work schedules has some some negative consequences for the quality and stability of marriages and both positive and negative consequences for other aspects of family functioning.

Marital Quality

Staines and Pleck (1983) have shown that shift work affects the quality of family life and leads to greater marital conflict. Updated research based on data from the National Survey of Families and Households on families shows that evening and rotating shifts allow for less quality time together for spouses, compared with working daytime shifts (Presser, in press).

Marital Stability

Research conducted by White and Keith (1990) suggests that nonstandard work schedules have a negative effect on marital stability. Furthermore, Presser (2000) looked at the National Survey of Families and Households to consider whether nonstandard work schedules increase the likelihood of martial instability. This research looked at the effects of different shifts, as well as the gender of the spouse and the spouse's respective gender ideologies, conditioned by the duration of the marriage and the presence of children. This research showed that night and rotating shifts significantly increased the odds of marital instability for couples with children. Specifically, separation or divorce over a five-year period is about six times higher among couples in which fathers work nights (and have been married less than five years). In similar couples in which mothers work nights, separation or divorce is three times as high. One could speculate that individuals who are already in troubled marriages choose nonstandard work, but, in fact, the data do not suggest this direction of causality (Presser, 2000). Rather, some types of nonstandard shifts may place stress on relationships that then heightens the likelihood of divorce.

Two mothers describe the time crunch that work entails:

[My job] was too far . . . I would have to get up at four o'clock in the morning in order to be at work at seven. [I] leave work at three-thirty and still wouldn't make it home until eight o'clock. And it was too far when I wasn't making anything. . . . I didn't have no time for my kids, no time for myself (Jarrett, 1994).

You see I work ten hours a day. . . . I take two hours to travel to work, two hours to travel back. . . . So that's like, fourteen hours a day I'm out of the house (Cook and Fine, 1995:127).

Family Functioning

Nonstandard work has an effect on the ways in which families function and interact. Parents working nonstandard hours often suffer from irregular and limited sleep, contributing to increased parental stress, greater family conflict, and poorer relationships with their children (Simon, 1990; Rahman and Pal, 1994). One indicator of family involvement is having dinner together: it often allows for consistent family interaction and an opportunity for family organizing. Presser (2001) found that parents who work evenings and rotating shifts are significantly less likely to have dinner with their children than parents who work day shifts. Working nights, however, has not shown the same effects on full family involvement in dinner.

In an examination of employment schedules and the division of household labor by gender among married dual-earner households, Presser (1994) found that when husbands work a nondaytime or rotating shift and their wives work a day shift, the men are significantly more likely to do traditionally female household tasks than couples in which both spouses work day shifts. These tasks include preparing meals, washing dishes and cleaning up after meals, cleaning house, and washing, ironing, and mending clothes. Based on this research, it appears that a husband's being home alone, particularly during the day, is an important factor in increasing his share of traditionally female household tasks.

SUMMARY

One fundamental and very important finding drawn from the literature is that more parents, particularly mothers, are working. American family life has changed dramatically as the result of this increased labor force participation of mothers. Mothers are now more often employed right up to the birth of their child and are increasingly likely to return to paid work in the first year of their child's life. In addition, the proportion of preschool-age children who spend at least some hours per week in nonparental care settings has risen rapidly for employed and nonemployed mothers alike. An increasing proportion of children live in households in which all available adults are in the labor force, either in single-parent families or in two-parent, dual-earner families. The result of this trend is a heightened demand for nonmaternal care for children, particularly very young children.

We might have expected less maternal time with children, on average, as mothers' employment has increased. However, there have been offsetting trends. In two-parent families, fathers appear to have increased their time with children. Mothers often do not work full time, although a growing number of mothers are the main economic provider in their household, either because they are a single parent or because they are the primary earner in a two-parent family. Mothers appear to have decreased time spent in housework, leisure, and personal care in order to maintain a given level of involvement in their children's lives. These types of choices may have consequences for the well-being of children and adolescents in these families.

Another important finding is that a sizable number of families with young children work nonstandard hours. Working nonstandard hours complicates child care arrangements and may place additional strains on the family. Marital quality is lower and marital disruption is higher when couples work evening or rotating shifts. Evening shifts also reduce time together as a family; families are less likely to eat dinner together on a regular basis when one of the parents works evenings or a rotating shift. However, nonstandard work shifts may be part of the explanation for greater father involvement in family life, as fathers are more involved in housework and child care when they work rotating or nonday shifts.

3

Trends in the Care of Children

orking parents in the United States use a variety of child care providers, including care by family members (parents, grandparents, other relatives, and self-care), care by neighbors and friends (nonrelative care in the child's home or in the provider's home), family day care homes (care for a small group of children in a provider's home), child care centers, and other organized activities. In this chapter, we describe the types of care used by parents, the supply of care, family expenditures on child care, and quality. Given the evidence presented in Chapter 2 showing a rise in the labor force participation among mothers, we focus in this chapter on child care usage by families in which the mother is employed.

PATTERNS OF CHILD CARE USE

The evidence presented is drawn from the Survey of Income and Program Participation (SIPP) from spring 1999. We first discuss children of preschool age, defined here as ages 0 to 5, and then children of school age, ages 6 to 14.

Preschool-Age Children

According to data from the 1999 SIPP, there were an estimated 22.0 million children ages 0 to 5 in the United States in spring 1999 (March-June), of whom 12.2 million (55 percent) had an employed mother. More than a third of the preschool children (39 percent) of working parents had more than one child care arrangement during the week, and the average number of arrangements per child was 1.6. The primary child care arrangement was defined as the arrangement used for the most hours per week.[1] Average hours per week in the primary arrangement were 32.2, and total hours in child care per week, including primary and other arrangements, were 39.1.

Working parents traditionally often relied on relatives to care for their children. Evidence suggests that the use of relatives for child care declined during the last half of the 20th century as parents began to rely more on family day care homes and child care centers (Hofferth et al., 1991; Uttal, 1999). However, in 1999, almost half the preschool children of working mothers in the United States were cared for by relatives (48 percent) for their primary arrangement (see Table 3-1). This included care by parents (20 percent), grandparents (21 percent), and other relatives (7 percent). In 1999, a little more than half of the preschool children of employed mothers (52 percent) were in some type of nonrelative care, including children in day care centers, nursery schools, or kindergarten (31 percent), family day care homes (11 percent), and nannies or babysitters in the child's home or other nonrelative arrangements (10 percent).

Table 3-1 shows the distribution of primary child care arrangements of preschool age children for families classified by various characteristics. The proportion of children whose primary care arrangement is nonrelative care and the distribution of children across types of care vary substantially by household structure, education, race, ethnicity, nativity, income, location of the household, age of the child, and job characteristics of the mother. Unmarried mothers who were previously married use more nonrelative care than do married mothers, particularly center care. In total, 56 percent of their primary child care is in nonrelative arrangements compared with 53 percent for married mothers. This difference is probably due in part to lack of availability of the spouse to provide child care while the mother is at work.

Black mothers are about 7 percentage points more likely to use center care than are whites, but blacks are less likely to use other forms of nonrelative care than whites. Hispanic mothers are less likely to use center care and family day care homes than whites. These patterns have been noted in other data sources, and they persist when other household charac-

---

[1]When there were two (or more) arrangements with the same number of hours per week, the primary arrangement was assigned in the following order of priority: center, family day care home, school, organized before- or after-school activity, other nonrelative, grandparent, other adult relative, sibling, mother while at work, child's other parent, self-care.

WORKING FAMILIES AND GROWING KIDS

TABLE 3-1 Percentage Distribution of Employed Mothers' Primary Child Care Arrangements for Children from Birth to Age 5, Spring 1999

Demographic Characteristic	Center	Family Day Care	Other Nonrelative	Parent	Grand-parent	Other Relative
All	31	11	10	20	21	7
Married	31	12	10	24	18	6
Widowed, divorced, separated, married spouse absent	36	12	8	12	24	8
Never married	28	8	10	11	32	11
White	32	14	9	22	18	5
Black	39	5	8	13	26	9
Hispanic	20	7	13	21	24	15
Other	24	3	7	20	40	7
Noncitizen	19	4	14	25	23	16
Native	32	12	9	20	20	6
Native citizen	28	7	9	15	33	8
< High school	24	5	10	15	23	20
High school	23	8	8	24	25	7
Some college	30	12	12	18	22	7
College graduate	36	16	9	20	15	3
Full time	33	13	10	15	21	7
Part time	25	8	8	31	21	8
Day shift	35	13	9	15	20	7
Nonday	19	5	10	33	24	9
< poverty	30	7	11	17	24	12
1-2 poverty	24	7	8	24	25	11
2+ poverty	34	13	10	20	19	5
Public assistance	33	8	9	10	30	11
No public assisstance	31	11	10	21	20	7
Age 0	17	11	9	29	26	8
Age 1	19	14	14	22	25	7
Age 2	24	13	11	23	23	7
Age 3	27	12	8	20	23	11
Age 4	42	10	9	15	18	7
Age 5	51	7	7	15	14	5
South	37	10	8	15	23	7
Non-South	28	12	10	23	20	8

(continued)

TABLE 3-1 Continued

Demographic Characteristic	Center	Family Day Care	Other Nonrelative	Parent	Grand-parent	Other Relative
Metro	31	10	10	21	21	7
Nonmetro	30	17	10	16	20	8

NOTES: Data are weighted. Unweighted sample size is 3,066. Other nonrelative excludes school and includes babysitters, nannies, and other unspecified nonrelatives. Hispanics are excluded from the white, black, and other race categories. Public assistance includes Temporary Aid for Needy Families, food stamps, and other programs such as General Assistance and SSI. Full time = 35+ hours each week in the month prior to the survey. Part time = 1-34 hours each week.

SOURCE: Tabulations from SIPP 1996 panel, wave 10 (Spring 1999).

teristics are held constant (see Blau and Hagy, 1998; Chaplin et al., 1999). Nonnaturalized immigrants use less center care and family day care homes than natives, but noncitizens use more care by other nonrelatives.

Use of center and family day care arrangements increases with the mother's education. Only 24 percent of primary care arrangements for children of employed high school dropouts were in centers, compared with 30 percent for college attendees and 36 percent for college graduates. Family day care use rises from 5 percent for high school dropouts to 16 percent for college graduates. More educated mothers may be more aware of the potential benefits for child development of market child care and may be better able to afford such care.

Nonrelative care is much more heavily used by mothers who work full time (56 percent) rather than part time (40 percent), and by mothers who work a day shift (58 percent) rather than some other work schedule (34 percent). The day/nonday difference is entirely due to higher use of centers and family day care homes by day shift workers, and it is no doubt explained by the fact that many centers and family day care homes do not offer care at nonday shift hours.[2] The full-time/part-time difference is also mainly in use of centers and family day care homes, and it is probably due

---

[2]Kisker et al. (1991:45) report that 10 percent of centers and 6 percent of regulated family day care homes in the Profile of Child Care Settings (explained further in the section on child care supply) sample offered weekend care, and 3 percent of centers and 13 percent of regulated family day care homes offered evening care.

to the fact that relative care arrangements may be easier to make for a few hours per day than for eight to nine hours per day.

Families with incomes below the poverty line use more center care than families with incomes between one and two times the poverty line. This is probably due to greater access to child care subsidies through the welfare system. Families with incomes more than twice the poverty line also use more center care than the poor and the near-poor. This is probably due to the greater ability of higher-income families to pay for center care.

Overall use of nonrelative care increases sharply with the age of the child after age 1, from 47 percent at age 1 to 65 percent at age 5. Most of this increase is accounted for by center care, rising from 17 percent at age zero to 51 percent at age 5. The developmental benefits of center care may be perceived by parents to be strongest beginning at age 3, as children approach school entry age. Moreover, families have fewer options for nonrelative care when their children are infants and toddlers, or they may prefer to have their very young children cared for by a family member given the convenience, proximity, and reliability that they may feel is more easily attainable using family members or friends (Folk and Yi, 1994).

Patterns of nonrelative care use across regions of the United States are generally quite similar. The main exception is that center care is more heavily used in the South than in other regions. This pattern has been widely noted and has persisted over time (see Hofferth et al., 1991:Table 2.15; see also Capizzano et al., 2000a, for evidence on variation in child care use across states). It is also the case that the rate of full-time employment by mothers of young children is higher in the South than in other regions (Blau, 2001:Chapter 2, note 4), but the connection between these two facts and the direction of causality are not clear. Patterns of nonrelative care use across metropolitan and nonmetropolitan areas are fairly similar.[3]

In summary, relative care is more often used by Hispanic families, families with less education, families with a mother who works part time, families with younger children, and families with lower incomes. Furthermore, working nonstandard hours is associated with a greater reliance on relatives for child care (O'Connell, 1993; Casper, 1997; Casper and O'Connell, 1998). Among married, dual-earner households, split-shift work increases father participation in child care responsibilities, thus decreasing child care costs and increasing parent involvement (Presser, 1994; Brayfield,

---

[3]SIPP has been collecting data on child care since 1985, so in principle it is possible to examine trends in child care use over the period 1985-1999. However, there have been several important changes in survey design that make comparisons over time difficult. Smith (2002) shows trends in child care use in the SIPP data for children ages 0-4 (not 0-5, as in Table 3-1) with employed mothers. The results show substantial fluctuation over time in the use of nonrelative care (as defined here), with some suggestion of a decline in recent years.

1995; Garey, 1999; Hoffman et al., 1999). Grandparents are particularly involved in child care for single mothers who work nonstandard hours (Presser, in press; see Hofferth et al., 1991, for similar findings on use of relative care by Hispanics).

Finally, as noted earlier, 39 percent of preschoolers with employed mothers had more than one child care arrangement: 28 percent had two arrangements, and 12 percent had three or more arrangements. The percentage of children in multiple arrangements is especially high when mothers work nonstandard hours; for example, 51 percent when mothers work a rotating schedule (Presser, in press). In 1999, the majority (60 percent) of secondary arrangements were in relative care, compared with 49 percent of primary arrangements. Use of multiple arrangements is most common when the primary arrangement is a parent (45 percent have a secondary arrangement) or a center (48 percent). Average hours per week in secondary arrangements are 15.

School-Age Children

There were an estimated 35 million children in the United States ages 6 to 14 in spring 1999, of whom 22 million (63 percent) had an employed mother. For the great majority of the children of employed mothers (80 percent), the primary child care arrangement was school. School serves as a child care arrangement in most cases for six to seven hours per day during the school year. As noted later, unsupervised care increases during the summer months.

Table 3-2 classifies children ages 6 to 14 according to their primary arrangement other than school. Arrangements for school-age children are classified as center, nonrelative (including family day care homes), organized activities, parent, grandparent, other relative, and self-care. Organized activities include before- and after-school programs, lessons, sports, and clubs. The distribution of primary nonschool arrangements for children ages 6 to 14 was 5 percent in center care, 9 percent in nonrelative care, 12 percent in organized activities, 37 percent by parents, 14 percent by grandparents, 12 percent by other relatives, and 12 percent by self-care. Average hours per week in the primary care arrangement were 14.4, with longer hours in centers and nonrelative care (21.4 and 18.8, respectively) and shorter hours in organized activities (10.4). Average hours per week in all arrangements other than school totaled 20.7. Thus, the typical school-age child is in some kind of child care for a significant amount of time.

Use of the different types of child care for school-age children did not vary much by marital status, but married mothers were more likely than other mothers to use organized activities. This pattern appears throughout the table: use of organized activities is higher for more advantaged families,

TABLE 3-2   Percentage Distribution of Employed Mothers' Primary Child Care Arrangements Other Than School for Children Ages 6-14, Spring 1999

Demographic Characteristic	Center	Other Nonrelative	Organized Activity	Parent	Grand-parent	Other Relative	Self
All	5	9	12	37	14	13	12
Married	5	8	12	42	10	11	12
Widowed, divorced separated, married spouse absent	6	10	11	24	20	16	14
Never married	5	11	10	22	26	19	8
White	5	8	13	39	11	11	14
Black	5	8	12	31	19	17	9
Hispanic	4	13	8	33	17	19	7
Other	4	9	8	37	19	13	10
Noncitizen	3	10	5	43	12	20	6
Native	5	9	13	36	13	12	13
Native citizen	8	13	8	38	14	12	7
< High school	3	8	6	37	14	24	8
High school	5	8	9	37	17	13	12
Some college	5	10	11	36	14	12	13
College graduate	6	9	18	37	9	9	13
Full time	6	10	11	32	15	14	13
Part time	2	7	12	49	11	11	9
Day shift	5	9	13	35	13	13	13
Nonday	3	9	8	44	16	13	7
<poverty	5	8	8	37	19	16	8
1-2 poverty	3	9	10	37	15	18	9
2+ poverty	5	9	13	37	12	11	14
Public assistance	4	10	7	25	24	22	8
No public assistance	5	9	12	37	13	12	12
Age 6	11	17	10	35	18	9	1
Age 7	8	12	12	35	21	11	1
Age 8	6	12	12	38	16	13	2
Age 9	5	14	10	37	17	13	5
Age 10	5	9	13	40	13	14	6
Age 11	5	8	13	36	13	15	11
Age 12	2	5	11	37	11	15	19
Age 13	0	2	12	37	7	15	27
Age 14	1	2	10	34	6	11	33
South	7	8	12	32	15	15	10
Non-South	9	10	10	39	13	12	13

(continued)

TABLE 3-2   Continued

Demographic Characteristic	Center	Nonrelative	Organized Activity	Parent	Grand-parent	Other Relative	Self
Metro	5	9	12	37	13	13	12
Nonmetro	3	9	12	36	14	14	13

NOTES: Data are weighted. Unweighted sample size is 6,489. Nonrelative includes family day care homes, babysitters, nannies, and other unspecified nonrelatives. Hispanics are excluded from the white, black, and other race categories. Public assistance includes Temporary Aid for Needy Families, food stamps, and other programs such as General Assistance and SSI. Full time = 35+ hours each week in the month prior to the survey. Part time = 1-34 hours each week.

SOURCE: Tabulations from SIPP 1996 panel, wave 10 (Spring 1999).

regardless of whether advantage is measured by marital status, race/ethnicity, education, income, receipt of public assistance, or nativity. Nonrelative care use for school-age children increases with the mother's education, and the gap in the use of organized activities is especially large by maternal education, with only 6 percent of high school dropouts compared with 18 percent of college graduates using organized activities. Nonrelative care is used more often by mothers who work full time (27 percent compared with 21 percent for part time) and by day shift workers (27 percent compared with 19.7 percent for nonday shift workers). The biggest differences that appear in the table are by the child's age, with 38 percent of 6-year-old children in nonrelative care, 27 percent of 10-year-old children in nonrelative care, and 13 percent of 14-year-old children in nonrelative care. These differences undoubtedly reflect parental perceptions of differences in children's needs and capabilities by age, as well as the changing interests of children and the availability of appropriate programs for those age groups.

Finally, self-care, or care without adult supervision, has been a major policy concern for school-age children. According to the 1999 SIPP data, the extent to which children spend at least some time caring for themselves varies somewhat by family characteristics, although these differences are small. For example, a higher proportion of children with married mothers spend time in self-care (12 percent) than children of never-married women (8 percent); white children spend more time in self-care (14 percent) than black (9 percent) or Hispanic (7 percent) children; children of full-time working mothers spend more time in self-care (13 percent) than children of part-time working mothers (9 percent); and children with mothers working the day shift spend more time in self-care (13 percent) than children with mothers working nonday shifts (7 percent). The use of self-care varies more by age of child than it does for family characteristics. For example, a third of 14-year-old children spent time in care without adult supervision compared with less than 1 percent of 6-year-olds.

Overall, the data on self-care should be interpreted with caution. The estimates of the number of children without adult supervision have varied across reports and depends somewhat on the month the question is asked (whether school is in session or not), the parents' interpretation of the term "self-care," and the parents' willingness to admit that their children are left home alone. For example, a study released by the Urban Institute based on data from the 1999 National Survey of America's Families (Capizzano et al., 2002) found that while 1 in 10 children under age 13 spent time alone, these children spent twice as much time unsupervised in the summer than during the school year.

CHILD CARE EXPENDITURES

In 1999, there were an estimated 21.8 million families with an employed mother and at least one child ages 0 to 14. Table 3-3 (first row) shows that 43 percent of these families reported making a cash payment for child care for at least one child. The average weekly payment for all child care arrangements for all children among families that made any payment was $76.[4] The average percentage of family income spent on child care was 7.5 percent, almost identical to the figures for 1997 and 1995 and up slightly from 7.3 percent in 1993, 7.1 percent in 1991, 6.8 percent in 1988, and 6.3 percent in 1986 (Smith, 2000).[5] The fact that only 43 percent of employed mothers paid for child care may seem surprising, but the rate of use of nonrelative care by employed mothers of children, averaged over all children ages 0 to 14, is 42.1 percent. The rate of use of paid care was 56.8 percent for families with children ages 0 to 5 only, and 31.1 percent for families with children ages 6 to 14 only. The former group averaged $89 per week in child care expenditures (9 percent of family income), and the latter group averaged $55 per week (5.3 percent).[6]

---

[4]This is sharply lower than the average weekly payment of $85 reported in the 1995 SIPP (Smith, 2000). This may be a result of the change from a fall interview in 1995 to a spring (March-June) interview in 1999. Smith (2002) suggests that the spring interview period includes months in which children were off from school and may not have been in their regular arrangement.

[5]The SIPP questions on child care expenditure are intended to measure out-of-pocket cash expenditure by families. Since most child care subsidies do not take the form of cash, we can be reasonably confident that subsidies are not included in reports of cash expenditure.

[6]These payments include a variety of hours of care, ranging from less than five hours a week to more than 40 hours a week. See Smith (2002) for a breakdown of payments by different characteristics.

TABLE 3-3 Total Family Child Care Expenditure in Families with an Employed Mother, Spring 1999

Demographic Characteristic	All Families			Families with Children 0-5 Only			Families with Children 6-14 Only		
	% Pay	Weekly Expenditure	% of Income	% Pay	Weekly Expenditure	% of Income	% Pay	Weekly Expenditure	% of Income
All	43.0	76	7.5	56.1	89	9.0	31.1	55	5.3
Married	44.7	78	5.6	58.0	95	6.8	31.9	55	3.7
Widowed, divorced separated, married spouse absent	37.5	71	12.4	63.5	90	16.2	22.5	58	9.3
Never married	40.9	66	13.1	48.4	69	12.5	28.1	53	9.8
White	45.9	75	6.3	61.4	92	7.5	33.0	52	4.5
Black	35.9	71	10.6	45.4	73	11.8	24.2	56	7.5
Hispanic	41.3	80	11.5	48.0	89	16.4	31.3	65	8.5
Other	30.6	88	7.3	38.4	83	5.4	24.6	83	5.8
Age of youngest child									
0-2	56.3	96	10.1	54.7	98	10.2			
3-5	58.5	82	7.7	58.3	74	7.1			
6-8	43.7	66	7.0				43.7	66	7.0
9-11	31.0	52	4.1				31.0	56	4.1
12-14	16.9	31	2.9				16.9	31	2.9

(continued)

TABLE 3-3 Continued

Demographic Characteristic	All Families			Families with Children 0-5 Only			Families with Children 6-14 Only		
	% Pay	Weekly Expenditure	% of Income	% Pay	Weekly Expenditure	% of Income	% Pay	Weekly Expenditure	% of Income
< High school	30.0	73	15.2	49.4	75	19.2	18.1	62	11.5
High school	36.7	67	8.5	50.2	73	9.9	24.6	57	6.4
Some college	43.6	71	7.4	54.8	81	8.2	32.9	54	5.6
College graduate	55.7	88	5.1	65.5	111	6.6	43.0	54	3.0
Full time	45.8	79	7.2	63.9	93	8.6	32.6	59	5.4
Part time	37.5	63	6.2	41.1	77	5.7	28.2	42	4.6
Day shift	45.3	79	7.3	62.5	93	8.4	32.0	56	5.3
Nonday	35.2	63	8.5	38.1	71	11.8	27.3	50	5.3
Mother's earnings									
< $18,000	34.7	64	10.5	46.5	66	11.5	21.6	50	8.3
$18-35,999	48.3	73	6.1	65.1	93	7.6	35.7	52	4.6
$36-53,999	56.0	97	5.0	69.9	126	6.5	45.1	61	3.3
$54,000+	57.4	108	3.6	71.3	147	5.0	46.9	74	2.3
Family income									
< $18,000	35.1	65	22.8	51.0	58	22.2	20.8	52	19.5
$18-35,999	36.3	70	10.6	47.9	81	11.9	26.5	58	8.9
$36-53,999	43.2	67	5.9	57.4	81	7.2	29.5	48	4.2
$54,000+	49.0	84	3.9	62.2	106	5.0	36.7	57	2.5

NOTES: Data are weighted. Unweighted sample size is 5,864. Hispanics are excluded from the white, black, and other race categories. Full time = 35+ hours each week in the month prior to the survey. Part time = 1-34 hours each week.

SOURCE: Tabulations from SIPP 1996 panel, wave 10 (Spring 1999).

The other rows of the table illustrate how family child care expenditures differ by child and household characteristics. In most cases, married mothers are more likely to pay for child care than are nonmarried mothers and spend more if they do pay, but the percentage of family income spent by married mothers on child care is less than half the percentage for nonmarried mothers. White families are 5 percentage points more likely to pay for child care than Hispanic families, who are in turn 5 points more likely to pay for care than black families. Black and Hispanic families who do pay for care pay a greater share of income than others (10.6 percent to 11.5 percent compared with 6.3 for whites). The rate at which families use paid child care peaks when the youngest child is ages 3 to 5, but the amount and the percentage of family income paid are highest when the youngest child is ages 0 to 2, at $96 per week and 10.1 percent of family income.

The percentage paying for care increases with education, from 30 percent for high school dropouts to 55.7 percent for college graduates. The amount paid is higher for college graduates at $88 than for the other education groups ($67-73), while the percentage of income spent on child care falls monotonically with education, from 15.2 percent for high school dropouts to 5.1 percent for college graduates. These patterns also appear for families with only children ages 0 to 5 and for families with only children ages 6 to 14. Similar patterns are evident when families are classified by income or by the mother's earnings, with the single difference being the much sharper gradient in the percentage of income spent on child care. For example, 22.8 percent of income is spent on child care by families with annual incomes less than $18,000, while only 3.9 percent of income is spent on child care by families with income over $54,000 per year. It is interesting to note that the amount paid rises more sharply with increases in the mother's earnings than with increases in family income. For example, among families with only children ages 0 to 5, the average payment rises from $58 to $106 from the lowest to the highest income group, and from $66 to $147 from the lowest to highest mother's earnings group. This pattern suggests a higher propensity to spend on child care out of the mother's earnings than out of other income sources. This is consistent with findings that income controlled by mothers is spent disproportionately on child-related goods and services compared with other sources of family income (for some evidence on this from studies done in the United Kingdom, see Lundberg et al., 1997, and in Brazil, see Thomas, 1990).

Of mothers who are employed full time, 45.8 percent pay for care; of mothers employed part time, only 37.5 percent pay for care. The differential is even larger in families with only young children (63.9 compared with 41.1 percent). Part-time workers spend less on child care, but not in proportion to their hours worked. This suggests that part-time care is significantly more costly per hour than full-time care, a finding confirmed by data from other sources (Hofferth et al., 1991). If child care is priced by the week or the month, then families using part-time care may be forced to pay for a full-time slot. It is also possible that families seeking full-time care choose less expensive care. The day/nonday shift differences are similar to the full-time/part-time differences.

CHILD CARE SUPPLY

The simplest way to measure the supply of child care is to consider the licensed capacity of existing day care centers and family day care homes. However, this approach is problematic for our purposes for several reasons. First, many family day care homes and some centers and preschools are legally exempt from licensing and registration requirements, and therefore they are not found in state licensing lists. Second, the availability of babysitters, nannies, and relatives cannot be estimated in this manner. Third, licensed capacity does not distinguish between care provided during working and nonworking hours of employed mothers. Fourth, and most important, licensed capacity is a short-run measure that reflects the existing level of demand as well as supply. Should demand for nonrelative care rise in the future, one would expect licensed capacity to increase as well, through expansion of existing facilities and entry of new establishments.

Bearing in mind the shortcomings of licensed capacity as a measure of supply, the following data provide an overview of the supply of nonrelative care. The Profile of Child Care Settings (PCS) survey of day care centers and regulated family day care homes estimated that in 1990 there were 80,072 day care centers with a licensed capacity of 5,333,067 children; and 117,995 registered family day care homes with a licensed capacity of 859,506 children (Kisker et al., 1991). The National Child Care Survey (NCCS) of 1990 estimated that 6,104,000 children under 13 were enrolled in a day care center in 1990 for their primary child care arrangement (Hofferth et al., 1991).[7] The excess of enrollment over licensed capacity

---

[7]The PCS was a telephone survey of a sample of centers and family day care homes drawn from state lists of licensed facilities. A stratified random sample of counties was selected (with probability proportional to the number of children under age 5), and a stratified random sample of early education and care providers was drawn from the licensing list for each county. Counties were stratified by region, metropolitan status, and poverty level. Providers were stratified by whether they were home-based, Head Start, public school-based, or other center-based. The PCS data are over ten years old, but there have not been any nationally representative surveys of providers since the PCS. The data from the PCS should be interpreted with the caveat that we do not know whether the patterns documented in 1990 have changed significantly. Failure to regularly collect data on providers is a significant shortcoming of the U.S. child care data collection system, as we discuss in Chapter 9 of this report. The NCCS was a telephone survey of households with children under age 13 located in the same counties drawn for the PCS survey. The sample was selected randomly from telephone numbers in the selected counties.

may be accounted for by day care centers and preschools exempt from licensing. The NCCS also estimated that in 1990 3,193,000 children were enrolled in a family day care home as the primary child care arrangement. The large difference in this case between licensed capacity and enrollment undoubtedly reflects the fact that a large majority of family day care homes are believed to be unlicensed (National Research Council, 1990). A total of 37 percent of centers were for profit, of which 28 percent were independent and 9 percent were part of a national or local chain. Of the 63 percent of nonprofit centers, 6 percent were Head Start programs, 7 percent were based in public schools, 18 percent were religious-sponsored, 7 percent were sponsored by other groups (government agencies, community agencies, employers, etc.), and the remaining 25 percent were independent. These data are more than 12 years old, and there has not been a more recent national data collection that would reflect current licensed capacity.

More recent data collected by the Children's Foundation (CF) indicate that there were 113,506 licensed day care centers in 2001, and 306,246 regulated family day care homes (Children's Foundation, 2002). However, the Children's Foundation does not provide data on licensed capacity. It has gathered data for over a decade on the number of centers listed with licensing agencies, and its figures for 1990-1991 can be compared with data from the PCS. The Children's Foundation estimate of the number of centers in 1991 was 86,212, compared with an estimate of 80,072 by the PCS in 1990. This is a reasonably close correspondence. However, the Children's Foundation figure for family day care homes in 1990 was 223,351, much larger than the PCS estimate of 117,995. The reason for this large discrepancy is unclear.

Another source of information on availability of child care is the Census of Services, conducted every five years by the U.S. Census Bureau. The 1997 Census of Services found a total of 62,054 day care centers (establishments with payroll), which is only about two-thirds the 97,046 figure for 1997 from the Children's Foundation (U.S. Census Bureau, 2002b). The 1992 Census of Services estimated 489,054 family day care homes (establishments without payroll), compared with 265,347 in the Children's Foundation 1992 survey. The former figure applies to all family day care homes, while the latter refers only to regulated homes. The large differences across sources in estimates of the number of centers and family day care homes as well as the absence of recent information on licensed capacity illustrate the problems in measuring availability of private child care, thus making it difficult to draw any firm conclusions about the availability of private child care services.

Yet another source of information related to the supply of child care is the recent estimate of the size and components of the U.S. Child Care Workforce and Caregiving Population conducted by the Center for the

Child Care Workforce and the Human Services Policy Center at the University of Washington (May 2002), which was funded by the U.S. Department of Health and Human Services. Focusing on paid caregivers for children ages 0 to 5, the study estimates that there are 2.3 million such caregivers in the United States at a single point in time, including 550,000 (24 percent) working in child care centers, 650,000 (28 percent) providing family day care, 804,000 (35 percent) functioning as paid relatives other than family day care providers, and 298,000 (13 percent) as paid nonrelatives other than those working in centers or family day care programs (i.e., nannies). In addition to the paid child care workforce, the study estimated that approximately 2.4 million individuals provide unpaid child care during a given week. Most (93 percent) of these individuals are unpaid relatives, and the remainder are volunteers in centers or unpaid, nonrelative caregivers.

No current national data track how much time and effort working families spend trying to find child care at a price they are able to pay. Several recent reports (U.S. General Accounting Office, 1997; Mezey et al., 2002) suggest, as would be expected and is implied by data reported earlier in this chapter, that the lack of adequate supply is especially trying for parents of infants and toddlers, for children with special needs, for older schoolchildren, and for children of families working nonstandard hours. It is important that the requisite data be collected for the nation on a regular basis.

CHILD CARE QUALITY

Two main approaches have been used to characterize the quality of child care. One is based on structural features of the child care setting that are thought to affect the developmental appropriateness of the care for children. These features include the size of the group in which care is provided, the ratio of adult caregivers to children, the overall education level and specialized early childhood education and training of the providers, and the stability of the setting as measured by the turnover rate of the care providers. The other approach to measuring quality uses direct observation of the developmental appropriateness of the care received, as recorded by trained observers using standardized instruments. The ratings made by the observers are subjective in the sense that the observer makes a judgment about where on a given ordinal scale a child care setting lies (for example, a 1-7 ordinal scale or a "not at all," "somewhat," or "highly" characteristic scale). However, raters can be trained to produce ratings that are highly correlated with ratings of the same settings by other observers. And these process measures are believed to be more directly related than structural measures to child outcomes of interest.

The most recent nationally representative data on the structural measures are from 1990, and no nationally representative data are available on the process measures. Once again, failure to collect such data is a significant shortcoming of the child care data collection system in the United States. Here, we summarize the available information on quality.

The Profile of Child Care Settings (Kisker et al., 1991) collected information on structural classroom characteristics from a nationally representative sample of child care centers and regulated family day care homes through a telephone survey in 1990. There are limitations to telephone surveys for the purpose of measuring the structural characteristics, compared with recording them by direct on-site observation. Child care classrooms are in flux during the day, with groups often changing composition and merging with other groups for some activities for part of the day and teachers moving among classrooms (Helburn, 1995). The PCS telephone survey provided a static snapshot of a typical period during the day, but it did not capture the dynamics of classroom composition throughout the day. Nevertheless, these data provide a useful overview of the distribution of quality characteristics. It is also important to bear in mind that regulated family day care homes are unlikely to be representative of unregulated day care homes, and that the latter are thought to be far more numerous than the former.

Table 3-4 summarizes characteristics of centers and family day care homes (see Kisker et al., 1991, for more details). Average group size was 16 in centers and 7 in regulated homes. Group size increased with the age of children in centers, but not in family day care homes. The average group size in centers was 7 for infants, 10 for 1-year-olds, 12 for 2-year-olds, and 17 for 3- to 5-year-olds, which were within the range of maximum group size recommended by the National Association for the Education of Young Children (NAEYC) (see National Research Council, 1990) at that time. The average child-staff ratio was 9:1 in centers and 6:1 in regulated homes. The ratio of 4:1 for infants was at the high end of the range recommended by NAEYC at that time, and the ratios of 6.2:1 for 1-year-olds and 7.3:1 for 2-year-olds exceeded the NAEYC recommended ranges for these age groups. The average of 9.9 for 3- to 5-year-old children was at the high end of the NAEYC recommended level. The great majority of children in centers are 3 to 5 years old, so the majority of classrooms were (barely) within the range recommended by NAEYC.

The annual turnover rate of teachers reported by centers was 25 percent (half the centers in the sample reported no turnover, and the other half reported turnover averaging 50 percent annually). With regard to education of the teachers, almost half (47 percent) had a four-year degree, 39 percent had some college education, 13 percent had a high school diploma or graduate equivalency degree (GED), and there were virtually no high

TABLE 3-4   Characteristics of Day Care Centers and Regulated Family
Day Care Homes, 1990

Characteristic	Day Care Centers	Regulated Family Day Care Homes
Average group size[a]	16	7
Infants only	7	7
1-year-olds only	10	7
2-year-olds only	12	7
3-5-year-olds only	17	8
Average child-staff ratio[a]	9	6
Infants only	4	6
1-year-olds only	6	6
2-year-olds only	7	6
3-5-year-olds only	10	7
Annual rate of teacher turnover	25%	
Percentage of centers with any turnover	50%	
Turnover rate in centers with turnover	50%	
Average percentage of teachers with:		
At least a BA/BS degree	47%	11%
Some college	39%	44%
High school degree or GED	13%	34%
No degree or GED	1%	11%
Percentage of teachers who have had:[b]		
CDA training	25%	6%
Teacher training	35%	
Other education training	40%	
Child care workshops or courses	54%	43%
Child development or psychology courses	36%	28%
Nurse or health training	26%	
Training by a R&R or government agency	5%	5%
Social service training	4%	2%
Other training	6%	

[a] Excludes programs that serve primarily handicapped children.
[b] The training information for center refers only to private, nonreligious-sponsored centers.
SOURCE: Kisker et al. (1991).

school dropouts (1 percent). Operators of regulated family day care homes
had much less education, with only 11 percent having graduated from
college, 40 percent with some college education, 34 percent with a high
school diploma or GED, and 16 percent who were high school dropouts.
Specialized training in early education, child development, or child care is
also more common among center staff than in family day care homes. One-
quarter of day care center teachers had earned a child development associ-

ate (CDA) credential, compared with only 6 percent of family day care home operators.

Many studies (summarized in National Research Council and Institute of Medicine, 2000) have found that more formal education and specialized training for caregivers, a higher ratio of caregivers to children in their care, and lower caregiver turnover rates are, other things being equal, associated with a higher quality experience for children. Whether these correlations represent causal effects is uncertain, but it is likely that better working conditions, including higher wages and smaller group size, attract caregivers with more formal education and specialized training, and the associated better outcomes for children are the result.

As indicated earlier, there are no nationally representative samples of child care centers with measures of process quality. Two studies with reasonable sample sizes have measured process quality in site-specific samples of child care centers that may be representative of centers in the selected sites.[8] The Cost, Quality, and Outcomes (CQO) study and the National Child Care Staffing Study used the same instruments to rate quality—the Early Childhood Environment Rating Scale (ECERS) and its infant-toddler counterpart (ITERS). These instruments take about three hours to complete and rate each observed classroom on 30 to 35 items using a scale of 1 to 7 for each item. As a guide to the intended interpretation of the scores, ratings of 1, 3, 5, and 7 are designated by the instrument designers as representing inadequate, minimal, good, and excellent care, respectively (see Harms and Clifford et al., 1980, and Harms et al., 1990). Summary scores are obtained by averaging over the items. Table 3-5 presents descriptive statistics on quality ratings in day care centers from these two studies by site, age of children in the classroom, and the auspices of the center (for profit or nonprofit).

It is important to bear in mind that the samples in these two studies are drawn from a small number of states, and while they are likely to be reasonably well representative of centers in those states, we have no way to determine whether they are nationally representative. The overall average rating in both studies is just under 4, or about halfway between minimal and good. The authors of the CQO report refer to this level of quality as "mediocre" (Helburn, 1995). Quality varies substantially across locations, with the highest quality sites (Boston, California, Connecticut) rated almost a full point above the lowest quality sites (Atlanta, North Carolina, Seattle). Classrooms with preschool-age children are almost always rated to be of higher quality than infant-toddler rooms, by a fairly wide margin in the

---

[8] A third study, discussed below, is based on a sample of children and consists of the centers and all other child care arrangements in which the sample children were enrolled.

TABLE 3-5 Distribution of Child Care Quality in Day Care Centers as Measured by the Early Childhood and Infant Toddler Environment Rating Scales: Mean (and Standard Deviation)

	All Centers	For Profit		Nonprofit	
		Preschool	Infant-Toddler	Preschool	Infant-Toddler
		Cost, Quality, and Outcomes Study (1993)			
All Sites	3.99 (1.07)	4.07 (0.99)	3.33 (1.02)	4.41 (0.96)	3.57 (1.07)
California	4.36 (0.96)	4.27 (0.88)	3.86 (0.70)	4.66 (0.97)	3.60 (1.07)
Colorado	3.94 (0.95)	4.09 (0.85)	3.40 (0.89)	4.25 (0.89)	3.66 (1.04)
Connecticut	4.24 (1.05)	4.46 (1.02)	4.00 (1.07)	4.33 (0.99)	3.85 (1.13)
North Carolina	3.44 (1.08)	3.28 (0.83)	2.54 (0.60)	4.31 (0.95)	3.29 (1.02)
		National Child Care Staffing Study (1989)			
All Sites	3.92 (0.99)	3.59 (0.90)	3.43 (0.98)	4.39 (0.97)	4.09 (1.07)
Atlanta	3.57 (0.96)	3.32 (0.84)	3.04 (0.86)	4.30 (0.87)	3.89 (1.05)
Boston	4.44 (0.72)	3.66 (0.86)	3.16 (0.57)	4.72 (0.61)	4.51 (0.72)
Detroit	3.96 (1.24)	4.23 (1.04)	3.86 (1.37)	4.14 (1.40)	3.69 (1.45)
Phoenix	4.09 (0.90)	3.74 (0.75)	3.84 (0.83)	4.79 (0.89)	4.48 (0.97)
Seattle	3.62 (0.84)	3.30 (0.86)	3.37 (1.06)	3.99 (0.73)	3.63 (0.96)

NOTES: See Cryer et al. (1995) for description of the CQO Study, and Whitebook et al. (1989) for description of the NCCSS. Sample size is 731 classrooms in 401 centers for the CQO study and 665 classrooms in 227 centers for the NCCSS. The public release data set from the NCCSS does not include the scores on the individual ECERS and ITERS items or the average score. Rather, it includes two summary measures derived from factor analysis of the underlying items. The figures presented here are the unweighted average of the two summary measures. This has the same scale as the ECERS and ITERS scores from the CQO but was derived differently, so comparisons between the CQO and NCCSS should be made with caution.

SOURCES: Tabulations from the Cost, Quality, and Outcomes Study (CQO) and the National Child Care Staffing Study (NCCSS).

CQO data.[9] With only a few exceptions, nonprofit centers received higher average quality ratings than for-profit ones.[10]

The National Institute of Child Health and Human Development has been leading a longitudinal Study of Early Child Care (SECC) since the early 1990s. This study selected a sample of births in hospitals in 10 sites around the United States and has been following the children and their families ever since. Among other features of the study, the child care arrangements in which the study children were enrolled were visited and assessed for quality. Because this study was not limited to centers, a new quality assessment instrument was developed that could be used in a variety of different settings. This instrument, known as the Observational Record of the Caregiving Environment (ORCE), focuses on the caregiver's interaction with the study child, rather than on the overall quality of the arrangement. Like the ECERS and the ITERS, the ORCE takes about three hours to administer, and the final score is an average over the various observations during the recording period. The scale for this instrument is 1 to 4, with 1 indicating that a particular dimension of positive caregiving was "not at all characteristic," 2 indicating "somewhat uncharacteristic," 3, "somewhat characteristic," and 4, "highly characteristic."

Table 3-6 summarizes the distribution of ORCE scores at three different observation ages—15, 24, and 36 months—separately by type of child care arrangement (NICHD Early Child Care Research Network, 2000a). The most striking feature of the data is the relatively low quality of centers and family day care homes compared with care by the father, grandparent, or in-home babysitter. At age 15 months, positive caregiving is somewhat or highly characteristic of 28 percent of centers and 50 percent of family day care homes compared with 60 to 71 percent of fathers, grandparents, and in-home babysitters. The quality of the more informal types of care

---

[9]The ECERS and ITERS instruments are similar but not identical. It is not clear whether quality differences by age of children in the classroom are real or reflect different scales of the instruments.

[10]There is little systematic information on process quality in family day care homes. Kontos et al. (1995) studied about 200 family day care homes and relatives providing child care. They concluded that the majority of providers were providing care of adequate quality, about one third were providing inadequate quality care, and only 9 percent were providing good quality care.

There is no published breakdown of quality by family characteristics in the CQO study. The NCCSS reported some quality breakdowns by a measure of socioeconomic status (SES) of the families, as reported by the center director. This is not a very useful measure, because directors were not given any instructions on how to define SES. Quality tends to be highest in centers reporting the highest family SES, lowest in the middle SES, and in-between for centers reporting the lowest SES (many of which are Head Start or other heavily subsidized programs).

TABLE 3-6 Percentage Distribution of Observed Positive Caregiving in the NICHD Study of Early Child Care

Child Age	Positive Caregiving Rating			
	Not at all Characteristic	Somewhat Uncharacteristic	Somewhat Characteristic	Highly Characteristic
15 months				
Father	5	36	35	25
Grandparent	5	24	46	25
In-home	3	36	37	24
Family day care	7	44	34	16
Center	10	62	23	5
24 months				
Father	5	45	30	20
Grandparent	5	31	49	15
In-home	8	34	34	24
Family day care	9	50	28	14
Center	11	66	19	4
36 months				
Father	5	48	37	10
Grandparent	2	53	37	8
In-home	5	39	45	12
Family day care	2	63	29	5
Center	4	62	30	3

NOTES: The ORCE instrument has a rating scale of 1-4. The ratings here are based on averages over several time periods, with the following assignments: not at all characteristic = mean rating < 2; somewhat uncharacteristic = mean rating 2 to < 3; somewhat characteristic = mean rating 3 to < 3.5; highly characteristic = mean rating = 3.5.

SOURCE: NICHD Early Child Care Research Network (2000a:Table 5).

declines with the age of the children, as does the quality of family day care, while the quality of centers is lower at 24 than at 15 months but higher at 36 months than at either 15 or 24 months. By age 36 months, positive caregiving is somewhat or highly characteristic of 33 percent of centers and 34 percent of family day care homes compared with 47 percent of fathers, 45 percent of grandparents, and 56 percent of in-home babysitters. This differential may be due to the fact that the ORCE instrument emphasizes responsiveness to the individual child, and thus it might tend to produce higher quality ratings in small groups or individual care settings. It is important to emphasize that the figures presented in Table 3-6 are averages, and that there is substantial variation in quality within each type of care. This is illustrated for centers in Table 3-5 by the fact that the standard deviations within states and within type of child care center are on average about one point on a seven point scale.

SUMMARY

The evidence reviewed in this chapter highlights several important findings. The type of child care used by parents in the United States is very diverse in terms of setting, quality, and cost. Child care settings range from institutional arrangements, such as child care centers and preschools, to smaller family day care homes and in-home arrangements, with one adult hired to care for one child, to relative care. Child care is very diverse in quality, both within and across types of arrangements. About 56 percent of employed-mother families with preschool-age children only and 31 percent of families with older children only pay for child care. Among families that pay for child care, in 1999, the average percentage of family income spent on child care was 7.5 percent, for families with preschool age children only it was 9 percent, and it was 5.3 percent for families with school-age children. However, while low-income families are less likely to pay for care, child care is a major expenditure for those families who do pay, consuming about 23 percent of family income for families with annual incomes under $18,000. The average quality of child care in centers has been characterized as "mediocre," and the quality of child care by relatives, in-home babysitters, and other informal providers has not been highly rated either (Kontos et al., 1995).

Three implications of this portrait of child care are important for child development and public policy. First, the child care market has grown rapidly in the last 20 to 25 years, and **many children and adolescents are spending many hours in the care of someone other than their parent.** Nonrelative care is now the dominant source of child care in the United States, although relatives still play an important role in the care of children, particularly while they are very young. With regard to child care centers, the for-profit sector has grown the most rapidly. Thus the context in which public policy about child care will be made in the United States for the foreseeable future will in all likelihood include continued heavy reliance on a range of providers, rather than on a single delivery system. Most proposals for reform of public policy about child care are based on the presumption that the bulk of child care in the United States will continue to be provided though this diverse delivery system, perhaps with greater subsidies from the public sector (e.g., Barnett, 1993; Helburn and Bergmann, 2002; Blau, 2001; Gormley, 1995; Walker, 1996; Lombardi, 2003). New combinations of financing child care are emerging, which build public supports into the child care that is delivered in a variety of child care settings (Vast, 1998; Stoney, 1998; Lombardi, 2003). While these new financing strategies are promising, they are currently too small in scale to address the large amount of additional financing that may be needed to address problems in the child care market.

Second, the major federal welfare reform of 1996 required or induced many low-income mothers to enter the labor market. Some of the reforms discussed during the debate over reauthorization of federal welfare legislation in 2002 would impose even stricter work requirements for participation in welfare. **Child care during the mother's work hours is crucial for a successful transition from welfare to work.** While many low-income mothers are able to find child care at no monetary cost from relatives and other sources, many other low-income mothers who do pay for child care spend a large fraction of their income on such care. The welfare reform of 1996 increased funding for child care subsidies, but the amount of child care subsidy funds available remains much lower than the amount that would be needed to serve the population eligible under the federal child care subsidy program. Thus an important implication is that **funding for public child care subsidies may have to increase substantially if low-income families are to participate in the private market for child care in the new welfare environment.** Chapter 9 discusses further the importance of expanding public subsidies for child care.

Finally, the quality of child care is likely to have important consequences for the development of young children. A substantial amount of research on the impact of child care quality on development indicates that there is an effect, although the size of the effect is variable. The fact that the average quality of child care is mediocre in day care centers thus warrants concern. More generally, the lack of data on child care quality from a nationally representative sample of child care arrangements makes it difficult to draw firm conclusions about the adequacy of child care quality in the United States, although indicators of structural aspects of quality raise serious concerns. Given the mediocre average for centers in large-scale but local studies, we are reasonably confident that a substantial portion of center care is in fact of minimal or inadequate quality. The child development literature does not provide clear guidance on the threshold, if any, below which child care quality becomes a serious risk to the development of children. But it seems safe to conclude that low quality is potentially an important concern in the child care market in the United States. Moreover, **given the amount of time that children are spending in care, including a growing number of very young children, child care provides an important opportunity to promote their healthy development and overall well-being** (Lombardi, 2003).

Part II

Implications for the Development of Children and Adolescents

Part II considers the implications of the employment, family, and child care trends described in Part I. It reviews the science in a few specific areas. Chapter 4 reviews the research on maternal employment and its effects on the family. It describes how maternal employment is associated with a wide range of both positive and negative patterns of development for children and considers the ways in which it affects different subgroups of children.

Chapter 5 looks at early child care and school-age child care settings and considers the effects of care on children. It reviews conceptual and methodological advances that have informed recent research, reviews a set of large-scale studies that have examined the implications of child care quality on child developmental outcomes, and reviews evidence on associations between child care quality and various dimensions of the care.

Chapter 6 reviews the evidence on parental employment and a particular group of children—adolescents. It includes an overview of the salient tasks of adolescence, highlighting the opportunities and challenges that adolescents with working parents face.

Chapter 7 reviews evidence on the effects of welfare reform on the family, with particular attention to employment, earnings, poverty, fertility, and marriage, as well as the effects on children and adolescents.

4

Maternal Employment and the Family Environment

he evidence presented on trends in work and child care indicates that more mothers work and children and adolescents spend significant time in nonparental care. The committee's next step was to explore the extent to which these trends affect the development and well-being of children and adolescents in these families. This chapter reviews evidence on how maternal employment, particularly employment of low-income families, appears to affect the home environment of children and how that, in turn, affects children. Chapter 5 goes on to focus on the effects of child care environments on young children, while Chapter 6 focuses on the effects of care environments on adolescents.

The basis historically for research on maternal employment and children was premised with a straightforward and negative question: Does a mother's employment harm her children's development (Bianchi, 2000b; Gottfried et al., 1995)? This question emerged when more mothers, especially mothers with young children, began to enter the workforce. There was growing concern that substantial periods of time when a mother is inaccessible to her child, especially a young one, could affect the child's sense of his or her relationship with the mother as a source of comfort and as a safe base for exploring the environment (Ainsworth et al., 1978; Bowlby, 1969). It was hypothesized that not having reliable access to the mother would have unfavorable implications for the child's social, emotional, and cognitive development.

A RANGE OF PATTERNS

As the research on maternal employment has accumulated over a period of decades, it has become increasingly clear that the evidence does not support this negative hypothesis. The findings do not fall into a straightforward unidirectional pattern. Rather, the research indicates that:

1. maternal employment is associated with a wide range of patterns of development for children, ranging from positive to neutral to negative; and
2. the differences in developmental status that have been found for children of employed and nonemployed mothers have generally been found for specific and delineated population subgroups—for example, for specific age ranges but not others, for boys but not girls (or vice versa), and for children in families at some socioeconomic levels but not others.

Reviews of the research show key patterns (see, for example, Hoffman, 1979, 1984, 1989; Hoffman and Youngblade, 1999; National Research Council, 1982; Zaslow and Emig, 1997). In their recent review, Hoffman and Youngblade (1999) found evidence to support the following patterns: on the positive side, school-age and adolescent daughters of employed mothers show higher academic aspirations and achievement and are more likely to make nontraditional role choices than are daughters of nonemployed mothers, and both sons and daughters of employed mothers have less traditional attitudes about gender roles. The evidence further indicates that when preschool and school-age children in poverty show differences in development in light of their mothers' employment status, they also show more favorable cognitive and socioemotional outcomes.

On the negative side, some findings indicate lower school performance and academic achievement during middle childhood for middle-class sons of employed mothers. Hoffman and Youngblade (1999) point to an emerging pattern of findings suggesting that maternal employment may be associated with unfavorable developmental outcomes for children when the employment is resumed in the child's first year and is extensive (full time rather than part time). Findings providing further evidence of such a pattern have continued to emerge since the publication of that review (Brooks-Gunn et al., 2002; Han et al., 2001; Waldfogel et al., 2002).

As the research on maternal employment has evolved, the possible reasons for this more complex patterning of results have become increasingly clear. Three potential explanations have been identified:

• *Maternal employment influences family life in multiple ways simultaneously, with influences sometimes in counterbalancing directions.* A clearly articulated hypothesis in the research on maternal employment is

Parents not only affect their children's psychological development, they also introduce them to the world of work (Galinsky, 1999:355):

You have to work and teach your children how to work. Also, let them know how to do something they'll enjoy. You have to work to get what you want in life.

that this "status" variable (i.e., whether mothers are employed or not) does not affect children directly, but rather affects them to the extent that it brings about changes in their immediate experiences (Gottfried et al., 1995). Furthermore, maternal employment appears to affect multiple aspects of children's environments simultaneously, and it may do so in contrary directions. In recent ethnographic work, mothers making the transition from welfare to work themselves articulated this idea of multiple counterbalancing influences of their employment on their children (London et al., 2000). For example, mothers moving from welfare to employment see themselves as providing resources for the family and better role models for their children. At the same time, they perceive themselves as less available to their children and express concern about their ability to supervise them. Findings of neutral or small associations of maternal employment with child outcomes may actually reflect counterbalancing influences in the family rather than an absence of influences.

• *Families actively adapt to the mother's employment patterns.* The evidence suggests that families do not respond passively to the mother's employment, but rather actively compensate for hours the mother is away from the child, for example, through a reallocation by mothers of time spent in leisure to time spent with children and a redistribution of household tasks between parents (as explained in Chapter 2). The extent to which maternal employment is associated with children's outcomes (or instead shows limited or neutral patterns of association) may reflect the resources that the family has to make such active adaptations. Families with low incomes and complex work schedules that do not permit flexibility, or single-mother families with fewer resources to draw on, may have less capacity to make active adaptations.

• *Maternal employment is not a unitary variable in itself, but rather reflects key variations in employment circumstances.* Studies that distinguish simply whether a mother is employed or not (or employed full time, part time, or not at all), may overlook other key variations in employment circumstances that are important to children. Recent research suggests, for example, whether hours of employment are standard or nonstandard and such job characteristics as degree of autonomy on the job may be linked to family processes and child outcomes (Menaghan and Parcel, 1995; Han, 2002a). It is becoming increasingly clear that we need to move beyond the simple identification of employment status to capture such variation in job characteristics in order to understand influences on children.

STRENGTHS AND LIMITATIONS OF THE RESEARCH

Recent research has made substantial strides in examining maternal employment and child outcomes in low-income families. Whereas earlier research focused mostly on middle-class families, the focus more recently has been on families participating in the transition from welfare to work (Grogger et al., 2002; Morris et al., 2002; Zaslow et al., 2002) as well as low-income families in general (Phillips, 2002; Tout et al., 2002). The research on welfare-to-work programs studies what happens to children and families in light of whether the mother participated in a welfare-to-work program, rather than her transition to employment per se. Across a range of program approaches (for example, programs that mandate work without providing strong supports for employment, programs that combine work mandates with financial incentives for working, programs with time limits on welfare receipt), these programs have brought about increases in maternal employment. As such, these studies provide a context for considering child outcomes when employment increases as a result of welfare-to-work programs.

Another important development in the research is an explicit focus on the processes underlying associations between maternal employment and child outcomes, such as family economic resources, maternal parenting behavior, father involvement, and maternal psychological well-being. While this is an important step in the research, it is necessary to acknowledge that this approach is as yet limited. There is not a literature that can point to key underlying processes across the full range of child ages and population subgroups. And studies tend to provide fragments of the picture, linking maternal employment to underlying processes, and maternal employment to child outcomes, but not completing the picture by examining whether and how the underlying process helps to explain the association between maternal employment and child outcomes (or even a step further, considering how multiple processes function simultaneously). For example, a study may consider whether father involvement differs in families with and without an employed mother, but not whether father involvement is a key process in explaining the link between maternal employment and child outcomes. We are limited to a small set of studies that explicitly test the role of specific underlying processes in explaining the associations between maternal employment and child outcomes.[1]

A persisting issue in this body of work is whether differences by employment status in family processes or outcomes for children reflect differences in the characteristics of families in which the mother did and did not become employed rather than differences due to employment (see the discussion of these "selection effects" in Blau, in press; Vandell and Ramanan, 1992). Zaslow and colleagues (1999) note the substantially differing conclusions that are reached when a study simply describes differences in child outcomes in light of mother's employment status, or whether it seeks to control for the child, family, and broader social context factors that can predict to both maternal employment and child outcomes.

In this chapter, we reserve the terms "effects" and "impacts" to describe the results of studies using experimental designs (see Box 4-1 for elaboration on research terms used in this chapter and the rest of the report), specifically evaluations of welfare reform programs that sought to encourage or require employment. When discussing findings from non-experimental studies of maternal employment, because of concern with variation across studies in how well selection effects are accounted for, we do not use the terminology of "effects" of maternal employment on families or children, but rather restrict ourselves to describing "associations" of maternal employment or of "implications" of maternal employment for families and for children. And we restrict our focus to studies that, at the least, control for background characteristics that may predict both maternal employment and child outcomes.

MATERNAL EMPLOYMENT AND THE FAMILY ENVIRONMENT

Hoffman and Youngblade's review of the research (1999) hypothesizes that there are three key aspects of the family environment that differ in light of the mother's employment status and that in turn may be important to children's development: parenting behavior and the home environment, father involvement, and mother's psychological well-being. In addition, the work on maternal employment in the context of welfare reform adds a fourth key element to this list: family economic resources, which may in turn affect any of these three factors. We provide a brief overview of the evidence here, starting with the findings on family economic resources, and returning to the set of factors hypothesized by Hoffman and Youngblade.

---

[1]These studies use the statistical approach to studying mediation developed by Baron and Kenny (1986).

BOX 4-1
Research Terms

Experimental design: involves the random assignment of individuals to either a treatment group (in this case, participation in the program being assessed) or a control group (a group that is not given the treatment). Many believe that the experimental design provides some of the strongest, most clear evidence in research evaluation. This design also affords the highest degree of causal inference, since the randomized assignment of individuals to an intervention condition restricts the opportunity to bias estimates of the treatment effectiveness.

Nonexperimental design (also known as correlational methods): does not involve either random assignment or the use of control or comparison groups. These designs gather information through such methods as interviews, observations, and focus groups, and then examine relations or associations among variables in an effort to learn more about the individuals receiving the treatment (participating in the program) or the effects of the treatment on these individuals. Nonexperimental studies sometimes use statistical techniques to control for such factors as maturation, self-selection, attrition, or the interaction of such influences on program outcomes. The concern, however, is that unmeasured factors or variables may account for obtained relationships.

Multivariate analysis: any analysis in which two or more dependent variables are included in a single analysis.

Hierarchical regression: predictors are entered in analyses in a sequential order in which "control" variables are entered first followed by the selected variables of interest. Researchers are seeking to answer the question, "Does variable x predict outcome y after variables a, b, and c are controlled?"

Psychometrics: the branch of psychology that evaluates the reliability and validity of different measurement techniques. Reliability refers to the consistency of measurement over time, across raters or observers, or across individual items of a survey. Validity refers to whether the measure is assessing the construct of interest.

Effect size: calculated as the difference in means between the treatment and the control group divided by the standard deviation of the control group or the difference between the value specified in the null hypothesis and the research hypothesis. The larger the effect size, the more powerful the test because the difference between the sample and the null hypothesis mean will be farther apart, thus increasing the probability of rejecting the null hypothesis.

Econometrics: The branch of economics that applies statistical methods to analyze data.

Family Economic Resources

A mother's employment may affect children through the economic resources she provides for the family (Huston, 2002). Researchers hypothesize that the relative importance of the economic contribution from maternal employment is greater in lower-income than higher- income families (Desai et al., 1989), and that this may help account for the tendency of maternal employment to have positive implications in lower income families (Zaslow and Emig, 1997). Recent work (Dearing et al., 2001) indeed provides evidence that changes (both increases and decreases) in families' income-to-needs ratio (the ratio of total family income to poverty threshold for the appropriate family size) are much more important for cognitive and social outcomes of children in poor than nonpoor families.

A child warns parents that neglected children could become problems to society now or in the future (Galinsky, 1999:350):

> *It is good to work, and it definitely makes finances better for a family with two sources of income. Just don't alienate your children or let them do whatever they want whenever they want because that could get them in trouble.*

Economic resources can derive not only from earnings, but also through benefits intended to support employment, such as financial work incentives, including the federal and state earned income tax credits and child care subsidies (Zedlewski, 2002). The mother's contribution to overall family income may be of importance to children by influencing the adequacy of food, clothing, and housing; safety from injury and from dangerous elements in the physical environment (for example, from environmental toxins and violence); and by ensuring health care services (Huston, 2002). Family economic resources also contribute to the number and variety of toys and books available to the child in the home and the extent to which the family can engage in stimulating outings (e.g., Bradley, 1995; Bradley and Caldwell, 1984b; Bradley et al., 1988).

While there is substantial research looking at the link between family economic resources and child outcomes (Duncan and Brooks-Gunn, 2000; Duncan et al., 1994; Chase-Lansdale et al., 2003), very little research has looked at the role of economic resources in transmitting the implications of maternal employment to children, despite the fact that this is one of the main reasons for working and may help to shape other changes in the family (such as changes in maternal mental health).

Experimental studies of welfare reform programs provide evidence suggesting the importance of the economic implications of employment for children. Evidence looking across multiple evaluation studies of programs to encourage or require employment among families receiving welfare (Grogger et al., 2002; Morris et al., 2002; Zaslow et al., 2002) concludes that favorable impacts on children's development tend to occur in programs in which an increase in maternal employment was accompanied by an increase in family income. This pattern of increases in both employment and income occurred most consistently in programs that provided strong financial incentives for working (for example, through earned income disregards, which allow parents to keep more of their welfare benefits while working). Examples of programs with strong financial work incentives with positive impacts on young school-age children include the Minnesota Family Investment Program (Gennetian and Miller, 2000), New Hope (Bos et al., 1999), and the Canadian Self-Sufficiency Program (Morris and Michalopoulos, 2000).[2]

This pattern of favorable impacts on children did not typically occur in programs that increased employment without increasing overall family income (except in instances in which there was a program impact involving an increase in maternal educational attainment, for example, in a subset of the six JOBS programs, studied in the National Evaluation of Welfare-to-Work Strategies Child Outcomes Study; McGroder et al., 2000). Beyond the studies in which mothers increased their educational attainment, there are also indications that in programs in which the families did not make economic progress or actually experienced a setback on one or more of these economic outcomes, impacts for children fell in the neutral to unfavorable range (for example, in the New Chance Demonstration and selected sites of the Teenage Parent Demonstration, welfare reform programs for adolescent mothers; Quint et al., 1997; Kisker et al., 1998).

Recent reviews of research on welfare reform programs noting links between the economic impacts for families and the impacts for children have particularly found outcomes for children related to cognitive development and academic achievement, but also for behavioral outcomes. There were few impacts at all in these evaluations on outcomes related to children's health. Although health outcomes were studied in the least detail in these evaluations, the pattern of findings in these evaluations parallels the pattern of findings linking economic resources and child outcomes directly: outcomes related to intellectual achievement are most consistently found to be

---

[2]Experimental evaluations of welfare reform programs done in five of the states that were granted welfare waivers in the years prior to the 1996 welfare reform (Connecticut, Florida, Indiana, Iowa, and Minnesota) reported similar findings.

related to family income, with less evidence of a link with behavioral adjustment or health and safety outcomes (Dearing et al., 2001). Effect sizes of the impacts on children in the experimental evaluations of welfare reform fell in a range from about 0.10 to 0.80, with most falling at the lower end of the range. As discussed by Zaslow and colleagues (2002), while the effect sizes tended to be smaller than those found in the most successful programs aimed directly at improving the development of young children (such as the Abecedarian and High/Scope programs), they are comparable to the effect sizes for other programs focusing on young children (such as Early Head Start and the Tennessee STAR class size reduction program). These findings suggest that, beyond employment per se, the circumstances that surround and follow from it, including the implications of employment and associated benefits for families' overall economic circumstances, are important for children.

Zedlewski (2002) finds the evidence on economic resources of families following welfare reform to provide a complicated picture. Labor force participation has increased among single mothers with young children overall, among welfare recipients, and among families leaving welfare. Concerning the economic well-being of these families, however, findings differ according to what elements are included in the calculation of family economic resources. With only cash income taken into consideration, poverty has declined in the years since welfare reform. However when total family income is considered, including noncash benefits as well, studies suggest that a portion of families are faring worse in the years since welfare reform. The evidence indicates that while participation in the earned income tax credit is strong among eligible families, a substantial proportion of eligible families are not receiving food stamps, Medicaid, or child care benefits for which they are eligible. An important step for the research on maternal employment will be to take a closer look at how family economic resources are defined, in order to determine which approach best helps to explain associations between maternal employment, family resources, and children's outcomes.

Parenting Behavior

In studying the implications of employment for family life, particular emphasis has been placed on parenting behavior. This appears to be the case for two reasons: first, parenting behavior and the home environment appear to serve as conduits through which a broader set of influences on the family are conveyed to the child. For example, McLoyd (1990) summarizes evidence from a range of studies indicating that family economic stress is conveyed to children partially through the psychological distress it creates in parents and a resulting tendency to show harsher and less supportive parenting, which in turn predicts children's social and emotional outcomes.

Second, in studies that simultaneously examine the role of the home environment and of children's experiences in child care, results point to a relatively greater influence of the home environment (National Institute of Child Health and Human Development, 2001b). Thus, if maternal employment leads to changes in children's relationships and interactions with parents, this is likely to be an important pathway through which their development is influenced (Huston, 2002).

Much of the research on parenting has focused on maternal rather than paternal behavior. We next review evidence on the links between maternal parenting behavior and the quality of stimulation and support available to children in the home environment. The issue of father involvement is covered in a subsequent section.

Maternal Parenting

Chase-Lansdale and Pittman (2002) identify six dimensions of parenting: (1) gatekeeping, (2) warmth and responsiveness, (3) control and discipline, (4) cognitive stimulation, (5) modeling, and (6) family routines and traditions. In a review of the evidence on parenting behavior in light of welfare reform, these researchers note that initial expectations were that there would be a range of effects on parenting behavior, including an increase in family routines when mothers were employed and more positive role modeling. Focusing on the findings on parenting in the experimental evaluations of welfare reform programs, they find that employment in the context of reform has actually had limited effects on parenting. Rather than cutting across the differing dimensions of parenting, Chase-Lansdale and Pittman see the effects for preschool and school age children in these studies as concentrated primarily in terms of an enhancement in the gatekeeping aspects of parenting, which involve not direct interactions or structuring of the home environment, but rather oversight and guidance of the child's activities outside the home. For example, gatekeeping encompasses selection of child care contexts and out of school lessons and activities, as well as monitoring the child's whereabouts, activities, and friendships.

Their review finds that mothers of young children in a number of welfare reform programs (though not all) were more likely to make use of formal child care arrangements for their young children. They note that use of more formal child care may be related to better academic school readiness and, for school-age children, adjustment and progress in school. For example, mothers in the New Hope program were more likely to place their children, especially their sons, in structured after-school programs; sons in particular in this program showed positive program impacts in terms of teacher-rated measures of behavior in the classroom and the children's own educational and occupational aspirations (Bos et al., 1999).

An important extension of the gatekeeping hypothesis for preschool and school-age children comes from the recent work of Gennetian and colleagues (Gennetian et al., 2001; Crosby et al., 2001). These researchers distinguish between two types of welfare reform programs in terms of child care benefits: those that provide enhanced child care supports for families in the program group, and those that simply offer more of the same child care supports and benefits as employment increases, not distinguishing the nature of supports for those in the program and the control groups. Enhanced child care supports in the former group include any one (or a combination) of the following: (1) provide information and support specific to child care through case management or access to resource and referral agencies, (2) improve the process of reimbursement for child care, (3) continue eligibility during the transition off welfare, (4) promote the use of formal child care through financial or other means, and (5) restrict the provision of subsidies to regulated care.

In analyses of data from multiple welfare reform programs, this research finds that while such programs generally increase reliance on child care (as mothers increase their work preparation and employment activities), it is specifically in the programs with enhanced child care supports that mothers increased their reliance on formal child care settings, such as child care centers and organized after-school programs (showing larger absolute impacts on use of formal care and larger relative impacts of center compared with home-based child care). The pattern of differential increase in center compared with home-based care was apparent for preschool-age and school-age children, although the evidence for the older children was less extensive.

These findings are important in indicating that the nature of the supports available to parents matter for their choice of type of care; that is, resources and information help parents guide their children's experiences. While some researchers have noted that the relatively greater reliance of low-income families on home-based child care may reflect a preference for such care, these new findings raise the possibility that this pattern reflects, at least in part, a resource constraint. Lowe and Weisner (2001) provide ethnographic data suggesting that low-income families recognize the strengths of formal care arrangements but also have some concerns about this type of care (e.g., suspicion about care provided by someone without an existing relationship with the family). The results of the analyses using data from experimental studies suggest that when resources and information are available, low-income families will make relatively more use of formal child care and activities.

Turning to the dimensions of parenting other than gatekeeping, program impacts on the more dyadic/interactional aspects of parenting (cutting across the dimensions noted by Chase-Lansdale and Pittman of warmth and responsiveness, control and discipline, and cognitive stimulation) did occur in families with preschool and school-age children, albeit in a less concentrated pattern when looking across multiple measures of parenting in a particular study. Zaslow and colleagues (2002) report that of 20 analytic comparisons (involving program variations or different subgroups of families participating in 7 experimental evaluation studies), impacts on at least 1 in 16 parenting measures were found, although this usually involved an impact on only 1 or a few of multiple parenting measures examined.

There is some evidence that the direction of impacts on these more dyadic aspects of parenting (whether favorable or unfavorable) corresponded to the pattern of economic progress for families. The strongest evidence for this comes from looking at patterns of parenting in the evaluations of specific programs in which economic impacts differed for subgroups or variants of the program. In the Minnesota Family Investment Program (Gennetian and Miller, 2000), for example, long-term recipients of welfare assigned to the program group showed increases in income as well as employment. For this subgroup, the version of the program that involved financial incentives without a work requirement decreased harsh parenting of school-age children as reported by mothers. In contrast, the version of the program used with recent applicants resulted in increased employment but not increased family income. For this subgroup, the result was an increase in harsh parenting.

McGroder and colleagues (2002) provide exploratory evidence that the impacts on dyadic aspects of parenting, when they did occur, helped to explain program impacts on child outcomes for the school-age children in the JOBS program. For example, two years after assignment to the Atlanta labor force attachment JOBS program (a program emphasizing work first rather than starting with education or training before attempting to locate employment), there was a positive program impact on 5- to 7-year-old children's school readiness scores. Positive parenting and mothers' verbal interactions with the child, both of which improved as a result of the program, were found to partially mediate this favorable child impact. While the labor force attachment program in Atlanta increased mothers' employment and decreased the proportion of families in the program group relative to the control group living in deep poverty, the same program approach at another site, Grand Rapids, Michigan, had different economic impacts, with no increase in employment and a decrease in the proportion of program group families living at or above the poverty line. The Grand Rapids labor force attachment program increased children's antisocial behavior problems at the two-year follow-up, and McGroder and colleagues found this impact to be completely mediated by decreases in maternal reports of warmth in parenting as well as increases in maternal depression. McGroder and colleagues caution that these mediational analyses, carried out in an experimental framework, should be viewed as exploratory, in that while covariates controlled for selection factors (and the extensive set of baseline variables made it possible to control for a broad range of initial characteristics), the possibility nevertheless remains that further (unobserved) variables should have been taken into account.

Regarding these more dyadic aspects of parenting, Chase-Lansdale and Pittman (2002) also note that a substantial number of states are allocating temporary assistance for needy families (TANF) funds to provide parenting education programs or home visitation to families. It is interesting to note that one of the demonstration programs, New Chance, involves a parenting education component. One study (Zaslow and Eldred, 1998) found positive program impacts on parental support and cognitive stimulation of mother-child interaction. However, the program group children did not, over time, show positive program impacts on outcomes, and behavior at the final follow-up in the evaluation showed some negative impacts. While positive parenting behavior did predict more favorable child development outcomes in this sample over time, there were important negative influences on development that appeared to counterbalance positive parenting, including very low income, difficult life circumstances, residential mobility, and isolation or lack of social support for the very young welfare-receiving mothers in this study.

These results suggest that parenting education has the potential to influence parenting behavior positively, even among very disadvantaged welfare-receiving families (in this case, adolescent mothers who had dropped out of school), yet that the broader social context of these families in contributing to child outcomes needs to be taken into account as well. Chase-Lansdale and Pittman further caution that features of parenting education programs, such as the skill level and training of program providers, the dosage (amount of time spent in care) of the program, and the motivation of the parents to participate, are all likely to be important to the impacts on parenting of such programs.

It is also important to consider the implications of maternal employment for parenting in relation to differing developmental periods as well as the challenges and resources maternal employment may provide in specific socioeconomic contexts.

Parenting of Adolescents

Experimental studies of welfare reform and children have had an intensive focus on preschool-age children (with follow-up into their school years) rather than on older or younger children. As in the broader set of studies on maternal employment, the research focusing specifically on transition to work in the context of welfare reform has followed (and sometimes raced to catch up with) changes in demographics and policy. The focus on preschool-age children in studies conducted in the 1990s occurred because the wave of welfare reform in 1988, for the first time, required mothers of children age 3 years and older (and younger only at state option) to participate in work-related activities. There was concern that changes in employment would necessitate changes in the care routines of these children to a greater extent than children already in school, and that any changes in the home environment would also be of greater significance for younger than older children.

Only a limited number of experimental evaluations have included measures of adolescent development, and the measures included have generally been brief indicators of adjustment rather than the kind of in-depth measures used for younger children. There was little anticipation that changes in mothers' employment status or assignment to a welfare reform program could change adolescents' experiences or development in a substantial way. But results from these studies have moved the focus on this age group from peripheral to central. Across a number of very different programs (in which employment and income impacts varied, and for whom impacts for younger children tended to correspond with these economic patterns), findings for adolescents, when they did occur, were consistently unfavorable (Brooks et al., 2001; Gennetian et al., 2002b). These occurred on such outcomes as parent report of adolescent school achievement, behavior problems in school, adolescent participation in delinquent activities, and substance use (see, for example, Bloom et al., 2000; Gennetian and Miller, 2000; Hamilton et al., 2001; Morris and Michalopoulos, 2000).

The unfavorable impacts for adolescents have led researchers to ask what the underlying processes for such a pattern might be and to consider the possibility that relationships and roles in the family may change when mothers become employed during the transition from welfare to work. Brooks and colleagues (2001) view the findings in the context of particular developmental tasks of the adolescent period, especially the need to move toward greater autonomy and assumption of responsibility, yet with an appropriate range of parental oversight and monitoring (Eccles et al., 1993). The possibility exists that the assumption of a demanding employment role by the mother alters relationships in the family in such a way that the balance of autonomy, responsibility, and parental oversight is pushed beyond an appropriate range, especially in school and neighborhood contexts in which increased autonomy may also involve increased exposure to negative influences (see Chapter 6).

While this work is in early hypothesis-building phases, Brooks and colleagues examined preliminary evidence for three different patterns that might be indicators that the balance has tipped beyond an appropriate range: (1) an increase in harsh parenting in families participating in a welfare reform program, hypothesized to occur if there is increased friction surrounding adolescent autonomy; (2) diminution in parental monitoring among mothers in welfare reform program groups as a result of employment demands, which could result in too great autonomy, particularly in high-risk neighborhoods; and (3) increased assumption of adult-like roles by adolescents to help the family function after the mother becomes employed, but to an extent that exceeds a positive range (that is, regularly caring for siblings for prolonged periods).

Some evidence exists for each of these possibilities in the experimental evaluation studies, although the evidence regarding monitoring is mixed. For example, regarding the first hypothesis, in the Canadian Self-Sufficiency Project, one of the programs in which adolescents showed negative program impacts, program group mothers reported an increase in their use of harsh parenting with their adolescents ages 15 to 18 (Morris and Michalopoulos, 2000). Regarding monitoring, studies to date have examined this aspect of parenting for the younger children in the family but not adolescents. In order to be seen as pertaining to adolescents, it must be assumed that there is a general tendency in families for mothers to show increased or decreased monitoring across *all* the children in the family when they participate in a welfare reform program (whereas issues of monitoring may well be specific to age groups). While one program (the Florida Transition Program) did lead to a slight decrease in the monitoring of younger children (Bloom et al., 2000), another (the Minnesota Family Investment Program; Gennetian and Miller, 2002) increased monitoring of younger children for the group of long-term welfare recipient families. Regarding the hypothesis of more adult-like roles, in the Canadian Self-Sufficiency Project, adolescents were more likely to be working 20 or more hours a week and performed household chores more frequently when their mothers were in the program group. In the Florida evaluation, mothers were more likely to report that their younger children were being cared for by a sibling (presumed to be an adolescent). Gennetian and colleagues note that the unfavorable impacts on adolescents in the experimental evaluations were concentrated among the adolescents with a younger sibling, suggesting that responsibility for sibling care may be one contributing factor.

The implications of these differing hypotheses for programs and policies differ. For example, the monitoring hypothesis suggests the need for out-of-school youth activities to provide supervision and meaningful activities to adolescents. Yet the hypothesis of assumption of adult-like roles suggests that the adolescents may not be able to participate in youth activities if they have substantial responsibilities at home during the hours that younger siblings are out of school. Further research is needed, focused on which one or more of these hypotheses helps to explain the unfavorable program impacts on adolescents, to help clarify appropriate program and policy responses.

Recent work by Brooks and colleagues (2001) is taking a first step in this direction. Research is considering mothers' employment status, family processes, and adolescent outcomes with the new cohort of the National Longitudinal Survey of Youth (NLSY, the 1997 cohort). This work focuses on single mothers in low-income families (below 200 percent of the federal poverty level) with 12- to 14-year-olds. These are nonexperimental analyses seeking further insight into the pattern found in the experimental evaluations. Findings thus far underscore the importance of examining maternal employment separately in three groups of families: those with current or recent welfare receipt, those with welfare receipt in the past five years, and those with no previous welfare receipt. Maternal employment was related to teens' reports of more favorable relationships with their mothers and lower delinquency in families currently or recently receiving welfare.

In contrast, mothers' employment was related to adolescents' reports of lower quality relationships with their mothers and less maternal monitoring—although not to differences in adolescent outcomes—in families with previous but not recent welfare receipt. In considering why maternal employment might have differing implications for families with differing histories of contact with the welfare system, Brooks and colleagues (2001) raise the possibility that those with current receipt may have more access to resources and caseworker support than those previously but not currently associated with the welfare system, though they note that it is impossible to rule out differences in selection into employment and welfare as helping to account for these patterns.

With this new focus on maternal employment and adolescent development, Chapter 6 reviews the evidence on adolescent development in light of mothers' employment status for more economically heterogeneous samples.

Parenting of Infants

The experimental studies of welfare reform and children have another important gap with respect to child age: these studies rarely considered program impacts on infants and, when they did so, did not use extensive or in-depth measures (see the review of these measures and findings in Zaslow et al., 2002). This is a serious gap, given the work requirements in the 1996 welfare reforms imposed on mothers with infants and toddlers. A recent set of studies using data from major longitudinal studies with in-depth measures of young children's development as well as parenting suggest that early and extensive maternal employment may have negative implications for the cognitive development of children in specific population subgroups.

They suggest that a key aspect of parenting for the infancy period, maternal sensitivity, may be affected over time when maternal employment is both early and extensive.

It is important to note that these new studies do not focus specifically on the transition from welfare to work.

Brooks-Gunn and colleagues (2002), in a study focusing on white non-Hispanic families in the Study of Early Child Care of the National Institute of Child Health and Human Development (NICHD), found that when mothers worked 30 or more hours per week by the 9th month of a child's life, the mothers scored lower on sensitivity to the child at 36 months than those who did not work this extensively early on. This pattern held even when controlling for previous maternal sensitivity. Furthermore, children of mothers who worked 30 or more hours per week by the 9th month scored lower on a measure of cognitive school readiness at 36 months than children of mothers who did not work full time early on. Maternal sensitivity and the quality of the home environment as well as the quality of child care helped to explain the relationship between extensive early maternal employment and children's scores on the school readiness measure.

In analyses with another dataset, the National Longitudinal Survey of Youth-Child Supplement, Waldfogel and colleagues (2002) found negative implications of maternal employment of 21 or more hours per week in the first year of life for the cognitive development of children in white (though not Hispanic or black) families. Negative implications persisted through age 7 or 8 and were stronger for mothers who worked more hours. The pattern differed by income group, with the strongest pattern found for children in the lowest income families. While sensitivity was not measured in this survey, a measure of the home environment (including supportiveness of the mother toward the child) was included. Taking into account the quality of the home environment reduced but did not eliminate the association of early maternal employment with children's cognitive outcomes.

These findings suggest that maternal employment, if resumed early and extensively, may for some families hinder the emergence of mother-infant sensitivity. There may be insufficient time for mothers to learn their infants' cues and develop patterns of responding to them. It is important to note that the findings in these studies do not cut across subgroups but tend to pertain to specific and delimited groups (as, for example, white but not Hispanic or black families in the NLSY analyses). It is important to pursue further the question of why these patterns are occurring in some subgroups and not others and in general to test the generalizability of the pattern.

A study focusing explicitly on length of maternity leave during the first year of life and mother-child interaction (Clark et al., 1997) found differences according to whether the return to employment occurred at 6 weeks or at 12 weeks. Interestingly, the study for this sample was predominantly white (as well as middle class). In observations of mother-child interaction when the babies were 4 months old, mothers with the shorter (6 week) maternity leave showed more negative affect and behavior with their infants than mothers with the longer (12 week) maternity leave. While there was a direct relationship between the timing of leave and negative maternal behaviors with the infant, this was not the case for positive maternal behaviors. However, statistically significant interactions were found between mothers' depressive symptoms and length of leave, as well as between infant temperament and length of leave, for positive maternal behaviors. Among mothers with higher levels of depressive symptoms, those who had taken a shorter maternity leave were observed to show less positive behavior with their infants than those who had taken longer leaves. In contrast, there was no difference in the positive behaviors of mothers according to the timing of leave when depressive symptoms were low. Similarly, when infants had more difficult temperament, the extent of maternal positive behaviors in interactions varied by length of leave, but this was not the case when infants did not show difficult temperament.

While the study by Clark and colleagues (1997) suggests that the timing of return to employment even in the first months of the infant's life may be important to the quality of mother-infant interaction, other work suggests that time together may continue to be important to the quality of mother-child interaction even beyond the first year. The NICHD Study of Early Child Care reports findings suggesting that "the amount of time that mothers and children spend together is associated with the ease of their interaction and communication" (1999a:1410). It also appears that the presence of a husband/partner is positively associated with maternal sensitivity. However, the pattern reported in the NICHD study, of more hours in child care predicting less maternal sensitivity in interactions with the child, held across the first three years (rather than pertaining specifically to extensive use of child care during the first months of life). Thus, further work is needed examining whether time together contributes to maternal sensitivity and the affective quality of mother-child interaction specifically (or perhaps more strongly) during the first months of a child's life, or beyond this period as well.

Parenting in Very-Low-Income Families

The findings we have reviewed to this point, focusing very heavily on low-income families, with much of the evidence reviewed coming from the welfare reform experimental evaluations, underscore the importance of taking child age into account in considering the implications of maternal employment and parenting. There are, perhaps, the rough outlines of an extension of the "stage environment fit" hypothesis proposed by Eccles and colleagues (1993) regarding the development of young adolescents. This hypothesis suggests that development in early adolescence will depend on the fit of the environment with the developmental tasks of the period, such as the degree to which the social context permits adolescents an increasing role in decision making (on which middle school classrooms are found to vary substantially).

Extending this rubric of fit to the maternal employment research, such employment may provide a context that poses challenges to the salient parenting tasks of some developmental periods but fosters the salient tasks of other developmental periods, depending on the broader context in which parenting occurs.

In very-low-income families, maternal employment may foster the tasks of parenting that involve directing the child to positive out-of-home care environments during the preschool years and middle childhood (gatekeeping) when employment results in increasing resources or information for identifying such care. However, for parenting in the earliest years, the possibility exists that extensive hours of employment begun early may hinder the emergence of sensitive responding to the infant in some groups of families and that adequate time together is necessary for the parenting task of establishing early reciprocal responsiveness. For parenting during adolescence, the possibility exists that maternal employment may, for some families, result in too fast or too extensive movement toward autonomy and assumption of responsibility, either granted by the mother because of needs for adolescent participation in responsibilities in the family, or taken by the adolescent in the mother's absence and a source of friction.

It is important to note that the findings on which this rough hypothesis is based are drawn from studies of very-low-income families (the experimental studies of welfare reform programs) or are particularly strong in the lowest income families studied in broader samples (the findings for infants). There may be particular challenges facing these families, for example, in terms of economic resources and the neighborhood context, that contribute to the patterns of parenting noted, perhaps posing other challenges that make it difficult to establish mutual responsiveness with infants, or confronting adolescents with dangerous environments when they push for greater autonomy.

It is important to complement these findings with results from further studies of maternal employment and parenting that look at patterns in a wider range of economic groups. In these further studies, the low-income and working-class families are a more heterogeneous group than the more economically restricted samples of families studied in the welfare reform experiments.

Parenting Beyond the Infancy Period

Focusing on results beyond the infancy period in studies of more socioeconomically diverse samples, two further patterns regarding maternal employment and parenting behavior can be seen: (1) studies find more positive patterns of parenting in families with employed than nonemployed mothers, with only slight indications of this patterning in middle-class families, but stronger indications of the pattern in groups of working-class and lower income families. This patterning of results anticipates findings in the area of maternal employment and mothers' mental health (summarized below) and maps onto the pattern of child outcomes that Hoffman and other reviewers have summarized for low-income families (of outcomes for children of employed mothers falling in a neutral to positive range); and (2) there are patterns of association of parenting and the home environment among employed mothers according to the characteristics of employment.

Regarding the first pattern, a longitudinal study of maternal employment in middle-class families that followed a sample of children from infancy to adolescence (Gottfried et al., 1995) found evidence that maternal employment showed only a few limited associations with parenting behavior. In infancy, employed mothers engaged in more attempts at toilet training than nonemployed mothers. During the early elementary school years, employed mothers had higher educational aspirations for their children, their children were engaged in more out of school lessons, and they and their children watched less television. However, this study did not find evidence of differences by employment in the extent of nurturance or stimulation that children received. The researchers emphasize the active adaptations to the mothers' employment in the families in this sample, including greater involvement of fathers.

A study encompassing both middle income and lower income families with 3rd and 4th grade children extends this set of findings, suggesting that associations of maternal employment and parenting practices may be stronger in lower than higher income families (Hoffman and Youngblade, 1999). Overall, employed mothers in this study were found to rely less on authoritarian, power-assertive disciplinary styles. Less coercive discipline styles and more overt affection toward the child were linked with more positive social adjustment for children of employed mothers, particularly among working-class families in this study. Employed mothers' less authoritarian parenting was linked to higher scores for the 3rd and 4th grade children on tests of reading and math achievement and to teacher ratings of more effective learning patterns. Linkages to children's school outcomes were stronger in single-parent than two-parent families.

Work by McLoyd and colleagues (1994) also found an association between maternal employment and disciplinary approach. This work, focusing on black families headed by single mothers, found more authoritarian parenting among unemployed than employed mothers of 7th and 8th graders. These findings are discussed in further detail below in relation to mothers' psychological well-being in relation to employment. As in the work of Hoffman and Youngblade, disciplinary approach was found to be related to children's outcomes, with the more power assertive discipline shown by unemployed mothers predicting less favorable adjustment in the young adolescents.

While the studies noted above contrast families with employed and nonemployed mothers, other studies do not contrast employment categories but look at variations in parenting in light of the nature or extent of employment. For example, focusing on a demographically diverse sample of families, Menaghan and Parcel (1995) provide evidence that maternal employment has differing implications according to the work circumstances of the mothers. Building on the work of Kohn and Schooler (1983), these researchers present the hypothesis that specific features of parents' jobs influence the behaviors that they value and encourage in their children (Menaghan and Parcel, 1995; Parcel and Menaghan 1990, 1994; Rogers et al., 1991). For example, they hypothesize that jobs that are repetitive and unstimulating and permit little self-direction will be associated with parental childrearing values that emphasize obedience rather than initiative. Such jobs provide limited cognitive stimulation to the parent, which may, in turn, influence the extent of stimulation in parent-child interaction. In contrast, when parents have jobs that involve greater variety, stimulation, and self-direction, they may be more likely to use strategies of reasoning in discipline with their children and to expect self-direction and internalization of adult norms.

Some of the existing research designs do a better job of handling selection effects than others. One of the designs that is particularly helpful is one used in the study by Menaghan and Parcel (1995), looking at changes in employment status and related changes in the home environment. This design takes into account the initial characteristics of the mother and more fully isolates changes that occur with changes in employment status by the same mothers. (This approach found deterioration in the home environment particularly when single mothers started jobs low in complexity and wages). Other studies have been able to take into account (control for) cognitive or literacy test scores administered to the mothers at the start of a welfare reform evaluation or survey data collection. For example, mothers were administered the AFQT in the NLSY; this is often used as a control variable in analyses examining employment in this dataset. Mothers were administered tests of literacy at the start of the Child Outcomes Study of the National Evaluation of Welfare-to-Work Strategies; this measure is used as a control variable in many analyses with these data.

In a further examination of work circumstances of employed mothers, Han (2002a) focused on the issue of nonstandard work hours (work that occurs during the evenings, nights, and weekends; see Chapter 2 for more information on trends around nonstandard work schedules). Using data from the NICHD Study of Early Child Care, Han found less positive cognitive and social developmental outcomes over time for children whose mothers had ever worked nonstandard hours by the child's third year of life in comparison with those who had not, controlling for extent of employment. This study also found differences in parenting and maternal psychological well-being in relation to work schedule. The quality of the home environment was less optimal at 36 months when the mother had ever worked nonstandard hours, mothers experienced more depression at specific time points in the longitudinal study (though not others), and children had less exposure to center care when mothers had worked this schedule. The relationship between work schedule and children's developmental outcomes was attenuated, although it did not disappear, when the home environment and type of child care was taken into account.

When he entered school, Nancy's son was often left home alone either before or after school. Nancy describes one particular week (Heymann, 2000:42):

My boss made me work the six o'clock shift while Andrew was six or seven—maybe seven. I would leave him in the morning, and he got up that week and he was on his own. He was scared. And he got in trouble a couple of times that week . . . arguing with a teacher, fighting with a classmate. I shouldn't have did what my boss wanted. . . . They changed my hours without any notice. . . . It didn't work for my son because he couldn't handle being in the house alone at that age.

Other research focusing on nonstandard work hours provides mixed findings. On one hand, there is evidence that for some occupations, working nonstandard hours allows parents to spend more time with their children, providing increased supervision and involvement (Garey, 1999; Grosswald, 1999; Hattery, 2001). Further research finds working nonstandard hours to be associated with higher proportion of employed parents being home when children are leaving and returning from school. Depending on the specific work schedule, gender of the parent, and activity considered, parent-child interaction may be greater when parents work nonstandard schedules (Presser, in press). On the other hand, Heymann (2000), in her research examining the circumstances of a range of working families in the United States, found work during nonstandard hours and work by spouses during different shifts (strategies used by many families to juggle the needs of work and child rearing) had unfavorable implications for the well-being of the children. Further work is needed looking at the specific circumstances in which nonstandard work hours support or hinder supervision of children and children's development. Such work should consider marital status, whether one or both spouses are working nonstandard hours, and the specific nonstandard schedule worked.

Father Involvement

While there has been much focus on maternal parenting behavior and the home environment, existing research extends the picture of parenting to father involvement as well. As was described in more detail in Chapter 2, father involvement in parent and family household tasks may change as a result of maternal employment. Hoffman (1989) observed that "probably the most clearly demonstrated effect of maternal employment is a modest increase in the participation of fathers in household tasks and child care" (p. 286). Some research has found father involvement to increase not only in keeping with the mothers' employment status, but also with their hours of employment (Gottfried et al., 1995).

These findings generally pertain to father involvement in dual-earner families. We note that research to date focusing on father involvement in single-parent families in welfare reform programs has tended to examine the economic contributions of the father, through formalized or informal child support (and paternity establishment as a prerequisite to formalized child support), rather than involvement in the care of the child or the household (McLanahan and Carlson, 2002). Existing studies show substantial increases in paternity establishment and child support payments in the years following welfare reform. McLanahan and Carlson note that there is a new generation of programs aimed at improving not only employment and the economic contribution that low-income fathers have the potential to make, but also parenting skills and direct involvement of nonresident fathers with their children. To date, however, there is little evidence on the efficacy of such programs or on the direct involvement of fathers in the care of their children when they do not reside with them, in light of the mothers' employment. Accordingly, we focus here on father involvement in the household in dual-earner families.

In the research on dual-earner families, studies distinguish between contributions to housework and child care on one hand, and playful or educational joint activities or interaction with the child on the other. Two recent studies (Crouter et al., 1999; Hoffman et al., 1999) found mothers' work hours to be related to the division of labor in two-parent families in terms of household tasks and physical care and supervision of children, but not in terms of educational or playful interactions with children. The NICHD Study of Early Child Care also found differing predictors of father involvement in caregiving and of father sensitivity in play with the child. Greater work hours by the mother and fewer work hours by the father predicted greater paternal involvement in caregiving, but work hours were not associated with paternal sensitivity during play (National Institute of Child Health and Human Development, 2000c).

This distinction between caregiving and household tasks and the quality and quantity of nonobligatory interactions with the child perhaps helps to explain the findings of observational studies of fathers and their very young children, which have not reported increased interactions of fathers with their children in dual-earner families when family interaction is sampled for discrete periods of time (e.g., Stuckey et al., 1982), or a difference in the quality of observed parenting behavior by fathers in light of the mother's employment status (e.g., Grych and Clark, 1999).

Findings from the observational study of father-infant interaction by Grych and Clark (1999) suggest that while maternal employment during the first year of a child's life does not seem to affect the quality of father-infant interaction directly, it may do so indirectly by influencing the context in which fathers and their infants interact. For fathers in this study whose wives were not employed, increased involvement in caregiving both early and late in the infant's first year (at 4 and 12 months) was accompanied by greater expression of positive affect during interactions with the infant. A similar pattern of greater positive affect occurring with greater paternal involvement in caregiving was also found for fathers of wives employed part time, although only at the later point during the infant's first year. In contrast, for husbands whose wives were employed full time, greater involvement in caregiving was accompanied by more negative interactions with the infant at the earlier time point.

The findings suggest the hypothesis that when the mother is not employed, greater father involvement in caregiving is at the volition of the father and is pleasurable, while this is not the case, at least early on, for fathers of wives employed full time (who may feel that the caregiving is obligatory and not pleasurable). This hypothesis is consistent with results reported by Vandell and colleagues (Vandell et al., 1997) that fathers whose wives were employed reported more anger when they were more involved in the caregiving of their 4-month-old infants. Grych and Clark (1999) caution that the sense of being pressed into greater responsibility for child care early on by fathers of wives employed full time does not appear to be sustained through the end of the first year in their sample, "suggesting that they may have become more proficient at balancing work and family responsibilities" (p. 900).

Turning to families with older children, Hoffman and colleagues (1999) provide the most detailed examination of whether and how increased father involvement in dual-earner families is associated with child outcomes. In a study of stable maternal employment (consistent employment status over a three-year period) in low- and middle-income families with 3rd and 4th grade children, they found that the greater the father's involvement in household tasks and child care, the less stereotyped were the children's attitudes about appropriate roles for men and women. Children's less stereotyped gender roles, specifically their perception of women's competence in traditionally male domains, predicted achievement test scores in the 3rd and 4th grade for both boys and girls. These researchers also tested a model regarding daughters' scores on tests of academic achievement. They found that maternal employment was associated with greater participation in household and child care tasks by fathers, which in turn predicted daughters' less stereotyped attitudes about women's competence. This in turn predicted a greater sense of efficacy and higher scores on tests of reading and math achievement. Thus, greater father involvement in dual-earner families may help to explain the findings for girls of greater aspirations and achievement. The researchers note the key limitation of their work is that the examination of interrelationships involved concurrent rather than longitudinal data.

We have noted the paucity of work laying out and testing such models. While the research of Hoffman and colleagues is clearly a step forward, there is a need for more work of this kind, using longitudinal data and examining patterns across key subgroups (for example, considering whether models are similar or different according to gender, race/ethnicity, and socioeconomic status).

Maternal Psychological Well-Being

Mothers who are employed have been found to show better psychological well-being on measures of depression, stress, psychosomatic symptoms, and life satisfaction (Kessler and McRae, 1982; McLoyd et al., 1994; Repetti et al., 1989). Mothers' psychological well-being, in turn, has been shown to be important to children's development, influencing development through the quality of mother-child interactions (Downey and Coyne, 1990; Goodman and Brumley, 1990; Harnish et al., 1995, Hair et al., 2002; National Institute of Child Health and Human Development, 1999c).

Some work suggests that this pattern holds only or more strongly for lower income than middle-class families (Warr and Parry, 1982). In recent research, Hoffman and Youngblade (1999) found evidence of better maternal psychological well-being for employed than nonemployed working-class mothers of school-age children, using measures of depressive symptoms and morale. However, no parallel difference by employment status was found for middle-class mothers.

Maternal psychological well-being has also been shown to be related to job characteristics. Fuller and colleagues (2001) found maternal depressive symptoms to be lower among low-income mothers working in higher quality jobs (as indexed by the provision of health benefits). Han (2002b) found that mothers who worked nonstandard hours (evenings, nights, or rotating shifts) had higher scores on a measure of depression by the time their child was 15 months old than mothers working standard hours.

McLoyd and colleagues (1994) found maternal unemployment to be associated with greater depression among black mothers of adolescent children in single-parent families. Employed mothers perceived less financial strain and greater instrumental social support. Their 7th and 8th grade children perceived their relationships with their mothers to be more positive, perceived less economic hardship, and had lower anxiety levels. The increased depressive symptomatology among unemployed mothers was associated with increased use of harsh punishment with their adolescent children, which in turn predicted greater difficulty concentrating and more depression among the adolescents.

A similar set of linkages is reported for 3rd and 4th grade children in the work of Hoffman and Youngblade (1999). For example, among working-class mothers, employment was predictive of fewer depressive symptoms, which in turn were found to be associated with more authoritative (firm but warm), rather than power-assertive, parenting. Such parenting in turn was predictive of children's higher achievement test scores in reading and math, fewer learning problems as rated by teachers, and more positive social skills on teacher ratings of peer social skills and acting out behavior. Maternal depressive symptoms partially mediated the relationship between maternal employment and parenting style in these analyses.

We note the important caution that causal direction is not entirely clear in this work and in other work showing an association between maternal employment and maternal mental health. It is indeed possible that mothers may derive a sense of competence from their work, that contact with coworkers serves as a source of social support, and that the income derived from employment may reduce anxiety about family economic resources. However, it is also possible that mothers with poor mental health may find it more difficult to find or maintain employment, and that this is the source of the employment-mental health link (see findings in Vandell and Ramanan, 1992). Indeed, in recent research with families with a history of welfare receipt, mother's depressive symptoms were found to predict subsequent employment (Hair et al., 2002).

If employment is the cause of improved maternal psychological well-being, then one might expect that mothers would show improved well-being in the welfare-to-work evaluations in which mothers showed an increase in employment. In an overview of the findings on maternal psychological well-being in these evaluations, Ahluwalia et al. (2001) examined findings regarding impacts on depressive symptoms in 20 analytic groups in 7 programs (with separate analytic groups in some of the evaluations for families with children of differing ages, for variations in the programs, and for subgroups of families such as recent or long-term welfare recipients). Impacts on maternal depressive symptoms were found in only seven of these groups. In most instances (for five of the programs in which statistically significant impacts were found), these impacts were unfavorable rather than favorable.

Interestingly, in most of the programs in which the unfavorable impacts (increases in depressive symptoms) occurred, overall family income did not increase despite the family's participation in a welfare reform program. In some of these programs, employment increased while income did not increase; in others, neither employment nor income increased. The possibility exists that in some programs and for some families, maternal psychological well-being may decline when participation in a welfare reform program intended to increase employment does not result in employment or an improvement in the family's economic situation.

It is also possible that employment in the context of a welfare reform program differs substantially from employment in other circumstances. Most of the programs evaluated involved mandatory participation in employment-related activities (with the possibility of sanctions for noncompliance). The link between mothers' mental health and employment may well exist and follow a causal sequence in which employment results in better maternal well-being, but only when the mother can choose the timing and nature of the employment. Employment in the context of a mandate may not show the hypothesized benefits. Yet the results from the welfare reform evaluations suffice to caution that the causal direction of the maternal employment-psychological well-being link needs closer examination. Huston (2002) suggests that such an examination encompass the possibility of a recursive relationship, with maternal psychological well-being perhaps helping to determine employment outcomes, which in turn may contribute to mothers' psychological well-being.

ADAPTATION TO MATERNAL EMPLOYMENT

Bianchi (2000b) observes that despite the increases in rates of maternal employment in recent decades, time use studies show substantial consistency in maternal time with children. Greater demands of household tasks in earlier decades limited the time that mothers at home actually spent in interactions with their children. Also, families had more children in the past, so time per child has changed less. In addition, the evidence indicates that families actively adapt to employment in ways that maximize parental time with children, for example, through mothers choosing part-time employment, a reallocation of mothers' time away from leisure activities and toward time with children, and greater father involvement (as noted above) when the mother is employed.

Recent research continues to provide a picture of active adaptation to maternal employment in which families seem to protect parental time with children. At the same time, new work poses the possibility that there may be constraints in some families in making such adaptations.

Aronson and Huston (2001) examined time use data for mothers with infants in the NICHD Study of Early Child Care. They found that employed mothers did spend less time overall with their infants. However, employed mothers were more likely to make reductions in other activities than infant care and to compensate for time away from their infants through time use on weekends.

The tendency to maximize time with children when the mother is employed emerges especially in recent findings on two-parent low-income families. National survey data indicate that there have been increases in these families in the percentage of young children cared for only by parents when the parent most involved in the care of the child (almost always the mother) is employed. Data from the National Survey of America's Families (NSAF) indicate that from 1997 to 1999 the percentage of children under age 5 in such families cared for only by parents increased from 28 to 33 percent. This increase is not found in single-parent low-income families or in higher income families (Zaslow and Tout, 2002).

Data on parental activities with young children suggest that active adaptation may be more difficult in single-parent than two-parent low-income families. Phillips (2002), also using NSAF data, found that full-time employment in single-parent low-income families was associated with a reduction in parent involvement in reading and outings with preschool children. In two-parent families, however, high levels of parental work were not found to be associated with diminished parent involvement in activities with preschoolers.

The evidence suggests that maternal employment is not a circumstance to which families respond passively, but rather one that they actively seek to shape (Gottfried et al., 1995). A hypothesis that seems to be emerging in the research is that there may be some groups of families, such as low-income single-parent families, who are more constrained in this adaptation process.

SIMULTANEOUS INFLUENCES ON MULTIPLE ASPECTS OF FAMILY LIFE

We have considered the implications of maternal employment for aspects of family life separately, without considering how influences on different aspects of family life might operate jointly to affect children's development. Yet it may be important to take into account how multiple influences of employment on family life operate simultaneously.

McGroder and colleagues (2000) examined the mediators of the impacts on young children of mothers' assignment to JOBS welfare-to-work programs. They found that these programs tended to affect families in multiple ways, and not always in the same direction. Impacts on children reflected the net effect of these influences.

For example, one of the six programs examined in this evaluation, the JOBS labor force attachment program in the Atlanta site of the study, had a favorable impact on children in reducing their externalizing behavior problems. This program had a positive impact on a summary rating of mothers' parenting behavior. However, the program also increased mothers' feelings of time stress and perceptions that the welfare office pushed parents to go to school or get training. While positive parenting predicted fewer externalizing behavior problems, time stress and feelings of being pushed by the welfare office predicted more such problems. The favorable impact of the program on children's externalizing behavior reflected the balance of these influences: the impact on children's externalizing behavior was mediated by favorable parenting, but would have been even more favorable without the counterbalancing influence of mothers' subjective sense of time stress and pressure. McGroder and colleagues note that while these analyses controlled for a range of family characteristics prior to random assignment in this experimental evaluation, the possibility nevertheless exists that further (unobserved) factors were contributing to the patterns noted; thus the findings should be viewed as exploratory.

Our understanding of how maternal employment influences family life and children's development would be deepened by further research looking at multiple aspects of family life simultaneously, taking into account the possibility that these may have counterbalancing influences.

SUMMARY

On the basis of evidence presented in this chapter, we conclude that the effects of maternal employment depend on a range of factors and may vary by subgroup. Very young children may be particularly affected by maternal employment. **For newborns, outcomes for mothers and children are better when mothers are able to take more than 12 weeks of leave, and outcomes** for children may be better when mothers are able to return to work part time or to delay returning to work full time until after the first year.

A family's income also appears to affect material well-being, which in turn affects children and adolescents. The research on maternal employment and the family environment for children has recently been extended by studies of families enrolled in a range of programs to support the transition from welfare to employment. Findings regarding the impact of the family environment of children from studies of low-income families differ in a number of ways from studies of maternal employment in more heterogeneous samples of families.

For example, while findings in broader samples suggest that maternal employment is associated with better mental health for mothers, this pattern is not found with any consistency among mothers participating in welfare-to-work programs. Findings in broader samples indicate that employed mothers tend to use less power-assertive discipline, and that this has favorable implications for children's development. In the welfare-to-work evaluations, there is limited evidence of effects on dyadic aspects of parenting (like expression of warmth or disciplinary practices), although when these occur they appear to play a role in shaping program impacts on children. Instead, impacts on parenting in the welfare-to-work evaluations are concentrated in the gatekeeping aspects of parenting, such as enrollment of children in child care and after-school activities. There are indications in the welfare-to-work evaluations of the particular importance of economic resources associated with employment in shaping positive impacts for young children of mothers making the transition to work (although these same factors do not seem to contribute to positive impacts for adolescent children in these families, who show a pattern of unfavorable impacts irrespective of whether increased employment was associated with increased family income). The role of economic resources has been hypothesized as important in explaining the implications for children in a broader range of families, but little work has been carried out focusing explicitly on this issue in more heterogeneous samples. While there are some indications that relationships and roles in families with adolescents are affected negatively during the transition from welfare to work, there is no parallel pattern for adolescents in broader samples of low-income families, and indeed there are indications that employment is related to more positive patterns of mother-adolescent relations. Studies of maternal employment vary substantially in how well they have addressed selection effects.

One possible interpretation is that the differences in findings primarily reflect methodological differences across the studies of welfare and nonwelfare families. The former have been studied in experimental evaluations of welfare-to-work programs, while the more heterogeneous samples have been studied in descriptive research that looks at associations of employment with family life and child outcomes either concurrently or over time. Perhaps the experimental evaluations have more fully isolated the effects of employment from selection effects, and a truer picture emerges of the implications of employment in these studies.

A number of further differences across the sets of studies need to be kept in mind as possibly contributing to the differences in findings noted. The families studied in the welfare evaluation studies are more disadvantaged than the low-income families in broader samples. In the latter, "low income" may be defined as including families up to 200 percent of the poverty line (as in analyses in light of income in the National Survey of America's Families, Phillips, 2002). Families in the welfare reform evaluations, in nearly all of the studies, did show increases in employment on average, but the evaluations reflect the impacts of assignment to a welfare-to-work program rather than the impacts of employment per se. Families making the transition to work in the welfare reform context were experiencing mandates to work or incentives to work that affected the speed with which they needed to find employment and the benefits from employment. In broader samples, while there are clearly constraints operating, mothers are somewhat freer to choose the timing of employment and the nature of the job. They may, for example, take into account to a greater extent their own satisfaction with a child care arrangement, the availability of other adults to help, job characteristics, and issues concerning their children's well-being, such as health.

In future work, it would be particularly helpful to look systematically in heterogeneous samples at whether maternal employment is associated with different family processes and child outcomes in light of history of welfare receipt and socioeconomic circumstances. In addition, while all of the studies included in this review took background characteristics of the families into account, future work would be particularly informative if it grappled more fully with selection effects.

Even given these needs for further work, the set of studies reviewed here does provide some guidance as to where further supports for low-income working families might be targeted. Those instances in which unfavorable associations of maternal employment and family life occurred can help to identify contexts in which supports might be helpful. In the work reviewed, these include: a very early and extensive resumption of employment after the birth of a child for some groups of families (although, as noted above, there is a need to understand why this pattern is occurring for some subgroups of families but not others), and employment (especially by single mothers) in jobs that involve low complexity, lack benefits, or involve working nonstandard hours. For families making the transition from welfare to work, the research suggests that supports might be helpful in connecting families with the full set of benefits (such as child care subsidies) for which they are eligible and targeting families struggling to make the transition to work. The research also suggests that a particular focus be given to the needs of adolescent children in these families.

5

Effects of Child Care

ne by-product of the increase in women's employment in the United States has been a transformation in how children are cared for. This transformation has affected children of all ages—from the youngest infants to adolescents. Children in the United States typically begin full-time (i.e., 40 hours a week) nonmaternal care during their first year and this often lasts through elementary school, since the regular school day is typically shorter than parents' workdays. A critical issue for parents, educators, and policy makers is whether these care experiences are a source of enrichment that contributes positively to children's developmental outcomes or are a source of risk that undermines development.

Substantial progress has been made in the past 15 years in determining the effects of child care on children's cognitive and social functioning. This progress reflects a convergence of conceptual and methodological advances and the availability of several large-scale research projects (see Box 5-1). From this research base, it is possible to specify the effects of nonmaternal care on children's development with greater confidence and precision than was possible when the National Academies published the 1990 report entitled *Who Cares for America's Children?* (NRC, 1990).

This chapter reviews the conceptual and methodological advances that have informed recent research. Then we evaluate the research evidence pertaining to the effects of three aspects of early child care—quality, type of care, and quantity—on a wide range of child developmental outcomes. Included in this review is consideration of experimental studies of center-based early education programs, which fulfill both child care and educa-

BOX 5-1
Multisite Child Care Studies

1. National Institute of Child Health and Human Development (NICHD) Study of Early Child Care

The Study of Early Child Care (SECC) is a prospective longitudinal study of 1,364 children recruited at birth from 10 research sites: Little Rock, Arkansas; Irvine, California; Lawrence, Kansas; Boston, Massachusetts; Morganton, North Carolina; Philadelphia, Pennsylvania; Pittsburgh, Pennsylvania; Charlottesville, Virginia; Seattle, Washington; and Madison, Wisconsin. The sample includes ethnic minority children (24 percent), mothers without a high school diploma (10 percent), and single mothers (14 percent). The recruited families did not differ from the eligible families on any of a substantial number of variables, except that mothers in the study were more likely to plan to be employed in their infant's first year. Of the 1,364 families who began the study, 1,216 continued through 36 months, 1,062 continued through 1st grade, and 1,033 continued through 3rd grade.

Extensive information was collected about child care, families, and child functioning (see Annex Table A5-4). Extended observations of children's primary child care arrangements were conducted at 6, 15, 24, 36, and 54 months. Mothers reported amount and types of care during phone interviews every three to four months. In addition, extensive information about the children's families and homes was obtained during home and lab visits at 1, 6, 15, 24, 36, and 54 months. Child developmental (cognitive, social, academic, and health) outcomes were assessed using multiple methods (standardized tests, observations, questionnaires) and multiple respondents (mother, father, teacher).

The study's design has made it possible to examine quality, quantity, and type of child care in the same analyses in order to estimate the unique contributions of each factor. It also is possible to examine effects of timing (see Brooks-Gunn et al., 2002) and trajectories of care (see NICHD Early Child Care Research Network, 2002c). Another strength is that it is possible to include extensive controls for family factors, including controls for such observed factors as mother-child interaction and the home environment. The longitudinal data have permitted examinations of changes in scores (NICHD Early Child Care Research Network and Duncan, 2002).

Although it is a remarkably rich dataset, the NICHD study is limited in some important respects. The sample is not nationally representative. Compared with Census Bureau figures from all births in the United States in 1991, white, non-Hispanic children are somewhat overrepresented in the sample and children from ethnic minority groups are somewhat underrepresented (NICHD Early Child Care Research Network, 2001c). Mean household income and maternal education also were higher than the U.S. average. There also are indications (NICHD Early Child Care Research Network, 2000a) that poorer quality child care settings were less likely to have been observed, meaning that effects associated with quality of child care may be underestimated.

2. Cost, Quality, and Outcome Study

The Cost, Quality, and Outcomes Study (CQO; Peisner-Feinberg et al., 1999) was conducted in four states (California, Colorado, Connecticut, and North Carolina) that varied in the stringency of their child care regulations. The initial sample was recruited in 1993 and consisted of 579 children (30 percent ethnic minority) who were enrolled in 183 preschool classrooms. At the start of the study, the children were in their next-to-last year of preschool before entering school. Classrooms were observed and rated for quality of the classroom environment, teacher sensitivity, and teaching style. These quality indicators were combined into a single process quality composite. Children were followed through two years of child care and the first three years of school (kindergarten through 2nd grade) and completed tests of receptive language ability, reading ability, and math skills. Child care staff and schoolteachers rated the children's cognitive and attention skills, sociability, and problem behaviors yearly.

3. The Three-State Study

The Three-State Study (Scarr et al., 1994) was conducted in Georgia, Massachusetts, and Virginia, three states that varied in child care regulations. The sample consisted of 120 centers that included randomly selected programs from national chains, with nearby nonprofit programs, local for-profit centers, and church sponsored centers situated. Each program was observed during a single full-day visit that included observations of an infant classroom, a toddler classroom, and a preschool classroom. A total of 718 children (176 infants, 291 toddlers, and 251 preschoolers) were observed at the centers. Mothers and fathers completed questionnaires about the study child's problem behaviors, as well as information about family income, education, parenting attitudes, and parenting stress.

4. The National Day Care Study

The National Day Care Study (Ruopp et al., 1979) included a quasi-experiment that was conducted at 49 publicly funded centers in three cities (Atlanta, Georgia; Detroit, Michigan; and Seattle, Washington) and a random assignment experiment that was conducted in eight centers (29 classrooms). In the quasi-experiment, ratios were improved in some centers, high ratios were maintained in some centers, and low ratios were maintained in other centers. In the experiment, classrooms were assigned to one of three levels of staff education (master's degree, completed 2-year training program, had not completed 2-year training) and one of two ratios (5:1 versus 7:1). Outcomes included observed teacher and child behavior at the centers and child performance on standardized cognitive assessments.

5. Family and Relative Care Study

This study was conducted in three communities (San Fernando Valley, California; Charlotte, North Carolina; and Dallas, Texas) that differed in the stringency of their child care home licensing regulations (Kontos et al., 1995). Participants were identified from random digit phone calls, birth records, and referrals for child care providers. A total of 820 families and 226 child care homes and providers of relative care were contacted. The final sample of children consisted of 145 cases (35 percent ethnic minority, 54.7 percent low or very low income) in which both mother and provider agreed to participate. Three-hour observations were conducted at each home by trained field staff, and quality of care was assessed using the Family Day Care Rating Scale (FDCRS).

6. The National Child Care Staffing Study (NCCSS)

The National Child Care Staffing Study (NCCSS) was conducted in 1988 in 227 centers in five metropolitan areas in the United States (Atlanta, Georgia; Boston, Massachusetts; Detroit, Michigan; Phoenix, Arizona; and Seattle, Washington). Approximately 45 centers were randomly selected from the licensed full-day programs in each city. In each center, an infant, toddler, and preschool classroom was randomly selected, and two teachers in these classrooms (six per center; total number of teachers = 1,309) were interviewed about their training, education, wages, experience, and personal background. The selected classrooms also were observed by the research staff, who rated process quality using the Early Childhood Environment Rating Scale (ECERS), the Infant/Toddler Environment Rating Scale (ITERS), and the Arnett Scale of teacher sensitivity.

tional functions. We then examine the effects of different types of child care during middle childhood.

CONCEPTUAL AND METHODOLOGICAL ADVANCES

Various aspects of child care have informed the advances of researchers working to understand the effects of child care on the cognitive and social functioning of children.

Relationship Among Contextual Factors

Bronfenbrenner's ecological systems theory (1979, 1989; Brofenbrenner and Morris, 1998) has guided much of the research by developmental psychologists who study child care effects (see NICHD Early Child Care Research Network, 1994; Vandell and Posner, 1999). A key element of the theory is a framework of nested relations among contextual factors, which are conceptualized as microsystems, mesosystems, and exosystems. A *microsystem* is described as "a pattern of activities, roles, and interpersonal relations experienced by the developing person in a given setting with particular physical and material characteristics" (Bronfenbrenner, 1979:22). Consistent with the formulation, child care researchers have developed detailed descriptions of children's activities, roles, and interpersonal relations at centers and day care homes, and with nannies and grandparents (see Clarke-Stewart, Gruber, and Fitzgerald, 1994; Howes, 1983; NICHD Early Child Care Research Network, 1996, 2000a). These descriptions proved instrumental in the development of measures that distinguish high-quality and low-quality care.

Bronfenbrenner conceptualizes the *mesosystem* as "the interrelations among two or more settings in which the developing person actively participates, such as, for a child, the relations among home, school, and neighborhood peer group" (1979:25), and this also has influenced research in this area. One child care and family linkage that has been extensively investigated is families' selection of care arrangements. In some cases, selection reflects active decision making, which occurs when parents visit several providers and then select one. In other cases, parents may use an arrangement because it is the only one that they can afford, even if they have concerns about it. The critical point is that family preferences and circumstances influence the particular care that children receive.

Child care and the family also are interconnected because child care may affect family functioning. An example of such effects was reported in the Wisconsin Family and Work Project. Early and extensive child care was related to maternal and paternal emotional well-being (Vandell et al., 1997). Increases in maternal and paternal depression, anger, and anxiety were found in parents whose infants were in full-time child care during the first four months, but not in parents whose children were not in early and extensive child care.

These associations between child care and the family highlight a challenge for child care research, namely, to distinguish between aspects of the family that influence placement into care and aspects of the family that change in response to child care. Only the former reflect selection differences, whereas the latter may be indicative of changes in family functioning that mediate child care effects. Longitudinal studies have begun to track the interplay between child care and the family over time.

Bronfenbrenner conceptualizes the *exosystem* as "one or more settings that do not involve the developing person as an active participant, but in which events occur that affect, or are affected by, what happens in the setting containing the developing person" (1979:25), and this also has guided research about child care. For example, as discussed earlier, the mother's work environment (her schedule, working conditions, etc.) has implications for the child's development even if the child is not typically cared for at the mother's work site (Hoffman and Youngblade, 1999). Such effects are consistent with the conceptualization of the exosystem.

Multidimensional Aspects of Child Care

A second advance that has occurred in child care research since the mid-1980s is the move from simple comparisons of day care versus no day care to studies that focused on *quality*, *quantity*, and *type* of child care (see Lamb, 1998, for a comprehensive review). Studies of child care quality have asked whether structural and caregiver characteristics as well as more process-oriented indicators of caregiving are related to child developmental outcomes. Studies of child care quantity have asked if cumulative hours in child care as well as when care begins are related to child outcomes. Type-of-care studies have primarily focused on the effects of center care, although some research has considered the effects of child care homes, nannies, and relatives on child outcomes.

A limitation of much of the research in this area is that these three aspects of care (quality, type, and quantity) have been studied in isolation, that is, without consideration of the other aspects. Thus, quantity of care has been investigated without consideration of the quality of care, and quality of care was studied without consideration of quantity. Findings in these studies are sometimes difficult to interpret because it is not possible to rule out alternative explanations for purported effects (Phillips et al., 1987a; Vandell and Corasaniti, 1990). Several recent projects, described below, have sought to disentangle effects associated with quality, amount, and type of care by including measures of all three aspects of care in their design and analyses.

Multiplicity of Child Care Arrangements

A third advance is the recognition that children in the United States often have multiple child care arrangements, both simultaneously and sequentially (see Chapter 3). This multiplicity of arrangements means that researchers have needed to collect information about child care over time and include secondary and tertiary arrangements as well as the primary arrangement. Otherwise, key aspects of these arrangements may not be measured adequately.

Surveys such as the National Child Care Survey and the National Household Education Survey have asked parents to report both primary and secondary arrangements, and the Survey of Income and Program Participation (SIPP) asks parents to report all child care arrangements used by each child. The NICHD Study of Early Child Care obtained reports from mothers every three to four months to document the types and amount of care that were used.

Correlational Versus Experimental Designs

Although research examining the effects of high-quality center-based interventions on children from low-income families (e.g., Ramey et al., in press) has relied on experimental and quasi-experimental designs, most of the research examining the effects of child care quality and quantity has used correlational designs. As is the case with any correlational study, there are important concerns that unmeasured factors may account for reported effects (Blau, 2001). In some cases, child care researchers have sought to address possible selection bias by including multiple controls for family and child characteristics (examples of such studies appear in the annex at the end of this chapter, see Tables A5-1, A5-2, A5-3). In other cases, investigators (Blau, 2000; NICHD Early Child Care Research Network and Duncan, 2003, discussed below) have considered the robustness of findings using other statistical methods to control for biases introduced by unobserved factors.

Characteristics of the Child

A final advance reflected in much of the recent research is the recognition that child characteristics also may influence placement in child care. A long line of scholarship has shown that children (and parents) actively seek out environments that are consistent with children's maturity, interests, and skills (Scarr and McCartney, 1983). For child care researchers, the issue is whether children with particular characteristics, dispositions, or skills are more likely to be placed in some settings and not others, and if these selection differences account for the observed findings.

In some instances, it is relatively easy to identify child characteristics that affect placement. Placement based on age, for example, is easy to determine; infants are more likely to be placed in relative care, whereas preschoolers are more likely to be placed in centers. Identifying child dispositions and competencies that influence placement in early child care is more difficult, because of the absence of reliable and robust measures of social and cognitive functioning for young infants that can be obtained before they begin child care. In several reports, the NICHD investigators used maternal reports of child temperament collected at 6 months of age as an indicator of child disposition, but by 6 months, 75 percent of the children had already been in care for 3 months (or half their lifetime). Measures of child functioning obtained after care begins may reflect the effects of that care and thus may not be measures of child selection. Measuring child adjustment and functioning for older children is more feasible because there are numerous psychometrically strong measures of social and cognitive functioning that are appropriate for preschoolers and young school-age children.

QUALITY OF EARLY CHILD CARE

In this section, we consider the research evidence pertaining to the effects of child care quality on developmental outcomes. First, we describe how quality is measured, focusing on measures of process quality, structural characteristics, and caregiver characteristics. Next, a model is presented that describes the interactions among various dimensions of child care experiences. This model has guided much research on the effects of child care quality on children's developmental outcomes. Three sets of research findings related to this model are explored. These include: (1) relations between structural characteristics and process quality, (2) relations between process quality and child outcomes, and (3) relations between structural measures and child outcomes. Both concurrent and longer term associations are presented.

Measuring Child Care Quality

Process quality refers to the kinds of experiences that children have with caregivers and other children, opportunities for cognitive, linguistic, and social stimulation, and opportunities to use interesting and varied materials. Process quality is typically assessed by trained personnel who observe the arrangement for an extended period of time. Particular experiences are evaluated because developmental theory and research have identified them as important for children's healthy development. There are several robust measures of process quality that have been used by researchers. Each of these measures is designed to serve somewhat different purposes. All of these measures are strong measures that have particular uses and strengths.

One of the most commonly used measures of process quality is the Early Childhood Environment Rating Scale (ECERS) (Harms and Clifford, 1989), an instrument used to assess center-based care for preschool-age children. It consists of 37 items and evaluates 7 areas: personal care routines, furnishings, language reasoning experiences, motor activities, creative activities, social development, and staff needs. Detailed descriptors are provided for each item, which is rated on a scale from 1 to 7 in which 1 = inadequate, 3 = minimal, 5 = good, and 7 = excellent. Ratings are completed after at least two hours of observation in a classroom.

The Infant/Toddler Environment Rating Scale (ITERS) (Harms et al., 1990) is a related measure for use in classrooms serving children under the age of 2½ years. The Family Day Care Rating Scale (FDCRS) rates process quality in child care homes (Harms and Clifford, 1989), and the School-Aged Care Environment Rating Scale (SACERS) is appropriate for before-school and after-school programs serving school-age children. All of these measures have good internal consistency, and field staff can be trained to use them fairly easily

The Observational Record of the Caregiving Environment (ORCE) was developed by the NICHD Early Child Care Research Network (1996, 2000a) to assess all types of child care settings. Age-appropriate versions are available for children ages 6 months to 5 years.[1] Observers complete both time-sample behavioral counts and qualitative ratings during a series of 44-minute observation cycles collected over a 2-day period. The observer records the frequency or amount of specific caregiver behaviors, such as *responds to child vocalization* and *asks questions,* and makes qualitative four-point ratings of caregiver sensitivity to the child's needs, cognitive stimulation, positive regard for the child, emotional detachment, and negative regard. The positive caregiving composite score is the mean of the qualitative scales, after reflecting the ratings of detachment and negative regard.

Annex Table A5-4 provides the distribution of child care quality (categorized as poor, fair, good, excellent) that was derived from positive caregiving composite scores of the ORCE in the NICHD Study of Early Child Care. In these analyses, poor quality care was defined as a composite

---

[1]Coding manuals, including detailed descriptions of scales at each age, can be found at http://secc.rti.org.

score of less than 2, fair quality care as a score of 2 or more, but less than 3, good quality care was a score between 3 and 3.5, and excellent quality care was a score of 3.5 or higher. Because there is no nationally representative study that has assessed process quality in the United States, the observations from the NICHD study and other multisite studies (described in Annex Table A5-2) are the only available estimates of process quality in the United States. In the NICHD study, 7 percent of the settings observed were of poor quality and 12 percent were of excellent quality. Most of the settings provided care that was only of fair quality. In Chapter 3 we estimated the process quality of child care from these studies.

As shown in Annex Table A5-4, children in low-income families were more likely than children in high-income families to receive poor-quality child care: 11 percent of the low-income children compared with 4 percent of the high-income children. Children in low-income families also were less likely than children in high-income families to receive excellent quality child care: 8 percent of low-income children compared with 15 percent of high-income children. Disparities in quality associated with family income were more evident in child care homes and informal care arrangements than in centers, perhaps because children in low-income families have access to publicly supported programs such as Head Start.

It is likely that these observations overestimate the amount of high-quality care and underestimate the amount of poor-quality care. Informal care settings and settings that serve children from low-income families were more likely to refuse to participate in the observations, and outcomes are lower for children whose care was not observed even after controlling for an extensive array of family covariates (NICHD Early Child Care Research Network and Duncan, 2003). The sample in the NICHD Study also did not include some groups of children (e.g., children of adolescent mothers, mothers who do not speak English, and mothers who were known substance abusers).

Other measures of process quality are the Caregiver Interaction Scale (Arnett, 1989), which focuses on teachers' sensitivity during interactions with children, and the CC-HOME scale, which assesses overall quality of child care homes (Clarke-Stewart et al., 2002). All of these measures have excellent psychometric properties and predict child developmental outcomes.

Another approach to the assessment of child care quality is consideration of *structural characteristics,* such as child-adult ratio, and *caregiver characteristics,* such as caregivers' specialized training as indicators of child care quality. Structural-caregiver characteristics are the only indicators of quality in studies such as the National Longitudinal Survey of Youth, the National Child Care Survey (Hofferth et al., 1991), and the National Household Education Survey (Hofferth et al., 1998). Both structural-caregiver characteristics and process quality measures were collected in the NICHD

Study of Early Child Care, in the Cost, Quality and Outcome Study, and the Child Care Staffing Study.

Structural-Caregiver Characteristics, Process Quality, and Child Outcomes

The conceptual model that has guided much of the research on the effects of child care quality on children's developmental outcomes is shown in Figure 5-1 (Blau, 2001; Lamb, 1998; NICHD Early Child Care Research Network, 2002b; Vandell and Wolfe, 2000). This schema posits that process quality is directly related to child developmental outcomes, whereas structural-caregiver characteristics are posited to affect child outcomes indirectly through their impact on process quality. In this model, appropriate structural-caregiver characteristics are seen as providing necessary, but not sufficient, conditions for high-quality care. Also reflected in the model is the recognition of the importance of family factors for child developmental outcomes and selection into child care.

For the most part, individual studies (see Annex Tables 5-1, 5-2, and 5-3) have focused on one or another component of the overall model, while positing that the other pathways exist. One report, however, has formally tested the overall model (NICHD Early Child Care Research Network, 2002b). In that study, structural equation modeling (SEM) was used to test relations between structural-caregiver characteristics and process quality as predictors of child developmental outcomes. Two main findings were found: (1) process quality measured by the ORCE predicted children's cognitive competence and social competence at 4½ years, controlling for

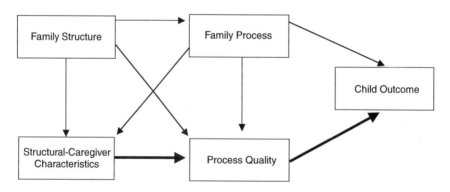

FIGURE 5-1 A conceptual model of relations among structural-caregiver chateristics, process quality, and child outcomes.
SOURCE: Blau (2001).

family income, maternal education, and parenting quality; and (2) there was a connection between structural qualities such as caregiver training and child-staff ratio and cognitive competence and social competence that was not accounted for by family variables. As noted above, other research studies have focused on one or another pathway in the overall model. In the following sections, we review these studies, starting with studies that consider relations between structural-caregiver characteristics and process quality. Then we examine research pertaining to process quality and child developmental outcomes. Finally, we consider relations between structural-caregiver characteristics and child developmental outcomes.

Structural-Caregiver Characteristics and Process Quality

Blau (2001) and Vandell and Wolfe (2000) reviewed the research examining associations between structural-caregiver characteristics and process quality. (These studies also are summarized in Annex Table A5-1.) Four structural-caregiver characteristics—child-adult ratio, group size, specialized training, and general education level—have been the focus of much of the research. Although early research studies were criticized for various methodological limitations (small samples, single site, simple bivariate analyses), recent research (Burchinal et al., 2002; NICHD Early Child Care Research Network, 1997b, 2000a) has examined relations between structural-caregiver characteristics and process quality using multivariate techniques, multiple study sites, and large samples.

As shown in Annex Table A5-1, many studies have reported associations between child-adult ratios and process quality. When child-adult ratios are lower, caregivers spend less time managing children in their classrooms, children are less apathetic and distressed (Ruopp et al., 1979), and caregivers are more stimulating, responsive, warm, and supportive (Clarke-Stewart et al., 1994; NICHD Early Child Care Research Network, 1996, 2000a; Phillipsen et al., 1997). Lower child-adult ratios also are associated with higher process quality scores on the ECERS and the ORCE (NICHD Early Child Care Research Network, 1996, 2002b,c). For the most part, these findings are derived from correlational research designs, although one study (Ruopp et al., 1979) used a random assignment experimental design to assess the effects of varying child-adult ratios.

The number of children in the group (or group size) also is associated with process quality. In multivariate analyses that included ratio, group size, caregiver training, and caregiver education, caregivers appeared more responsive, more socially stimulating, and less restrictive when there were fewer children in the group (NICHD Early Child Care Research Network, 1996, 2000a; Ruopp et al., 1979). Process quality is higher in child care homes that are in compliance with recommended group sizes dependent upon the age of the children (Clarke-Stewart et al., 2002).

Caregivers' education—both formal education and specialized training pertaining to children or early education—is related to process quality. When caregivers have more formal education and more specialized training, the care they provide is more likely to be stimulating, warm, and supportive, to offer better organized materials, and to provide more age-appropriate experiences (Howes, 1997; NICHD Early Child Care Research Network, 1996, 2000a; Phillipsen et al., 1997).

Analyses based on the Cost, Quality, and Outcome (CQO) dataset also indicate that ratio and caregiver education are related to observed quality. The chapter in the CQO Technical Report by Mocan et al. (1995) showed consistent findings when hierarchical regressions (preferred by psychologists) and econometric analyses were conducted. Both sets of analyses showed ratio, caregiver education/training, and caregiver wages (especially wages for lower paid employees or employees with less education) to predict observed quality.

Associations between caregiver wages and process quality also have been reported in the Child Care Staffing Study (Howes et al., 1992) and the Three-State Study (Phillips et al., 2000). There is evidence that low wages are associated with high turnover rates, another indicator of poorer quality care (Whitebook et al., 1998, 2001).

These relations among wages, process quality, and turnover are worrisome because wages for child care staff tend to be low. For example, whereas the incomes for kindergarten, elementary, middle, and secondary teachers ranged from $37,610 to $42,080 in 2000, the median earnings for prekindergarten teachers were $17,810 (U.S. Bureau of Labor Statistics, 2003:203). Furthermore, the salaries of child care teachers tend to be even lower than prekindergarten teachers.

Finally, there is some evidence that relations between structural-caregiver characteristics and process quality vary by child age. In a study that observed children from 6 though 36 months, group size and child-adult ratios were stronger predictors of process quality for infants, whereas caregiver educational background and training were stronger predictors of process quality for preschoolers (NICHD Study of Early Child Care, 1996, 2000a).

Blau (1997, 2000) has argued that the research evidence pertaining to structural-caregiver characteristics and process quality must be viewed with caution because unobserved characteristics may be confounded with the structural-caregivers characteristics, causing biased estimates. Thus, it seems likely that better structural-caregiver characteristics can facilitate improved process quality, but research to date leaves uncertainty about the magnitude of the effects.

Process Quality and Child Outcomes

Since the publication of the report, *Who Cares for America's Children* (National Research Council, 1990), a substantial body of research has found significant associations between process quality and child developmental outcomes (see Blau, 2001; Love et al., 1996; Vandell and Wolfe, 2000). Findings from these studies are summarized in Annex Tables 5-2 and 5-3. First is an examination of relations between process quality and child functioning in the child care setting. Then process quality and concurrently assessed child functioning in other settings is considered, including laboratory assessments, standardized tests, and maternal reports. Finally, we review research evidence pertaining to relations between process quality and subsequent child developmental outcomes and relations between structural-caregiver characteristics and child developmental outcomes.

Children's Behaviors in the Child Care Setting. Nine studies examined relations between process quality and child behavior in the child care setting (see Annex Table A5-2). Five of these studies had relatively small samples (less than 100 children), and five studies did not include controls for family background. Within these constraints, a consistent pattern of findings is evident. Children were more likely to display positive affect and to appear securely attached to their caregivers in child care settings in which process quality is higher (Elicker et al., 1999; Hestenes et al., 1993; Howes et al., 1992; Howes and Smith, 1995). Children appear more prosocial and positively engaged with peers when their caregivers are sensitive and positive to them (Holloway and Reichhart-Erickson, 1988; Howes et al., 1992; Kontos and Wilcox-Herzog, 1997). Finally, children are rated as more cognitively competent during free play in child care settings that offer more opportunities for art, blocks, and dramatic play (Kontos and Wilcox-Herzog, 1997). Relations between process quality and child functioning were more consistently reported in studies that used assessments with strong psychometric properties (Vandell and Pierce, in press).

Child Functioning in Other Settings. A total of 17 studies examined concurrent relations between process quality and child functioning in laboratory assessments, maternal reports, and teacher reports (see Annex Table A5-2). Five of these studies had relatively small samples (less than 100 children), and seven studies did not include controls for family background. The research evidence across the 17 studies, however, suggests that higher process quality is associated with better cognitive and social-emotional development. In particular, children whose child care is higher in process quality score higher on standardized language and cognitive tests (Burchinal et al., 1996; Dunn et al., 1994; Goelman, 1988; McCartney, 1984; NICHD Early Child Care Research Network, 2000a, 2002c; Peisner-Feinberg and Burchinal, 1997; Schliecker et al., 1991). Higher process quality also has been related to fewer behavior problems (Hausfather et al., 1997; Peisner-Feinberg and Burchinal, 1997) and to higher social competence (Phillips et al., 1987b), as reported by mothers and teachers.

Longer Term Associations Between Process Quality and Child Functioning. Relations between process quality and children's subsequent development also have been reported (see Vandell and Wolfe, 2000, and Annex Table A5-3). Significant associations are more evident in research studies that assessed process quality at several time periods (Burchinal et al., 2002; NICHD Early Child Care Research Network, 2000a, 2002c) and less apparent in studies that relied on a single assessment (Chin-Quee and Scarr, 1994; Deater-Deckard et al., 1996). Because children in the United States typically experience multiple arrangements and because caregivers change as children move from one class to another and as caregivers leave the program, it is not surprising that effects are less evident in studies that measured child care on only a single occasion or at a single age. Multiple assessments are more likely to yield more reliable indicators of children's care.

In the NICHD Study of Early Child Care (2000a, 2002c), cumulative scores of process quality (the ORCE positive caregiving composite) obtained from child care observations at 6, 15, 24, 36, and 54 months predicted children's performance on standardized cognitive and language assessments at these same ages, controlling for other aspects of child care (quantity and type) and family factors (maternal IQ, family income, observed quality of the home environment, and observed maternal stimulation). In the Cost, Quality, and Outcomes Study, process quality (assessed with the ECERS) predicted cognitive, language, and social development during the early grade school years, controlling for maternal education and ethnicity (Peisner-Feinberg et al., 2001). Children who had closer relationships with their preschool teachers appeared more sociable in kindergarten. Children who attended higher quality child care demonstrated better math skills prior to school entry, in kindergarten, and in 2nd grade. The children had better receptive language skills during the preschool period. These relations were stronger for children whose mothers had less education.

Other longitudinal analyses also have reported longer term associations between process quality and social developmental outcomes. In analyses of the Cost, Quality, and Outcome sample, Howes (2000) reported that preschoolers who attended centers in which there were closer teacher-child relationships were subsequently rated by their 2nd grade teachers to be more socially competent with peers, controlling for family factors and previous child functioning. Other research also has found relations between process quality and children's social-emotional outcomes. Children who had caregivers who were involved and invested in positive socialization practices during the first three years were reported by their kindergarten teachers to have fewer behavior problems and better verbal IQs (Howes, 1990).

Both economists and developmental psychologists (Blau, 1999b; Burchinal et al., 1995, Duncan and Gibson, 2000) have worried, however, that the relations between process quality and child functioning are biased estimates because of omitted variables. To more definitively address the question of causality, random assignment experiments are needed, but randomly assigning some children to low-quality child care is unethical and unlikely to be acceptable to parents, institutional review boards, or researchers. Consequently, investigators have turned to a variety of statistical strategies to address this problem.

One strategy has been to expand the list of family covariates in an effort to better capture omitted variables. In the NICHD Study of Early Child Care (2002c), for example, child care effects were tested in models that had nine covariates (such as maternal education, ethnicity, family structure, income-to-needs ratio, maternal depressive symptoms, observed parenting quality, observed home environment quality) and then 15 family covariates (the 9 covariates plus measures of child temperament, maternal psychological adjustment, maternal report of social support, maternal separation anxiety, and maternal beliefs about the benefits of maternal employment). The effects associated with child care did not differ in the two models, suggesting that omitted family variables did not account for the child care effects. In these analyses, effect sizes between process quality and preacademic skills and between process quality and language skills were 0.24 and 0.17, respectively.

A second strategy has been to test effects of early child care experiences after controlling for concurrent quality (NICHD Early Child Care Research Network, in pressb). In these analyses, the quality of care from 6 to 36 months was found to predict child cognitive outcomes at 4½ years when process quality at 4½ years was statistically controlled. Social outcomes, in contrast, were predicted by concurrent child care quality, but not earlier quality.

A third strategy has been to examine changes in child functioning associated with changes in child care quality (NICHD Early Child Care Research Network and Duncan, 2002). Modest but statistically significant impacts of process quality were observed when children were 6-24 and 36-54 months. An increase of 0.5 point on the 4-point ORCE scale (representing an increase of one standard deviation in child care quality) between 36 and 54 months was associated with an increase of 2.4 points on standardized cognitive tests. Effects of quality between 6 and 24 months were found to have had an independent and additive impact on outcomes at age 54 months that were of similar magnitude, suggesting that higher quality care between 6 and 54 months was associated with a 5.0 point increase in cognitive scores. Effect sizes were considerably higher for children with low early cognitive scores.

Structural-Caregiver Characteristics and Child Outcomes

Consistent with the conceptual model delineated in Figure 5-1, a third body of research has examined relations between structural-caregiver characteristics and children's developmental outcomes (see Annex Tables 5-2 and 5-3). In one study (Ruopp et al., 1979), effects of structural-caregiver characteristics on child outcomes were tested both quasi-experimentally and experimentally. Children assigned to classrooms in which teachers had more education and training displayed greater gains in cooperative behavior, task persistence, and school readiness over a nine month period relative to children assigned to classrooms in which teachers had less education and training.

Other studies have adopted correlational designs to examine relations between structural-caregiver characteristics and child outcomes. Infants who attended programs with smaller observed child-adult ratios had better receptive and expressive language skills (Burchinal et al., 1996; Vernon-Feagans et al., 1997), higher cognitive scores (Burchinal et al., 1996), and better social knowledge and social skills (Holloway and Reichhart-Erickson, 1988) than children who were attending programs with higher observed child-adult ratios. When teachers were better educated and had more recent child care training, children displayed better expressive language skills (Burchinal et al., 1996; Howes, 1997) and higher scores on cognitive inventories (Dunn, 1993; Clarke-Stewart et al., 2000). A limitation of much of this research, however, is that it relied on small samples (less than 100) and did not control for family background.

Child developmental outcomes also have been examined in relation to aggregated scores of structural-caregiver characteristics. Some programs, for example, seek to trade off teacher training and group size by having better trained teachers care for more children. In other programs, more highly trained teachers are assigned fewer children. And in still other programs, centers fail to meet any recommended standards. In one report (NICHD Early Child Care Research Network, 1999b), centers were scored in terms of the age-based guidelines for group size, child-adult ratio, caregiver training, and caregiver formal education recommended by the American Public Health Association. If a particular guideline was met, a point was awarded. If a guideline was not, no point was given. The number of points was then summed. Controlling for family income and maternal sensitivity, children who attended centers that met more recommended guidelines had fewer behavior problems at age 2 and 3 years and higher school readiness and language comprehension scores at 3 years.

Compliance with specific guidelines also was related to child scores. Children displayed fewer behavior problems and more positive social behaviors when centers were observed and met the recommended child-adult ratio at 2 years. Children exhibited fewer behavior problems and obtained higher school readiness and language comprehension scores at 3 years if caregivers reported levels of specialized training and education that met the recommended guidelines for specialized training and formal education.

Longer term relations between structural-caregiver characteristics and children's subsequent social and cognitive development also have been reported (see Love et al., 1996; Vandell and Wolfe, 2000). Howes (1988), for example, examined structural-caregiver characteristics (amount of teacher training, child-adult ratio, group size, a planned curriculum, and space) when children were 3 years of age in relation to the children's functioning in 1st grade. During the intervening period, the children attended the same university lab school, meaning that they experienced classes with the same or similar structural and caregiver characteristics. Controlling for maternal work status, family structure, and maternal education, children whose early care met more structural-caregiver guidelines had fewer behavior problems and better work habits compared with children whose early care had met fewer guidelines.

In a different sample, Howes (1990) found significant relations using a composite score of structural-caregiver indicators (child-adult ratio, caregiver training, caregiver stability) at 18, 24, 30, and 36 months. Controlling for family sociodemographic factors and socialization strategies, children with a history of poor-quality structural-caregiver indicators were rated as more difficult by their preschool teachers and as more hostile by their kindergarten teachers. Recent research from the Otitis Media Study also has focused on specific structural and caregiver characteristics in relation to subsequent child developmental outcomes (Burchinal et al., 2002). Children whose child care classrooms met recommended guidelines for child-staff ratios exhibited better receptive language and communication skills, controlling for child gender, family poverty, and cognitive stimulation and emotional support in the home. Girls whose caregivers had at least 14 years of education (with or without early childhood training) had better cognitive and receptive language skills over time.

Blau (1997, 1999b, 2000) has been critical of the fact that research in this area has relied on nonrepresentative samples and has failed to control adequately for family factors and other child care features. To address these concerns, random assignment experiments are needed to establish whether the reported associations between caregiver characteristics, structural characteristics, and child social and cognitive functioning are causal.

EFFECTS OF DIFFERENT TYPES OF EARLY CHILD CARE

Research that has considered the effects of different types of child care has taken several forms. One set of studies has used experimental designs and quasi-experimental designs to evaluate the effects of high-quality early education programs on children in families with low incomes. The primary purpose of these programs is the improvement of the developmental outcomes of children who are at risk for school failure, although the programs also can function as child care, especially if they are full-day programs. Well-known examples of such programs include Head Start, which provides preschool educational services, nutrition, a health component, social services, and parent involvement for families with 3- and 4-year-old children (Zigler and Styfco, 1993), and the Chicago Parent-Child Centers (Reynolds, 2000). Other types of early child care that have been studied include comparisons of the effects of child care centers, child care homes, and relative care. In this section, we first review the research pertaining to the effects of high-quality early education programs and then turn to consideration of the effects of different types of child care typically used by families, including child care centers, family child care, in-home care (i.e., nannies), and grandparent care.

Early Center-Based Intervention Programs

Early childhood intervention programs have been categorized according to three overall models: those that provide educational services to children; those that provide parenting, vocational, and other supports to parents; and those that combine these two components (Brooks-Gunn et al., 2000; Seitz, 1990; National Research Council and Institute of Medicine, 2000; St. Pierre et al., 1995; Yoshikawa, 1995). In this section, we do not consider programs that provide services to parents only, because the focus of this chapter is on child care; we review evidence on the two other forms of early childhood intervention. We do not aim to provide a comprehensive review of effects of each type of intervention program, but rather to summarize patterns of effects by type of program, review evidence on these programs' coverage of working parents in the United States, and consider the quality of these programs. We exclude programs serving solely families with children with disabilities.

Child-Focused Programs

The provision of educational services to low-income, preschool-age children, most often in center-based programs, is the main focus of this set of early childhood interventions. Beginning with evaluations of educational preschools prior to the 1960s, this kind of program has demonstrated consistent short-term benefits on measures of cognitive development and early school performance in randomized evaluations (Barnett, 1995; Bryant and Maxwell, 1997). However, few of these experimental studies have been of large-scale programs; the vast majority of studies have been conducted in single-site, demonstration-quality programs. For example, of 21 large-scale programs reviewed by Barnett (1995), none was evaluated using random assignment designs. Similarly, although state prekindergarten programs have expanded tremendously in the recent decade, no randomized evaluations of these programs yet exist.

Head Start is the most well-known example of this type of intervention. Although a variety of quasi-experimental studies have shown short-term gains from Head Start in areas of cognitive ability and school performance, with some showing some longer term effects into early adolescence (e.g., Currie and Thomas, 1995; Garces et al., 2000), no experimental evaluations of Head Start exist. A random assignment evaluation of the Head Start program is now under way.

Some recent work on the Chicago Parent-Child Centers, a large-scale preschool program tied to follow-on transition services through 3rd grade, attempted to adjust for selection biases by utilizing sample selection models. This work demonstrated long-term effects of the program in reducing rates of delinquency and raising levels of school achievement (Reynolds, 2000). Another program, which enhanced Head Start with a social skills component and parent training, has shown short-term effects in reducing aggressive behaviors among Head Start children in a randomized evaluation (Webster-Stratton et al., 2001).

One of the best known early intervention projects is the Carolina Abecedarian Project (Campbell and Ramey, 1995; Ramey et al., 1998, in press). This clinical trial began at 6 weeks postpartum and included: (1) a randomized control group (n = 54) that received family support social services, pediatric care, and child nutritional supplements, and (2) an experimental group (n = 57) that received the services of a high-quality center-based intervention for the first five years. The center operated 5 days a week for 50 weeks a year. Child-adult ratios were 3:1 for infants and 6:1 for older children. The curriculum emphasized language development. IQ scores at ages 8 and 15 years were significantly higher for the children who received high-quality center-based care during the first five years (4.5 point difference at 8 years and 4.6 point difference at 15 years). The effect sizes, calculated as the difference in means between treatment and control subjects divided by the standard deviation of the control group, were similar at the two ages (0.36 and 0.35, respectively) (Campbell and Ramey, 1995). Children who had participated in the early intervention program also had higher scores on tests of reading and mathematics achievement at age 15 and were less likely to be retained in grade by age 15 (31.2 compared with 54.5 percent, p < 0.02), and they were less likely to be placed in special education (12 compared with 47 percent). The most recent follow-up report from this research team (Ramey et al., 1999) includes findings to age 21. Intervention children were reported to be older, on average, when their first child was born and to have been more likely to attend a four-year college.

Another demonstration project that has reported beneficial effects of a high-quality early education program is the Perry Preschool Project (Schweinhart et al., 1993), which involved 123 black children who were followed to age 27. The experimental group consisted of 45 children who entered the preschool program at age 3 and an additional 13 who entered at age 4, attending a half-day center-based program and receiving teacher home visits. The researchers report that the experimental group had a somewhat lower probability of ever being arrested by age 27 (57 compared with 69 percent), but a larger difference in the average number of lifetime arrests by age 27 (2.3 compared with 4.6). Differences in the proportion receiving public assistance by age 27 were also large—15 compared with 32 percent. Mean earnings were far higher for the experimental group than the control group at age 27—monthly reported mean earnings were $1,219 for the experimental group and $766 for the control group.

Participation in the Chicago Child-Parent Centers (CPC) also has been related to long-term beneficial effects (Reynolds et al., 2000). This project has followed the educational and social development of 1,539 black (93 percent) and Hispanic (7 percent) children as they grew up in high-poverty neighborhoods in the central city of Chicago. Some of the children (n = 989) participated in government-funded (Title I) early childhood programs in 1985-1986, whereas others did not (n = 550). A rich array of data, including surveys from teachers, parents, school administrative records, standardized tests, and the children themselves has been collected since that time. Reynolds (1994) reported (at the end of the program in 3rd grade), that extended program participation was related to one half of a standard deviation improvement in reading and math scores over the comparison group, even after controlling for family risk status, child gender, and later program participation. Reynolds and Temple (1998) obtained similar effects of extended program participation on reading and math performance at age 13. At age 20, participants in the CPC were more likely to have completed high school (49.7 compared with 38.5 percent, p < 0.01) and to have lower rates of juvenile arrests (16.9 compared with 25.1 percent, p < 0.001) (Reynolds et al., 2001).

Even though only a few studies have followed children into adulthood, it is notable that all find some evidence of long-term gains. For instance,

Heckman (2000) looks at long-term effects of each education program on long-term success in the job market. In this discussion of early center-based interventions, it is relevant to explore whether these programs provide adequate coverage for low-income families. Head Start served 858,000 children in 2000, with a budget of $6.2 billion. The program served just over 40 percent of eligible families. Only a quarter of Head Start programs are full-day programs (Administration for Children and Families, 2002). Experimental data from welfare-to-work evaluations shows no effect of mandated employment programs on Head Start use, while the use of other forms of center care appeared to increase (Chang et al., 2002); this difference in effects may be due to the high proportion of part-day Head Start programs or the fact that Head Start centers may already be full. Data from a random sample of 40 Head Start programs (comprising 518 classrooms) found that the average observed quality of services in classrooms was in the "good" range of the ECERS, with under 2 percent of classrooms in the minimal-to-inadequate range and 17 percent of classrooms in the excellent range (a score of 6 or 7; Zill et al., 1998). Researchers noted that this was a somewhat higher average than in most studies of center care for low-income families, with fewer classrooms at the bottom of the distribution on the measure (i.e., fewer classrooms in the "minimal" or "inadequate" ranges of the ECERS).

In 1999, state prekindergarten funds served over 4.5 million children in 32 states (Gilliam and Zigler, 2000). A higher percentage of these programs are full-day (just under 50 percent). However, the quality of these programs is largely unknown. One study in Michigan found its sample of preschools to fall in the range of medium to high quality on a measure developed from the state's performance standards; subscales in the areas of administration, supervision, program philosophy, and use of funding were related to child development ratings in kindergarten in predicted directions (Florian et al., 1997).

Gilliam and Zigler's (2000) review of state-sponsored prekindergarten evaluations discusses serious shortcomings with the designs of all the existing evaluations. For example, only the evaluation in New York used a reasonable method of selecting a control (using other children from the waiting list), and none used random assignment.

Parent-Focused Programs and Combination Child- and Parent-Focused Programs

The combination of services to parents (whether in job training, adult education, parenting information and support, or other social services) with child-focused enrichment has been termed the "two-generation" approach (Smith, 1995). The most prevalent forms of parent-focused services in this program model are parenting support and vocational/educational support. In parenting support models, professional or paraprofessional staff (most often home visitors) provide informational support about parenting and child development, as well as some general support for vocational and educational goals, to low-income parents. As of 1999, a conservative estimate was that 550,000 children were participating in these programs (totaling across selected programs with national offices only; Gomby et al., 1999). However, few of these programs combine home visiting with a part- or full-day, educational, child-focused component in a two-generation approach. No national estimates exist regarding the numbers of children served overall in two-generation programs.

Demonstration-quality programs that have combined these approaches have shown impressive effects in experimental evaluations, not only on child school performance, but also on antisocial behavior in late childhood and adolescence and some measures of parenting and parent employment (Bryant and Maxwell, 1997; Yoshikawa, 1995; National Research Council and Institute of Medicine, 2000). However, it is unclear to what extent these same programs, if scaled up, would retain these effects.

The largest federal initiative taking this program approach is the Early Head Start program, which in 2000 served 55,000 children ages 0 to 3 in 664 communities. This program, which provides parent education and educational child care, is implemented in center-based, home-based, and combination versions, depending on the site (each must adhere to a set of performance standards). A three-year follow-up, in a randomized evaluation of families in 17 sites, documented an overall pattern of impacts at age 3. For children, positive impacts were found in cognitive development, language development, and social-emotional development. For parents, positive impacts were in parenting, home environment, participation in education and job training, and subsequent births (mothers less likely to have a second child). There were also some positive effects specifically related to fathering and father-child interactions, but not all of the programs had a father-oriented component and participated in father studies. All effects were in the small range (between 0.10 and 0.20 of a standard deviation).

An eight-site experimental evaluation was conducted on a program with a somewhat similar combination of parent-focused home visits beginning at birth and high-quality child care beginning at 12 months, the Infant Health and Development Program (Brooks-Gunn et al., 1992, 1994; McCormick et al., 1993). This program showed positive effects on IQ and other cognitive measures among a sample of low-birthweight infants when they were 36 months old. However, assessments at ages 5 and 8 showed that the control group had improved in its levels of cognitive outcomes, and no experimental effect was found on cognitive or behavioral measures of child development (McCarton et al., 1997), although positive cognitive outcomes have been found for children receiving higher dosages (i.e., attending more days) (Hill et al., 2003). This was an unusually large-scale demonstration program, rather than a randomized evaluation of an existing large-scale program.

What constitutes quality in two-generation programs and what the effects of variation in program quality are on child development remain largely unstudied. The Early Head Start evaluation, rating each of the 17 programs on level of implementation, found that experimental effects were largest in the group that was judged to have achieved the highest level of implementation (Love et al., 2002). Evaluations of a model home visiting program that was developed by David Olds and colleagues have shown that the proportion of home visit time focused on parenting issues was positively associated with HOME scores of parenting quality and observed measures of mothers' empathy toward children (Korfmacher et al., 1998). It is unknown how the most widely available two-generation programs score on such measures of quality.

Child Care Centers, Child Care Homes, and Grandparent Care

In addition to the evaluations of the early childhood intervention programs, investigators have studied the effects of participating in different types of child care, such as child care centers, child care homes, in-home care (including nannies), and grandparents. As noted by Clarke-Stewart et al. (1994), these care arrangements differ in a myriad of ways, including their physical facilities, the number and kinds of materials, the flexibility of the daily schedule, the number of children in the arrangement, the child-adult ratio, and caregivers' education, training, and reasons for providing care. In comparison to child care homes and nannies, center-based care typically offers more highly educated caregivers, larger group sizes, more time spent in lessons, more structured activities, and more child-oriented materials, activities, and toys. Caregivers are more likely to have a more professional orientation and less likely to provide care as a favor for the family. In child care homes, children spend more time in free exploration, casual learning, and watching TV than in centers. Consistent with the more educational focus of the centers, Clarke-Stewart et al. (1994) found that center-based care was associated with higher scores on standardized cognitive assessments, controlling for family demographic characteristics and observed parenting. Children in center-based care also were more competent with strangers and independent of mothers in a laboratory playroom.

Research conducted by the NICHD Early Child Care Research Network (2000a, 2002b) also has considered the effects of center-type experience on child developmental outcomes. Children who had more experience in center-based care received higher cognitive and language scores at age 2 years (2000) and 3 years (2000), and higher language and memory scores at 4½ years (2002), controlling for quality and quantity of child care and for family background characteristics. Effect sizes in these analyses ranged from 0.21 to 0.43, indicating expected differences in standard deviations on cognitive outcomes between children who attended centers and those who did not. The NICHD Early Child Care Research Network and Duncan (2003) report that children who attended centers between the ages 27 and 54 months (but not earlier) scored 4.1 points higher on cognitive tests than children who never attended centers during this period, controlling for family factors and previous child performance (effect size = 0.27).

The developmental consequences of other relative care arrangements are more equivocal. Dana cares for her young grandson, and they spend much of their time watching television (Newman, 1999:203).

Grandma Dana is not particularly attentive to Anthony's emotional needs, even though she keeps him fed and safe. He is never left alone, he does not run the streets, and his clothes are clean.

Participation in child care homes does not appear to confer similar cognitive advantages. In a study of low-income families in the National Longitudinal Survey of Youth (NLSY), Yoshikawa (1999) found that number of months in child care homes in the first five years of life was associated with lower standardized math and reading achievement at ages 7 and 8, controlling for months in relative care and center care as well as family background characteristics.

Evidence of center-type effects also was found in the area of social development. Children whose care settings contained more children were reported by caregivers to be more sociable but also to have more negative interactions with their peers (National Institute of Child Health and Human Development, 2001a, in pressd). Children's experiences in child care homes were less consistently related to cognitive and language development.

An early study by Baydar and Brooks-Gunn (1991) is one of the few studies to consider explicitly the effects of grandmother care on child developmental outcomes. In a study of white children in infancy whose mothers were employed, grandparent care was associated with fewer behavior problems at age 4 years than children who attended child care homes and centers. Additional research is needed to clarify the conditions under which relative and other informal care arrangements are supportive of children's development.

EFFECTS OF QUANTITY OR AMOUNT OF CHILD CARE

A third aspect of early child care that has been subject to considerable research is quantity or amount of child care (see Lamb, 1998, and Belsky, 1999, for reviews). A related literature has considered amount (and timing) of maternal employment (see Chapter 2 of this report and Brooks-Gunn et al., 2002). One of the most hotly debated issues is whether extensive hours in early child care (or extensive hours of early maternal employment) place children at risk. In a series of papers, Belsky (1986, 1988, 1999) argued that early and extensive hours place young children at risk for insecure relationships with mothers and heightened behavior problems, including aggression and noncompliance. Other scholars (Brazelton, 1986; Egeland and Heister, 1995) made similar arguments based on the need for mothers and infants to have sufficient time to build emotionally attuned relationships that serve as a basis for subsequent social competencies. These views were countered by other scholars, who argued that the effects of early and extensive care might be explained by other factors, such as: (a) the quality of the child care (Phillips et al., 1987b), (b) differences in family background that accounted for different amounts of child care and differences in child developmental outcomes (Richters and Zahn-Waxler, 1990; Thompson, 1988), or (c) a failure to distinguish between avoidance and independence in assessments of infant attachment relationships and between assertiveness and aggressiveness in the assessments of older children (Clarke-Stewart, 1989). Much of the initial research that reported effects associated with quantity of care did not control for quality of care and had only limited controls for family selection.

The NICHD Study of Early Child Care, initiated in 1991, afforded the evaluation of these alternative positions. Key elements included in the design of that study were consideration of the effects of early and extensive hours in a prospective longitudinal design that had: (1) a sufficiently large sample to detect effects; (2) robust measures of child care quality, type, and quantity; (3) extensive and repeated measures of family characteristics and processes that could be used to detect family characteristics associated with child care selection as well as family characteristics that changed as a function of child care; and (4) a diverse set of child developmental outcomes that were assessed at multiple ages.

The NICHD Early Child Care Research Network has considered the effects of amount and timing of child care on children's social and cognitive development, including attachment to mother (1997a, in pressd), behavior problems (1998, 2002c, in pressa), social competence (1998, 2002c, in pressb), and cognitive, language, and preacademic performance (2000b, 2002b). Infants with extensive child care experience did not differ from infants with little or no child care experience in their distress during separations from the mother in a strange situation (1997b). There were no significant effects of amount of care on attachment security at 15, 24, or 36 months (1997b, in pressb). Amount of care also was not related to children's cognitive, language, or academic performance assessed at 24, 36, or 54 months (2000b, 2002a).

Amount or hours of care were related to children's social development at age 24 months, 54 months, and in kindergarten. In particular, children who had more hours of care had more behavior problems, according to their caregivers (NICHD, 1998), and were less socially competent, according to their mothers (2002a). In kindergarten, children who had more hours in care were reported by both mothers and teachers to have more externalizing problems and, by teachers, to have more conflict relationships (in pressd). This finding held when type of care was controlled.

Examination of the proportions of children with substantial behavior problems (defined as one or more standard deviations above the mean) revealed that only the group of children in care for more than 45 hours a week displayed higher than expected rates of substantial problems: 19 percent of this group had elevated behavior problems, according to kindergarten teachers, and 21 percent had elevated behavior problems, according to mothers. In contrast, 9 percent of the children who had been in care for 0 to 9 hours were reported by kindergarten teachers to have substantial behavior problems. By definition, on this normed instrument, 17 percent of the children are expected to score one standard deviation above the mean.

Additional research is needed to identify the processes or mechanisms that mediate relations between quantity of care and behavior problems. By and large, in the NICHD analyses, effects were not attenuated when the positive caregiving composite (the ORCE measure of process) and maternal sensitivity were included in the regression analyses, suggesting that the quantity findings were not mediated by the quality of caregiving provided by child care providers or mothers, at least as measured by the study investigators. Further research is needed to consider other aspects of the child care environment beyond those reflected in the measure of process quality used in the NICHD study. For example, the specific strategies that caregivers use to promote children's social skills and to handle noncompliance and aggression or experiences with peers may help to explain the effects associated with quantity of care.

Recent research by Watamura et al. (in press) found elevated cortisol levels at the end of the day when children were in centers all day, suggesting that the experiences were taxing for them. Other findings from this laboratory (Dettling et al., 1999) have shown that the largest increases in cortisol over the course of the child care day were observed in children who had the most difficulty regulating their negative emotions and behavior.

Other issues warranting additional study pertain to the timing of early child care. In general, reports from the NICHD study have found cumulative indicators of child care quantity are stronger predictors of child developmental outcomes than age-segmented predictors (see NICHD, 2000a). One exception is that kindergarten teachers reported higher levels of behavior problems for children in care for more hours in the first 6 months of life, controlling for amount of care in later time periods. A recent study by Brooks-Gunn et al. (2002) also found age-specific relations in analyses involving the NICHD dataset. In analyses of European-American children in the sample, children whose mothers were employed for 30 or more hours a week by 9 months had lower preacademic skills at 36 months than children whose mothers worked less than 30 hours a week. These effects were not evident in the children's cognitive performance at 15 or 24 months or in the cognitive performance of ethnic minority children at 15, 24, or 36 months. The findings of associations between extensive maternal employment in the first year and lower cognitive performance of European-American children are, however, similar to findings from the Child Supplement of National Longitudinal Survey of Youth (Baydar and Brooks-Gunn, 1991).

These findings suggest that amount as well as quality and type of child care need to be considered in relation to child developmental outcomes. While children appear to benefit cognitively (and perhaps socially) from high-quality child care and from center-type experiences, extensive hours in child care are associated with increased problem behaviors. Additional research is needed to determine why extensive hours are related to problem behaviors.

EFFECTS OF CHILD CARE ARRANGEMENTS DURING MIDDLE CHILDHOOD

Because parents' workdays are typically longer than the school day, needs for child care do not disappear when children begin elementary school. Families of school-age children have adopted a variety of strategies to cover the nonschool hours when parents are at work, including self-care, before- and after-school programs, extracurricular activities, and informal care by sitters and relatives. These different care arrangements are often used in combination, and children move from one type of care to another in the course of an afternoon and across the week.

These arrangements vary in their opportunities for children to engage in activities that they enjoy and care about (Larson, 2000), to develop physical, social, and cognitive skills (Larson, 1994), and to be with friends, adult mentors, and parents (McLaughlin et al., 1994; Posner and Vandell, 1994). For example, children who attend after-school programs have a chance to spend more time in academic enrichment, arts, and sports activities, whereas children in informal settings spend more of their after-school hours watching television and hanging out with friends (Posner and Vandell, 1999). Extracurricular activities and lessons offer opportunities for substantial engagement in activities that children care about. In this section, we consider research findings pertaining to effects of different types of before- and after-school care on developmental outcomes during middle childhood.

Self-Care

Self-care, sometimes called latchkey care (Steinberg, 1986; Woods, 1972), refers to various unsupervised circumstances, including children being home alone, being cared for by older siblings, providing care for younger siblings, and hanging out with unsupervised peers (Belle, 1997; Galambos and Maggs, 1991; Vandell and Su, 1999). The notion of self-care stirs mixed reactions. The goal for many parents in the United States is for children to become independent and capable of functioning without parents or other adults directly supervising their activities. Toward this end, children often experience a gradual transition from direct parental supervision to self-care. At the same time, it is clear that young children lack the maturity and judgment to care for themselves. Thus, an important issue is how children and families navigate the transition from close supervision to independent self-care and a determination of the circumstances under which self-care is beneficial for children's development and the conditions under which it is detrimental.

Self-care is predicted by a number of child, family, and community factors. It is more likely to be used by older children versus younger children and by children who previously exhibited fewer internalizing and externalizing problems. White children are more likely than black children and Hispanic children to be in self-care (Capizzano et al., 2000b). Self-care also more likely if mothers are employed (Smith, 2002) and family incomes are higher (Capizzano et al., 2000b), reflecting perhaps the greater availability of relatives and other adults in lower income households and greater concerns about the dangers of leaving children alone in low-income neighborhoods. Self-care is more common in suburban and rural areas than in urban areas (Hofferth et al., 2000) and more likely when parents and children perceive their neighborhoods to be safe places (Vandell and Posner, 1999).

Evidence of relations between self-care and children's developmental outcomes indicates that these associations vary depending on: (1) the child's age and previous functioning, (2) family characteristics, (3) neighborhood characteristics, and (4) the amount and type of self-care (for reviews, see Vandell and Shumow, 1999; Vandell and Su, 1999; Powell, 1987). Self-care appears to be more problematic when combined with such child factors as previous behavior problems (Pettit et al., 1997, 1999), such family factors as poverty (Marshall et al., 1997; Pettit et al., 1997) and low parental monitoring (Galambos and Maggs, 1991; Steinberg, 1987; Pettit et al., 1999), and unsafe neighborhoods (Pettit et al., 1999).

Retrospective data on Anthony Hayes, "a high achiever," illustrates how children assume adult-like responsibilities when their parents work (Clark, 1983:67-68):

We all had responsibilities even when I was in second or third grade. I had my own door key. My mother and father would go to work and it was up to us to come home and do what we were supposed to do. And during lunch periods, I came home and ate lunch and went back to school. When school was over, I came home and cleaned up and did whatever I had to do.

Pettit and colleagues (1997) found some longer term effects of early self-care. Children whose mothers retrospectively reported more unsupervised care (alone or with a sibling) in 1st and 3rd grade were less socially competent in 6th grade, according to teacher reports. They also received lower grades and achievement test scores in comparison to their classmates who had experienced less self-care, even after controlling for family characteristics and children's functioning in kindergarten. Self-care (alone or with siblings) in 5th grade was not related to the children's functioning in 6th grade, consistent with the proposition that these forms of self-care are more problematic for younger children than for young adolescents. Pettit et al. also found interactions between self-care and previous child adjustment and between self-care and family income. The highest levels of behavior problems in 6th grade were evident in those children who had extensive self-care in 1st grade as well as high levels of behavior problems in kindergarten. The combination of low family income and early self-care also predicted higher levels of behavior problems in 6th grade.

In a subsequent report, Pettit and colleagues (1999) distinguished among three forms of unsupervised care during 6th grade—time with unsupervised peers, time alone, and time with siblings. Children who spent more time with unsupervised peers in 6th grade displayed more externalizing problems in 7th grade, controlling for family background factors and 6th grade behavior problems. The greatest risk was found for unsupervised children who were less closely monitored by parents and who lived in less safe neighborhoods. Time alone, time with unsupervised siblings, and time with supervised peers during 6th grade did not predict externalizing problems in 7th grade.

McHale et al. (2001), however, have reported evidence that both time alone and time with unsupervised peers is related to problematic development during middle childhood. Children who spent more time alone at ages 10 and 12 reported more depression than children who spent less time alone. Children who spent more time with unsupervised peers, in contrast, had lower grades and more externalizing behavior problems.

After-School Programs

Increases in maternal employment, beliefs about children's needs for supervision and enrichment during the nonschool hours, stories in the popular press about the negative effects of self-care, and concerns about lagging academic achievement in children who are growing up in poverty have contributed to the substantial growth in after-school programs (Vandell and Su, 1999). These programs are housed at schools, community centers, and child care centers. Historically, school-based programs and day care centers have been funded by parental fees and served children of middle-income families, whereas community centers historically served children of low-income families (Halpern, 2002).

The 1990s have been marked by a substantial increase in after-school programs serving children of low-income families. A number of program models have emerged, including a range of program activities such as community service, academic enrichment, recreation, arts, mentoring, and child care.[2] One of the best known programs is the 21st Century Community Learning Centers (CCLC), a school-based after-school program initially administered by the U.S. Department of Education. Funding for the program grew from $40 million in 1997 to $1 billion in 2002. In 2001, 1.2 million elementary and middle school students participated in programs located in 3,600 schools.

Even with the growth in programming, a General Accounting Office (GAO) study estimates that as little as 20 percent of the demand for programs is met in urban areas (U.S. General Accounting Office, 1997). It is estimated that only about one-third of the demand for programs is being met in rural areas (Larner et al., 1999). The GAO report and other studies (Mezey et al., 2002) indicate shortages of care in certain critical areas, including for infants and toddlers, children with special needs, older school-age children, and children of families working nonstandard hours. While the GAO study predates the expansion of child care opportunities available

---

[2]Descriptions of many of these federal, state, and local after-school initiatives can be found at http://www.gse.harvard.edu/hfrp/projects/afterschool/mott/mott1.html.

through the 21st Century Community Learning Centers, in the 2000 competition for funding for these programs, 2,252 communities sought funds to establish or expand after-school programs, but funds were available to support only 310 grantees.

Evidence pertaining to the effects of after-school programs on children's developmental outcomes is mixed, with some studies reporting positive effects (Grossman et al., 2002; Marshall et al., 1997; Pettit et al., 1997; Posner and Vandell, 1994; Vandell and Corasaniti, 1988; Welsh et al., 2002), other studies reporting no effects (Pettit et al., 1997), and still others reporting negative effects (Vandell and Corasaniti, 1988). Findings are related to family factors (Posner and Vandell, 1994; Vandell and Corasaniti, 1988; Marshall et al., 1997), program quality (Pierce et al., 1999), and dosage (Cosden et al., 2001; Vandell and Pierce, 1999). After-school programs have been more consistently associated with positive effects for children from low-income families than for children from middle-income families (Grossman et al., 2002; Marshall et al., 1997; Pettit et al., 1997; Posner and Vandell, 1994; Vandell and Corasaniti, 1988; Welsh et al., 2002) and for children whose parents have limited English proficiency (Cosden et al., 2001; Welsh et al., 2002).

In a large-scale evaluation of 96 programs serving low-income students in New York City (25,909 program participants and 39,780 students who did not participate in a program), Welsh et al. (2002) reported that low-achieving students, black students, Hispanic students, and English language learners were especially likely to benefit from active participation in the programs, as evidenced by greater gains in math achievement relative to their peers. In the Boston After-School Study, Marshall et al. (1997) found that children of low-income families (but not middle-income families) had fewer behavior problems if they regularly attended after-school programs. Similarly, in a study conducted in a context of low family income and unsafe neighborhoods, Posner and Vandell (1994) found that children who attended after-school programs had fewer antisocial behaviors and better reading and math grades, work habits, emotional adjustment, and peer relationships than children who were in self-care, sitter care, or parental care after school. The after-school programs appeared to serve as a safe haven for children in neighborhoods in which crime rates are high and unsupervised time after school exposed them to deviant peers and violence.

The evaluation of the Extended Services School Initiative (Grossman et al., 2002) found changes in school engagement for students who regularly participated in after-school programs in comparison to students who participated less regularly in the programs. Controlling for students' baseline performance in the outcomes of interest and family background characteristics such as family income, household structure, parental education, and the quality of the parent-child relationships, students who regularly attended the after-school programs were more likely to show positive changes in school engagement and attentiveness in class and less likely to start skipping school and drinking alcohol in comparison to students who attended programs less regularly. As noted by the study authors, a limitation of the dose/response analysis strategy is that participation patterns may have been the result of unmeasured factors that might be the result of self-selection, not program participation.

As is the case in early child care, there is wide variation in the quality of after-school programs. In terms of structural-caregiver characteristics, child-staff ratios ranged from 4 to 1 to 25 to 1 in the National Survey of Before- and After-School Care (Seppanen et al., 1993). Staff education ranged from less than a high school diploma through graduate degrees. Although some programs reported no staff turnover during the previous year, turnover averaged 60 percent a year. Consistent with the model outlined in Figure 5-1, effects on school-age children are related to the quality of the after-school programs. Structural-caregiver characteristics predict process quality. When child-staff ratios were higher, staff appeared more negative and hostile toward the children in the program (Rosenthal and Vandell, 1996). Staff were warmer, more sensitive, and more supportive in programs in which child-staff ratios were lower (Pierce et al., 1999). Children also spent less time waiting and in transition and more time interacting positively with staff when child-staff ratios were lower. Staff education was also associated with observations of process quality. In programs in which staff were more highly educated, staff members used more positive behavior management strategies and were less harsh with children (Pierce et al., 1999; Rosenthal and Vandell, 1996).

Variations in process quality in after-school programs, in turn, predict child developmental outcomes (Pierce et al., 1999). Boys who attended after-school programs in which there was a positive emotional climate were reported by their 1st grade teachers to exhibit fewer problem behaviors at school in comparison to boys who attended programs with less positive climates. More negative emotional climate in the after-school programs was related to boys' poorer academic performance at school. Boys who attended programs rated as fostering autonomy and choice among activities had better social skills, according to their 1st grade teachers.

Amount or dosage of program experience also is related to program effects (Cosden et al., 2001; Vandell and Pierce, 1999; Welsh et al., 2002). Educationally at-risk students who attended a three-year homework club for more sessions scored higher on reading, math, and language achievement tests than children who participated less consistently (Cosden et al., 2001). Welsh et al. (2002) used a quasi-experimental design to examine program effects associated with participation in The After-School Corporation (TASC) programs. Changes in reading and math achievement for highly active participants (n = 12,973), active participants (n = 17,805), nonactive participants (n = 8104) and nonparticipants (n = 39,870) were examined. Students who were active participants in TASC programs for more than a year showed significantly greater gains in math achievement than did similar nonparticipating classmates. In a smaller scale study of four after-school programs located in high-crime neighborhoods, children who attended after-school programs for more days during the school year demonstrated improvements in their academic grades and work habits, whereas the performance of children who attended the programs for only a few days did not improve (Vandell and Pierce, 1999). Interestingly, many of these programs have an enrichment focus and are not limited to tutoring and homework help.

In an effort to evaluate the implementation and impact of after-school programs supported by 21st Century Community Learning Center funds, the U.S. Department of Education and the Charles Stewart Mott Foundation provided support for a two-year evaluation of several of the CCLCs across the nation. The evaluation was conducted by Mathematica Policy Research, Inc. The initial evaluation report, released on February 3, 2003, describes first year findings from samples of elementary and middle school students assessed during the 1999-2000 school year (U.S. Department of Education, 2003). The report purports that the CCLCs had little impact on the academic or social behavior of the participants.

There are, however, several notable limitations with the National CCLC Evaluation. For instance, the elementary school sample involved a small number of sites that agreed to have students randomly assigned to participate or not to participate in the CCLC's after-school programs. These schools were not representative of the larger population of elementary schools receiving CCLC funds. In the middle school sample, a matching design was used to compare after-school program participants and nonparticipants. The matching, however, was based on limited information about the students at the initial assessment, and the resulting comparison groups were dissimilar. In particular, the after-school participant group showed heightened risk at baseline in several areas, including markedly lower achievement test scores, more behavior problems, and greater socioeconomic disadvantage. In light of these initial differences, it is interesting to note that by the end of the school year the program participants and nonparticipants were reported to have similar levels of academic and social competence. The absence of certain baseline data, treatment and comparison group contamination, and issues surrounding the evaluation's timing and measurement are also methodological concerns in the National CCLC Evaluation.

An ongoing debate in the after-school arena is how best to organize and structure programs, and it centers on how academically oriented programs should be. Some contend that programs should emphasize homework help, tutoring, and preparation for mandated tests. Others contend that programs should emphasize extracurricular enrichment activities. Still others have argued that after-school programs should provide a safe place for youth to relax and hang out. The effects of these different approaches (or hybrids of these approaches) to after-school programming have not been systematically evaluated. Research is needed to determine if these approaches are differentially associated with improvements in school attendance, student achievement, emotional well-being, positive youth development, and decreases in problem behaviors.

Structured Voluntary Activities

Another source of supervised experiences for children during the after-school hours is structured activities, a term that encompasses lessons and extracurricular activities, such as piano lessons, coached sports, and scouts. Structured activities are typically funded by fees, which are paid by participants. Consequently, it is not surprising that children of higher income families are more likely than children of lower income families to participate in these activities. According to the National Child Care Survey, 20 percent of the children in families with incomes over $50,000 (1990 dollars) are enrolled in lessons, whereas only 6 percent of children whose families earned between $15,000 and $25,000 have these experiences (Miller et al., 1997). Updated data from the 1999 SIPP reports indicated a similar discrepancy, with 8 percent of youth (ages 6 to 14) whose families earned less than $18,000 a year being reported to participate in lessons, clubs, and sports, whereas 20.4 percent of the youth whose families earned more than $54,000 a year were reported to participate in these activities

Most of the research examining the effects of structured activities was conducted with adolescents (see Chapter 6). However, indications are that these types of activities also benefit school-age children (ages 6 to 12). Controlling for child prior performance, ethnicity, and gender as well as family demographics and parenting, children who consistently participated in extracurricular activities during kindergarten and 1st grade obtained higher reading and math scores at the end of 1st grade than children who sometimes or never participated in extracurricular activities (NICHD Early Child Care Research Network, 2002b). For the most part, the children were not "overprogrammed." Children typically participated in a single activity for less than three hours each week. Few children (less than 4 percent) were involved in extracurricular activities for more than five hours each week.

Pettit et al. (1997) also have found moderate amounts of structured activities to be beneficial. Children who engaged in structured activities for one to three hours a week in 1st grade were more socially competent in 6th grade than children who had either no structured activities or high amounts of these activities (more than four hours a week) in 1st grade, controlling for family factors and child behavior in kindergarten.

In addition, extracurricular activities have been related to functioning in older school-age children. Time spent in extracurricular time during 3rd, 4th, and 5th grades predicted children's emotional well-being in 5th grade, controlling for emotional adjustment in 3rd grade and family background (Posner and Vandell, 1999). Time spent in sports activities and hobbies was associated with fewer depressive symptoms at age 10 and age 12, controlling for family factors (McHale et al., 2001).

Larson's (2000) research suggests why structured activities may be beneficial for children. In his studies, adolescents were more likely to report concentrated effort and intrinsic motivation during structured activities, which Larson posits is particularly conducive to the development of initiative. In contrast, adolescents report low concentration but high choice while they are hanging out and high concentration and low choice while at school.

SUMMARY

Conceptual and methodological advances have contributed to a substantial research literature that has considered the effects of child care quality, quantity, and type on children's developmental outcomes. This research literature has begun to specify the conditions in which child care can enhance positive developmental outcomes for children as well as the conditions in which it can be problematic and associated with poorer developmental outcomes. These findings are based on several multisite projects as well as single-site studies that have utilized psychometrically strong measures of child care. Cognitive, language, social, and behavioral outcomes have been assessed. Efforts to address concerns about selection bias and omitted variables have resulted in expanded lists of family factors, analyses of change scores, and controls for prior child performance.

Studies of the effects of early child care quality have considered both process quality and structural and caregiver characteristics. Process quality refers to the experiences that children have with their caregivers, with other children, and with age-appropriate activities and materials, and structural and caregiver characteristics refer to such factors as child-adult ratio, the number of children in the class or group, the amount of formal education that caregivers have, caregivers' specialized training related to children, and caregivers' wages. Consistent with the conceptual model shown in Figure 5-1, many of the studies reviewed have found that:

(1) structural and caregiver characteristics predict observed process quality;

(2) process quality predicts children's cognitive, language, and social competencies both concurrently and over longer periods of time; and

(3) structural and caregiver characteristics predict children's cognitive, language, and social competencies.

When process quality is higher, children display better performance on a range of cognitive, language, and social assessments. By the same token, when process quality is lower, children demonstrate poorer performance in these areas. Relevant to these findings is evidence from the NICHD study of early child care that almost 60 percent of the observed child care settings in that study were of either poor or fair quality, rather than of good or excellent quality. In comparison to their higher income peers, children of low-income families appear more likely to receive poor-quality child care and less likely to receive excellent quality child care, especially in the early years.

The available research indicates that type of child care arrangement also is related to children's developmental outcomes. Both experimental and correlational studies have found that center-type experiences are associated with higher scores on cognitive and language assessments, particularly for 3- and 4-year-olds. Experience in child care homes and relative care, in contrast, has been less consistently related to cognitive and language performance and does not appear to convey the same benefits for preschool-age children.

Quantity or amount is the third aspect of early child care that has been studied in relation to child developmental outcomes. In several studies, children who are in care for more hours per week are reported to have more behavior problems than children who are in child care for fewer hours a week. Substantial behavior problems, defined as a score of one or more standard deviations about the mean on a normed measure of problem behaviors, have been reported by both teachers and mothers for the group of children who averaged more than 45 hours a week of care up to age 4½ years. Rates of substantial behavior problems are less than expected for children who averaged less than 10 hours per week and are at the norm for children who averaged 10 to 45 hours a week. There is some evidence that more extensive hours in the first 6 to 9 months of life is associated with heightened behavior problems and lower cognitive scores for some groups of children. Additional research is needed to determine the processes or mechanisms that mediate these effects.

Studies of the effects of child care on school-age children (6- to 12-year-olds) have considered three types of before- and after-school care: self-care, programs, and extracurricular activities. This research literature is less extensive than the available evidence pertaining to early child care. Nonetheless, findings have emerged that begin to delineate the conditions in which the child care experiences during middle childhood serve as positive influences on developmental outcomes and conditions in which experiences are problematic. These findings are consistent with those reported for young children in that three aspects of care—quality, type, and amount—are important considerations. Effects also appear to vary by family circumstances, neighborhood safety, and children's previous adjustment.

Self-care is increasingly common for children as they move through middle childhood. Self-care is not associated with poor academic or social outcomes if it occurs in limited amounts, takes place in safe neighborhoods, is accompanied by parental monitoring, and is used by competent children who are emotionally ready for the experience. Self-care appears more problematic when used by younger school-age children, when unsupervised time is spent in the company of peers, when neighborhoods are unsafe, when children have previous behavioral problems, and when families have low incomes.

The effects of after-school programs on children's developmental outcomes also are variable. Positive effects on children's emotional well-being, academic performance, and peer relationships are more evident when program quality is high and the children attend regularly. Children of low-income families and children who reside in unsafe neighborhoods appear to derive greater benefit from participation in after-school programs than do children of more affluent families, perhaps because their opportunities to participate in fee-based extracurricular activities and lessons are so limited. An issue that requires additional research is the determination of how best to organize and structure after-school programs to meet the developmental needs of school-age children.

Studies that have examined the effects of voluntary structured activities (i.e., extracurricular activities) on child developmental outcomes suggest a model for after-school programs that may be particularly effective. Time spent in extracurricular activities, such as organized sports, music, and art, is associated during middle childhood with positive developmental outcomes, including higher grades and higher standardized test scores, even when family factors and previous child adjustment are controlled. These findings are consistent with findings that extracurricular activities during adolescence (discussed in Chapter 6) were particularly conducive to positive youth development.

In summary, the quality of child care is likely to have important consequences for the development of children during the early years and middle childhood. The research presented in this chapter shows that the impact of child care quality on child development depends on such variables as the activities children experience in care, caregiver training and education, type of setting, and amount of time in care.

ANNEX TO CHAPTER 5 FOLLOWS

TABLE A5-1   Relations Between Structural-Caregiver Characteristics
and Process Quality

Citation[a]	N	Type of Care	Structural-Caregiver Variables
Arnett (1989)	59	Centers	CG training: (1) no training; (2) two courses Bermuda college; (3) four-course training program; (4) four-year college degree in ECE
Berk (1985)	37	Centers	CG formal education and CG specialized training
Blau (1997)	5 cities; 204 centers; 1,094 teachers; 567 classrooms (reanalysis of the National Child Care Staffing Study)	Centers	37 center characteristics including group size, ratio, caregiver education, different types of training
Blau (2000)	548 classrooms (reanalysis of CQO data)	Centers	Group size, ratio, CG experience, job tenure, ethnicity, formal education, specialized training
Burchinal, Howes, and Kontos (1999)	Total = 244 Florida Child Care Study = 144 California Licensing Study = 100	Family child care	CG education, formal and informal training experiences, experience as a child care provider, group size, business practices Points (sum of number of children, weighted by age of children)

Process Quality[b]	Analysis	Findings
Parental Modernity Scale, CIS (positive interaction, punitiveness, detachment, permissiveness)	ANCOVA	CG with half or all the Bermuda College training less authoritarian in childrearing attitudes than CG with no training, rated higher on positive interaction and lower on detachment in interactions with children. CG group with 4-year ECE degree differed from other 3 groups: childrearing attitudes less authoritarian, interactions with children rated higher on positive interaction and lower on punitiveness and detachment.
Observations of caregiver behavior	ANOVAs and correlations	College-educated caregivers had more encouraging behaviors, more suggestions, less restrictive actions.
Ratings on Arnett Scale (sensitivity, harshness, detached), appropriate caregiving, developmentally appropriate activities	Ordinary least squares regressions; fixed effects analyses	OLS regressions indicate that formal education associated with caregiver sensitivity and appropriate caregiving. Effects were reduced and nonsignificant in many of the FE analyses.
ECERS, ITERS	Pearson correlations, regressions with and without a fixed effect control for center ID	Simple correlations and regressions that did not include the fixed effect—center control found lower group size, lower C:A ratio, and more CG training to be related to better ECERS scores. These relations were substantially reduced when the center fixed effect control was added to the model.
FDCRS, CIS	Pearson correlations	CG education and experience better predictors of CC quality than C:A ratios. CG with more education → more sensitive and rated higher on global quality. More experienced CG slightly more detached and provide lower-quality care.
Regression		CG with more education tended to have settings with higher global quality ratings.

(continued)

TABLE A5-1 Continued

Citation[a]	N	Type of Care	Structural-Caregiver Variables
Burchinal, Roberts, Nabors, and Bryant (1996)	79	Centers	Director and observer reports of group size and C:A ratio; teacher report of training and experience
Burchinal et al. (2000)	27	Centers	C:A ratio, CG education, group size
Clarke-Stewart et al. (2002)	15 months = 133 24 months = 146 36 months = 131	Child care homes	Group size, group size points, CG education, amount of specialized training, recent training
Dunn (1993)	30	Day care centers	CG education, child major, training, center experience, field experience, CG age, group size, C:A ratio, ECERS

Process Quality[b]	Analysis	Findings
		CG experience was negatively related to observed quality in the licensed Family Child Care Study. Group size or ratio not related to observed quality of care.
ITERS	Pearson correlations	Higher observed and reported C:A ratios were associated with lower ITERS scores. Higher CG training was associated with higher ITERS scores.
ITERS, ECERS	Pearson Correlations	Higher C:A ratios were related to lower global quality at 12, 24, and 36 months. Higher group size was related to lower global quality at 24 and 36 months. Higher teacher education was related to higher global quality at 12 and 36 months.
ORCE-Positive Caregiving CC-HOME	Correlations HLM	Both correlational analyses and HLM analyses indicated overall quality of care measure by CC-HOME and by ratings of observed CG, behavior was higher when CG was more highly educated, had more specialized training pertaining to children, and had received training in the past year, with the strongest effects evident at 36 months. CG exhibited more positive caregiving when age-adjusted group sizes were smaller.
Play space, variety, divergent/elaborative interact, praise/ nurturance/ redirection, clear limits, total limits	Pearson correlations	CG with more experience in the field and larger group sizes was positively related to higher ECERS scores. Larger group size was positively related to more variety in classes. Higher ECERS scores were related to more divergent/elaborative interactions and less total limits.

(continued)

TABLE A5-1 Continued

Citation[a]	N	Type of Care	Structural-Caregiver Variables
Dunn et al. (1994)	30	Day care centers	Group size, C:A ratio, CG education, CG experience in field, CG experience in centers, CG certification
Elicker, Fortner-Wood, and Noppe (1999)	23	Family day care	Group size, C:A ratio
Goelman (1988)	74	Center day care Family day care	Caregiver education
Holloway and Reichhart-Erickson (1988)	15	Preschools and day care centers	Group size, C:A ratio
Howes (1983)	40	Center day care and family day care	C:A ratio, group size, number of adults, CG years experience, training child development

Process Quality[b]	Analysis	Findings
Language/reasoning (ECERS), developmentally appropriate activities (ECERS), variety, literacy activities, literacy quality	Pearson correlations, simultaneous regression	Only one structural quality variable correlated with quality of environment. CG who held some form of teacher certification provided classes rated higher on literacy quality scale.
Caregiver-Infant Involvement-AQS	Pearson correlations	Smaller group size and fewer children per adult → more CG-child involvement. CG years of experience, CG educational level, income, overall work satisfaction, work-related stress, control over work schedule, work and family conflict not significantly correlated with CG-child involvement or infant-CG attachment.
Learning activities, social development, language development, creative activities, total quality	Pearson correlations	Higher CG education correlated with higher total quality scores in both family day care and center day care.
ECOI	Pearson correlations	Smaller group sizes were related to higher ratings on the Interaction Quality Composite and accommodation of varied groups. C:A ratio was not related to any ECOI Indicators.
CG behavior (facilitative social, express positive affect, negative affect, restrictiveness, responsivity)	Pearson correlations	Caregivers in both settings with fewer children in their care, who worked shorter hours, with less housework responsibilities engaged in more facilitative social stimulation, expressed more positive affect, were more responsive, and less restrictive and negative. Family day care caregivers who worked in spaces specifically designed to be safe and appropriate for children were less restrictive of toddler activity.

(continued)

TABLE A5-1   Continued

Citation[a]	N	Type of Care	Structural-Caregiver Variables
Howes (1997)	Total = 1,065 Cost, Quality, Outcome Study (CQOS) = 655 Florida Quality Improvement Study (FQIS) = 410	Child care centers	C:A ratio, CG education, CG ECE training
Howes, Phillips, and Whitebook (1992)	143	Child care centers	C:A ratio, group size
Howes and Rubenstein (1985)	Total = 50 Home = 23 Center day care = 11 Family day care = 16	Home, center day care, family day care	C:A ratio, group size
Howes and Smith (1995)	150	Child care centers	CG characteristics (years of education + specialized training in ECE), C:A ratio, group size
Howes, Phillips and Whitebook, (1992)	1,300	Child care centers	CC experience, specialized training, education

Process Quality[b]	Analysis	Findings
CIS, AIS	ANOVA	CQOS: CG with BA or higher degree in ECE rated more sensitive than CG with AA degrees in ECE, who were more sensitive than CG with other backgrounds. CG with at least AA degree less harsh than CG in other backgrounds. CG in classes in compliance with ratio standards rated more sensitive, less harsh, and less detached. FQIS: CG with at least BA in ECE rated more sensitive than CG with CDA training who were rated as more sensitive than all other CGs. Caregivers with most advanced education → most effective.
Appropriate caregiving, developmentally appropriate activities	Chi-square	Classrooms with higher child:adult ratios were more likely to be rated as inadequate in caregiving and activities. Large group sizes also were more likely to be rated as inadequate in caregiving and activities. Smaller group sizes were more likely to be rated as developmentally appropriate.
Caregiver-child interaction (talk and play, restrictiveness and cry, touch and laugh)	Pearson correlations, one-way ANOVA	Lower C:A ratio was associated with higher quality of CG-child interactions.
ITERS, ECERS	Pearson correlations	Classes with more educated and trained teachers had higher ITERS and ECERS scores.
ECERS, ITERS, Arnett teacher sensitivity measure	Pearson correlations, multiple regression	CG formal education and specialized training was associated with behavior. Formal education better predictor than specialized training. Infant/toddler CGs need more college-level specialized training than preschool teachers to be competent teachers.

(continued)

TABLE A5-1   Continued

Citation[a]	N	Type of Care	Structural-Caregiver Variables
Iutcovich et al. (1997)	Total = 675 Center = 561 Group home = 70 Family = 44	Center, group home, family	CG education, CG years in field, CG salary, CG long-term educational goal, training characteristics, organizational climate
Kontos, Howes, and Galinsky (1997)	Training group = 130 Regulated providers = 112	Family day care	CG training, C:A ratio, group size
NICHD Early Child Care Research Network (1996)	576	Center, child care homes, in-home sitters, grandparents, fathers	Group size, C:A ratio, physical environment CG characteristics (formal education, specialized training, child care experience, beliefs about childrearing)
NICHD Early Child Care Research Network (2000a)	612	Center, child-care homes, in-home sitters, grandparents, fathers	C:A ratio, group size, CG education, CG specialized training, CG beliefs, CG experience
Phillipsen, Burchinal, Howes, and Cryer (1997)	Total = 749 228 = I/T 521 = P	Child care centers	CG background (educational level and experience), class structure (C:A ratio)

Process Quality[b]	Analysis	Findings
ITERS, ECERS, FDCRS	Pearson correlations	Higher CG salary → higher ITERS and ECERS scores. Younger CG, CG with more long-term educational goals, evaluating appropriateness, and evaluating usefulness → higher FDCRS scores. CGs with higher long-term educational goals, more likely to evaluate appropriateness and usefulness → higher FDCRS scores. CG higher ratings of professional growth, clarity, reward system, goal consensus, and task orientation → higher ECERS scores.
Process quality: Arnett Scale of Provider Sensitivity, Adult Involvement Scale Global quality: FDCRS	Chi square, t-test	Training group and comparison group were similar on structural, process, and global quality. Providers in comparison group cared for slightly more children per adult than training group. Effects of training → no changes on Arnett scale but increases on the FDCRS.
ORCE: caregiver interactions	Pearson correlations and multiple regression analyses (backward elimination procedure)	Caregivers rated as providing more positive caregiving when group sizes and C:A ratios were smaller and when CG held less-authoritarian beliefs about childrearing. Seen in all five types of care.
ORCE (positive caregiving frequency, positive caregiving rating) Global quality rating	Pearson correlations and multiple regressions	Positive caregiving ratings higher when CG had more child-centered beliefs (all ages), higher levels of education, and more experience providing care (at 24 and 36 months), and more specialized training (15 months), and when lower C:A ratio and smaller group sizes (15 and 24 months).
ITERS, ECERS, TIS, CIS	MANOVA Hierarchical regressions	Structural measures predicted process quality more strongly in preschool than in infant/toddler classes. Infant/toddler process quality higher in

(continued)

TABLE A5-1   Continued

Citation[a]	N	Type of Care	Structural-Caregiver Variables
			(C:A ratio and group size) CG education x A:C ratio, lead CG wages, center structure, direct background, economic characteristics of center, state, and sector
Ruopp, Travers, Glantz, and Coelen (1979)	National Day Care Study = 57 preschool day care centers in 3 cities; Infant/Toddler Substudy = 74 caregivers in 38 centers	Centers	C:A ratio, group size, CG years of education, child-related training, education, physical environment
Scarr, Eisenberg, and Deater-Deckard (1994)	363	Child care centers	C:A ratio, group size, CG training in child development and child care, CG education, highest wage paid to a CG in the center, staff turnover
Stallings and Porter (1980)	303	Child care homes, included sponsored, regulated, and unregulated homes	Observed C:A ratio

Process Quality[b]	Analysis	Findings
		classes with moderate experience and better paid teachers and more experienced directors. Preschool process quality higher in classes with CG having more education, moderate amount of experience, and higher wages. Better C:A ratios, lower center enrollment, and lower proportion of infant/toddler and subsidized children in center also predicted higher process quality for preschool. Teacher wages strongly related to process quality in infant/toddler classes.
Caregiver behaviors, including management, social interaction; child aimless wandering	Multiple regression	For 3-, 4-, and 5-year-olds, smaller groups consistently related to more socially active children. Smaller C:A ratios = less time in child behavior management. More child-related training associated with more teacher-child interaction. For children < 3 years: group size and ratio are strongly related to process quality.
ITERS, ECERS, APECP	Pearson correlations	Highest CG wages were highly correlated with process measures of quality (ITERS/ECERS and Profile Score). Lower C:A ratios, more teacher education, and more teacher training were correlated with higher process measures of quality, however, less correlated with process quality criteria.
Specific caregiver behaviors including teaches, plays, directs, converses, comforts, tends to physical needs, housekeeping, not involved	Pearson correlations Multiple regressions	Higher child:adult ratios associated with less caregiver teaching, playing with child, and facilitating child activities, and more efforts to control child behavior. Relations stronger when children < 35 months.

(continued)

TABLE A5-1   Continued

Citation[a]	N	Type of Care	Structural-Caregiver Variables
Stith and Davis (1984)	30	Employed mothers, substitute CG unemployed moms	Group size
Vandell and Powers (1983)	53	Center	Structural composite (C:A ratio and toys accessible + CG education + space allotment per child)
Volling and Feagans (1995)	36	Center	Group size C:A ratio

[a] For full references, see the report reference list.

[b] Process quality measures alphabetized by acronym: AIS: Adult Involvement Scale; APECP: Assessment Profile for Early Childhood Programs; AQS: Attachment Q-Set; CIS: Caregiver Interaction Scale; ECERS: Early Childhood Environment Rating Scale; ECOI: Early Childhood Observation Instrument; FDCRS: Family Day Care Rating Scale; HOME: Home Observation for Measurement of the Environment; ITERS: Infant/Toddler Environment Rating

Process Quality[b]	Analysis	Findings
Yarrow, Rubenstein, and Pedersen's (1975) infant environment observational scale	Pearson correlations	Larger group sizes → less expression of positive affect and less contingency of responses to distress.
Positive and negative behavior with adults, total adult-directed behavior	ANOVA	Higher quality structural composite related to more positive interactions with adults.
Positive adult-child interaction, nonsocial activity, positive peer interaction, negative peer interaction	Pearson correlations	Smaller group sizes and C:A ratios related to more time in positive staff-child interactions and less time in nonsocial activities. Larger C:A ratios related to more frequent negative interactions with peers.

Scale; ORCE: Observational Record of the Caregiving Environment; TIS: Teacher Involvement Scale; CG = caregiver; ECE = early childhood education; C:A ratio = child:adult ratio; CC: child care.

NOTE: Vandell and Wolfe (2000) served as the source for studies prior to 2000.

TABLE A5-2   Concurrent Associations Between Child Care Quality and
Child Developmental Outcomes

Citation[a]	N	Age	Process Quality Measure[b]	Structural Quality Measure[b]
Burchinal, Roberts, Nabors, and Bryant (1996)	79	12 months	ITERS	Group size, C:A ratio, CG training, CG experience
Clarke-Stewart, Vandell, Burchinal, O'Brien, and McCartney (2002)	15 months = 242 24 months = 248 36 months = 201	15-36 months	ORCE CC-HOME	Group size adjusted for child age; CG education, specialized training, recent training
Dunn (1993)	60	51.85 months	ECERS Goals, strategies, and guide child's emotional development	Group size, C:A ratio, CG education, CG center experience, CG field experience, CG age
Dunn, Beach, and Kontos (1994)	60	51.85 months	ECERS Language and reasoning environment, physical environment and available learning activities	CG education training, certification, experience, C:A ratio, group size
Elicker, Fortner-Wood, and Noppe (1999)	41	14.8 months	FDCRS	CG experience caring for infants and toddlers, group size, income
Goelman (1988)	105	CDC = 50.5 LFDC = 38.3 UFDC = 39.8	ECERS DCHERS COF	

Family Controls	Child Developmental Outcomes[c]	Quality Findings
None	MDI: (cognitive) SICD-R and CTBS: (language skills)	ITERS related to better cognitive development, language and communication skills. Lower C:A ratio related to higher Bayley scores, more advanced receptive language development and communication skills. Better educated CG → children higher on expressive language.
Family income, observed maternal sensitivity	Bayley MDI, Bracken School Readiness, Reynell language, mother and CG report of social competence, mother and CG report of behavior problems	Controlling for income and sensitivity, higher ORCE and CC-HOME scores related to higher cognitive scores, better language comprehension, and more cooperation. CG education and training associated with better cognitive and language scores, controlling for family income and education.
Child age, SES, parental age and education, day care history	CBI: (Socand Intelligence) PBQ: (social competence) PSI; (Cog) PPS (soc play) CPS and POS (cog play)	Controlling for child age, DC history, SES, parent age and education, higher ECERS, CG child major, less experience in the center → higher CBI intelligence.
SES	CBI: (language) PSI (cognitive)	Controlling for SES, process quality predicted children language development. Literacy environment predicted significant portion children's language development controlling for SES.
None	AQS: (attachment) Adult-child IRS: (CG-child involvement)	Smaller group size and smaller C:A ratio predicted more infant-CG interactive involvement. Higher global CC quality related to better infant-CG attachment security, but not interactive involvement.
	PPVT-R EOWPVT (language)	Higher global quality in family day care (DCHERS) significantly predicted higher children's PPVT and EOWPVT scores.

(continued)

TABLE A5-2 Continued

Citation[a]	N	Age	Process Quality Measure[b]	Structural Quality Measure[b]
Hausfather, Toharia, LaRoche, and Engelsmann (1997)	155	55 months	ECERS ECOS	ECOS
Hestenes, Kontos, and Bryan (1993)	60	52 months	ECERS teacher engagement	C:A ratio, group size
Holloway and Reichhart-Erickson (1988)	55	53 months	Early childhood observation, process composite	Class size, C:A ratio, number of hours of substitute care
Howes (1997) Study 1	760	4.25 years	CIS, AIS	C:A ratio, group size, ECE training, CG education
Howes (1997) Study 2	410		CIS, AIS	CG background in ECE

Family Controls	Child Developmental Outcomes[c]	Quality Findings
	SCS: (soc comp) PBC: (behavioral problems)	Low-quality DC significantly contributes to children's anger and defiance. HMR: additive risk for aggressive behavior (early entry to DC, low-quality stress in parenting, males, stressful life events). High quality → no relation with behavior problems. HMR: high quality, early attendance, favorable family circumstances → children's level of interest and participation. Quality of care mediates positive or negative effects of age of entry.
Gender, SES	BSQ: (emotional expression, temperament)	MR: DC quality predicted measure of effect acting for temperament (controlling for SES and gender). In DC centers with more appropriate caregiving, children displayed more positive effect. Neither structural related to effect. High level CG engagement → children had higher intensity positive effect. Lower level CG engagement → children display more intense negative effect.
SES	SSPS (social problem solving)	Children in high-quality interaction with CG → more prosocial responses and mentioned more prosocial categories. In larger classes, children gave more antisocial responses and used more antisocial categories. Children in classes with larger C:A ratios spent less time in solitary play. Controlling for SES, most still remained signficant.
	Language, preacademic, social development	CG with at least AA in ECE → higher PPVT-R scores, children in classes complying with C:A ratio → higher prereading.
	Cognitive play, peer play	CG with BA or child development associate degree → greater child language, play and most complex play with peers, most language activity. CG with BA ECE → children engaged in most complex play with objects and more creative activities.

(continued)

TABLE A5-2 Continued

Citation[a]	N	Age	Process Quality Measure[b]	Structural Quality Measure[b]
Howes and Olenick (1986)	89	18, 24, 30, and 36 months		Low quality (higher C:A ratios, no formally trained CG, < 2 primary CG)
Howes, Phillips, and Whitebook (1992)	414	14-54 months	ECERS Infant-Toddler Environment Rating Scale, Developmentally appropropriate activities	C:A ratio, group size
Howes and Smith (1995)	840	34.07 months	ECERS, ITERS, AIS, Attachment	
Howes and Stewart (1987)	55	20.2 months	Family Day Care Rating Scale, Adult Play with Child Scale	C:A ratio, group size
Kontos (1991)	138	53 months	Overall environmental quality, COFAS, ECERS	C:A ratio, group size, CG training, child development program evaluation indicator check

Family Controls	Child Developmental Outcomes[c]	Quality Findings
	Compliance, control	High-quality centers → children more compliant and less resistant, and children more likely to self-regulate. M.R.: for girls compliance best predicted by combination of high quality DC, low life complexity, and low parental involvement. Task-resistance best predicted by combination of low quality DC, high life complexity, and high parent involvement. CC quality best predicted self-regulation in boys.
	AQS- (attachment) Peer Play Scale (social orientation, interaction with peers)	CG who practiced more appropriate caregiving → child more secure with CG. CG engaged in more developmentally appropriate activities → children were more socially oriented with CG. Regulatable quality on social competence mediated through process quality variables and through children's relationship with adults and peers. Process mediated through children's relationship with adults and peers rather than direct influence on peer competence.
	Cognitive Activity Scale	HMR: (1) positive social interact with CG, attachment, and play activity (2) ECERS or ITERS. Classroom quality did not result in significant → change. Quality → indirect effect.
Family characteristics (nurturance and support, restrictiveness and stress)	Peer Play Scale Play with Objects Scale	Girls: controlling for family characteristics (nurturance and support, restrict and stress), higher quality CC → higher level play with peers, objects, and adults. Boys: controlling for family characteristics: higher quality care → higher play with objects.
Child age, child care history	Language, intelligence, social, behavior problems	Higher quality CC → poorer intelligence, and poorer language. HMR (child age, CC history controls): quality did not predict language or intellect; family background did. HMR (child age, CC history control): higher quality CC (CDPE-IC: structural measure) → children better socially adjusted and more sociable.

(continued)

TABLE A5-2   Continued

Citation[a]	N	Age	Process Quality Measure[b]	Structural Quality Measure[b]
Kontos and Wilcox-Herzog (1997)	114	51.7 months	CG responsive involvement CG verbal stimulation	
McCartney (1984)	166	36-68 months	DCEI, ECERS	
McCartney, Scarr, Phillips, and Grajek (1985)	166	2 years	ECERS, verbal interact with CG	C:A ratio
McCartney, Scarr, Rocheleau, Phillips, and Abbott-Shim, (1997)	718	Infant = 14.7 months Toddler = 27 months Preschool = 47.9 months	ECERS, ITERS, CG-C interaction	
NICHD Early Child Care Research Network (1999a)	97 118 163 250	6 months 15 months 24 months 36 months	None	C:A ratio, observed group size, CG training, CG education

Family Controls	Child Developmental Outcomes[c]	Quality Findings
Child age	Cognitive competence, social competence	Controlling for child age, more CG involvement → lower cognitive competence, but not social competence even when controlling for age. MR: More contact with CG and more CG involvement → higher social competence. Less contact with CG and more involvement in high yield activities → higher cognitive competence.
Child age, parent as educator interview (values conformity, values social)	PPVT-R, PLAI, ALI, experimental communication task	HMR: Controlling for child age, values conformity, and values social, higher total quality of center care scores (ECERS) → children had higher PPVT, PLAI, ALI scores and performed better on communication task. Quality of DC → positive effect on language development. Controlling for total number of functional utterances by CG to child, family background and group care experience, more verbal interaction with CG → higher PLAI, ALI scores and better performance on communication task.
	PPVT-R and ALI: (intellect, language) CBI and PBQ: (social skills)	Intervention center highest quality rating. Intervention center higher language, IQ, and social ratings than other centers.
Mother's education	AQS and Separation-Reunion Quest: (attachment) CBS Q-sort (social behavior, behavior problems; Harter: (competence and social acceptance)	Partial correlations, controlling for mother's education, more CG-C interaction related to more social bids (toddlers and preschoolers), more solitary play (preschoolers) and fewer CG ratings of negative separation/reunion for toddlers. HMR: CG-C interactions not related to child outcomes.
Income to needs, maternal education, concurrent single-parent status, child gender, maternal sensitivity	Bayley MDI Bracken School Readiness Reynell Dev Lang CBCL, ASBI (social behavioral)	Outcomes (cognitive, language, and social) better when children attended classes, meeting recommended C:A ratio at 24 months and CG training and CG education at 36 months. More standards met, better school readiness, language comprehension, and less behavior problems at 36 months. Older children more likely to be in classes meeting recommended standards.

(continued)

TABLE A5-2 Continued

Citation[a]	N	Age	Process Quality Measure[b]	Structural Quality Measure[b]
Peisner-Feinberg, and Burchinal (1997)	757	4.3 years	ECERS, CIS, AIS, UCLA ECOF	
Phillips, McCartney, and Scarr (1987b)	166	36-68 months	ECERS, DCEI	C:A ratio, director's years of experience
Ruopp, Travers, Glantz, and Coelen (1979)	Natural study = 64 centers Experiment = 57 centers	3- and 4-year-olds	Observations of staff-child interactions; observation of child behavior	C:A ratio, group size, staff education, training
Schliecker, White, and Jacobs (1991)	100	4 years	ECERS	
Vernon-Feagans, Emanuel, and Blood (1997)	67	24 months		High and low quality defined by a composite of C:A ratio, group size, and CG training

Family Controls	Child Developmental Outcomes[c]	Quality Findings
Mother's education, ethnicity, and child gender	PPVT-R, WJ-R (prereading, pre-math), CBI (social skills)	Controlling for child and family characteristics, the observed quality index and the STRS CG-child closeness score related to better PPVT-R scores (both quality indices), better WJ-R prereading scores (individually, observed quality index), better CG ratings of child's cognitive/attention skills on CBI (individually, CG rating of closeness), and fewer behavior problems (individually, CG rating of closeness), and higher sociability ratings. Higher quality CC → better language, preacademic, sociability, and fewer behavior problems.
	CBI, PBQ: (social development)	Higher overall quality → higher social competence ratings. Better C:A ratio → higher social competence ratings, but lower social adjustment (anxious). More CG-C interaction → better social competence ratings.
Looked at changes in child performance over time as a function of systematic changes in ratio and staff training	Preschool Inventory (PSI), Peabody Picture Vocabulary Test (PPVT-Revised)	Children had larger gains on PSI and PPVT when groups were smaller. Centers with higher proportions of caregivers with child-related training had greater gains on the PSI.
SES	PPVT-R (verbal)	Controlling for SES, higher center quality → higher PPVT. Family structure analyses: 2-parent families: Controlling for mother's education, mother's and father's age, and occupational prestige, children whose fathers have more prestigious occupations and are enrolled in high-quality DC have higher PPVT-R scores. 1-parent families: Controlling for mother's age, education, and occupational prestige, children whose mothers were older and are enrolled in high-quality DC have higher PPVT-R scores.
All middle-income, dual earner, white households	Sequenced Inventory of Communiction Development (SICD)	Poor-quality child care associated with poorer expressive language scores. Poorest scores obtained when poor-quality care coupled with chronic otitis media.

(continued)

TABLE A5-2   Continued

Citation[a]	N	Age	Process Quality Measure[b]	Structural Quality Measure[b]
Volling and Feagans (1995)	36	18-24 months		C:A ratio, group size

[a] For full references, see the report reference list.

[b] Quality measures alphabetized by acronym: COF: Child Observation Form; DCEI: Day Care Environment Interview; DCHERS: Day Care Home Environment Rating Scale; ECERS: Early Childhood Environment Rating Scale; ECOI: Early Childhood Observation Instrument; ECOS: Early Childhood Observation Scale; FDCRS: Family Day Care Rating Scale; ITERS: Infant-Toddler Environmental Scale.

[c] Child developmental outcome measures alphabatized by acronym: AQS: Attachment Q-Set; Adult-Child IRS: Howes and Stewart's Adult-Child Involvement Rating Scale; ALI: Adaptive Language Inventory; BSQ: Behavior Style Questionnaire; CBI: Classroom Behavior Inventory-Preschool Form; CBS Q-Sort: Child Behavior Survey, Q-Sort version; CPS: Cognitive Play Scale; CTBS: Comprehensive Test of Basic Skills; EOWPVT: Expressive One-Word Picture Vocabulary Test; Harter: Pictorial Scale of Perceived

Family Controls	Child Developmental Outcomes[c]	Quality Findings
Child's age, age of entry, hours/week in care	IBQ: (Temp) TBAQ and Vandell and Powers Quest: (social competence)	Controlling for child's age and age of entry, higher C:A ratios predicted more nonsocial play and less positive adult interactions. Controlling for child's age and hours/week in care predicted more nonsocial play and less positive adult interactions. Child's temperament (social fear) interacts with quality of care. High-quality care may act as a buffer for socially fearful children in positive peer interactions and nonsocial play with peers.

Competence and Social Acceptance for Young Children; MDI: Mental Developmental Index; PBC: Preschool Behavior Checklist; PBQ: Preschool Behavior Questionnaire; PLAI: Preschool Language Assessment Instrument; POS: Play with Objects Scale; PPS: Peer Play Scale; PPVT-R: Peabody Picture Vocabulary Test-Revised; PSI: Preschool Inventory-Revised; SCS: Social Competence Scale; SICD: Sequence Inventory of Communication Development; SSPS: Spivack and Shure's Social Problem Solving Skills; TBAQ: Toddler Behavior Assessment Questionnaire; CG = caregiver; ECE = early childhood education; C:A ratio = child:adult ratio; CC: child care; DC = day care; SES = socioeconomic status.

NOTE: For articles published before 2000, Vandell and Wolfe (2000) was used as the source.

TABLE A5-3   Longitudinal Relations Between Child Care Quality and
Child Developmental Outcomes

Citation[a]	N	Age	Process Quality Measure[b]	Structural Quality Measure[b]
Blau (1999b)	N = 2,503 to 4,031, depending on outcome	Variable	None	Mother report of group size, C:A ratio, CG training; averaged 0-2 and 3-5
Broberg et al. (1990)	84 children in Sweden	Time 1 = prior to care; M age = 16 months. Time 2 = 1 year later; Time 3 = 2 years later	Positive and negative events Belsky and Walker Spot observation checklist	None
Broberg et al. (1997)	Initial sample of 146 was recruited at 12-24 months. 123 assessed at 8 years. 123		Composite: adult child interaction at 16, 28, and 40 months	Composite: C:A ratio, number of in care per day: 16, 28, and 40 months
Burchinal et al. (2000)	89	Recruited in first year; reassessed at 12, 24, and 36 months.	ITERS, ECERS	C:A ratio, group size, teacher education

Other Child Care Measures	Family Controls	Child Developmental Outcomes[c]	Quality Findings
Type of care, number of arrangements, hours, cost	30 items	BPI (behavior problems index) beginning at 4 years PIAT (math and reading achievement) collected beginning at 5 years PPVT (language) collected beginning at 3 years	Simple correlations: CG training related to all 4 outcomes. OLS regressions: individual coefficients for the 3 structural variables were generally not significant.
Type of care	Social status, quality home environment, parents' perceived social support, child temperament, child sociability	Griffith's Developmental Scales-Scale C (verbal/linguistic ability at 28 and 40 months)	ANOVA: no care group difference in verbal abilities at 28 or 40 months. PLS: no effect of child care quality nor type of care on verbal ability at 28 or 40 months.
Time in child care	Social status, inhibition, paternal involvement, home environment	Griffith's Developmental Scales-(language subscales) Standardized School Readiness Test (numerical subscales)	Structural quality related at 40 months (.30*) and 80 months (.22*) with math in 2nd grade. Verbal in 2nd grade predicted by (1) verbal at 40 and 80 months, (2) number of months in CC, (3) consistent high paternal involvement. Math in 2nd grade predicted by (1) math at 80 months, (2) structural quality, (3) inhibition scores, (4) process quality. Not predicted by number of siblings, gender, quality of home. SES not entered in equation.
	Child age, child gender, poverty status, home environment	Bayley (Cognitive: 12, 24, 36 months) Language: receptive and express (vocabulary) Communication skills (12, 24, 36 months Communicative, social affective,	HLM analyses controlling for sex, poverty, home quality, higher process quality over time related to better cognitive, receptive language, expressive language, and overall communication skills. Associated with expressive language increase with age.

(continued)

TABLE A5-3   Continued

Citation[a]	N	Age	Process Quality Measure[b]	Structural Quality Measure[b]
Chin-Quee and Scarr (1994)	127	Recruited preschool, follow-up 5-9 years	ECERS amount and type of verbal interaction of child and CG	
Deater-Deckard et al. (1996)	141	Time 1 = toddler or preschooler Time 2 = 4 years later	Composite of ITERS, ECERS, Profile, CG education, wages	C:A ratio
Field (1991) Study 1	28	5-8 years in full time care by 2	Not assessed All high quality	C:A ratio CG education CG stability
Field (1991) Study 2	56	6th grade (M = 11.5) full-time care by 2	Not assessed All high quality	C:A ratio, CG education, CG turnover

Other Child Care Measures	Family Controls	Child Developmental Outcomes[c]	Quality Findings
		symbolic skills (12, 18, 24 months)	Lower C:A ratio related to higher scores over time on receptive language and overall communication skills, controlling for family factors. Teacher education: related to higher cognitive and receptive language skills for girls only.
Child's experiences in CC, age of entry into CC, number of hours in attendance	Maternal education and IQ (PPVT-R), values conform, value social skills	Report cards (social and cognitive development) Teacher report peer relations, cooperative behavior, academic achievement	HMR: (1) maternal education, maternal IQ, values conform, values social skills; (2) CC experience: age began care, total time in care; (3) Quality: ECERS. Quality of care in infant and preschool years → not related to school-age outcomes.
	SES, child sex, child age, parenting stress, harsh parental discipline	Composite scores of mother-reported behavior problems and social withdrawal and teacher-reported behavior problems and social withdrawal	No significant correlations between Time 1 process quality and Time 2 child outcomes or between Time 1 C:A ratio and Time 2 child outcomes. Also Time 1 process quality and C:A ratio did not predict Time 2 outcomes in hierarchical regressions that controlled for Time 1 adjustment.
Amount time in care	Maternal extraversion → child outcome	BRS: (sociability, socioemotional adjustment) Piers-Harris (self-concept) Buck I/E scale	Partial correlations (maternal extraversion): amount time spent in high-quality, stable care and later adjustment (5-8) associated with all child outcomes.
Amount time in care	No family variables associated with time in care	BRS (socioemotional adjustment and sociability) Piers-Harris (self-concept) Peer interactive behavior Academic measures: gifted program, language arts, math grades	Simple correlations: amount of time in high-quality programs. Stable care and later adjustment at 6th grade. Amount of time in high-quality care associated with all child outcomes.

(continued)

TABLE A5-3 Continued

Citation[a]	N	Age	Process Quality Measure[b]	Structural Quality Measure[b]
Howes (1988)	87	45-57 months followed for 2 years		CG training in child development, small group size, low C:A ratio, planned and individual educational program, adequate physical space
Howes (1990)	80 children	45 center care, b-4 1 year; other full-time between 1 and 4	CG involvement/ investment in child compliance (toddler period: 18, 24, 30, 36 months)	Composite: C:A ratio, CG training, CG stability (toddler period)
Jacobs and White (1994)	36 kindergartners, 4 years at recruit 32 kindergartners, not enrolled	Kindergarten	ECERS	None
NICHD Early Child Care Research Network (1998)	1,085 1,041	24 and 36 months	ORCE positive caregiving rating at 6, 15, 24, and 36 months	

Other Child Care Measures	Family Controls	Child Developmental Outcomes[c]	Quality Findings
Age of entry, length of day, number of different arrangements	Maternal education, family structure, maternal employment	Academic progress (1st grade CG report) CBP: (behavior problems, school skills)	Controlling for family characteristics, higher quality predicted better academic skills (for boys), better social skills for both girls and boys, and fewer behavior problems in both girls and boys. Smaller number of arrangements → better academic skills for boys and girls.
	Family social, family structure, child age	CBCL CBI	Process quality (longitudinal), age partialled out. Preschool: CG involvement/investment → observed social play, social pretend play, positive affect, less CG rate difficult and hesitant. Kindergarten: CG involvement → less parent ratings of internalizing and externalizing; less CG rate of distract, hostile, higher rate verbal IQ, consideration.
	SES	PPVT-R: (receptive language) SSC: (social)	MANOVAs (same results with no covar and with SES and PPVT cov). Children in center care higher on interest-participation than children in no care; no difference between high- and low-quality care. No care effect on cooperation-compliance. Children in high-quality center highest on receptive language, followed by no care and then low quality.
Quantity, entry age, stability, group type	Income/needs, psychological adjustment, child's gender, child's temperament	Mother-reported behavior problems and social competence; caregiver report of	Children in higher-quality child care during first 3 years → more compliant and cooperative during observations; CG reported

(continued)

TABLE A5-3 Continued

Citation[a]	N	Age	Process Quality Measure[b]	Structural Quality Measure[b]
NICHD Early Child Care Research Network (2000b)		6, 15, 24, 36 months	Positive CG composite, language stimulation	
NICHD Early Child Care Research Network (2001c)	669 612	24 and 36 months	Positive caregiving (ORCE)	
Peisner-Feinberg et al. (2001)	CQO Study: n = 733 in year 1; 499 in year 2; 399 in kindergarten, 345 in 2nd grade	Preschool to 2nd grade	ECERS CIS ECOF AIF	

Other Child Care Measures	Family Controls	Child Developmental Outcomes[c]	Quality Findings
		problems; laboratory observations of compliance and negativity	fewer behavior problems.
Quantity, type	Maternal PPVT-R, child gender, HOME and maternal stimulation	Bayley MDI , Bracken School Readiness, Macarthur CDI; Reynell Developmental Language	Process quality significantly related to cognitive and language outcomes at 24 and 36 months, controlling for family factors.
Amount of time in CC, available other children	Maternal education, maternal attitude toward employment, child gender, cognitive/ linguistic performance at 24 and 36 months, maternal sensitivity in play, maternal psychological adjustment, family structure, number of children in home	Mother and caregiver report of peer competencies; observed peer interaction in child care and structured task	More positive caregiving → child more positive sociability at 24 months, lower proportion negative interaction with peers observed.
	Family income, education, marital status, child's gender, child's ethnicity	PPVT-R WJ-R CBI (classroom behavior inventory) STRS (teacher-child relationship)	Higher ECERS scores predicted higher language and math scores, but the magnitude of the association declined over time. A significant interaction between maternal education and quality of classrooms indicated that better quality child care had stronger association when mothers had less education. Higher quality practices were significantly associated with fewer problem behaviors in Year 1, but this association declined in subsequent years.

(continued)

TABLE A5-3   Continued

Citation[a]	N	Age	Process Quality Measure[b]	Structural Quality Measure[b]
Pierrehumbert et al. (1996)	47 Swiss	1-5, recruited 3-9 months	Positive contact (Ainsworth interactive scale)	None
Vandell et al. (1988)	20	Observed at 4 and 8 years	None	C:A ratio, group size, space, materials available, CG education
Vernon-Feagans, Emanuel, and Blood (1997)	67	Recruited before age 1, followed until 4		Adults present (C:A ratio), group size

[a] For full references see the report reference list.

[b] Quality measures alphabetized by acronym: AIS: Adult Involvement Scale; CIS: Caregiver Interaction Scale; ECOF: UCLA Early Childhood Observation Form; ECERS: Early Childhood Environment Rating Scale; ECOI: Early Childhood Observation Instrument; IEOS: Instructional Environment Observation Scales; ITERS: Infant-Toddler Environmental Scale; ORCE: Observational Record of the Caregiving Environment; STRS: Student-Teacher Relationship Scale.

[c] Child developmental outcome measures alphabetized by acronym: ASBI: Adaptive Social Behavior Inventory; ASB: Teacher Assessment of Social Behavior; BCL: Behavior Checklist; Boehm: Test of Basic Skills; BPI: Behavior Problems Index; BRS: Behavior Rating Scale; BSQ: Behavior Screening Questionnaire; Buck I/E Scale: Buck Internalizer/Externalizer Scale; CBCL: Child Behavior Checklist; CBI: Child Behavior Inventory; CBP: Child Behavior Profile; CTBS: Comprehensive Test of Basic Skills; MacArthur CDI:

Other Child Care Measures	Family Controls	Child Developmental Outcomes[c]	Quality Findings
	SES, child gender, attachment with mother, positive contact with mother	Developmental Quotients WPPSI CBCL	Attach security, SES, and positive contact with CG predicted increase in cognitive index between 2 and 5 years.
	Family structure, age of entry in full-time care, family social class	PRS Harter PCS Parent ratings socioemotional adjust (Santrock and Warshak)	Controlling for social class, positive interaction with adults at 4 years was related to more competent behavior at 8 years. Aimless wandering at 4 years was related to less social competence at 8 years.
		SICD: (receptive and expressive language)	Children in high-quality centers → better expressive language and receptive language.

Communication Development Inventory; MDI: Mental Development Index (Bayley II); MSCA: McCartney Scale of Children's Abilities; ORCE: Observational Record of the Caregiving Environment; PBQ: Preschool Behavior Questionnaire; PEI: Parent as Educator Interview; PIAT: Peabody Individual Achievement Test; PPS: Peer Play Scale; PPVT-R: Peabody Picture Vocabulary Test-Revised; PRS: Peer Relations Scale; RCSA: Rutter Child Scales (A and B); SCS: Social Competence Scale; SICD: Sequence Inventory of Communication Development; SRA: Science Research Associates Achievement Battery; TBQ: Toddler Behavior Questionnaire; WJ-R: Woodcock-Johnson Tests of Achievement-Revised; CG = caregiver; ECE = early childhood education; C:A ratio = child:adult ratio; CC: child care; DC = day care; SES = socioeconomic status.

NOTE: Vandell and Wolfe (2000) was the source for articles published prior to 2000.

TABLE A5-4 Distribution of Child Care Quality by Type of Care and Family Income

For All Nonparental Care	Low Income N	(%)	Moderate Income N	(%)	High Income N	(%)	Overall N	(%)
6 months (n = 471)								
Poor quality	11	(13)	14	(9)	12	(5)	37	(8)
Fair quality	39	(44)	67	(41)	89	(40)	195	(41)
Good quality	31	(35)	60	(37)	74	(33)	165	(35)
Excellent quality	7	(8)	21	(13)	46	(21)	74	(16)
15 months (n = 494)								
Poor quality	10	(9)	15	(9)	14	(6)	39	(8)
Fair quality	59	(55)	74	(45)	96	(43)	229	(46)
Good quality	27	(25)	55	(34)	76	(34)	158	(32)
Excellent quality	11	(10)	19	(12)	38	(17)	68	(14)
24 months (n = 537)								
Poor quality	13	(13)	30	(15)	10	(4)	53	(10)
Fair quality	62	(63)	99	(51)	126	(52)	287	(53)
Good quality	19	(19)	49	(25)	76	(31)	144	(27)
Excellent quality	5	(5)	17	(9)	31	(13)	53	(10)
36 months (n = 587)								
Poor quality	11	(7)	9	(5)	6	(2)	26	(4)
Fair quality	102	(67)	122	(65)	134	(54)	358	(61)
Good quality	36	(24)	50	(26)	87	(35)	173	(29)
Excellent quality	3	(2)	8	(4)	19	(7)	30	(5)
54 months (n = 795)								
Poor quality	25	(12)	21	(7)	12	(4)	58	(7)
Fair quality	90	(44)	142	(46)	112	(40)	344	(43)
Good quality	65	(32)	96	(31)	113	(40)	274	(34)
Excellent quality	26	(13)	48	(16)	45	(16)	119	(15)
Overall (n = 2,884)								
Poor quality	70	(11)	89	(9)	54	(4)	213	(7)
Fair quality	352	(54)	504	(50)	557	(46)	1,413	(49)
Good quality	178	(27)	310	(31)	426	(35)	914	(32)
Excellent quality	52	(8)	113	(11)	179	(15)	344	(12)
TOTAL	652		1,016		1,216		2,884	
For Father Care	Low Income N	(%)	Moderate Income N	(%)	High Income N	(%)	Overall N	(%)
6 months (n = 87)								
Poor quality	1	(6)	1	(2)	0		2	(2)
Fair quality	5	(29)	18	(38)	4	(18)	27	(31)

TABLE A5-4 Continued

For Father Care	Low Income N	(%)	Moderate Income N	(%)	High Income N	(%)	Overall N	(%)
Good quality	8	(47)	18	(38)	13	(59)	39	(45)
Excellent quality	3	(18)	11	(23)	5	(23)	19	(22)
15 months (n = 107)								
Poor quality	1	(3)	5	(11)	0		6	(6)
Fair quality	15	(45)	13	(28)	11	(41)	39	(36)
Good quality	12	(36)	18	(38)	7	(26)	37	(35)
Excellent quality	5	(15)	11	(23)	9	(33)	25	(23)
24 months (n = 89)								
Poor quality	2	(8)	2	(6)	0		4	(4)
Fair quality	15	(60)	16	(44)	10	(36)	41	(46)
Good quality	4	(16)	13	(36)	11	(39)	28	(31)
Excellent quality	4	(16)	5	(14)	7	(25)	16	(18)
36 months (n = 83)								
Poor quality	3	(9)	2	(6)	0	5	(6)	
Fair quality	21	(62)	12	(36)	8	(50)	41	(49)
Good quality	10	(29)	16	(49)	3	(19)	29	(35)
Excellent quality	0		3	(9)	5	(31)	8	(10)
54 months (n = 36)								
Poor quality	4	(27)	2	(13)	1	(20)	7	(19)
Fair quality	8	(53)	7	(44)	1	(20)	16	(44)
Good quality	2	(13)	6	(38)	3	(60)	11	(31)
Excellent quality	1	(7)	1	(6)	0	2	(6)	
Overall (n = 402)								
Poor quality	11	(9)	12	(7)	1	(1)	24	(6)
Fair quality	64	(52)	66	(37)	34	(35)	164	(41)
Good quality	36	(29)	71	(39)	37	(38)	144	(36)
Excellent quality	13	(10)	31	(17)	26	(27)	70	(17)
TOTAL	124		180		98		402	

For Grandparents	Low Income N	(%)	Moderate Income N	(%)	High Income N	(%)	Overall N	(%)
6 months (n = 94)								
Poor quality	0		0		0		0	
Fair quality	7	(33)	6	(16)	6	(17)	19	(20)
Good quality	10	(48)	22	(59)	15	(42)	47	(50)
Excellent quality	4	(19)	9	(24)	15	(42)	28	(30)

(continued)

TABLE A5-4 Continued

For Grandparents	Low Income N	(%)	Moderate Income N	(%)	High Income N	(%)	Overall N	(%)
15 months (n = 77)								
Poor quality	1	(4)	2	(7)	1	(4)	4	(5)
Fair quality	12	(48)	6	(21)	3	(13)	21	(27)
Good quality	9	(36)	14	(48)	10	(43)	33	(43)
Excellent quality	3	(12)	7	(24)	9	(39)	19	(25)
24 months (n = 66)								
Poor quality	1	(5)	2	(8)	0		3	(5)
Fair quality	13	(68)	6	(23)	5	(24)	24	(36)
Good quality	3	(16)	14	(54)	13	(62)	30	(45)
Excellent quality	2	(11)	4	(15)	3	(14)	9	(14)
36 months (n = 61)								
Poor quality	3	(12)	0		0	3	(5)	
Fair quality	15	(58)	8	(44)	12	(71)	35	(57)
Good quality	7	(27)	8	(44)	3	(18)	18	(30)
Excellent quality	1	(4)	2	(11)	2	(12)	5	(8)
54 months (n = 34)								
Poor quality	1	(6)	0		1	(14)	2	(6)
Fair quality	8	(50)	8	(73)	2	(29)	18	(53)
Good quality	6	(38)	2	(18)	3	(43)	11	(32)
Excellent quality	1	(6)	1	(9)	1	(14)	3	(9)
Overall (n = 332)								
Poor quality	6	(6)	4	(3)	2	(2)	12	(4)
Fair quality	55	(51)	34	(28)	28	(27)	117	(35)
Good quality	35	(33)	60	(50)	44	(42)	139	(42)
Excellent quality	11	(10)	23	(19)	30	(29)	64	(19)
TOTAL	107		121		104		332	

For in-Home Care (not parents or grandparents)	Low Income N	(%)	Moderate Income N	(%)	High Income N	(%)	Overall N	(%)
6 months (n = 83)								
Poor quality	1	(6)	1	(8)	3	(6)	5	(6)
Fair quality	9	(56)	5	(38)	13	(24)	27	(33)
Good quality	5	(31)	4	(31)	22	(41)	31	(37)
Excellent quality	1	(6)	3	(23)	16	(30)	20	(24)
15 months (n = 95)								
Poor quality	1	(7)	0		2	(3)	3	(3)
Fair quality	11	(73)	10	(48)	17	(29)	38	(40)

TABLE A5-4 Continued

For in-Home Care (not parents or grandparents)	Low Income N (%)		Moderate Income N (%)		High Income N (%)		Overall N (%)	
Good quality	2	(13)	7	(33)	25	(42)	34	(36)
Excellent quality	1	(7)	4	(19)	15	(25)	20	(21)
24 months (n = 78)								
Poor quality	3	(23)	3	(19)	0		6	(8)
Fair quality	7	(54)	6	(38)	16	(33)	29	(37)
Good quality	2	(15)	4	(25)	19	(39)	25	(32)
Excellent quality	1	(8)	3	(19)	14	(29)	18	(23)
36 months (n = 66)								
Poor quality	2	(18)	0		1	(2)	3	(5)
Fair quality	8	(73)	6	(50)	14	(33)	28	(42)
Good quality	1	(9)	5	(42)	21	(49)	27	(41)
Excellent quality	0		1	(8)	7	(16)	8	(12)
54 months (n = 16)								
Poor quality	1	(20)	0		1	(13)	2	(13)
Fair quality	3	(60)	3	(10)	5	(63)	11	(69)
Good quality	0		0		2	(25)	2	(13)
Excellent quality	1	(20)	0		0		1	(6)
Overall (n = 338)								
Poor quality	8	(13)	4	(6)	7	(3)	19	(6)
Fair quality	38	(63)	30	(46)	65	(31)	133	(39)
Good quality	10	(17)	20	(31)	89	(42)	119	(35)
Excellent quality	4	(7)	11	(17)	52	(24)	67	(20)
TOTAL	60		65		213		338	

For Child Care Homes	Low Income N (%)		Moderate Income N (%)		High Income N (%)		Overall N (%)	
6 months (n = 192)								
Poor quality	7	(18)	5	(7)	7	(9)	19	(10)
Fair quality	19	(48)	34	(46)	37	(47)	90	(47)
Good quality	13	(33)	26	(35)	23	(30)	62	(32)
Excellent quality	1	(3)	9	(12)	11	(14)	21	(11)
15 months (n = 197)								
Poor quality	5	(11)	5	(7)	5	(6)	15	(8)
Fair quality	23	(51)	34	(47)	33	(41)	90	(46)
Good quality	13	(29)	26	(36)	29	(36)	68	(35)
Excellent quality	4	(9)	7	(10)	13	(16)	24	(12)

(continued)

TABLE A5-4 Continued

For Child Care Homes	Low Income N	(%)	Moderate Income N	(%)	High Income N	(%)	Overall N	(%)
24 months (n = 210)								
Poor quality	5	(14)	10	(12)	4	(5)	19	(9)
Fair quality	21	(57)	44	(52)	45	(51)	110	(52)
Good quality	9	(24)	23	(27)	29	(33)	61	(29)
Excellent quality	2	(5)	8	(9)	10	(11)	20	(10)
36 months (n = 168)								
Poor quality	3	(7)	1	(2)	1	(2)	5	(3)
Fair quality	31	(72)	47	(76)	30	(48)	108	(64)
Good quality	7	(16)	12	(19)	28	(44)	47	(28)
Excellent quality	2	(5)	2	(3)	4	(6)	8	(5)
54 months (n = 76)								
Poor quality	9	(41)	3	(9)	1	(5)	13	(17)
Fair quality	7	(32)	20	(57)	13	(68)	40	(53)
Good quality	4	(18)	7	(20)	3	(16)	14	(18)
Excellent quality	2	(9)	5	(14)	2	(11)	9	(12)
Overall (n = 843)								
Poor quality	29	(16)	24	(7)	18	(5)	71	(8)
Fair quality	101	(54)	179	(55)	158	(48)	438	(52)
Good quality	46	(25)	94	(29)	112	(34)	252	(30)
Excellent quality	11	(6)	31	(9)	40	(12)	82	(10)
TOTAL	187		328		328		843	

For Centers	Low Income N	(%)	Moderate Income N	(%)	High Income N	(%)	Overall N	(%)
6 months (n = 102)								
Poor quality	3	(27)	8	(21)	2	(4)	13	(13)
Fair quality	4	(36)	22	(58)	33	(62)	59	(58)
Good quality	3	(27)	8	(21)	14	(26)	25	(25)
Excellent quality	1	(9)	0	4	(8)	5	(5)	
15 months (n = 125)								
Poor quality	3	(14)	8	(20)	6	(10)	17	(14)
Fair quality	13	(59)	24	(59)	43	(69)	80	(64)
Good quality	3	(14)	8	(20)	12	(19)	23	(18)
Excellent quality	3	(14)	1	(2)	1	(2)	5	(4)
24 months (n = 183)								
Poor quality	4	(13)	15	(22)	6	(7)	25	(14)
Fair quality	21	(70)	43	(63)	60	(71)	124	(68)
Good quality	5	(17)	8	(12)	15	(18)	28	(15)
Excellent quality	0	2	(3)	4	(5)	6	(3)	

TABLE A5-4 Continued

For Centers	Low Income N	(%)	Moderate Income N	(%)	High Income N	(%)	Overall N	(%)
36 months (n = 292)								
Poor quality	3	(4)	8	(8)	4	(3)	15	(5)
Fair quality	48	(67)	61	(63)	78	(63)	187	(64)
Good quality	21	(29)	25	(26)	35	(28)	81	(28)
Excellent quality	0	3	(3)	6	(5)	9		(3)
54 months (n = 669)								
Poor quality	14	(9)	18	(7)	9	(4)	41	(6)
Fair quality	72	(44)	111	(43)	92	(37)	275	(41)
Good quality	55	(34)	87	(34)	10	(42)	247	(37)
Excellent quality	22	(14)	42	(16)	42	(17)	106	(16)
Overall (n = 1371)								
Poor quality	27	(9)	57	(11)	27	(5)	111	(8)
Fair quality	158	(53)	261	(52)	306	(54)	725	(53)
Good quality	87	(29)	136	(27)	181	(32)	404	(29)
Excellent quality	26	(9)	48	(10)	57	(10)	131	(10)
TOTAL	298		502		571		1,371	

6
Parental Employment and Adolescent Development

*T*his chapter considers the effects of parental employment on the salient developmental tasks of young people past middle childhood, between the ages of 12 and 18. An overview of opportunities and challenges associated with parental employment during adolescence is considered in terms of adult supervision and child care arrangements and responsibilities, adolescents' use of time after school, and parent-adolescent relationships. Also included is an overview of developmental tasks during adolescence in order to highlight the unique needs of this group of teens.

DEVELOPMENTAL TASKS DURING ADOLESCENCE

Modern developmental theories underscore the holistic nature of the developmental process (e.g., Bronfenbrenner and Morris, 1998; Cairns, 1979; Magnusson and Stattin, 1998). According to the holistic perspective, all aspects of an adolescent's functioning are interdependent. Any single factor—such as parental employment—gains meaning through its functional relationship with other aspects of the developing system. In this view, internal changes at one level (e.g., biological changes associated with pubertal maturation) have implications for developments at other levels (e.g., psychological functioning and social relationships) (Stattin and Magnusson, 1989). At the same time, internal functions are influenced by the social contexts of which the adolescent is a part. Because increasing participation in multiple settings characterizes adolescence, it is imperative that individual-environment interactions across contexts are assessed and related to changes in psychosocial adjustment (Bronfenbrenner, 1979). Accordingly, understanding adolescent development requires attention to the whole person and her or his interaction with multiple aspects of the environment, and persons therein, over time.

The notion of salient developmental tasks essentially refers to the attainment of age-appropriate competencies. The acquisition of such competencies increases the likelihood that an individual will be able to take advantage of personal and environmental resources at a specific point in the developmental process. This permits the attainment of positive developmental status in the present and increases the likelihood for healthy adjustment in the future (Waters and Sroufe, 1983). The attainment of competencies always involves a complex history of interactions among aspects within the individual, and the individual's interaction with available resources and opportunities in the environment, over time. Accordingly, competence during adolescence is tied to previous functioning, and it may be defined somewhat differently according to individual differences, contexts, and changing historical conditions (Elder et al., 1993; Mahoney and Bergman, 2002).

During middle childhood, salient developmental tasks include forming a positive orientation toward school and achievement, developing and maintaining conventional relationships with peers and adults outside the family, and acquiring appropriate value systems about rules and conduct across different contexts (Masten and Coatsworth, 1998). These tasks remain important during adolescence and are typically renegotiated in light of interdependent transitions and developments in biological and physical maturation, cognitive functioning, social-emotional abilities and relationships, and social contexts (Eccles et al., 1993).

Early theories of adolescent development, such as Erikson's (1968) age-graded psychosocial theory, described the processes of identity formation, individuation and autonomy, and personal mastery/efficacy, as the salient tasks for youth. The importance of these tasks has been anchored by empirical support and also refreshed by new challenges and opportunities that face today's youth. For example, studies of adolescent time use show that youth spend significantly more time in the company of peers than is reported during childhood (Larson, 2001). Dyadic friendships expand to peer networks and crowds that tend to form on the basis of particular values, norms, attributes, and behaviors (Brown, 1990; Cairns and Cairns, 1994). Intimacy in relationships becomes more central (Berndt, 1982), the social influence of peers for positive and negative behaviors increases (Brown et al., 1986), and interest in romantic relationships intensifies

(Levesque, 1993). Relationships with parents continue to be a critical source of support during adolescence (Laursen et al., 1998), and relationships with unrelated adults, such as teachers, coaches, mentors, and employers, become increasingly important influences as well (National Research Council and Institute of Medicine, 1999; Rhodes, 1994).

Academic performance continues to be important across adolescence and attains new consequence with regard to prospects for postsecondary school education and employment. Although schoolwork is viewed as challenging, many adolescents report low levels of motivation and excitement during in-class learning experiences (Larson, 2000). Time spent in social relationships and experiences in activities outside the classroom become a more typical source of satisfaction for young persons. Greater responsibilities at home, including the care of younger siblings, characterize the adolescent experience for many youth (Burton et al., 1995). Devoting significant time to involvement in after-school enrichment activities and service learning experience is common (National Survey of America's Families, 1997; Youniss and Yates, 1997), and paid employment becomes the norm for most young persons by the end of high school (Steinberg and Cauffman, 1995). These nonschool learning experiences contribute to the development of several important competencies during adolescence, including agency and personal initiative, civic and community engagement, forming a sense of industry, and making plans for the future.

Overall, it appears that most adolescents negotiate the salient tasks of adolescence successfully (National Research Council and Institute of Medicine, 2002), even under conditions of adversity (Luthar and Chicchetti, 2000). However, some young persons do not develop adequate competencies and engage in a variety of problem behaviors. Consistent with holistic theories of development, problem behaviors during adolescence tend to come in packages rather than in isolation (Jessor, 1993). This is of particular concern because adolescence is a developmental period in which many problem behaviors escalate in frequency, severity, and consequence.

By way of example, the prevalence of criminal arrests increases dramatically across adolescence, with a lifetime peak for boys and girls occurring between ages 16 and 19, and the daily peak time for juvenile violence occurring between the hours of 3:00 and 8:00 p.m. (U.S. Department of Justice, 2001). While juvenile arrests have decreased in recent years, the arrest rate for females under age 18 in 2000 was 25 percent higher than in 1991. Rates of substance use remain a concern as well. Among high school seniors surveyed nationally about substance use during the past 30 days, approximately 30 percent report smoking cigarettes, 33 percent report drinking alcohol to the point of intoxication, and 26 percent used illicit substances (Johnston et al., 2002). The national estimate of high school dropout for young persons ages 16-24 was 10.9 percent in 2000; the rate for Hispanic youth was 27.8 percent (National Center for Education Statistics, 2001). Sexual activities and the associated risks also increase markedly with the onset of puberty. Recent estimates from the Centers for Disease Control and Prevention (CDC) in 1999 indicate that roughly 50 percent of high school students have had sexual intercourse (Centers for Disease Control and Prevention, 2002a). Among sexually active high school students, the use of a condom or birth control pill before the last sexual intercourse was reported by 58 percent and 16.2 percent, respectively. Moreover, while adolescence is often viewed as a time of health and vitality, 16 percent of high school students may be classified as at risk for obesity or being overweight (Centers for Disease Control and Prevention, 2002b). Finally, the prevalence of various mental health problems, such as anxiety (Albano et al., 1996), depression (Birmaher et al., 1996), suicide (Kachur et al., 1995), and aspects of conduct disorder (Achenbach, 1991), is increased significantly during adolescence.

PARENTAL EMPLOYMENT AND ADOLESCENT ADJUSTMENT

As described in Chapter 2, the percentage of employed mothers with school-age children has grown markedly over the last several years (see Blau, 2001, Figure 2-1). Among families with children ages 6-17, 78.7 percent of mothers and 93.5 percent of fathers were employed in 2001 (Bureau of Labor Statistics, 2002). The majority of parents (both mothers and fathers) were employed full-time.

Given the preceding discussion, the remainder of this chapter focuses on how parental employment during adolescence may impede or facilitate important developmental tasks during adolescence. There are three main ways by which parental employment may influence adolescent adjustment: (1) parental supervision, child care arrangements, and responsibilities while parents are working; (2) access to supervised activities and contexts; and (3) parenting practices that may affect the parent-adolescent relationship.

Parental Supervision, Child Care Arrangements, and Responsibilities

Self-Care

Self-care generally involves an arrangement in which the child cares for himself or herself in the absence of adult supervision. Self-care is an increasingly common arrangement during adolescence. Whereas 11 percent of 10-year-olds experience some self-care while their mother is at work, the percentage rises to 25 percent for 12-year-olds and 40 percent for 14-year-olds, according to the Survey of Income and Program Participation (SIPP,

1999).[1] The time spent in self-care also increases with age: 14-year-olds spend approximately 9.5 hours per week in this arrangement compared with 8 hours for 12-year-olds and 6 hours for 10-year-olds. Ethnic differences reveal that self-care is consistently most prevalent for white children and least prevalent for Hispanic children ages 10 to 14; however, ethnic differences diminish with the child's age as self-care becomes more common for young persons in all ethnic groups by the age of 14. By contrast, the average number of hours that 10- to 14-year-olds spend in self-care does not differ markedly by ethnicity.

Self-care is less common among families below or near the poverty line, and it becomes more common as hours of parental employment increase. Historically, self-care has become more prevalent in recent decades owing to a variety of possible factors, including increases in employment for single-parent and dual-earner families, dispersion of extended families, and lack of after-school programs serving children over the age of 12 (Stewart, 2001). However, the proportion of children experiencing self-care has been relatively stable across the early 1990s. Self-care can be divided into two broad categories: in-home self-care and out-of-home self-care.

Anita, 19 years old and living in New York City, further suggests the burdensome aspects of accelerated development (Williams and Kornblum, 1985:39):

> *Anita is . . . working her way through City College. Her mother works extremely long hours cleaning offices in midtown Manhattan. This leaves Anita with the responsibility for caring for her own 2-year-old as well as her four younger siblings. Often at wits' end with fatigue and anxiety, Anita's usual calm has failed her today. "I'm so worried about my brother, the 14-year-old. He's getting in with a rough crowd. I know he's going to get into serious trouble real soon if we can't get him into something that will help him."*

In-Home Self-Care refers to time spent in the home by oneself or in the company of siblings, while parent(s) are working. Children and early

---

[1]As was explained previously in Chapter 3, the data on self-care should be interpreted with caution. The estimates of the number of children without adult supervision has varied across reports and depends somewhat on the month the question is asked (whether school is in session or not), the parents' interpretation of the term "self-care," and the parents' willingness to admit that their children are left home alone.

adolescents in this category of self-care are frequently referred to as "latch-key children" (Rodman et al., 1985). Comparisons between adolescents in in-home self-care and those in adult-supervised arrangements have tended *not* to find substantial differences in adjustment (e.g., Galambos and Maggs, 1991; Rodman et al., 1985; Steinberg, 1986; Stewart, 2001). However, the unsupervised conditions that occur as part of in-home self-care may be conducive to loneliness and boredom, as well as to engagement in health-compromising behaviors (i.e., unhealthy dietary behavior; passivity; use of tobacco, alcohol, and other illicit substances; early sexual activity) (e.g., Coolson et al., 1985; Stewart, 2001; Zill et al., 1995).

The directionality of associations between adolescent self-care and problem behaviors is not clear. For instance, factors that affect the parental decision process in selecting self-care are often unaccounted for in the above studies. Moreover, longitudinal designs using appropriate compari-son groups are scarce. Future research might assess the frequency and duration of in-home self-care for adolescents, whether the arrangement is voluntary or required, and the extent to which visitors (e.g., peers) are present and focus more attention on the characteristics of the home envi-ronment when making comparisons with adolescents in other arrange-ments while their parents are at work.

A subcategory of in-home self-care involves caring for younger siblings. Approximately 1.4 percent of 6- to 10-year-olds and 1.9 percent of 11- to 14-year-olds are left primarily in the care of an older sibling (SIPP, 1999). In the majority of cases, the sibling providing care is at least 15 years of age and the care takes place in the child's home. Ethnic differences among adolescent caretakers reveal little variation. However, sibling care is, in general, a primary arrangement more often for black children (3.5 percent) compared with Hispanic (1.6 percent) or white (1.3 percent) children (SIPP, 1999). This form of care is most often provided by daughters (Zukow-Goldring, 1995) and is also most common in single-parent and low-income families (de Vaus and Millward, 1998; Laird et al., 1998) and may be more typical in families living in rural areas (Zukow-Goldring, 1995; Conger and Elder, 1994).

Evidence on the consequences of sibling care is limited and mixed. For example, some research suggests that children under the care of their sib-lings demonstrate poorer academic achievement and attitudes toward school than those in formal, supervised after-school programs (Miller and Marx, 1990). By contrast, other studies report no significant relationship between being under sibling care and later behavioral adjustment for higher-income families (Marshall et al., 1997).

To be sure, sibling care is valuable when family care arrangements are considered in an ecological context. For example, qualitative data suggest that in families with physically disabled or mentally ill children, siblings

---

Art's mother describes how sibling care worked during an earlier period (Fordham, 1996:168-169):

> *I had to work . . . [s]o they [the older siblings] would mind him— see I had to be at work at three, so the bus wouldn't bring him [home] til like six, so they would mind him, and I'd cook everything [and leave it] on the stove so they could fix it. . . . They mind themselves while I went to work—they went to school, and then I would cook and wash clothes at night when I come home. . . . Then I'd get about two or three hours' sleep or something. . . So, anyway, I made it. And they didn't give me any trouble. . . . And that's all they did—they stayed in the house. So they've never been in trouble, or jail, or stealing, or dope or nothing, yet. . . . I hope they don't.*

---

often provide essential caregiving assistance (Zukow-Goldring, 1995). Sibling care may also be of particular importance in high-risk, impoverished environments in which alternative child care arrangements are not possible. In such contexts, older siblings can represent an effective source of child monitoring, supervision, guidance, and positive modeling and assist with homework while parents are working (Burton and Jarrett, 2000; Jarrett, 1998b; Zukow-Goldring, 1995). Indeed, some researchers regard the responsible care of younger siblings as a salient task for adolescents (Mahoney and Bergman, 2002; Yoshikawa and Seidman, 2000; Werner and Smith, 1992).

An important gap in the knowledge base on sibling care concerns the impact on adolescent caregivers. Caregiving by adolescent siblings may facilitate such competencies as planfulness, responsibility, and maturity. It may also prematurely accelerate young persons into adult roles, augment negative emotions (e.g., stress, anger, anxiety, depression), and undermine opportunities for involvement in after-school enrichment activities or employment. It seems likely that both positive and negative consequences are possible and may depend on the particular individual and family considered. However, the empirical evidence needed to inform this issue is lacking.

Out-of-Home Self-Care can entail a wide variety of situations in which the adolescent is alone, or with others, outside her or his home and not under the supervision of an adult. Available research has not always been clear on whether a parent is working during out-of-home self-care, or whether this difference significantly moderates the association with adolescent adjustment. Nonetheless, research across the disciplines of psychology, criminology, leisure studies, education, and anthropology report associations between adolescent engagement in unsupervised and unstructured after-school endeavors and a range of problem behaviors (e.g., antisocial behavior, crime, substance use, early sexual activity). The likelihood that out-of-home self-care may be problematic depends on peer socialization and parental monitoring. While the majority of peer influence during adolescence appears to support conventional and prosocial behavior (e.g., Brown et al., 1986), after-school arrangements that feature a lack of adult supervision accompanied by affiliation with deviant peers in unstructured contexts are associated with negative outcomes (e.g., Dishion et al., 1999; Galombos and Maggs, 1991; Mahoney et al., 2001; McCord, 1978; Osgood et al., 1996; Steinberg, 1986; Aizer, 2001). On this score, the capacity of parents to influence adolescents' activities, peer relationships, and unstructured leisure when they are not present seems critical.

During childhood and adolescence, parental supervision is frequently conceptualized in terms of parental monitoring—the extent to which parents are knowledgeable about their adolescent's whereabouts, affiliates, and activities (Dishion and McMahon, 1998). Such knowledge may be obtained by solicitation of information, control and restriction of activities, or unsolicited child disclosure (Stattin and Kerr, 2000). Poor parental monitoring has been linked to a variety of negative behaviors and outcomes for young persons, including antisocial behavior and crime; use of tobacco, alcohol, and other illicit substances; poor school performance; and early sexual activity. The risks associated with poor parental monitoring appear greatest for young persons living in dangerous areas (Pettit et al., 1999) and are partly accounted for by an increased likelihood of deviant peer affiliation among unsupervised adolescents (Dishion et al., 1995; Reid and Patterson, 1989). Evidence indicates that the association between deviant peer affiliation and negative adjustment holds for both genders.

Walter's mother provides an example of the risks of sibling care (Burton, 1991:36):

I know he is out there [on the streets] when I'm at work. I don't have any other way right now to have someone watch my children . . . I hope and pray that I taught Walter the right things, though. He knows too that when I'm home he better be straight. The Lord only knows, I have to believe that what I taught him, the good I taught him, will bring him through and make him a good man.

It is important to note, however, that the relations may be reciprocal. Adolescents prone to deviant behavior may also be more difficult for parents to communicate with and to monitor. A detailed account of the selection process into unstructured and unsupervised after-school settings is not presently available. However, young persons with existing behavioral problems appear especially prone to difficulties when they experience out-of-home self-care (Pettit et al., 1997), and those with dissatisfying experiences in structured settings (e.g., family, school, organized activities) are more likely to select unstructured and unsupervised endeavors (Mahoney et al., in pressb).

The available research indicates a possible connection between maternal employment, monitoring, and adolescent adjustment. For example, data from the National Longitudinal Survey of Youth found a small association between previous or concurrent maternal employment characteristics and delinquency in early adolescence (Vander Ven et al., 2001) that was mediated by parental supervision. Similarly, Jacobson and Crockett (2000) found maternal employment to be a significant moderator between parental monitoring and adolescent delinquent and sexual behavior, particularly when mothers were employed full time. Large-scale, experimental comparisons of employed and unemployed mothers receiving welfare have also been conducted (Morris et al., 2002). While positive associations were found between adjustment and employment for younger children, maternal employment was negatively associated with school-related outcomes for adolescents (e.g., lower grade point average, grade retention, suspension, school dropout). However, the magnitude of these differences was generally small and primarily based on parent reports of child or adolescent adjustment. Moreover, many nonexperimental studies do not report a significant link between parental employment and adolescent adjustment (e.g., Orthner, 1991).

Access to Supervised Contexts and Activities

Although rates of self-care do increase across adolescence, most young persons are engaged in some form of structured, adult-supervised arrangement during the after-school hours while their parent(s) are working. The association between involvement in two prevalent supervised settings during the after-school hours—structured enrichment activities and paid employment—is considered in relation to parental employment and the salient developmental tasks of adolescence.

Structured Enrichment Activities. Involvement in structured after-school enrichment activities, such as sports teams, lessons, and clubs, is relatively common during adolescence. Adult reports[2] of youth ages 12 to 17 from

---

[2]Questions were asked of the adult in the household most knowledgeable about the child; this was most often a parent.

the National Survey of America's Families (1997) indicates that 57 percent participated on a sports team in or out of school, 29 percent participated in lessons, and 60 percent participated in clubs or organizations after school or on weekends during the past year.[3] Boys were more likely to be involved in sports activities than girls (64 versus 49 percent), while girls were more likely to be involved in lessons and clubs than were boys (34 versus 24 percent, and 68 versus 53 percent, respectively). White adolescents were more likely to participate in all categories of enrichment activities compared with black or Hispanic youth. Hispanic youth showed the lowest participation across these categories, although ethnic differences in sports participation are relatively small. Rates of participation are also higher among youth with married parents, and participation tends to increase with higher levels of family income and parental education (National Survey of America's Families, 1997).

The National Research Council and Institute of Medicine (2002) recently evaluated the science and research on community programs and associated adjustment of young persons. That report underscores the tremendous diversity of programs that serve adolescents in the United States, and that most existing programs have not been evaluated, rigorously or otherwise. Three programs were highlighted in the report as having been evaluated with an appropriate comparison group and deserving of further study. Each program is structured, adult-supervised, and focuses on the prevention of problem behaviors or the enhancement of psychosocial competencies. The programs are (1) the Teen Outreach Program (Allen et al., 1997), which involves a school-based curriculum focusing on life-skills education, parent-adolescent relationships, future orientation, and volunteer service in the community; (2) Big Brothers Big Sisters (Grossman and Tierney, 1998), which emphasizes one-to-one mentoring and life-skills training for at-risk youth; and (3) the Quantum Opportunities Programs (Hahn et al., 1994), which targets youth in high-risk areas and provides community service activities, educational and job preparation training, and personal and life-skills training.

The evaluation of the Teen Outreach Program involved a random assignment design of 695 students in grades 9 to 12 from 25 schools across the nation. The Quantum Opportunities Program evaluation used a random selection and random assignment design involving 50 8th grade stu-

---

[3]The NASF estimates are somewhat higher than percentages reported from the SIPP data. The difference is probably due to the fact that NASF estimates of participation in enrichment activities are reported over the last year, while SIPP estimates are based on current participation at the time of survey. Comparisons between NASF data and the National Education Longitudinal Survey (1988) are also available. However, the NELS data on enrichment activities represent high school seniors only.

dents from 5 sites whose families were receiving public assistance. The Big Brothers Big Sisters evaluation used a random selection and random assignment "waiting list" design comparing 959 students who were 10 to 16 years old and from single-parent homes; 8 program sites across the nation were involved in this evaluation.

The findings from these evaluations (and several other quasi-experimental investigations) indicate that engagement in after-school enrichment activities may prevent the development of problem behaviors and promote competencies during adolescence. For example, compared with control group members, participants in the Teen Outreach Program reported lower rates of school failure (31 versus 37 percent), school suspension (16 versus 21 percent), and teenage pregnancy (3.2 versus 5.4 percent). Similarly, participants of the Quantum Opportunities Program had higher rates of high school graduation (63 versus 42 percent) and postsecondary school attendance (42 versus 16 percent), and lower rates of criminal arrest (17 versus 58 percent) than control group members. Likewise, participants of the Big Brothers Big Sisters program reported lower rates of drug use, truancy, and physical aggression and perceived their ability to complete schoolwork and their relationships with parents to be more positive than control group members. Note, however, that the magnitude of effects for the Big Brothers Big Sisters evaluation is relatively small, and both the Teen Outreach Program and Big Brothers Big Sisters evaluations rely heavily on self-reported information. Self-reported information may be biased to the extent that the programs increase knowledge of appropriate responses without affecting actual behaviors.

The need and importance of youth activity and programs have been recognized in Congress through the proposed Younger Americans Act. It was introduced in the House of Representatives and the Senate in 2001 and is expected to be reintroduced. As proposed, the act would authorize $5.75 billion over five years to provide enrichment opportunities for young persons ages 10 to 19 in the form of state block grants, with special attention given to low-income families. Enrichment activities that could be supported include those fostering positive relationships with adults, structured after-school activities, those that promote job-related training and competence, and community and service learning activities.

While program content and goals differ across specific programs and activities, common denominators of effective programs include opportunities to form positive relationships with peers and competent adults, a safe environment that fosters a sense of belonging and connectedness to conventional values, and the development of valued skills through regular and structured engagement in challenging activities that are intrinsically interesting to the participants. Overall, programs that lack such features seem unlikely to benefit young persons, and some may actually increase the development of problem behaviors (e.g., Mahoney et al., 2001; McCord, 1978).

Research on how participation in enrichment activities promotes successful development during adolescence is rapidly emerging (e.g., Mahoney et al., in press), and empirical evidence for a variety of activity-related change mechanisms is available. For example, Larson and colleagues (Larson, 2000; Dworkin et al., in press) find that enrichment activities offer a balance between challenge and enjoyment and promote "initiative skills," such as learning to set goals, managing time, and regulating emotions. Such skills may ultimately promote an appreciation for work and prepare young persons for the transition to adulthood (Csikszentmihalyi and Schneider, 2000; Mahoney, 2002).

Peer relationships associated with structured after-school activities appear to mediate improvements in social status and popularity for children who previously experienced low peer acceptance in the classroom (Eder and Kinney, 1995; Sandstrom and Coie, 1999). Peer affiliations in structured after-school activities have also been shown to moderate the association between early profiles of problem adjustment and later school failure, dropout, and crime (Mahoney, 2000).

After-school activities may also help to establish constructive relationships between adults and participating adolescents. For example, parents are often required to play a role in supporting children's after-school activities, including the provision of transportation and social support. Parent engagement in child after-school activities has, in turn, been correlated with parent-child communication and trust (Csikszentmihalyi et al., 1993; Mahoney and Magnusson, 2001; Tierney and Grossman, 1995). Moreover, relationships with after-school activity leaders may also be beneficial. Because children spend a significant amount of time engaged in after-school activities, there is an opportunity to form meaningful and lasting relationships with unrelated adult activity leaders. Available evidence indicates that supportive relations with unrelated adults may reduce the likelihood for developing problem behaviors among high-risk young persons (e.g., Werner, 1993). This appears to include affiliation with after-school activity leaders, coaches, and mentors (e.g., Mahoney, 2000).

Barriers to Participation in Structured Enrichment Activities. Students who are at risk for social and academic failure by virtue of early profiles of psychosocial risk and disadvantage may benefit the most from engagement in after-school activities. However, these same students are ordinarily the least likely to participate in them (Howard and Madrigal, 1990; Hultzman, 1995; Lindsay, 1984; Mahoney and Cairns, 1997; Quinn, 1999).

Economic barriers are salient for some youth. The expense of participation, required transportation, and entrance fees can influence participation rates. These impediments may help to explain the lower rates of participation among adolescents from low-income families. Consistent with this proposal, findings from the New Hope Project (Huston et al., 2001) show that adolescents from poor families that were provided with wage supplements to raise income above the poverty line were significantly more likely to participate in enrichment activities compared with families that did not receive wage supplements.

A lack of competence and requisite skill is also an apparent obstacle to engagement in enrichment activities. Peer networks can discourage entry into after-school activities for some less competent children and adolescents (Eder and Parker, 1987; Evans and Eder, 1993; Eder et al., 1995; Jackson and Rucks, 1995; Kinney, 1993). Minimum academic requirements are sometimes needed to participate in after-school activities, and this also constrains opportunities for involvement among students struggling in the classroom (Braddock et al., 1991; Jacobs and Chase, 1989).

Because these multiple constraints are interdependent, opportunities for structured after-school activity involvement and its associated benefits may be more limited for young persons from low-income families and disadvantaged areas and those with social or academic problems. Moreover, early activity involvement may be required for some forms of later activity participation (McNeal, 1998). Therefore, children who do not (or cannot) become competent in the skills developed through after-school activities and programs early on may find that opportunities for structured after-school involvement diminish across adolescence.

Paid Employment During Adolescence

Adolescent employment is connected to family and work policies in several ways. First, like after-school enrichment activities, participation in the job force is an increasingly common activity in the after-school hours and during the summer while many parents are working. Second, parental employment, education, and income are positively associated with adolescent employment rates. Third, adolescent employment is positively associated with employment and earnings in young adulthood. Fourth, employment during adolescence appears to influence the psychosocial well-being of young persons (although the directionality of the association is mixed). Finally, while adolescents are much less likely to contribute their earnings to the family income than was true in previous generations, as many as 19 percent of employed high school seniors still may do so (Bachman et al., 1987).

Rates of Adolescent Employment. Data from the 1997 National Longitudinal Survey of Youth (NLSY97) indicate that 63.7 percent of 15-year-olds were employed. However, estimates of adolescent employment do vary by

Work and on-the-job training can facilitate personal skills (independence, initiative, discipline and structure, multitasking) and interpersonal skills (teamwork) (Newman, 1999:25):

> *Kyesha's experiences at Burger Barn reflect the positive aspects of youth employment: "My mother, she limits the money for clothes. . . . [S]o I had to get a job and get it myself. . . . My family was like, 'Ah, Kyesha's becoming independent. I'm proud of her.'. . . So I felt good. I didn't have to ask my mother for money."*

the data source considered (e.g., Stone and Mortimer, 1998), and the corresponding employment rates for 15-year-olds from the Current Population Survey (CPS) and Consumer Expenditure Survey (CE) are considerably lower (U.S. Department of Labor, 2000). The discrepancies are presumably explained by methodological differences among the CPS, CE, and NLSY97 surveys (i.e., differences in the frequency of assessments and the recall time considered, whether estimates include summer employment, definitions of employment utilized, whether self-reports or proxy reports were used, interview probes involved, etc.). Indeed, when the time frame and informant are the same, the results are more consistent across these surveys. Regardless of the data source consulted, however, it seems safe to conclude that most adolescents participate in paid labor by the end of high school.

Across surveys, rates of adolescent employment are found to differ according to demographics. Employment increases with age, and rates are typically higher during the summertime compared with the school year. Gender differences in overall rates of employment are not large; however, males are almost twice as likely as females to work more than 20 hours per week (Lerman, 2000). Ethnic differences are more substantial. Employment rates for white adolescents are considerably higher than for black or Hispanic youth. Foreign-born youth are also less likely to be employed compared with their native-born counterparts; however, foreign-born youth tend to work more hours than native-born youth.

Adolescent employment is also associated with parental employment and tends to increase as a function of family income when comparisons are made between low-income and other families. For example, 31 percent of adolescents in families on welfare worked, while 46 percent of adolescents in families at or above 200 percent of the federal poverty level were employed (Lerman, 2000). Likewise, the adolescent employment rate increases with parental education. Because ethnicity, family income, and maternal education are nested factors, it is difficult to sort out the individual contributions of these aspects to adolescent employment.

Work Experience and Adolescent Adjustment. Whether and to what extent adolescents should engage in employment continues to be a source of debate. A concern that young persons lack real preparation for work has prompted government initiatives to expand funding to support work-based learning, paid employment, and employer involvement for high school students—for example, the School-to-Work Opportunities Act of 1994 (e.g., see Donahoe and Tienda, 2000, and Ruhm, 1997). The empirical evidence on this matter is complicated and often mixed. The discussion below focuses on three major areas of adjustment studied in relation to adolescent employment: social behaviors and relationships; school engagement and related outcomes; and future employment, education, and earnings.

Social Behaviors and Relationships. An association between work intensity (number of hours working) and problem behaviors such as substance use and delinquency is reported in several studies (e.g., Bachman and Schunlenberg, 1993; Greenberger and Steinberg, 1986; Steinberg and Dornbusch, 1991). Adolescents who work long hours (e.g., more than 20 hours per week during the school year) are somewhat more likely to engage in problem behaviors. While most studies demonstrating this relation are cross-sectional and therefore cannot sort out directionality, some longitudinal work indicates that increases in work hours precede the increases in problem behaviors (Steinberg et al., 1993; but see also Mortimer et al., 1996).

Possible explanations for the link between intensive work and problematic adjustment include: (1) a premature acceleration to adult roles and responsibilities that compromises adjustment; (2) an increase in discretionary income that may be used to purchase alcohol and drugs; (3) a preference for disengagement from other conventional institutions and contexts (e.g., school, family, structured enrichment activities); (4) the possibility of forming peer relationships with deviant and older peer coworkers; and (5) unmeasured aspects involved in the selection process (Stone and Mortimer, 1998). It should be noted, however, that relatively little variance in problem behavior is accounted for by employment intensity, and that most employed young persons do not average over 20 hours of work per week. For instance, the NLSY97 reports that 8 percent of 14-year-olds and 17 percent of 15-year-olds worked during the school year and averaged over 15 hours of work per week. Similarly, the CPS data indicate that, across the school year and the summer, the average hours of work per week for adolescents ages 15, 16, and 17 was 11.6, 15.7, and 18.2, respectively. However, two subgroups of adolescents—high school dropouts and foreign-born youth—are more likely to work long hours (Grogger 2000, 2001). The CPS data indicate that, during the period 1996-1998, employed dropouts worked an average of 34 hours per week, compared with 15 hours for employed students. Similarly, foreign-born youth averaged 24 hours of work per week compared with 18 hours for native-born youth.

Steinberg and colleagues (Greenberger and Steinberg, 1986; Steinberg and Dornbusch, 1991) have also noted associations between adolescent employment and family involvement. Employed teenagers tend to provide less assistance with household tasks and spend more time away from the family (see also Manning, 1990). However, there is little basis to conclude that adolescent work disrupts family relationships. Indeed, Mortimer and Shanahan (1994) report a positive relationship between boys' work and closeness to father when the type of employment is perceived as promoting skills and responsibility. In this regard, the quality of employment—the type of work and employment conditions—seems critical. Employment that is perceived as high in quality is, for example, positively associated with the development of intrinsic values for work (Mortimer et al., 1996), mental health, and behavioral adjustment (Mortimer et al., 1992).

School Engagement and Related Outcomes. Under most circumstances, working long hours during the school year has been found to be negatively associated with school engagement and performance. This includes more school absence and tardiness, less time spent on homework and reduced grade point average (e.g., Steinberg and Cauffman, 1995; Steinberg and Dornbusch, 1991; Marsh, 1991; Mihalic and Elliot, 1997). These associations tend to be most apparent for boys (Lerman, 2000). However, not all studies find such relations (e.g., Mortimer et al., 1993), the magnitude of associations is often quite small, and selection effects have not always been addressed. Indeed, the negative associations between employment intensity and school performance (i.e., grades, time spent on homework) diminish when preexisting factors are taken into consideration (Schoenhals et al., 1998). Moreover, the association between employment intensity and adolescent adjustment is positive in some studies. For example, an increase in work hours is related to fewer hours spent watching television (Schoenhals et al., 1998), and moderately intense employment is associated with homework completion, school achievement, and low rates of truancy (Lerman, 2000; Stone and Mortimer, 1998).

For some adolescents, selection may explain the negative relation between long hours of employment and school success. Students who are less interested or engaged in school may commit themselves to other activities such as more intensive work. This could account for why some studies have found long hours of work to be negatively related to long-term educational attainment (e.g., Carr et al., 1996; Marsh, 1991). For other adolescents, spending long hours in employment contexts may affect the educational process through socialization. Because the employment experience is often unrelated to learning activities in the school, intensive employment could introduce a value system that deemphasizes the importance or benefits of schooling. Consistent with the socialization explanation, Stone and colleagues (Stone and Mortimer, 1998; Stone et al., 1990) have argued that schools should promote employment opportunities that are more directly connected to school learning experience. Cooperative vocational educational programs represent one possibility. Comparisons of students intensively employed in school-based work programs with those in jobs not connected to school find that students in the school-supervised arrangement may fare better in terms of achievement (e.g., Stern et al., 1997). The findings are suspect, however, because selection factors that predate choosing school-based or nonschool-based employment were not considered. Nonetheless, the notion of supervised work experiences that are connected to school, are structured, involve an adult mentor, and encourage skill development is consistent with the broader literature on positive youth development programs described above. See Donahoe and Tienda, 2000, and Lerman, 1996, for discussions of the types of school-to-work programs, the outcomes associated with participation these programs, and possible benefits of participation for disadvantaged and high-risk youth.

Future Employment, Education, and Earnings. In contrast to the possible negative associations between intensive employment during adolescence and secondary school adjustment, a long-term perspective shows that employment during high school is positively associated with future employment, earnings and benefits, and occupational status in the decade following high school graduation (e.g., Ruhm, 1997; Chaplin and Hannaway, 1996; Carr et al., 1996; Wright and Carr, 1995). For example, Ruhm (1997) found that seniors who worked an average of 20 hours per week earned 22 percent more in annual income 6 to 9 years after graduation than high school students who were not employed. Similarly, Chaplin and Hannaway (1996) found that the future earnings of youth who were low achievers in high school and worked at moderate intensity during their sophomore year was 25 percent higher 8 to 11 years later compared with similar students that did not work. The above studies are noteworthy since a variety of demographic and individual factors that predated adolescent employment were included to account for possible selection differences between employed and nonemployed adolescents.

However, it should be noted that both high-intensity employment during high school and lack of employment during high school are related to decreased levels of secondary or postsecondary education (Ahituv et al., 1998; Carr et al., 1996; Tienda and Ahituv, 1996; Ruhm, 1997). Thus, the possible long-term benefits of adolescent employment in terms of increased employment and income observed during the third decade of life must be weighed against the short-term negative associations of intense employment during adolescence. In addition, when econometric selection models are applied to consider unobserved heterogeneity and sample selectivity, the positive associations between adolescent employment and later employment and earnings are diminished (Hotz et al., in press). Finally, whether gains in employment or earnings associated with adolescent employment persist to the fourth decade of life (ages 30 to 40) is not yet known.

Parental Occupation and Adolescent Career Choice. A final point concerning the future employment of adolescents is the possibility that parent occupations affect young persons' career choices. Some research suggests that, for girls, maternal employment is related to high educational and career aspirations (Hoffman, 1974, 1989). This general finding may be partly dependent on the extent to which working mothers are satisfied with their employment arrangement, as the combination of maternal role satisfaction, educational attainment, and occupational prestige appears to be particularly indicative of high career aspirations for young persons (Castellino et al., 1998). However, studies have also reported small negative associations between maternal employment and boys' adjustment. Reasons for the gender difference may involve girls' being more likely to positively identify with and be influenced by maternal employment, more negative consequences of low supervision for boys, and the possible benefits of increased household responsibilities that are more likely to be taken on by girls when their mothers are working. Adolescents' perceptions of fathers' work, however, has been linked to adolescent work values (Galambos and Sears, 1998), which in turn influence adolescent career decisions and aspirations (Ryu and Mortimer, 1996).

Parental Employment, Parent-Adolescent Relationships, and Adjustment

Research on the link between parental employment, parent-adolescent relationships, and adolescent adjustment reveals a complex pattern of associations that varies according to family income level, economic strain, the features of employment, and the adolescent's gender (Crouter et al., 1990; Galambos and Sears, 1998). Most of the research has focused on maternal employment and adolescent adjustment. However, as fathers are also employed in most families, the studies tend to inform understanding of what happens when both parents work rather than pinpointing the role of maternal employment on adolescent functioning. It should also be noted that the literature on maternal employment and adolescent functioning is presently fragmented and often inconsistent, rendering it difficult to make strong conclusions concerning the conditions under which maternal employment may affect young persons. Employment has been defined in different ways; the characteristics of the family ecology, the parent(s), and the adolescent have typically not been assessed in tandem; and the characteristics of maternal employment (e.g., wages, work schedules, job satisfaction and complexity, etc.) have not been examined in detail.

Having noted the above limitations, overall, the difference in adjustment of adolescents whose mothers are employed and who are not employed seems marginal (Orthner, 1991; Armistead et al., 1990). For instance, in areas such as sexual attitudes or behaviors (Wright et al., 1990; Nelson and Keith, 1990), the use of illicit substances (Hillman and Sawilosky, 1991), social competence (Armistead et al., 1990), behavior problems (Ross Phillips, 2002a), and susceptibility to peer pressure (Hillman et al., 1993) adolescents with mothers who are employed are similar to adolescents whose mothers are not. However, as discussed earlier, the general association is more substantial when parental supervision and after-school arrangements are considered.

One area of adolescent adjustment that may be influenced by maternal employment is school achievement. The association varies by both income level and gender (e.g., Bogenschneider and Steinberg, 1994; Conger et al., 1994). Middle-class adolescent sons (but not daughters) of full-time employed mothers have been found to show lower overall grades (Bogenschneider and Steinberg, 1994; Bronfenbrenner and Crouter, 1982; Montemayor, 1984). Based on maternal reports, recent investigations among lower income families involved in welfare-to-work programs show that adolescents have somewhat poorer academic achievement, higher enrollment in special education, and increased rates of grade retention (Brooks et al., 2001; Schaefer, 2001). Using a meta-analytic strategy, Gennetian et al. (2002b) have demonstrated similar results. These negative findings, while small in magnitude and not entirely consistent across all studies, are surprising given that other studies have found that mothers who are employed full-time report spending more time on homework with their adolescents compared with mothers who are not employed (e.g., Maryse and Duckett, 1994). One possible explanation is that adolescents with employed mothers from low-income families spend more time assuming adult roles and responsibilities, including caring for younger siblings. Gennetian et al. (2002b) provide evidence consistent with this proposal. The negative association between maternal employment and school outcomes was most marked for adolescents with younger siblings.

While work-related stress for mothers does not appear to impact adolescent adjustment (Galambos and Maggs, 1991), the influence of employment (or the lack thereof) on the parent-adolescent relationship may partly explain the differences associated with gender and income. For instance, maternal employment for middle-income families has been associated with stronger father-adolescent relationships and more positive affect in mother-adolescent relationships (Richards and Duckett, 1994; Duckett and Maryse,

1995). The same may not be true for adolescents in low-income families (Paulson et al., 1990). In addition, changes in employment, work interruption, and financial strain may negatively affect parent-adolescent relationships, parenting practices, and adolescent adjustment (Gutman and Eccles, 1999; McLoyd et al., 1994). This may be particularly true for boys and when overt behaviors, such as achievement and aggression, are considered (Conger et al., 1997; Skinner et al., 1992; Elder et al., 1995).

SUMMARY

Adolescence is characterized by a number of salient developmental tasks that are negotiated in light of interdependent changes in individual functioning, expanding social contexts, and biopyschosocial transitions. While most young persons negotiate these tasks successfully, some do not. Because adolescence is also a time when many problem behaviors increase in severity and consequence, understanding how families and employment impede or facilitate success during adolescence is critical.

There are three main ways in which parental employment may influence adolescent adjustment: (1) parental supervision, child care arrangements, and responsibilities while parents are working; (2) access to supervised activities and contexts; and (3) parenting practices that may influence the parent-adolescent relationship.

While in-home self-care becomes increasingly common from late childhood through adolescence, there is little empirical basis for concluding that this arrangement is detrimental for adolescents. However, to the extent that young persons who experience self-care are prone to problem behaviors, or parents do not monitor their unsupervised endeavors, the risk for negative developmental consequences may increase.

Available research on adolescent engagement in structured enrichment activities suggests that beneficial programs offer opportunities to develop positive relationships with peers and adults, a sense of belonging and connectedness to conventional values, and the opportunity to develop valued skills. **Young persons who are able to engage in structured, supervised, and skill-focused activities show more favorable outcomes than their unengaged counterparts. Unstructured programs, however, may not only fail to offer these benefits, but they may also amplify existing problems or encourage the development of new problems.** Students who are at the highest risk for developing problems during adolescence tend to show low rates of participation in enrichment activities. Barriers to participation for these young persons are multiple (e.g., economic, social, lack of skills or experience).

Most adolescents will participate in the paid labor force by the end of high school. Although intensive work (e.g., more than 20-25 hours per week) has been linked to increased problem behaviors and low postsecondary educational attainment, this is not representative of most adolescents' work experience. In addition, moderately intense employment during adolescence is linked to positive adjustment during high school and to high rates of employment and earnings in young adulthood. Work that is moderate in intensity, connected to school, and offers an adult-supervised learning experience may be optimal.

In conclusion, the overall associations between parental employment, parent-adolescent relationships, and adjustment tend to be marginal. However, the magnitude and direction of association differs by gender and family income level and is likely to vary according to levels of parent supervision and the adolescents' after-school activities and social relationships.

7

Effects of Welfare Reform

ew federal public polices, which began to be enacted in the 1980s, have had a particularly significant effect on work and family trends among low-income families in the United States. The 1996 Personal Responsibility and Work Opportunity Reconciliation Act (PRWORA) replaced Aid to Families with Dependent Children (AFDC), the major program of cash assistance to families with children, with Temporary Assistance for Needy Families (TANF), a work-oriented time-limited program designed to encourage single mothers to become self-sufficient (see Box 7-1). This legislation ended what had become known as "welfare." Prior to the passage of welfare reform, efforts had been made to "make work pay" by increasing the federal minimum wage and expanding the earned income tax credit (EITC), which subsidizes the earnings of low-income families. Together, welfare reform and expansion of the EITC built on and furthered ongoing policy developments with origins in the federal 1988 Family Support Act, as well as 1980s and 1990s state welfare reform "waiver" programs that sought to increase assistance to low-income working families and to require, prepare for, and support labor market participation among welfare recipients and would-be recipients (e.g., Ellwood, 1988).

The 1996 act went beyond earlier reform efforts by turning responsibility for program design to the states, ending the entitlement to cash assistance to poor single mothers, and time-limiting eligibility for federal cash assistance. Proponents of welfare reform sought to increase employment among low-income single mothers with preschool-age children (who made

---

BOX 7-1
Key Provisions of Welfare Reform in Temporary Assistance for Needy Families (TANF)

1. Replaces welfare entitlement with block grants to states.

2. Establishes a 60-month limit on federal assistance for families with adults, with shorter time limits permitted at state discretion. However, up to 20 percent of a state's TANF caseload may be exempt from the time limit for hardship.

3. Requires states to ensure that recipients engage in work and work-related activities. For example, half of nonexempt single mothers must be engaged in work or work-related activities by 2002. Federal law requires 20 hours of work activity per week for single mothers with children under age 6 and 30 hours for those with only older children. However, states can offset the work requirement with a "caseload reduction credit" that reduces the percentage of the caseload required to be engaged in work activities by 1 percentage point for each percentage point reduction in the caseload since fiscal year 1994 for reasons other than changes in eligibility rules. States may exempt mothers of children under 1 year of age from work requirements.

4. Consolidates streams of federal assistance to states for child care and increases funding.

5. Makes legal immigrants ineligible for TANF for their first five years in the country, subject to limited exceptions.

6. Gives significant control over program design to the states.

---

up approximately two-thirds of AFDC cases). And, indeed, the years following welfare reform have seen major increases in labor force participation among single mothers with children.

This chapter reviews the evidence on the effects of TANF on working families, first by looking at its effects on adult employment, earnings, poverty, fertility, and marriage and then by looking at its effects on the well-being of parents which, in turn, affects the development of children and adolescents in these families.

EFFECTS OF TEMPORARY ASSISTANCE FOR NEEDY FAMILIES

Employment, Earnings, Income, and Welfare Use

Reviewers of evidence on the effects of the 1996 welfare reform observe, first, that dramatic changes occurred in the 1990s in the employment and welfare participation of adults at highest risk of welfare use and, second, that the 1996 reforms were not subject to experimental evaluation (Blank, 2002; Moffitt, in press).[1] As a result, the precise causal contribution of welfare reform to the behavioral changes observed in the 1990s is uncertain and likely to remain so.

Estimating the causal impact of policy changes such as welfare reform must begin with a clear statement of both the treatment and the counterfactual to treatment for those affected (see National Research Council and Institute of Medicine, 2000:Chapter 4 and Appendix B). Although impossible, the ideal study would allow an analyst to observe the same individuals exposed to and not exposed to welfare reform. Experimental evaluation approximates this ideal by randomly assigning individuals either to a treatment group subject to welfare reform policies or to a control group subject to some alternative policy, such as traditional AFDC. Because assignment to a policy regime is done at random, if the experiment is carried out correctly and successfully, characteristics of individuals—even characteristics difficult for analysts to measure—should be unrelated to assignment to treatment or control. In principle, the average effect of the policy on the treated group is simply the difference between the average outcomes (such as earnings or employment rate) of the treatment and control groups.

In the absence of random assignment, analysts use statistical procedures to simulate experimental evaluation. Analysts attempt to measure and control characteristics of individuals related both to the outcome of interest and to the probability of treatment. Failure to adjust for differences in such characteristics between treatment and comparison populations can lead to biased estimates of program effects (selectivity bias).

Despite the widespread understanding among social scientists and policy analysts of the importance of specifying a treatment and counterfactual to the treatment, in research on the effect of welfare reform, an explicit statement of the treatment and the counterfactual may be problematic (Blank, 2002). Specifying the treatment is difficult because welfare reform legislation has spawned a complex variety of welfare policy changes by states and substate entities (see the section below on state reactions to welfare reform). Indeed, a central purpose of welfare reform was to increase state control over program design and the ability of states to tailor programs to state-specific needs and environments.

Specifying the appropriate counterfactual to welfare reform has also proven difficult because it requires the analyst to project what would have

---

[1]This section draws on these two major recent reviews of TANF and the estimates of its impact, borrowing some organizational features from Blank (2002).

happened to those affected by welfare reform in the absence of the policy changes. For example, one possibility would be to compare behavior under the 1996 reforms to that under the traditional AFDC program. However, a before-after study of welfare reform will not always result in a comparison to traditional AFDC because about half the states had been granted major federal waivers under AFDC prior to the passage of the 1996 act. In short, both the treatment and the counterfactual vary across states. Furthermore, as noted, welfare reform was part of a broader social policy reform package, one intention of which was to end cash assistance to able-bodied adults, at the same time increasing the take-home pay of low-income working families through expansion of the EITC and increasing the minimum wage. This raises the question of whether it is appropriate to evaluate the effects of TANF provisions of welfare reform in isolation from (i.e., controlling for) the increased generosity of the EITC and other nonwelfare provisions intended to support low-income working families.

Because the 1996 welfare reforms were not subject to random assignment evaluation, it is difficult to know what the labor market outcomes and related behaviors of the population affected by welfare reform would have been in the absence of welfare reform. In the absence of experimental evaluation, analysts have attempted to draw causal inferences about the effects of the 1996 welfare reforms from three types of studies: nonexperimental (observational) statistical analysis; extrapolation of results from random assignment evaluations of earlier state waiver reform efforts that share features of the 1996 reforms; and "leaver studies" (studies of recipients who leave welfare after the implementation of welfare reform). Evaluations of the effects of welfare reform generally begin by reviewing aggregate trends in welfare caseloads and employment rates of single mothers over the 1990s that might plausibly be attributed to welfare reform.

State Reactions to Welfare Reform

Although research on the effect of welfare reform has properly estimated effects on recipient populations, federal welfare reform is mediated by the choices that states make in how they implement their welfare policies. As noted, the welfare reform "treatment" received by those on welfare or at high risk of welfare use depends importantly on the state of residence. Blank (2002) concludes that variability across states in program characteristics was generally increased by welfare reform. Some generalizations about policy choices are possible. Maximum benefit for families with no other income continued to decline in real value in the 1990s, as they had in the 1970s and 1980s. The maximum benefit for a family of three in the median state fell about 21 percent (adjusted for inflation) between 1995 and 2000 (Blank, 2000:Table 2). Many states opted to provide greater work incentives for those on welfare through smaller benefit reduction rates than had characterized AFDC immediately prior to reform. Reducing the benefit reduction rate increases the net income of women who work at the same time that they receive welfare, but it can also reduce incentives to leave welfare and thus jeopardize eligibility for federal assistance under time limits. Although earlier research on the AFDC program concluded that there was little evidence for effects on labor supply of more generous earnings disregards,[2] 1996 welfare reform included strong work requirements, so employment response to incentives might be different than under AFDC (Moffitt, in press, 1992).

The 1996 welfare reform act required increasing proportions of the caseload in each state to work or to participate in work-related activities. However, the act also provided a caseload reduction credit that allows states to reduce the percentage of the caseload subject to work requirements by 1 percentage point for each percentage point reduction in its caseload from fiscal year (FY) 1995 (for declines that are not attributable to changes in eligibility rules). Many states have met caseload work requirements through caseload reduction. By FY 1999, 38 percent of recipients were engaged in work or job-related activities (U.S. Department of Health and Human Services, 2000b), and nearly 30 percent were employed.

According to Blank (2002), most states have used "work first" approaches for work activities, which require participants to participate in limited job preparation services and then engage in job search. Little money has been spent on longer term education and training (Strawn et al., 2001). A total of 26 states have adopted the 60-month federal limit on assistance, whereas 8 states have no mandatory time limit to end all benefits (i.e., they may elect to provide benefits paid for with state funds to individuals who have exhausted eligibility for federal assistance). And 17 states have elected to impose limits shorter than 60 months, at least for some families.

Some states attempt to divert new applicants from participating in TANF either by requiring search for work prior to eligibility (10 states), or by providing short-term emergency cash payments intended to allow would-be recipients to return to or to maintain a job. States and the federal government dramatically expanded work support expenditures such as child care and wage subsidies (through earned income credits) along with welfare reform. States have also increased spending on transportation and job search assistance.

---

[2]Earnings disregards allow welfare recipients to keep a proportion of their welfare benefits as they increase their earnings, rather than reduce recipients' benefits dollar for dollar as earnings rise.

Aggregate Trends

Welfare Caseload and Employment

Two patterns are prominent in the data for the 1990s: a sharp decline in the welfare caseload and a surge in employment among single mothers (Table 7-1 and Table 7-2). As a percentage of the population of the United States, the number of welfare recipients increased by about 1 percentage point from 1990 to 1993 (to over 5 percent of the population, or an increase of more than 2 million persons), declined modestly between 1993 and 1996, and then plummeted between 1996 and 2000, falling to less than 3 percent of the population by 2000 (Moffitt, in press). Time limits were not directly responsible for this decline, as it began and took place prior to the date that recipients began to exhaust eligibility for benefits. In all, the caseload fell by more than half between 1994 and 2000, and the decline was widespread across the states.

The welfare caseload decline in many states began well before 1996. But in the late 1990s, caseloads declined at a faster rate than in any equivalent period. It is unlikely that the decline was merely the product of the strong economic recovery of the 1990s because the 1983-1989 recovery was not associated with notable reductions in the welfare caseload (Blank, 2002).

Employment of unmarried women with children increased strikingly in the 1990s. The employment rate of single mothers with children increased over 12 percentage points between 1993 and 1998, peaking in 2000 at 75.5 percent for those with children under 19. For unmarried women with children under age 6 who traditionally made up the majority of welfare recipients, the increase in labor force participation was even more dramatic: the employment rate for single mothers with children under 6 increased from 52.5 percent in 1995 to 69.1 percent in 2000. There were also large increases for those with children under age 3 and under age 1 (see Table 7-1). There were no corresponding increases in labor force participation this period for married women with young children (in fact, their participation rates declined somewhat over the second half of the 1990s). Although one might suspect that the surge in employment and labor force participation rates among single mothers with young children in the mid-1990s is solely a product of the economic recovery of the 1990s, single mothers saw little change in labor force participation and employment over the 1980s (Blank 2002). Furthermore, among those who received public assistance in the previous year, the proportion employed increased from 20 percent in 1990 to 44 percent in 2000 (Blank, 2002). Among adult TANF/AFDC recipients, the proportion working increased from about 7 percent in 1990 to about 28 percent in 1999 (administrative data cited by Ron Haskins in

TABLE 7-1 Employment Status of Mothers by Age of Youngest Child (annual averages) (% of population)

	1995		1996		2000		2001	
	Labor Force Participation Rate	Employment Rate	Labor Force Participation Rate	Employment Rate	Labor Force Participation Rate	Employment Rate	Labor Force Participation Rate	Employment Rate
Total mothers								
Youngest child < 6	58.9	53.9	59.4	54.6	60.4	56.8	60.2	56.0
Youngest child < 3	55.0	50.0	54.3	49.5	54.6	51.0	54.9	50.6
Youngest child < 1								
Mothers married with spouse								
Youngest child <6	60.4	60.9	60.3	61.0	58.0	59.9	57.5	59.5
Youngest child <3	57.0	57.2	55.9	57.5	53.3	55.8	53.9	55.0
Youngest child <1		53.6		52.9		51.0		51.3
Mothers not married with spouse								
Youngest child <6	54.3	52.5	56.8	55.2	67.9	69.1	68.5	67.5
Youngest child <3	49.0	44.4	49.4	46.1	58.8	59.6	58.3	59.2
Youngest child <1		38.9		39.0		50.7		48.5

SOURCE: U.S. Bureau of Labor Statistics (1997, 2002).

TABLE 7-2 Poverty Rates for Persons in Families Headed
by a Female Householder, No Husband Present

	All	Black	Hispanic
2001 (new weights[a])	28.6	37.4	37.8
2000 (new weights)	28.5	38.6	37.8
2000 (old weights)	27.9	38.7	36.5
1999	30.4	41.0	40.7
1998	33.1	42.8	46.7
1997	35.1	42.8	50.9
1996	35.8	46.4	53.5
1995	36.5	48.2	52.8
1994	38.6	50.2	54.8
1993	38.7	53.0	53.2
1992	39.0	54.0	51.5
1991	39.7	54.8	52.7
1990	37.2	50.6	53.0
1989	35.9	49.4	50.6
1979	34.9	53.1	51.2
1969	38.2	58.2	53.5[b]
1959	49.4	70.6	NA

[a] Beginning with data published for 2000, the Current Population Survey
used new population weights. For 2000, figures were published using both
old and new weights to indicate the effects of the revised weights.

[b] 1969 entry for Hispanics is data for 1972, the earliest available from the
Current Population Survey.

SOURCE: U.S. Census Bureau (2000).

Blank and Haskins, 2001) (with some proportion of this increase attributable to changes in eligibility rules that affected eligibility for working families).

Earnings, Poverty, and Income

Since employment increased substantially at a time when welfare caseloads were falling, analysts have attempted to determine whether employment improves the economic status of recipients and former recipients. Whether employment increases income depends importantly on wage rates and hours of work. More detailed analyses of wage rates of welfare leavers are discussed below. However, simple calculations indicate that half-time work at the minimum wage (plus the EITC) provides income that meets or exceeds the maximum benefit in the median state (e.g., Ellwood, 1999; Jencks, 1997; Jencks and Swingle, 2000). In states with high benefit levels or generous earnings disregards, more than half-time work would be required to improve income relative to welfare. These calculations also depend importantly on whether former recipients have major unreimbursed work expenses, particularly for child care. Combining employment and welfare unambiguously raises income for recipients in states that have adopted generous earnings disregards (see the section on state reactions to welfare reform), but it may not increase income in the absence of earnings disregards. Finally, although wages are low among the low-skilled women who make up the vast majority of welfare recipients, they do appear to increase with labor market experience (Gladden and Taber, 2000).

Poverty rates among single mothers fell sharply in the 1990s, especially after 1995. Poverty rates fell 15 percentage points among black and Hispanic single mothers from their early 1990s peaks to 2000. Perhaps more strikingly, more than half of this decline took place after 1996 (see Table 7-2). Census tabulations of poverty rates for 2001 are not strictly comparable to figures for the late 1990s due to the introduction of new population weights based on the 2000 census. However, it is possible to use the newly weighted data to compute changes between 2000 and 2001. Between 2000 and 2001, the poverty rate for all persons increased 0.4 percentage points, but for persons in families headed by single mothers, the increase was only 0.1 percentage points (on a much larger base). More strikingly, despite the slowing economy, the poverty rate for individuals in families headed by a black single mother actually declined by 0.8 percentage points, and the corresponding figure for Hispanic single mothers was unchanged. (Although poverty reduction is a key goal and therefore an important outcome for assessment of welfare reform, it must be noted that, while they are receiving welfare, virtually all welfare recipients are very poor, so it is possible for their income to improve substantially and still be in poverty.)

Poverty rates fell as income increased for single mother-headed families. Between 1993 and 1999, income increased across the entire distribution (Blank, 2002:Table 5, citing data from the Center on Budget and Policy Priorities), whereas between 1997 and 1999, income increased for all but single mother families in the lowest quintile. Specifically, single mothers in the lowest quintile saw their average real income decline by about 5 percent between 1997 and 1999, after having risen by over 10 percent in the first half of the 1990s. Consumption expenditures increased over the 1990s, even among families with very low income headed by women (Blank, 2002, citing Meyer and Sullivan, 2001).

Limitations of measures of income should be noted. Very few studies of changes in economic status use good measures of disposable income (Blank, 2002). Limitations include failure to measure accurately tax rates and EITC benefits (which are ignored or imputed by analysts); poor or absent measurement of the value of in-kind public assistance (housing, food, medical insurance); lack of information on income sharing within and between households; and failure to measure work expenses, including out-of-pocket child care expenses.

Causal Analysis

A variety of approaches have been taken to estimate causal effects of welfare reform.   Such attempts encounter several difficulties. Welfare reform was enacted in the mid-1990s and followed by a period of unusually strong economic growth.   Other programs intended to aid low-income working families were expanded, and it is difficult to know whether such programs should be considered a component of or separate from welfare reform.   Specifically, the federal EITC provided a 40 percent subsidy to earned income to low-income families with two or more children.   The maximum benefit, at about $4,000 per year, is comparable to the maximum AFDC benefit in many states. Because many related important factors changed contemporaneously with nationwide implementation of federal reform, isolating the causal contribution of federal welfare reform, either by cross-time comparisons within states or comparisons across states, is difficult.

Some analysts have taken advantage of the cross-state variation in the nature of welfare reforms enacted and implemented by states as a result of the 1996 act to estimate effects of specific program components. Estimating effects of specific welfare reform components requires an accurate and complete characterization of the components and the prereform policy environment (and other state-specific characteristics), which has proven difficult (Blank, 2002). Studies of the experiences of single states can provide better measures of both the welfare reform treatment and the counterfactual to welfare reform, but it is not clear that such results can be generalized to the nation.

Analysts also attempt to extrapolate from studies of prefederal reform statewide waiver evaluations that generally did conduct random assignment evaluations. However, for several reasons there are limits to generalizations to national welfare reform that can be drawn from evaluations of state waivers. First, waivers were not randomly assigned to states. For example, Blank (2002) notes evidence that waiver requests may have been more common among states with high unemployment rates (perhaps because states attempted to use welfare reform to curb welfare expenditure growth), but federal welfare reform was implemented in a strong expansion. Limitations of waiver evaluations for causal inference and especially inference about effects of TANF include

(1) waivers often involved multiple components that are not all well measured, making it difficult to determine the specific component of reform responsible for estimated effects; (2) possible "contamination" of control groups due to awareness of treatment, including a general understanding that the welfare system may become time limited or require work (Blank, 2002:29); (3) waiver states may not be representative (waivers were more common in Northern and Midwestern states); and (4) welfare reform may have affected behaviors related to entry, but such effects are generally not subject to experimental impact evaluation.

A second approach to evaluating welfare reform is leaver studies, which describe the economic and social status of welfare families that exited welfare in the years following welfare reform. Although these studies do not provide direct estimates of the effects of welfare reform (because many welfare leavers would have exited welfare even in the absence of reform), they provide useful descriptive information on the well-being of recent welfare recipients. Problems with leaver studies include (Blank, 2002): low response rates, loss to follow-up, issues in the quality of administrative matching, lack of comparability across states, and lack of ability to study entry effects or other effects of welfare reform on those not on welfare.

The third approach to the evaluation of TANF welfare reform uses econometric analyses of state panel data. A causal interpretation of estimates of effects of welfare reform or its components from such statistical analyses requires accurately specified state welfare policies and controls for characteristics relevant to the outcome that might be correlated with welfare reform or the specific reform measures taken. A key problem with econometric evaluations of welfare reform is insufficient variation in the timing of TANF implementation needed for identification of its effects, independent of other national policy and macroeconomic trends. As noted, it is also difficult to specify accurately state welfare policies. As a result of insufficient variation in the timing of implementation of TANF across states and widespread use of waivers prior to TANF, econometric models may be most appropriate for evaluation of the overall effect of policies benefiting low-income households in the 1990s, rather than effects of TANF specifically (Blank, 2002).

Research Findings

Welfare Use/Caseload Decline

The main concern of this literature has been to separate effects of the economy from those of welfare reform in explaining the dramatic (over 50 percent) decline in the welfare caseload in the 1990s, most dramatically in the second half. This literature has relied on cross-state time-series econo-metric analysis almost exclusively. The typical study regresses monthly state caseload on state unemployment rate and a measure of welfare re-form, such as implementation of a statewide welfare reform waiver. Such estimates have attributed 26 to 35 percent of the decline prior to 1996 and 8 to 10 percent of the decline between 1996-1998 to the economy, leading to the conclusion that the economy is an important contributor to but cannot explain the majority of caseload movement in 1990s, particularly after 1996 (Blank, 2002). The impact of policy is gauged by the inclusion of an indicator variable that "switches on" in the month or year when reform is implemented. Evidence from such studies suggests that an early statewide waiver accounted for 13 to 31 percent of the caseload decline in the first half of the 1990s. Effects on welfare use appear strongest among the least educated. Few studies have looked at TANF implementation but those that do find that its effects on the caseload are larger than the effects of early waivers (Blank, 2002). Results of TANF studies tend to be sensi-tive to the inclusion of year fixed effects, which is not surprising since TANF was implemented in all states within a year of passage of the 1996 legislation.

Criticisms of econometric studies of the caseload include that they focus on aggregate policy changes, not specific components of policy; that it remains very difficult to separate the effects of policy and the economy, especially in the case of TANF; and that these have been less useful in measuring additional impacts of related nonwelfare policy changes because national policies that take place in a given year (such as expansion of the EITC or increases in the federal minimum wage) are highly correlated with year effects. The impact of some related policy changes, such as those related to child support, child care, and health insurance, have rarely been accounted for in econometric studies of the caseload decline (Blank, 2002).[3]

Some studies have attempted to identify the specific policy components most responsible for the caseload decline. The welfare reform components most commonly investigated are time limits, family caps (which eliminate increases in benefits associated with additional births to families on wel-fare), the benefit reduction rate/earnings disregards, age-of-child work ex-emptions, timing of work requirements, and various sanctions (Blank, 2002). Although studies of components build credibility for causal infer-ence, only a limited set are measured. The most robust evidence of an effect of an individual component is time limits (Grogger, 2000, 2001). Grogger

---

[3]Exceptions are Huang et al. (2002a), who examine the effects of child support reforms on welfare caseloads, and Huang et al. (2002b), who find that stricter child support enforcement increases welfare exit rates and decreases entry rates.

(2001) reports that time limits account for about one-eighth of the decline in welfare use and about 7 percent of the large rise in employment of female household heads between 1993 and 1999, but they have little effect on earnings or income. Grogger (2001) also found a substantial effect of EITC expansions on labor supply and earnings.

Labor Force Participation

Implications of TANF, and the caseload decline in particular, for family work policies are most clearly related to induced changes in work behavior. Leaver studies find that approximately two-thirds of single mothers who have left welfare during the welfare reform period are employed at some future date (Cancian et al., 2002). The range of estimates of employment among leavers is wide: 50 to 90 percent. This wide range is due to to differences across studies in the period of follow-up, in the period of employment considered, and so forth. Studies typically find that about two-thirds of leavers are employed following exits from welfare; that they work about 30 hours per week on average; that their employment is fairly steady for about half of those leaving due to employment; and that their earnings, although low, grow with labor market experience at a rate comparable to the rate of other women (Cancian et al., 1999; Loeb and Corcoran, 2001; Brauner and Loprest, 1999). Wages of welfare leavers after 1996 typically average between $6.50 and $8.50 per hour (Loprest, 2001).

The insights shared by a former welfare recipient illustrate the positive impact of work (Edin and Lein, 1997:140):

> I'm . . . happier now. . . . [When I was on welfare] I was kind of upset because I had nothing to do. . . . [J]ust thinking about the bad times . . . of all the problems. . . . [N]ow that I'm working . . . I feel good.

As noted, leaver studies do not produce estimates of the effect of welfare reform on work behaviors. However, evidence from econometric studies supports some impact of welfare reform. Studies that control for state unemployment and income changes find that welfare waivers are associated with increased employment of single mothers, but they have not made clear whether or how much TANF contributed to the very substantial increase in employment of single mothers after 1995.[4]

---

[4]In contrast, Blank notes that there is "unambiguous agreement that EITC increased labor force participation among single parents" and concludes that "the lack of studies that effec-

Forming appropriate comparison groups for statistical analysis is problematic. Effects of welfare reform and related policy changes on employment have been estimated by comparing changes in employment of single mothers with and without children (Meyer and Rosenbaum, 2001; Kaushal and Kaestner, 2001), single mothers with older and younger children (Grogger, 2000), or single mothers with low and high levels of education (Schoeni and Blank, 2000; Kaushal and Kaestner, 2001). However, such characteristics as marital status, education level, and presence of young children are potentially influenced by welfare reform and therefore do not sharply delineate treatment and comparison populations.

The causes of employment increase and caseload decline are disputed. Some employment increase is attributed to the EITC expansion (Meyer and Rosenbaum, 2001). Economic expansion is also important but employment (and caseload) changes in the 1990s are unlikely to be due to the economic recovery alone, because caseload reduction and the employment response of single mothers are much greater in the 1990s than the earlier 1980 recovery. Reviews of this literature generally conclude that welfare reform played a role (Blank, 2002; Moffitt, 2002).

Evidence from welfare-to-work experimental evaluations indicates significant positive effects of such policies on labor market participation, although estimated impact sizes vary (see the discussion below).

Income and Poverty

The impact of welfare reform on income, poverty, and other measures of well-being has been studied less frequently than effects on the welfare caseload and employment. Clearly, it is more difficult to measure disposable income and poverty than employment and welfare participation. Particularly problematic has been the measurement of tax payments and transfer income, out-of-pocket work expenses, and access to income or in-kind assistance from family and household members and persons outside the household (e.g., child support or child care from a nonresident father). As noted, the aggregate data suggest increases in income and decreases in poverty for single mothers and their children over the 1990s.

Leaver studies most often find that half or more of welfare leavers remain poor.[5] The implication of these findings for understanding the

---

tively include both welfare reforms and EITC changes makes it difficult to talk about the comparative impact of these two policy changes" (Blank, 2002:53). Blank also notes that there are few studies of the impact of welfare reform child care provisions on employment.

[5] Blank (2002) cites the following results. Loprest (2001): 48 percent of welfare leavers are poor; Danziger et al. (2002): 50 percent are poor (annual income) two years after leaving; Moffitt and Roff (2000): 74 percent of leavers in three selected cities are poor; Cancian et al.

> Jasmine, a 35-year-old divorcee and mother of two children, describes how she manages with "odd jobs" (Seecombe, 1999:146-147):
>
> *I may have some extras, like my telephone, or cable bill, or something like that, but living in these days and time, children need those things. We need a phone for emergencies . . . To tell you the truth, I've been working little odd jobs on the side, like cleaning somebody's house or something like that to make ends meet. Also, there's a neighbor around the corner, and I've been taking him up to the grocery store, and I make money that way. . . . You just have to do that to survive.*

effects of welfare reform is unclear. On one hand, they clearly show that leaving welfare does not necessarily mean leaving poverty. On the other hand, the poverty rate of welfare recipients is near 100 percent when they receive welfare, and in many states only families with incomes far below the poverty line qualify for assistance. Therefore, it is possible that welfare reform could have improved the economic status of recipients even if it did not result in a reduction in the poverty rate among former or would-be recipients.[6]

Regression analysis of state panel data has also been used to study the effect of welfare reform on income and poverty. Moffitt (1999) found small effects of waivers on total income of single mothers; Grogger (2001) found that both waivers and TANF increased the income of single mothers; Schoeni and Blank (2000) found that waivers reduced poverty 2.4 points among less skilled women; and TANF reduced poverty 2 to 2.2 percentage points.

Experimental Evaluations of Specific Policy Choices

Experimental evaluations of specific policy components support the results of the general studies of welfare reform. Studies of welfare-to-work waiver programs of the 1980s and early 1990s (Gueron and Pauly, 1991; Friedlander and Burtless, 1995; Bloom and Michalopoulos, 2001; Michalopoulos and Schwartz, 2001) find significant increases in employ-

---

(2002): 55 percent are poor in the year following exit, and 42 percent are poor five years later; Loprest (2001): leavers in 1997-1999 fared better than leavers in 1995-1997.

[6]Danizger et al. (2002) estimate that monthly net income increases $2.63 for each additional hour of work effort associated with an exit from welfare to work.

ment and reductions in welfare usage and payments. Earnings increased approximately $200 to $600 per year. These studies found similar earnings increases for more and less advantaged single mothers. And, perhaps surprisingly (with the exception of those at high risk of depression), labor market effects among those with barriers to employment, such as child care problems, did not seem significantly worse, although these studies generally did not estimate the cumulative effects of multiple barriers.

Expectations (e.g., Pavetti, 1997) were that a large fraction of the caseload had multiple employment barriers and would have great difficulty finding steady employment. However, a study of employment barriers (Danziger et al., 2000c; Danziger, 2001) among recipients of welfare in Michigan after a nearly 50 percent decline in the caseload found that although many had multiple barriers, the majority were nonetheless employed half time or more at follow-up. Multiple barriers were associated with lower employment rates, but only with a very high number of barriers was employment substantially below 40 percent; only those with six or more barriers to employment (who made up 5 percent of the Michigan caseload) had very low employment rates (more than 20 percent).

Earnings Supplements

Other interventions tested the effects of earnings disregards and financial incentives to work, some of which were combined with work requirements. Studies of this type include those of Minnesota Family Investment Program (MFIP) (Miller et al., 2000; Gennetian and Miller, 2000), New York State's Child Assistance Program (NYCAP) (DeMarco and Mills, 2000), Milwaukee's New Hope (Bos et al., 1999), Vermont's Welfare Restructuring Project (WRP) (Bloom et al., 1998), and Canada's Self Sufficiency Project (SSP) (Michalopoulos et al., 2000). The MFIP and SSP interventions tested the effects of combined disregards and services by randomly assigning some recipients to receive neither, one, or both work requirement and financial incentives (Blank, 2002, summarizes these results; see also Blank et al., 2000).

For example, employment increased by 3.6 percent for MFIP recipients who were assigned to receive financial incentives only. In general, MFIP increased income and reduced poverty rates; earnings decreased slightly, but supplements resulted in increased income. MFIP did not reduce the cost or the use of public assistance, but shifted aid from nonworkers to workers. In reviewing the MFIP evaluation, Blank (2002:67) concluded that in "MFIP: employment effects depended on mandatory employment, anti-poverty effects depended on high earnings disregards."

Canada's SSP, which "required" 30 hours of work in order to be eligible to participate (although participation was voluntary) and included large earnings supplements, increased employment 7.2 percent relative to controls and reduced poverty rates by 9 percent. The Connecticut and Vermont programs also combined earnings disregards and strong work requirements. Both had strong earnings and employment gains but limited income gains. Many interventions also showed that gains in recipient income exceed $1 per $1 of government expenditure.

Some have concluded that financial incentives are among the most important welfare reform components. However, more evidence on this point is needed. The evidence most supportive of this inference comes from programs implemented in Minnesota and Canada, which may not be representative of U.S. states. More generally, the program designs were not randomly assigned to states, even if within states recipients are randomly assigned to different treatments or control groups. Interactions between the treatment and state characteristics may limit generalization to other settings with different populations or different economic or policy environments. As noted, welfare reform was intended to allow states to tailor programs specific to their economic, policy, and social environments as well as to their population's needs. In the absence of studies that jointly model states' policy choices and the interactions between state-specific characteristics and program outcomes, extrapolation of results to other settings is not justified.

Time Limits

Few recipients hit TANF time limits prior to 2001, so the direct effects of exhausting eligibility for federal assistance are not known. However, six states had early limits (Arizona, Connecticut, Delaware, Florida, Indiana, and Virginia). Studies of these states find no evidence for large effects of time limits on employment, although there is some evidence that recipients leave welfare faster to preserve their eligibility for assistance (Blank, 2002).

Marriage and Fertility

Changes to make welfare less generous reduced incentives for nonmarital birth. Aggregate trends, however, do not support a strong effect of the 1996 welfare reforms on marriage or fertility. Marriage and divorce rates continued a downward trend in the 1990s. Births to unmarried women stopped increasing and may have fallen in the 1990s, but these developments appeared to begin before major welfare reform was enacted. There is evidence of a decline in the proportion of children living with a single mother and an increase in the proporation of children living with married parents in the late 1990s; this trend is particularly noticeable among non-Hispanic black children (Dupree and Primus, 2001; Primus, 2002).

Causal analyses of the effects of TANF on fertility and marriage have been limited. The extensive literature on the effects of AFDC on marriage and fertility suggest small effects on these behaviors (Moffitt, in press; National Research Council, 1998). However, it is unclear whether the results of studies of the AFDC program apply to TANF reforms because the latter represent much larger changes in the incentives for nonmarital child-bearing and include additional provisions targeted to reducing nonmarital fertility.

Finally, experimental evaluations of welfare reform have found little effect on marriage and fertility, with one notable exception. The MFIP evaluation reported positive effects on marriage of welfare reform with financial incentives to support employment (Miller et al., 2000).

Conclusion

In the 1990s, welfare receipt declined and labor force participation increased markedly among single mothers. Even among single mothers with a child under 1 year of age, rates of labor force participation increased by nearly 10 percentage points in the five years following the passage of federal welfare reform (from 49 to 58 percent). Poverty rates for children fell dramatically in the late 1990s, especially in families headed by a single mother. The precise causal contribution of welfare reform to these developments is uncertain and is likely to be debated for many years. However, implications of these changes for family work policy may not depend importantly on causes. Whatever the cause, the fact remains that many more single mothers with young children are employed (Bureau of Labor Statistics, 2002), and, relative to the average worker, these employees have little work experience, low levels of education, and few economic resources.

EFFECTS ON THE WELL-BEING OF PARENTS, CHILDREN, AND ADOLESCENTS

Processes Through Which Welfare Policies Might Affect Children and Adolescents

Has the current wave of welfare reform affected child and adolescent cognitive or socioemotional development? If so, how? Many of the difficulties in inferring causality discussed in this report also apply to considering developmental effects of welfare policy changes (Blank, in press; Blau, 2003). For example, there are no experimental data demonstrating effects of different policy approaches, after 1996, on children. Of the three kinds of studies that have been conducted to estimate causal effects of PRWORA (leaver studies, econometric studies of state policy contexts, and random assignment studies of waiver and other programs prior to 1996), only one kind (the experiments) have collected data on child development. Thus the review here is limited primarily to those experiments, with some additional findings from nonexperimental studies that collected data on children both before and after 1996.

Theories from developmental research and policy analysis have been brought to bear on the question of how welfare reform might affect children (Chase-Lansdale et al., 2001; Duncan and Brooks-Gunn, 2000; Huston, 2002; Johnson and Gais, 2001; Moore, 2001; Yoshikawa and Hsueh, 2001; Zaslow et al., 1995). These theories converge on five main mechanisms: changes in employment, family resources, family processes, family structure, and child care.

As the parent behavior most directly targeted in the current legislation, increases in employment are most often cited as mediators of welfare policy effects on children. Longitudinal research on employment and development among low-income families, although largely nonexperimental, has shown small but consistent associations between increases in employment and better child school and cognitive outcomes (see Chapter 4 and Zaslow and Emig, 1997, for a review). There is other new evidence that shows no significant associations with mother's welfare and employment transitions for preschoolers or adolescents and, in fact, some evidence that mothers working may be related to improvements in adolescent mental health (Chase-Lansdale et al., 2003). However, these effects may vary by developmental period: recent evidence from national studies suggests that full-time maternal employment in a child's first year of life may be associated with decrements in cognitive abilities in middle childhood among non-Hispanic white families (Waldfogel et al., 2002; Brooks-Gunn et al., 2002). Few studies have examined the question of employment effects among adolescents, but these data suggest overall that variation in employment brought about by welfare reform approaches may have detectable, although generally small, effects on children, and that such effects may depend on age and gender.

Family resources, as potential mediators of the effects of welfare reform on children's development, have most frequently been measured as family income in developmental studies. Evidence from national studies, dating from the 1980s and 1990s, has shown that income poverty has negative effects on cognitive and socioemotional outcomes, particularly when experienced chronically or in early childhood (Brooks-Gunn and Duncan, 1997; Duncan and Brooks-Gunn, 1997). These data suggest that approaches to welfare reform that result in decreases in family income and other resources may harm children and that approaches resulting in increases may benefit children.

Family processes, such as parenting behaviors, family routines, and

Jervis keeps coming back to the power of character, to the dignity that real work bestows on people (Newman, 1999:254):

What people do about going to work or going on welfare depends on two things: their self-esteem and what's giving them the greatest benefit. Your self-esteem will definitely make you want to work. But at the same time, the welfare's giving you the greater benefit in dealing with your bills.

parent mental health, may be affected by increases in employment or changes in resources. Several hypotheses have been put forth regarding how such processes may be affected by welfare reform. Most of these have been hypothesized about welfare recipients making transitions to work. First, increases in employment brought about by TANF policies may result in higher levels of stress and family instability, due to the juggling of frequently shifting child care and work schedules and the pressures of low-wage employment. Second, increases in employment with regular hours may result in more regular family routines in the home. Third, engaging in employment may result in changes in self-concept, or self-esteem, or in improvements in mental health. Countervailing effects of these mechanisms, when considered in combination, may occur (London et al., 2001).

Family structure is targeted in the language of the 1996 legislation indicating that "marriage is the foundation of a successful society." The balance of the evidence indicates that TANF did not bring about large changes in rates of marriage. Some nonexperimental evidence suggests small associations between TANF implementation and subsequent changes in rates of marriage, but in opposite directions (Bitler et al., 2002; Schoeni and Blank, 2000). These data are subject to the cautions about causality described earlier. There are no clear overall patterns in the experimental evaluations. In the Minnesota Family Investment Program, one of the state waiver programs that provided a generous earnings disregard coupled with a work mandate, mothers in the experimental group who were single at the outset of the evaluation were more likely to be married three years later than their control-group peers; two-parent families in the experimental group stayed married at a higher rate than those in the control group (Gennetian and Miller, 2000; Knox et al., 2000). However, in an experimental evaluation of the Iowa waiver program, which also included a relatively generous earnings disregard together with an employment mandate, a reduction in the proportion married occurred among new applicants who were single at the time of random assignment (Fraker et al., 2002; the follow-up spanned from 2.5 to 6 years). Other experimental programs have shown some scattered effects, often in particular subgroups of the welfare caseload (Blank, in press).

Another dimension of family structure that may have been affected by the 1996 legislation is the birth of additional children; the law allowed states to institute family caps, which deny additional benefits upon the birth of subsequent children. A study taking advantage of variations in the timing of implementation of family cap policies across the states, however, found no evidence of an effect of these policies on fertility rates (Kearney, 2002).

Increases in employment have been associated with greater need for child care in many nonexperimental studies conducted both before and after passage of the 1996 legislation (Brady-Smith et al., 2001; Danziger et al., 2000a; Zaslow et al., 1998). The child care literature indicates, in turn, that type, stability, and quality of child care may affect cognitive and behavioral outcomes among children in poverty, and more specifically among children of parents on welfare (Blau, 2001; Helburn, 1995; NICHD Early Child Care Research Network, 2000b, 2001c; Phillips et al., 1994; Vandell and Wolfe, 2000; Yoshikawa, 1999). It is likely, therefore, that one mechanism through which welfare reform may affect children is through variation in type, stability, or quality of care.

Evidence of Effects

Which of these hypotheses are supported in the emerging data on effects of welfare policies on children and adolescents? No single study (or set of studies on the same data) has been able to test all of these rival hypotheses. Nonexperimental studies have begun to track the well-being of children and families across periods from just before 1996 through the end of the decade. In general, it appears that no strong trends have emerged, either negative or positive, in indicators of parent well-being or child development across the years just preceding and following the implementation of PRWORA (Cherlin and Fomby, 2002; Fuller and Kagan, 2002). For example, little change was found, before or after 1996, in rates of maternal depression, parent cognitive stimulation of young children, or developmental delays in children in one study of single mothers with very young children on welfare in California, Connecticut, and Florida (Fuller and Kagan, 2002). In one large study of welfare recipients in three cities, transitions from welfare to work, post-1996, appeared to have had few negative effects on children of preschool or young adolescent age. The one exception was that adolescents of mothers who entered the workforce reported small but significant declines in levels of psychological distress, particularly anxiety, across a period of 16 months (Chase-Lansdale et al., 2003). Thus far it has not been possible to draw causal conclusions about effects of welfare reform from such trend data (i.e., that it was in fact the implementation of the 1996 legislation that caused these trends), due to difficulties capturing relevant policy variation, difficulties defining a consistent counterfactual condition, and lack of variation in timing of TANF implementation (Blank, in press).

Experimental evidence provides preliminary support for the hypothesis that policies that raise parent income may benefit children in the primary grades. In a series of experiments conducted in the 1990s, a range of approaches to welfare policy drawn from responses to the Family Support Act of 1988 and the state waiver programs of the mid-1990s were tested, with random assignment of families to these policy approaches or to the existing state AFDC policy regimes. Although none of these experiments directly tested TANF programs post-1996, many incorporated aspects of policies that have become widespread in TANF programs, such as earnings disregards, mandated involvement in employment-related activities, or time limits. Data on adult economic outcomes, child school performance, parenting and family processes, and behavior problems were collected across follow-up periods of two to five years. The programs were divided into groups that represented three overall approaches to welfare and employment policy: (1) four earnings supplement programs, which either provided cash supplements contingent on full-time work or generous earnings disregards; (2) six mandatory employment programs, which mandated employment-related activities but did not include earnings supplements; and (3) two time-limit programs, which incorporated time limits on welfare receipt.

In middle childhood (ages 6 to 12), a pattern emerged of consistent (though small) positive impacts for children in the earnings supplement programs. In these programs, experimental group members not only worked more than their control group counterparts, but also received more income overall, as a result of take-up of earnings supplements (income was measured as the combination of welfare, earnings, food stamps, any earnings supplements, and state and federal earned income tax credits) (Bos et al., 1999; Huston et al., 2001; Gennetian and Miller, 2000; Morris and Michalopoulos, 2000). Moreover, in contrast to two programs that called for time limits and six programs that mandated employment or education without earnings supplements, the earnings supplement programs brought about significant (though small) increases in school achievement and reductions in externalizing (acting out) behavior problems among children in the early primary grades (Morris et al., 2001a). School achievement was measured in these studies through a mix of parent reports, teacher reports, and standardized measures; problem behavior was measured through a mix of parent and teacher reports. It was pointed out earlier that the programs that increased both employment and income consistently were associated with improvements in these middle childhood outcomes.

A rival hypothesis is that other features of the larger policy contexts of these programs may have accounted for these effects, rather than the earnings supplement approach. The Minnesota program's experimental design allowed for the testing of earnings supplements with and without mandated employment as separate experimental conditions, in addition to a control group, subject to then-existing AFDC rules. The research design enabled a test of the rival hypothesis that it was mandated employment that accounted for positive effects on children. Data from that program show that the positive effects on children were essentially of the same size in the earnings-disregard-only condition, suggesting that it may have been that element, rather than any added effect of mandated employment activities, that brought about the positive effects. In addition, one follow-up study on the Minnesota program investigated whether it was the rise in employment or in income brought about by an earnings supplement program that was more strongly associated with the improvements in outcomes for children. This study examined the rival hypotheses in the Minnesota Family Investment Program evaluation, using the two experimental conditions to conduct an instrumental variables analysis teasing apart the influence of the two mediators. The researchers found that parent income appeared to more strongly mediate the effects of MFIP on child school performance than employment (Morris and Gennetian, 2001).

Among the other hypotheses regarding mediators of welfare policy effects on children, data exist on employment, family processes, and child care. Although data on employment as a mediator of welfare policy effects is lacking (aside from the one study on MFIP just described), several ethnographic studies have examined experiences of welfare recipients as they made transitions to work after 1996. This qualitative evidence indicates that, for many welfare recipients, increased family stress has accompanied increased employment. Specifically, parents report worries stemming from spending less time with children, as well as worries about child care, following transitions to increased employment (Lowe and Weisner, 2002; Scott et al., 2001). This pattern extends to parents who experience rises in income following increased work; some of these parents find that as their earnings rise, they lose eligibility for federal programs and other supports for low-income parents (Lein et al., 2002; Scott et al., 2001). Some parents have also reported that they do feel better about themselves following transitions to increased work effort, citing benefits in terms of increased respect from children (London et al., 2001). The ethnographic work finds that parents typically use a blend of center-based, relative, and nonrelative home-based care. In studies of one experimental intervention that offered child care supplements (Gibson and Weisner, 2002; Lowe and Weisner, 2002), parents selectively took up child care supplements depending on beliefs about appropriate parenting, fears of "stranger care," child ages, ease of access to child care services, and interference with existing child care arrangements with kin or partners. Also, if child care supports are tied to work and work is episodic and unpredictable, then child care arrangements change too often for some parents (three times over 18 months on average in the New Hope earnings supplement program, for example; Lowe and Weisner, in press).

In general, no consistent impacts have emerged across welfare policy experiments on survey (self- or child report) measures of parenting, across such dimensions as monitoring, supervision, cognitive stimulation, control, or warmth (Bloom et al., 2000, 2002; Gennetian and Miller, 2000; Kisker et al., 1998; Morris and Michalopoulos, 2000; Quint et al., 1997). Very few of these studies assessed in-depth observational measures of parenting. One study that did was the New Chance demonstration, an intervention focused on human capital providing education, training, parenting, health and life skills classes, and child care to adolescents mothers on welfare and without a high school diploma. In a three-year post-program follow-up, researchers found small positive impacts of the program on measures of affective quality of mother-child interaction and cognitive stimulation in the home (Zaslow and Eldred, 1998). Another study examined observational measures of parenting in the Teenage Parent Demonstration, a human capital intervention for teenage mothers that provided relatively fewer support services than New Chance. No impacts on parenting were found (Aber et al., 1995). An analysis combining data from the 1977 to 1996 Current Population Surveys with state-level data on cases of child maltreatment, using a state-level, fixed-effects model, found that state welfare benefit levels were negatively related to rates of neglect cases (Paxson and Waldfogel, in press). More recently, Paxon and Waldfogel have analyzed the effects of welfare policies and welfare reforms on measures of child maltreatement over the period 1990 to 1998. The strongest evidence that welfare policies and welfare reforms matter comes from their results on the number of children in out-of-home care, which is negatively and significantly related to the level of welfare benefits and positively and significantly related to such welfare reforms as family caps, short lifetime limits, immediate work requirements, and tough sanctions for noncompliance (Paxson and Waldfogel, in press).

A surprising set of emerging findings on family process effects of welfare policies concerns mothers' reports of domestic violence. Among the experimental evaluations of welfare policies that measured this outcome, five of nine programs have found evidence of significant decreases in reports of domestic violence at follow-up periods from three to five years (the Minnesota Family Investment Program and four of six programs in the National Evaluation of Welfare-to-Work Strategies [NEWWS]; the other four programs showed no change, or nonsignificant decreases; Gennetian and Miller, 2000; Hamilton et al., 2001). It is not clear what mediating processes may explain these impacts on domestic abuse, although a set of nonexperimental analyses from the NEWWS evaluation suggests the roles of increases in employment and program caseworker attention to support services (Hamilton et al., 2001). However, another experimental waiver evaluation, in Iowa, testing a generous earnings disregard coupled with an employment mandate, was found to increase mothers' reports of domestic abuse (Fraker et al., 2002).

A meta-analytic synthesis of experimental welfare policy effects on child care use, across 13 experiments, suggests that policies that increase employment also increase use of all types of out-of-home care, including center-based care and home-based care (Crosby et al., 2001; Gennetian et al., 2001). Welfare and employment policies that included elements aimed specifically at increasing the use of child care, through subsidies, vouchers, or services to help locate and obtain child care, increased the use of center-based care more than other types of care. Interestingly, this was true regardless of whether these child care assistance approaches supported center-based care over other kinds of care. These programs that provided child care assistance also, as intended, reduced out-of-pocket expenses for child care, increased use of child care subsidies, and reduced reports of child care as a barrier to employment (Gennetian et al., 2002a). A separate analysis of effects on Head Start use revealed that welfare and employment policies did not increase or decrease use of Head Start, on average (Chang et al., 2002). However, for the subgroup of adolescent and young mothers (under age 25), a parallel meta-analytic study indicated that these policies did significantly decrease Head Start use, by an average of 7 percentage points (Gassman-Pines, 2002). This may be because Head Start remains, in the majority of sites, a part-day program and thus may not meet the needs of low-income parents who work full-time, nonstandard hours, or shifting work schedules.

Data have begun to emerge concerning subgroups differentially affected by welfare policies. Subgroups for whom data are available include those defined by developmental period (early childhood, middle childhood, adolescence), risk (particularly risk for being hard to employ and health risks), gender, and race/ethnicity.

Impacts in the policy experiments fielded in the 1990s on early childhood and adolescent outcomes differed from those found in middle childhood. In early childhood, small samples of very young children in the experiments reduced the number of program impacts available for analysis. In addition, almost no programs were available that had sufficient numbers of infants in the first year of life. Among the available programs, no experimental effects were found, either positive or negative, among children younger than age 5 at follow-up (Morris et al., 2001a). In adolescents, in contrast, a negative average effect on adolescent school performance (as rated by parents) was found across 10 experiments, as well as average increases in parent-reported grade repetition (12 experiments) and use of special education services (15 experiments). These findings were calculated using standard meta-analytic techniques across the available experiments; actual effect sizes ranged from zero to moderate and a very few large negative effects. However, no overall effects were found on rates of parent-reported dropout, suspensions, or high school completion (Gennetian et al., 2002b). The pattern of negative effects did not pertain to any particular kind of policy approach (time limit programs, earnings supplement programs, or those that mandated employment without earnings supplements) but occurred across all of them. In examining a range of hypothesized mechanisms that might account for these effects (including intensity of parent employment, parenting measures, or parent resources), the only clear pattern pertained to adolescents with younger siblings. For these adolescents, larger unfavorable effects on parent-reported school performance and receipt of special education occurred, as well as some not found in the full sample: increases in dropout, suspensions, and expulsions. These adolescents were also more likely to care for younger siblings, a responsibility that may have helped bring about the unfavorable pattern of impacts (Brooks et al., 2001). Ethnographic evidence from a study in four cities tracking urban welfare recipients, post-1996, has also suggested that sibling caregiving may be particularly harmful for adolescents in families affected by welfare reform (Gennetian et al., 2002b; Morris et al., 2001a).

Among other subgroups, concern has emerged about the effects of welfare reform on the hard-to-employ, that is, those parents who are least work-ready and may have the greatest difficulties in making transitions to work from welfare and advancing in low-wage job markets (Danziger et al., 2000a,b; Kalil et al., 2001). Evidence from the earnings supplement programs described above suggests that the positive impacts of these programs on middle childhood school performance and behavioral outcomes do not extend to children of the hardest to employ (Yoshikawa et al., in press). For the two U.S. earnings supplement programs, positive impacts on children were concentrated among the moderately hard-to-employ, with the very hardest to employ 25 percent of the samples experiencing neutral and negative effects (increases in behavior problems), despite equivalent and large increases in both employment and income. The unfavorable impacts on developmental outcomes among the children of the hardest to employ were accompanied by increases in maternal depression, decrements in the regularity of family routines, and smaller increases in center-based care, relative to the less at-risk other 75 percent of these samples.

Although little research has used reliable measures of child health status to examine how welfare policies affect children's health, some data exist on the experiences of welfare reform among families with existing health problems. Both survey and ethnographic research, post-1996, has found that families with health risks, whether of the parent or the child, appear to experience more difficulty responding to the work mandates of TANF programs (London et al., in press; Romero et al., 2002). In many families (40 percent in one three-city ethnographic study), both primary caregivers and at least one of the children have been rated to be in poor health (Burton et al., 2002). Bernheimer et al. (in press) found that mothers with children with significant disabilities or other child problems (in school achievement or problem behaviors) in the New Hope program—a circumstance characterizing perhaps 15 percent of families—struggled with work and child care.

Other studies have examined how subgroups defined by gender may be affected differently by welfare policies. The synthesis of primary grade outcomes of welfare policy experiments did not find consistent gender differences in school performance or behavior problems (Morris et al., 2001b). In the synthesis of impacts among adolescents, there was one notable difference in effects among boys and girls: across the welfare programs, there was no significant average effect on grade repetition among female adolescents, but there was a significant increase in grade repetition among the male adolescents (a significant difference in average impacts; Gennetian et al., 2002b). Research on other important subgroups, such as different racial and ethnic groups, families with children with disabilities, and immigrant families, is in process, with few studies completed as of this date (Rosman et al., 2002).

SUMMARY

Evidence to date on how welfare policies affect children and adolescents is relatively strong for some of the policies that immediately predated PRWORA. Certain elements of these policies are well represented in TANF programs, post-1996 (earnings disregards and other earnings supplements; mandated employment activities without earnings supplements; time limits). However, the need is urgent to obtain experimental evidence on impacts of welfare policies in current policy contexts. Given that caveat, several messages emerge from the data. Policies that increase the incomes of low-income parents, through earnings disregards or supplements, were more likely to be associated with improvements in children's school performance and reductions in their behavior problems in middle childhood than those that simply mandated employment. However, welfare policies, whether of the mandated employment or earnings supplement types, appeared to coexist with small but consistent decrements in parents' perceptions of adolescents' school performance. Policies that increased employment also increased use of out-of-home care, but increases in center-based care (the type of care associated most consistently with positive effects on low-income children) were brought about only by those policies that incorporate services or subsidies to increase child care use.

Part III

Supports for Working Families

Part III reviews the public supports currently available in the United States to families with working parents. Chapter 8 considers the public policies, including leave policies, tax policies, and education programs, available to working families and the implications of these policies for child and adolescent well-being. Chapter 9 summarizes the committee's findings and conclusions, as well as some policy options that are warranted, in the committee's view, by these trends and research evidence.

Policies to Support Working Families

his chapter reviews existing support policies available in the United States to families with working parents. The primary focus is on public policies—specifically leave policies, tax policies, education programs, and programs to assist families in paying for child care. For each major policy area, the support provided and the families who benefit from it are described. We conclude by briefly considering the implications of the current patterns of support for child and adolescent development and public policy. There is some evidence that family support policies have also been integrated into employment policies of private-sector companies (Galinsky et al., 1992; Galinsky and Friedmand, 1993). Only limited data are available on these employer policies and how well they meet the needs of children in working families. The data that do exist suggest that access to corporate policies and benefits is uneven, with lower-income workers less likely to have coverage (see Table 8-1). However, overall, the data are limited and do not provide a comprehensive understanding of who these policies affect and the extent to which they support the well-being of children in working families. The material presented here and the committee's findings and conclusions are therefore focused on public policies.

LEAVE POLICIES

Leave policies give working parents the right to take time off from work without the risk of losing their jobs. Evidence presented in Chapter 4

TABLE 8-1 Access to Corporate Work Place Policies by Employees with Children Under Age Six

Employee Group	Sample Size *	Percentage of Employees with Access to the Policy					
		Family Health Insurance (%)	Paid Vacation Days (%)	Paid Holidays (%)	Paid Leave for Sick Children (%)	Traditional Flextime (%)	Daily Flextime (%)
All parents with children under age six	513-536	86	85	84	49	44	26
Gender							
Mothers	228-231	78	78	80	N/A	39	20
Fathers	303-306	89	89	88	N/A	48	31
Work Status							
Part-time	69-72	57	57	63	34	N/A	N/A
Full-time	450-462	89	89	87	51	N/A	N/A
Marital Status							
Single	77-79	73	58	71	37	N/A	N/A
Married/partnered	443-456	86	89	86	51	N/A	N/A
Hourly Earnings							
≤$7.70	115-122	66	69	67	37	42	18
$7.71 to $19.25	247-254	87	88	87	48	35	19
≥$19.25	124-126	95	91	93	61	61	44
Family Income							
<$28,000 per year	109-116	69	78	74	36	31	13
$28,000 to $71,500	280-293	86	86	85	48	41	22
≥$71,600	106-120	93	88	93	66	62	47

*Sample sizes vary due to missing data on specific values. This sample includes employed mothers and fathers with children under age six from a randomly selected national sample of 3,552 employed men and women ages 18 and older. N/A indicates not available.

SOURCE: Galinsky and Bond (2000).

shows that very young children may be particularly affected by maternal employment, and, for newborns, outcomes for mothers and children are better when mothers are able to take more than 12 weeks of leave. Outcomes for children may be better when mothers are able to return to work part time or to delay returning to work full time until after the first year. There are many types of leave—vacation leave, personal leave, sick leave, leave for jury service, leave for bereavement, and so on. Here we consider family leave and medical leave—the major types of leave that working parents may need to take to care for their children and adolescents.

Family Leave

Family leave includes several types of leave that families use to care for children and adolescents, including most commonly maternity leave but also paternity leave, leave to care for a sick child or adolescent, or leave to arrange care for a child. In the area of family leave, as with other types of leave, the United States historically has not had many public policies; rather, leave policies have mainly been left to the discretion of employers. The United States had no national maternity leave legislation until the passage of the Family and Medical Leave Act (FMLA) in 1993.

Prior to 1993, the United States did have some state family leave laws, which provided the right to a job-protected leave for maternity and paternity to some mothers and fathers in some states. These state laws vary by their effective date, the type and size of firms covered, the number of weeks of leave provided, and the job tenure and working hours requirements that employees must satisfy in order to be eligible for coverage (Han and Waldfogel, 2002).

There is also a handful of states that have temporary disability insurance laws providing the right to a paid temporary leave for disability, including disability associated with maternity. In these states, employers are reimbursed for a share of the costs of providing a paid leave for maternity during the period of medically certified disability (usually 6 weeks, 8 weeks if delivery was by Caesarean section). Since 1978, with the passage of the Pregnancy Disability Act, the federal government has mandated that disability programs such as these must cover maternity like any other form of disability, but the act does not require firms or states to have disability programs in the first place.

Prior to the passage of the FMLA, as a result of the limited number and scope of state laws, many employed women had no right to job-protected maternity leave, and coverage levels were particularly low among part-time employees and those working for small firms (see Table 8-2). The share of men with paternity leave coverage was even lower, and it was lowest among those working part time or in small firms.

TABLE 8-2   Percentage of Private-Sector Employees with Family Leave
Coverage, 1991 to 1997

	1991	1993	1995	1997
A. *Full-time employees, medium-sized and large establishments*				
Maternity leave coverage:				
Percentage with unpaid leave	37	60	84	93
Percentage with paid leave	2	3	2	2
Total percentage with any leave	39	63	86	95
Paternity leave coverage:				
Percentage with unpaid leave	26	53	84	93
Percentage with paid leave	1	1	2	2
Total percentage with any leave	27	54	86	95
B. *Part-time employees, medium-sized and large establishments*				
Maternity leave coverage:				
Percentage with unpaid leave	19	36	42	54
Percentage with paid leave	1	1	0	0
Total percentage with any leave	20	37	42	54
Paternity leave coverage:				
Percentage with unpaid leave	14	32	42	54
Percentage with paid leave	0	1	0	0
Total percentage with any leave	14	33	42	54
C. *Full-time employees, small establishments*				
Maternity leave coverage:				
Percentage with unpaid leave	17	18	47	48
Percentage with paid leave	2	2	2	2
Percentage with any leave	19	20	49	50
Paternity leave coverage:				
Percentage with unpaid leave	8	8	47	48
Percentage with paid leave	0	1	2	2
Percentage with any leave	8	9	49	50

SOURCE: Bureau of Labor Statistics Employee Benefits Surveys (now called the National Compensation Surveys), various years, available from http://www.bls.gov/ebs/. The surveys define medium-sized and large establishments as those with 100 or more employees and small firms as those with fewer than 100 employees. Starting in 1994, figures are for family leave coverage rather than maternity or paternity leave.

The passage of the FMLA in 1993 led to dramatic increases in both maternity and paternity leave coverage (see Tables 8-2 and 8-3). By 1997, nearly all full-time employees in medium and large firms had the right to a job-protected family leave, that is, leave for maternity, paternity, or to care for a newborn or newly adopted or placed child. However, because the FMLA covers only those who work in firms with 50 or more employees and who have worked 1,250 hours or more in the past 12 months, coverage rates among part-time employees and employees in small firms are much lower.

TABLE 8-3   Percentage of Public-Sector Employees with Family Leave Coverage, 1990 to 1998

	1990	1992	1994	1998
A. Full-time employees				
Maternity leave coverage:				
Percentage with unpaid leave	51	59	93	95
Percentage with paid leave	1	1	4	4
Total percentage with any leave	52	60	97	99
Paternity leave coverage:				
Percentage with unpaid leave	33	44	93	95
Percentage with paid leave	1	1	4	4
Total percentage with any leave	34	45	97	99
B. Part-time employees				
Maternity leave coverage:				
Percentage with unpaid leave	28	32	62	56
Percentage with paid leave	1	1	1	1
Total percentage with any leave	29	33	63	57
Paternity leave coverage:				
Percentage with unpaid leave	18	24	62	56
Percentage with paid leave	1	1	1	1
Total percentage with any leave	19	25	63	57

SOURCE: Bureau of Labor Statistics Employee Benefits Surveys (now called the National Compensation Surveys), various years, available from http://www.bls.gov/ebs/. Starting in 1994, figures are for family leave coverage rather than maternity or paternity leave. Data for 1996 not available.

Overall, the FMLA covers only about 60 percent of private-sector employees, and only about 45 percent are both covered and eligible; about a quarter of those covered are not eligible due to short working hours or short job tenures (Commission on Family and Medical Leave, 1996; Cantor et al., 2001). Among all employees (public sector and private sector combined), the law covers about 75 percent, and just over 60 percent are both covered and eligible (Cantor et al., 2001). Coverage and eligibility rates vary a good deal by demographic characteristics, as shown in Table 8-4. Employees who are young (ages 18-24), have less than a high school education, or have low annual family income (less than $20,000) are much less likely to be covered and eligible than other employees.

In addition to not providing universal coverage, the FMLA is limited in that it provides for only 12 weeks of leave, which is unpaid. In contrast, other countries provide longer periods of coverage and generally provide at least some wage replacement during the leave (see Table 8-5).

Studies have found that women who have leave coverage are more likely to take a leave, and take longer leaves, but are also more likely to

TABLE 8-4 Family and Medical Leave Act Coverage by Demographic
Characteristics, 2000

| | Percentage of Employees in Each Demographic Category Who Are: | | |
	Covered	Covered and Eligible[a]	Noncovered
Gender*			
Male	74.9	62.3	25.1
Female	78.5	61.2	21.5
Age**+++			
18-24	83.3	43.8	16.7
25-34	77.3	63.0	22.7
35-49	76.7	66.8	23.3
50-64	74.0	66.7	26.0
65 and over	58.7	42.8	41.3
Race/ethnicity**+			
White non-Hispanic	73.5	59.7	26.5
Black non-Hispanic	93.3	71.8	6.7
Hispanic	80.2	66.2	19.8
Asian	92.0	73.4	—
All others	79.8	60.3	20.2
Marital status***++			
Married/living with partner	74.3	63.8	25.7
Separated/divorced/widowed	79.3	64.3	20.7
Never married	82.6	54.1	17.4
Children under 18 in household			
None	78.2	60.9	21.8
One or more	74.8	63.2	25.2
Education***++			
Less than high school	63.8	44.2	36.2
High school graduate	72.1	57.1	27.9
Some college	79.4	62.2	20.6
College graduate	77.1	65.3	22.9
Graduate school	88.0	73.8	12.0
Annual family income++			
Less than $20,000	71.8	38.6	28.2
$20,000 to less than $30,000	78.8	64.5	21.2
$30,000 to less than $50,000	77.9	63.9	22.1
$50,000 to less than $75,000	79.7	70.2	20.3
$75,000 to less than $100,000	81.1	70.9	18.9
$100,000 or more	81.4	74.0	18.6

TABLE 8-4   Continued

| | Percentage of Employees in Each Demographic Category Who Are: | | |
	Covered	Covered and Eligible[a]	Noncovered
Compensation type**++			
Salaried	78.7	70.8	21.3
Hourly	80.6	60.5	19.4
Other	52.1	37.7	47.9

[a]The "Covered and Eligible" column is a subset of the "Covered" column.

*Difference between covered and noncovered employees is statistically significant at p < 0.10.

**Difference between covered and noncovered employees is statistically significant at p < 0.05.

+Difference between covered and eligible employees and all other employees is statistically significant at p < 0.10.

++Difference between covered and eligible employees and all other employees is statistically significant at p < 0.05.

Column percentages may not total to 100% due to rounding.

SOURCE: Cantor et al. (2001:Table A2-3.4).

return to work for their prebirth employer, than women who lack coverage (Glass and Riley, 1998; Han and Waldfogel, 2002; Hofferth, 1996; Joesch, 1997; Klerman et al., 1998a, 1998b; Ondrich et al., 1996, 1998; Ross, 1998; Waldfogel, 1999b). Studies have also found that the lack of paid leave is a barrier to women's taking leave, or taking as much leave as they feel they need (Cantor et al., 2001; Waldfogel, 2001c).

Given that leave coverage is limited, unpaid, and of short duration, it is perhaps not surprising that mothers in America return to work much more quickly after birth than mothers in other comparable countries. A third of new mothers in the United States return to work within 3 months of giving birth, compared with only about 5 percent in Britain, Germany, and Sweden; half of new mothers in the United States are back at work within 4 to 6 months, compared with 15 months in Sweden, over 24 months in Germany, and over 36 months in Britain (Gustafsson et al., 1996; Klerman et al., 1990, 1994, 1999; Smith and Bachu, 1999;).

Data from the National Longitudinal Survey of Youth indicate that maternity leave coverage and usage vary somewhat by demographic characteristics of the family (Berger and Waldfogel, in press). Women with less than a high school education, for instance, are less likely than other new mothers to have the right to a job-protected maternity leave, less likely to

TABLE 8-5 Childbirth-Related Leave Policies in the United States and 10 Comparable Countries

Country	Type of Leave	Total Months	Payment
United States	12 weeks family leave	2.8	Unpaid
Canada	17 weeks maternity leave 35 weeks parental leave	12.0*	15 wks @ 55% pay 55% prior earnings
United Kingdom	18 weeks maternity leave 13 weeks parental leave	7.2	90% pay for 6 weeks, flat rate for 12 weeks if sufficient work history; if not, flat rate for 18 wks Unpaid
Denmark	28 weeks maternity leave 1 year parental leave	18.5	60% prior earnings 90% unemployment benefit rate
Finland	18 weeks maternity leave 26 weeks parental leave Childrearing leave until child is 3	36.0	70% prior earnings 70% prior earnings Flat rate
Norway	52 weeks parental leave 2 years childrearing leave	36.0	80% of prior earnings Flat rate
Sweden	18 months parental leave	18.0	12 months @ 80% pay, 3 months flat rate, 3 unpaid
Austria	16 weeks maternity leave 2 years parental leave	27.7	100% prior earnings 18 months @ unemployment, 6 unpaid
France	16 weeks maternity leave Parental leave until child is 3	36.0	100% prior earnings Unpaid for 1 child; flat rate (income-tested)
Germany	14 weeks maternity leave 3 years parental leave	39.2	100% prior earnings 2 years flat rate, 3rd unpaid
Italy	5 months maternity leave 6 months parental leave	11.0	80% prior earnings 30% prior earnings

*Canada extended its period of childbirth-related leave to 12 months in 2002.

SOURCE: Waldfogel (2001b).

A 29-year-old mother of two children describes the type of flexibility that would be needed to deal with family health problems (Harris and Lengyel, 2002:24):

Holding a job was very hard for two reasons. It was my weight and the other was my son's disability. I would often need days off for my son's doctor's appointments or even weeks if he was hospitalized. I knew there wasn't an employer on earth that would be that flexible or understanding. So needless to say, I lost a lot of jobs.

take any paid maternity leave, and more likely to return to work in the first six weeks after the birth. Never-married mothers, too, are more likely than other mothers to return in the first six weeks following birth.

Surveys conducted post-FMLA have found that not all new parents who are covered by the FMLA take the 12 weeks to which they are entitled, while others take more than 12 weeks (presumably because their employer offers a more generous policy). The 2000 Westat Survey of Employees found that among those who took a maternity leave, the largest group (40 percent) took a leave that lasted between 6 and 12 weeks, but with substantial numbers taking a leave of less than 6 weeks (31 percent) or more than 12 weeks (29 percent) (Cantor et al., 2001).

Medical Leave

The FMLA also provides medical leave—leave that an employee can take because of her or his own serious illness or because of the serious illness of a family member, including a child. Coverage is limited to those meeting qualifying conditions, the leave is limited to only 12 weeks per year, and it is unpaid. Thus, although the FMLA has extended medical leave coverage to some workers who previously lacked coverage, it has not provided universal coverage, nor has it provided paid coverage. As of 1999, 47 percent of employees in the private sector did not have paid sick leave, and the rate of noncoverage was strongly associated with job characteristics, with 62 percent of blue-collar and service employees and 41 percent of clerical and sales employees lacking paid sick leave in contrast with only 19 percent of professional, technical, and related employees (Bureau of Labor Statistics, 2001). Previous research has found that parents who lack paid sick leave are less likely to stay home with a sick child than parents who have paid sick leave (Heymann, 2000).

TAX POLICIES

In this section, we consider the major tax policies that help families with working parents to cover child care expenses. These include the child and dependent care tax credit and the Dependent Care Assistance Program. We also discuss the earned income tax credit, which although not a child care policy, is a major tax policy that supports low-income working families. We also briefly discuss the child tax credit, an important policy for families with children.

Child and Dependent Care Tax Credit and Dependent Care Assistance Program

Some relief for child care expenses of working parents through the tax code has been available in the United States since 1954. In fact, until recently, the dependent care tax credit, now known as the child and dependent care tax credit (CDCTC), and the employer-provided Dependent Care Assistance Program (DCAP) together constituted two of the largest federal programs for helping families with child care expenses.[1] However, as discussed below, an important limitation of both these programs is that they have not reached many low-income families and have provided only limited support to the families they do reach.

Currently, families are eligible for the CDCTC if they have earned income and maintain a household for a dependent under the age of 13 or for a spouse or other dependent (regardless of age) who is mentally or physically unable to care for himself or herself. In order to qualify, at least one spouse must be working and the other must be working or attending school full time. Also, the child care expenses must be work-related.

As of 2003, the total amount of child care expenses that can be used for the CDCTC is $3,000 for one child or $6,000 for two or more children. Families can receive credit for up to 35 percent of their child care expenses up to these limits, with the percentage declining as family income increases to a base of 20 percent of child care expenses. The maximum credit is $1,050 for one child and $2,100 for two or more children (see Internal Revenue Service, 2002, for details). Thus, for families that spend more than $3,000 per child per year on child care, the maximum credit will cover a smaller share of their child care expenses. As indicated in Chapter 3, the

---

[1]Until the early 1990s, the federal government spent more on child care tax credits than on Head Start. Here we focus on the federal CDCTC and DCAP programs. There are also state-level programs in about half the states. Information about these is available from the National Women's Law Center (at www.nwlc.org).

average cost per week of care for a family that paid for care in 1999 was $76—or an average of $3,952 per year. This figure, however, represents the average, and some families spend more.

The CDCTC is not refundable (and is thus not available to families whose incomes are so low that they do not pay taxes). Total CDCTC expenditures for 1999 were $2.675 billion distributed to 6.2 million households, for an average benefit of about $430 per family (Campbell and Parisi, 2001). Largely because the tax credit is nonrefundable, it is regressive for low-income families (those earning less than $10,000 receive next to nothing). However, the tax credit is progressively distributed over most of the income distribution above the lowest income quintile (Gentry and Hagy, 1995). Data from 1997 indicate that about 10 percent of the credit went to families with adjusted gross annual incomes of less than $20,000, 42 percent went to families with incomes of between $20,000 and $50,000, and 48 percent went to families with incomes above $50,000 (U.S. House of Representatives, 2000).

DCAP rules work somewhat differently. Basically, DCAP is a program that allows employees to choose to reduce their pretax income by a sum of up to $5,000 and use that money to pay for child care expenses. Thus, a DCAP benefits employees who will owe taxes by making a portion of their income (up to $5,000) tax exempt—but it does not offer any benefits to employees who will not owe taxes. Employers are not required to offer a DCAP program, but if they do, they must provide it as a part of an employee benefit package available to all employees. Examples of qualified child care and dependent care expenses include payments to child care centers, work-related babysitting, domestic help, and nannies. Even grandparents, uncles, aunts, and adult children qualify as child care providers if they are not also dependents of the tax filer. Federal expenditures on DCAP totaled nearly $1 billion in 2000 (Blau, 2001).

The same child care dollar cannot be claimed for both the CDCTC and DCAP. Whether a family benefits more from one or the other depends on their income and marginal tax rates, but DCAP is used by fewer families because it is offered by a limited number of employers and because its benefit exceeds the CDCTC only for those in higher income brackets. As indicated above, neither program benefits families whose incomes are so low that they do not pay taxes.

Earned Income Tax Credit

The earned income tax credit (EITC) is a refundable tax credit for low-income working families. While not a child care policy, the EITC is a potentially important source of support for child care expenses for low-income families, particularly for those families whose incomes are so low that they do not pay taxes and thus cannot benefit from the CDCTC or DCAP.

The EITC has grown 300-fold since its inception in 1975. Changes in the program have occurred in three major periods. Through the Tax Reform Act of 1986, the EITC increased by over 50 percent starting in 1987 and became indexed to inflation. With the Omnibus Budget Reconciliation Act (OBRA) of 1990, the value of the EITC increased by over 50 percent (phased in over three years, beginning in 1991), an additional credit was established for families with two or more children, and the EITC was no longer counted as income for most federal means-tested programs. With the Omnibus Budget Reconciliation Act of 1993, the EITC increased by over 50 percent (phased in over three years, starting in 1994), and a small EITC was established for taxpayers without children and age 25 or older.

The total amount spent per year on the EITC was about $30 billion in 1999, of which about $26 billion was refundable (i.e., paid to individuals whose earnings were so low that they did not have to pay taxes). The average benefit was over $1,500 per family. A number of states have also implemented their own state EITCs, usually set as a percentage of the federal tax credit.

Researchers are beginning to study the extent to which families know about and use the EITC, and how knowledge and usage vary by family characteristics; see, for instance, Ross Phillips (2002b), who found that low-income Hispanic parents are less likely than other low-income parents to know about and use the EITC. However, research on the extent to which the EITC is used to cover child care costs is limited. One study (Smeeding et al., 2000) asked families how they spent the money and found that few reported spending it on child care; however, in this study, some child care spending may have been reported under the category of education.

Child Tax Credit

The child tax credit (CTC) was until recently a nonrefundable tax credit available to families with children. In 2001, legislation was passed doubling the value of the CTC over the next 10 years (from a maximum of $500 per child to a maximum of $1,000 per child) and making the CTC partially refundable. Analysts from the Brookings Institution (Sawhill and Thomas, 2001) estimate that the new refundable benefits will provide about $540 per year on average to low-income families. The recent changes will mainly benefit families with annual incomes between $10,000 and $35,000 (and, to a lesser extent, large families with incomes above $35,000). Like the EITC, the CTC is not tied to child care expenditures, and little is known about how families use the credit.

EDUCATION PROGRAMS

Public education is the biggest public support program for working parents, providing care for children ages 5 to 18 (and sometimes younger) for a substantial portion of the working day, even if not year-round. Nearly $300 billion was spent on public elementary and secondary education in 1999, serving about 47.2 million children (including kindergarten and some prekindergarten). Although there has been little research on the effect of public education on employment decisions, one study found large effects of the availability of kindergarten on the employment decisions of single mothers with 5-year-olds (Gelbach, 2002). It is important to note, however, that school schedules do not provide care during all the hours that parents work. Indeed, the mean number of hours that school-age children of employed parents are in care other than school is 21 hours per week (see Chapter 3, this volume).

The education programs discussed here include public schools and preschool and after-school education programs, which are supported through general funds and a number of other federal, state, and local funding streams. In the following sections, we consider the major education programs that provide support for preschool or after-school care for working families, including full-day public kindergarten programs, Head Start, Title I preschool funding, the Individuals with Disabilities Education Act, and 21st Century Community Learning Centers.

Full-Day Public Kindergarten

Public kindergarten provides significant child care services for working families (85 percent of kindergarten is public) (Jamieson et al., 2001). Until recently, most kindergarten was provided for only part of the day (or part of the week). Since 1965, the number of children in kindergarten has fluctuated in a narrow range around 4 million; however, the rate of children in full-day (full school day hours) and full-week kindergarten has increased from about 1 in 10 to more than 1 in 2 (59 percent) in 1999 (Jamieson et al., 2001). Still, there are broad differences state by state (and sometimes from city to city) in the amount of full-day services offered (Mitchell, 2001). Eight states and the District of Columbia mandate full-day kindergarten programming in their public schools (Galley, 2001), but most leave it to local discretion.

The primary impetus for the move to full-day kindergarten has been to improve educational outcomes for children, particularly those from disadvantaged family backgrounds. Children who attend schools that have high proportions of children in poverty are much more likely to have full-day kindergarten programs, as are children who attend large schools (Love et al., 1992). In addition, with more mothers working full time and more children entering kindergarten having already attended preschool full time, families have increasingly come to expect full-day kindergarten from their schools. There is some research to indicate that children who attended full-day (as opposed to part-day or part-week) programs had higher achievement at the end of the year and in first grade (Fusaro, 1997; Gullo et al., 1986; Gullo and Clements, 1984; Koopmans, 1991).

Public Prekindergarten

As the number of children attending some form of preschool before kindergarten has increased,[2] states have become increasingly involved in providing publicly funded prekindergarten programs. In the last decade alone, state funding for public prekindergarten has increased from $700 million (Adams and Sandfort, 1994) to about $1.9 billion in 1999 (Schulman et al., 1999; Mitchell et al., 1998; Education Week, 2001). A total of 39 states and the District of Columbia provide public prekindergarten for at least some 3- to 5-year-olds, up from 10 states in 1980; 21 states and the District of Columbia use state funding to serve additional children in Head Start (Education Week, 2001). However, state investments in prekindergarten vary considerably from state to state and there is a variation in the range in these services in terms of such things as who they serve, teacher training, class size, and curriculum In 1999, three-quarters of state funding of prekindergarten was concentrated in just 10 states, while 11 states spent no money on public prekindergarten or state Head Start (Schulman et al., 1999). There is only limited research to date on the characteristics of state-funded prekindergarten programs and their effects on child outcomes (Gilliam and Zigler, 2000; Ripple et al., 1999; Zigler and Styfco, 1993).

Head Start and Early Head Start

Started in 1965 as part of the war on poverty, Head Start's goals are broad: "to promote school readiness by enhancing the social and cognitive development of low-income children through the provision of health, educational, social, and other services" (Head Start Act of 1998 U.S.C. 9801, et seq 1998). Head Start is federally funded with a 20 percent local match.

---

[2]Since 1965, the number of 3- and 4-year-old children attending some form of preschool has increased from 520,000 to 4,578,000 in 1999. The share of those services that is public has increased from less than 25 to 50 percent (Jamieson et al., 2001). Furthermore, a significant portion (a little less than half in 1999) of those publicly funded preschool services are provided on a full-time basis.

Some states invest their own funds above the required match. Head Start children receive free services, which include early education, social, and health and nutrition services.

Targeted at low-income families with 3- and 4-year olds (and also expected to serve children with disabilities), Head Start served 905,000 children in fiscal year (FY) 2001 at a cost of over $6 billion. Of the children served in 2001, 54 percent were age 4 and 35 percent were age 3; 13 percent were children with disabilities (Administration for Children and Families, 2002). Head Start has increased more than fourfold since the mid-1980s, but it does not serve all eligible children. Currie (2001) found that Head Start served 50 percent of eligible 3- and 4-year-olds. This is a higher percentage of eligible children served than in the past, reflecting both program expansions and also reductions in the numbers of poor children eligible for the program. Starting in 1995, an Early Head Start initiative has served children under age 3. Early Head Start has expanded rapidly and now has projects in all 50 states (U.S. Department of Health and Human Services, 2002). Early Head Start served 62,000 infants and toddlers in FY 2002 (U.S. Department of Health and Human Services, 2002). However, this represents a small share of eligible children under the age of 3.

Although Head Start is mostly a part-day, part-year program for poor families—only one-quarter of Head Start children receive full-day, full-year services (U.S. Department of Health and Human Services, 2002)—and one that involves a high level of parent involvement, many Head Start parents work. In 1995 (the most recent year for which data are available), 28 percent of Head Start parents were employed full time and 17 percent part time (Smith, 2000); these percentages are probably substantially higher now given the large increase in single mothers' employment in the 1990s. In 1995, almost one-third of enrollees used Head Start exclusively, and 79 percent used Head Start as their primary child care provider. For those who used multiple providers, most used relative care, primarily from grandparents. Among users of nonrelative care, very few used day care centers or nursery schools (Smith, 2000). There have been several recent community-based initiatives to combine Head Start services with other child care services in the community, to better meet the needs of working families while providing high-quality services for children (see Schumacher et al., 2001b; Lombardi, 2003). Findings from the Early Head Start evaluation indicate that such collaborations can improve the quality of care (Administration for Children and Families, 2002).

In accordance with its mandate, Head Start serves families with low incomes. The majority (77 percent) have incomes below $15,000 per year. Nearly equal proportions are black (34 percent), white (30 percent), and Hispanic (30 percent); relatively few were American Indian or Asian. Reflecting the program's mandate to serve disabled children, 13 percent of

Head Start children had some form of disability (Administration for Children and Families, 2002).

In recent years, there has been continued debate over the effects of Head Start on child outcomes. While there is a good deal of evidence to show that model early childhood intervention programs yield high and sustained benefits (see, for instance, Barnett, 1996; Ramey et al., 1999; Schweinhart et al., 1993; see also recent reviews by Currie, 2001; Karoly et al., 1998), the evidence on Head Start has been mixed. An early study (Westinghouse, 1969) found that gains in cognitive development faded after a few years in public schools, but subsequent research has found some positive long-term effects (Currie and Thomas, 1995, 1999, 2000; Garces et al., 2000). Currently, debate continues over the extent of positive effects associated with Head Start (U.S. General Accounting Office, 1997, 1998, 2000a,b). In large part, this debate stems from the lack of a randomized evaluation of Head Start. The U.S. Department of Health and Human Services recently launched such an evaluation—the National Head Start Impact Study, which is now under way (U.S. Department of Health and Human Services, 2002).[3]

Unlike Head Start, Early Head Start was implemented with a random assignment evaluation that included 17 programs in diverse communities around the country. Results indicate that at age 2 and at age 3 (when the intervention ended) the children in the program performed significantly better than control children on a wide range of measures of cognitive, language, and social-emotional development; in addition, the parents scored significantly higher than the control group on measures of the home environment, parenting behavior, and knowledge of infant and toddler development (Early Head Start Research Consortium, 2001; Love et al., 2002). While many of the effects were small (with effect sizes in the 10 to 20 percent range), the overall pattern of results, with significant differences across many types of outcomes for both children and parents, is indicative of the effectiveness of the program. Moreover, several subgroups demonstrated larger effects. For example, larger impacts were found among families in programs that used a mixed approach (a combination of home-based and center-based), especially programs that were fully implemented; families who enrolled during pregnancy; and families with a moderate number of risk factors (Administration for Children and Families, 2002.)

---

[3]The Department of Health and Human Services is also conducting a large-scale observational study of Head Start, involving a nationally stratified random sample of 3,200 children and families in 40 Head Start programs. This study has found that Head Start narrows the gap between disadvantaged students and other children in key components of school readiness, with the largest gains for the children who had the lowest cognitive skills to start with (U.S. Department of Health and Human Services, 2001b).

Title I Preschool

Title I was enacted under the Elementary and Secondary Education Act (1965) as a part of the war on poverty, to help schools meet the needs of children economically and educationally disadvantaged. Historically, most children served by Title I have been between the ages of 5 and 18, but recently Title I has expanded to include younger children. Much of the rise in services for preschoolers follows changes in eligibility regulations instituted in 1994. (Prior to 1994, only schools with 75 percent or more of their students living in poverty could use their funds to improve the whole school. The 1994 reauthorization lowered the poverty eligibility threshold to 50 percent.)

During the 1999-2000 school year, 17 percent of school districts that received Title I funding spent money on preschool services (U.S. General Accounting Office, 2000a,b). In that year, $407 million in Title I funds (out of more than $8.4 billion) went to an estimated 313,000 preschool children, or about 8 percent of children who will eventually enter kindergarten. Title I funds a variety of services for preschoolers, including education, meals, medical, dental, and social services. In the largest districts, most children served are minorities (45 percent black, 39 percent Hispanic, 11 percent white, 3 percent Asian, and 1 percent American Indian). In smaller school districts, a larger percent of those served are white (35 percent) and fewer black (21 percent) (U.S. General Accounting Office, 2000b).

Individuals with Disabilities Education Act

In 1975, Congress determined that millions of American children with disabilities were not receiving an appropriate education: more than half of handicapped children did not receive services that would enable them to have full equality of educational opportunity. The Individuals with Disabilities Education Act of 1975 was enacted to remedy this by requiring that all students with disabilities receive free and appropriate public education.

As the importance of early education for children's outcomes has become clearer, Congress has expanded the Act's mission to more fully serve younger groups of children with disabilities. The Education of the Handicapped Act Amendments of 1986 established the Early Intervention Program for Infants and Toddlers with Disabilities (Part C). In 1998-1999, nearly 189,000 children from birth through age 2 were served under Part C. In addition, more than 573,000 3- through 5-year-olds with disabilities are served in preschool (U.S. Department of Education, 1999). Evaluations of the impacts of the Individuals with Disabilities Education Act on child and family functioning are now under way (see Rosman et al., 2002.)

21st Century Community Learning Centers

The federal government funds expanded academic enrichment for children attending low-performing schools through 21st Century Community Learning Centers (CCLC). The CCLC programs also provide youth development activities, drug and violence prevention programs, technology education, art, music and recreation, counseling, and other services. Thus, CCLC programs are a potentially important resource to meet the after-school needs of children with working parents.

The CCLC program started in 1995 as a demonstration project with $750,000 appropriated by Congress. The program increased to $200 million in 1999 and to $1 billion in 2002 (U.S. Department of Education, 2002). In 2002, about 6,800 rural and inner-city public schools in 1,420 communities were participating as CCLCs. Eligible entities include local educational agencies, community-based organizations, other public or private entities, and consortia of two or more of such agencies, organizations, or entities.

As of January 2002, the No Child Left Behind Act converted the CCLC authority to a state formula grant. Until then, the U.S. Department of Education made competitive awards directly to designated lead agencies. Under the reauthorized authority, funds will flow to states based on their share of Title I, Part A, funds. Current CCLC grantees will continue to be administered by and receive funding through the U.S. Department of Education. States will use their allocations to make competitive awards to eligible entities. States are required to make awards only to applicants that will primarily serve students who attend schools with concentrations of poor students. Also, states must give priority to projects that will target services to students who attend low-performing schools (U.S. Department of Education, 2002).

While the CCLC permits funding to be used in support of after-school programs for adolescents, most funded programs provide service to children between the ages of 6 and 14, and attendance in after-school programs is typically highest for children under the age of 12 (Grossman et al., 2002; Vandell and Shumow, 1999). While participation in school-based or community-based programs is typical for adolescents overall, low-income youth and those from traditionally defined minority groups have relative low rates of participation (see Chapter 6, this volume).

State and Locally Funded School and Community-Based After-School Activity Programs

School and community-based programs are an important source of after-school care for children of employed parents. Government funds provide partial support for some youth activities (e.g., the Boys and Girls Clubs of America), but the federal government does not provide a stable source of funds to support enrichment activities for adolescents. A recent report (National Research Council and Institute of Medicine, 2002) described the funding for youth programs as fragmented and heavily dependent on grants from foundations and private agencies. Some after-school programs are funded mainly by parent fees or from other funding sources (such as charitable foundations), while others receive at least some support from state or local funding. Such programs have rarely had their own public policies or dedicated funding streams, but in recent years states are becoming increasingly involved in the funding of after-school programs. According to the National Conference of State Legislatures, in 2000-2001, at least 20 states passed legislation pertaining to after-school policies, including some that created new funding streams for after-school programs (National Conference of State Legislatures, 2002).

After-school programs that are sponsored by individual states include California's After School Learning and Safe Neighborhoods Partnerships, which serve almost 30,000 children, and the Ohio School Age Child Care Project, which serves 2,500 children. Programs sponsored by local governments, school districts, and private foundations include The After-School Corporation (TASC) in New York City (White et al., 2001), LA's Best Program in Los Angeles, San Diego's 6 to 6 Extended Day Program, and the Extended Services Initiative that has been implemented in 17 cities (Grossman et al., 2002).

CHILD CARE FUNDING

In this section, we consider the major child care funding streams that provide financial support to families or child care providers to offset the costs of child care used by families with working parents. These include the Child Care Development Fund, the Social Services Block Grant, Temporary Assistance for Needy Families child care funding and transfers, the Child and Adult Care Food Program, the Summer Food Program, and state child care programs. Most of these funding streams go to the states, where they are combined with state funds and then distributed, mostly through vouchers (with the exception of nutrition programs, which provide support to providers).

Child Care Development Fund

In 1996, the federal system of support for child care was overhauled with the passage of the Personal Responsibility and Work Opportunity Reconciliation Act (PRWORA). The act combined three separate federal funding streams for child care for low-income families—the Child Care Development Block Grant, Title IV-A at-risk child care, and other Title IV-A funding, which included Aid to Families with Dependent Children, job opportunities and basic skills training (JOBS), and transitional child care—into a new block grant, the Child Care and Development Fund (CCDF).

Under the CCDF, low-income mothers on welfare are no longer guaranteed child care assistance, and states have considerable latitude in defining the rules for low-income families to get help with their child care costs. In order to be eligible, children must be under the age of 13[4] and must reside with a parent who is working or participating in education or training or is in need of protective services. Under federal rules, children must be living in a family with income of at most 85 percent of the state median, but (as discussed below) states can set the income cutoff at a lower level, and in fact most do. Total expenditures in FY 2000 were $9 billion, including funds transferred from the Temporary Assistance to Needy Families (TANF) program (Mezey et al., 2002) (see below for a description of TANF and how funds can be transferred for child care).

The CCDF consists of three separate funding streams, each with its own set of requirements. The discretionary fund, essentially the old Child Care Development Block Grant, is 100 percent federal with no state match required. Congress sets aside a portion of discretionary funds for specific uses: quality improvements ($171.5.6 million in 2003), infant and toddler care ($99.3 million in 2003), education, technical assistance, and research ($9.9 million in 2003) and child care resource and referral, school-age child care, and an information hotline ($19 million in 2003). The second stream, the mandatory fund, is a rough equivalent of pre-PRWORA federal Title IV-A spending in each state. These funds are also 100 percent federal with no state match requirement. The third stream, also a mandatory fund but requiring a state match, is based on historical pre-PRWORA expenditures. If states want matching funds, they must meet a maintenance of effort requirement and obligate all of their mandatory unmatched funds.

The CCDF subsidizes child care services for eligible families mostly through certificates (vouchers), but also through contracts with providers. (States choose the extent to which they pay providers through vouchers or contracts, but parents must be given the option of receiving a voucher.) Parents can select any legal child care provider, as defined by each state. Providers may include family or friends, legal unlicensed family providers, and licensed family child care or child care centers. Providers must meet

---

[4]The regulations allow states to spend CCDF funds on children ages 13 to 19 if they have a physical or mental disability or are under court supervision.

minimum health and safety requirements as defined by the state. Relative providers may be exempted from some of the minimum regulations.

As mentioned earlier, each state sets eligibility guidelines, including the income cutoff for families. Nationwide, most states have set income eligibility levels below the maximum level allowed under the CCDF (85 percent of the state median income). According to states' plans for FY 2002 and 2003, eight states established eligibility at the maximum level; the remainder set their cutoffs at a lower level (Gish and Harper, 2002).

Eligibility does not guarantee that a family is served. Despite having flexibility in defining eligibility, no state serves all its low-income children. According to a study by the U.S. Department of Health and Human Services (DHHS), only 10 to 15 percent of eligible families received any form of child care subsidy through the CCDF in 1999 (Administration for Children and Families, 1999, 2000), and the percentage varies considerably from state to state. About one-fifth of states are serving less than 10 percent of the children eligible for CCDF subsidies as defined by state eligibility criteria. Three-fifths are serving between 10 and 25 percent; and one-fifth are serving 25 percent or more (Administration for Children and Families, 1999).[5] More recent studies have found similarly low percentages of children served (see, for instance, Collins et al., 2000, who found that states could serve 15 to 20 percent of eligible families, and Mezey et al., 2002, who estimated using DHHS data that states are serving 14 percent of eligible children.)

There are various reasons why such a small share of eligible families is receiving child care subsidies through the CCDF. Lack of funding for eligible families is a fundamental issue. In some states, there are waiting lists for subsidies. In other states, however, there are either no waiting lists, or program officials report that they have sufficient funding to serve all the eligible families who have applied (U.S. General Accounting Office, 2001). This could be the result of a small applicant pool if states set eligibility levels very low. Or it may be that some families do not know that they are eligible, or they do not believe that the type of child care they would like to use would be covered. Many families report that they find the system of child care subsidies complex and difficult to navigate (Adams et al., 2002b). Lack of outreach and administrative barriers have also been noted (Adams et al., 2002b; Schumacher and Greenberg, 1999). Most importantly, the ability of a state to serve all eligible families who apply does not necessarily mean that all eligible families who want services are getting them, since

---

[5]A small number of states (for example, Illinois) have made a commitment to serve all eligible families; however, they accomplish this by limiting eligibility to only very low-income families (Waldfogel et al., 2001).

there is evidence that when new funds become available, more families apply (Adams and Rohacek, 2002).

States set the copayment rates (the amount that parents will pay), on a sliding scale basis, which must take into account income and family size and may consider other factors as well. This fee can be waived for families below the federal poverty line and for children in protective services cases. CCDF regulations require that copayments must be affordable so that parents have access to a broad array of providers. In the past, DHHS has suggested that copayments should not exceed 10 percent of family income (Schumacher et al., 2001b); however, copayments differ widely around the country, and not all states have met this recommended level.

States also have considerable flexibility in setting reimbursement rates, the amount that providers will be reimbursed for services. Under the CCDF, parents are to be given a full range of choices of care that is in accordance with state regulations, although state regulations (and practices) vary considerably. As mentioned earlier, subsidized care can be provided by formal providers or by relatives and friends—that is, "informal care." If reimbursement rates are set too low, some providers will not accept subsidized children. So states must provide some evidence that their reimbursement rates meet the intent of federal law to provide choice to subsidized families and to provide equal access to care. States must conduct a market rate survey not more than two years prior to the effective date of the state plan and must establish payment rates for providers. DHHS guidance instructs states that a market rate set at the 75th percentile of the price distribution for care in that state will be considered adequate to meet the equal access requirement; however, many states do not meet that level. For instance, in a recent review of state plans, only 25 percent of the 56 states and territories included in the sample set their payment rates at or above the 75th percentile (Gish and Harper, 2002). Some areas set statewide rates, but payment rates can vary by location, type of care, and age of children. The rate at which states set the rate ceiling affects how much of the provider's costs are covered by the state, which in turn affects how much subsidized child care is available to families (Adams and Snyder, 2003).

Usage data on the CCDF is sparse and inconsistent from state to state. According to Administration for Children and Families 1999 data, the reason for care for almost 85 percent of children served was parent's employment or a combination of employment and training or education. A small percentage of children received care either because their parent was in training or education (10 percent), in protective services (3 percent), or for some other reason (4 percent). By law, states are required to spend 70 percent of their mandated funds on families receiving, transitioning from, or at risk of becoming eligible for TANF assistance. According to CCDF plans for FY 2000 and 2001, more than half the states list TANF and

TANF-transitional families either first or second on their priority list of families who are eligible for receiving child care subsidies. Notwithstanding these priorities, a recent DHHS study that examined child care for low-income families in 25 communities nationwide found that, while states' funding policies favor TANF families over non-TANF families for receiving child care subsidies, children of non-TANF families represented the largest percentage of children receiving child care subsidies in most of the states that were examined (Abt Associates, 2000). The larger number of non-TANF families may reflect the fact that, as welfare caseloads have declined (due to both increased exits from welfare and decreased entries into welfare), child care subsidies have increasingly been taken up by families who are not on welfare.

In FY 2000, approximately 1.7 million children were served by the CCDF (Child Care Bureau, 2000). Of these, just under a third (27 percent) were infants and toddlers, a quarter (26 percent) were older preschoolers, and over a third (36 percent) were school age. Most children were in state licensed or regulated care (74 percent), and the rest were in legally operating but unregulated care (a little more than half of this latter group consists of relatives). Most CCDF-funded children are in centers (58 percent), and another 30 percent served in family child care.

As discussed in Chapter 3, there is also some information on families receiving subsidies in the Survey of Income and Program Participation (SIPP). According to the latest published report on the SIPP data from the U.S. Census Bureau (2002), reporting data for 1997, only a small share of all families using child care receive subsidies or other government help toward the costs of the child care. Little is known at this point about the effects of child care subsidies on children and families. A small number of studies was conducted prior to welfare reform (see, for instance, Berger and Black, 1992; Meyers et al., 2002a; reviews by Blau, 2000, 2001). However, given the dramatic change in child care policies enacted under PRWORA, research that predates welfare reform is of limited use in understanding the likely effects of today's subsidy regime. Blau and Tekin (2001) provide some early evidence on the effects of child care subsidies post-PRWORA, finding that child care subsidies are associated with higher levels of employment and school enrollment. Bainbridge et al. (in press) also provide some early evidence, examining the period 1991 to 1996, finding that subsidies directed at low-income working families had a substantial positive effect on boosting single mothers' employment over that period.

As discussed in Chapter 3, an important characteristic of child care is its quality. Although the CCDF does not specify or control the quality of care that children receive, three of its provisions can affect the quality of services purchased with CCDF funds: health and safety protections, the quality set-aside, and the payment rates.

First, with regard to health and safety, states must document that they have established health and safety requirements that providers serving CCDF-funded children must meet (although most relatives would be exempt from these). At a minimum, these health and safety requirements must address the prevention and control of infectious diseases, immunizations, building safety, and training for providers in the area of health and safety.

Second, according to the federal law, 4 percent of CCDF funds must be set aside for quality improvements. According to a U.S. General Accounting Office (2002) study (based on case studies of 5 states plus a survey of states to which 42 states replied), the majority of states reported spending more than the minimally required 4 percent. Of the funds that states spent on quality improvements, most (61 percent) came from CCDF and TANF, with about a third (29 percent) coming from state funds. In the 34 states that tracked the type of providers receiving the quality improvement funding, two-thirds of the expenditures went to child care centers, and less than a third to family child care or after-school programs. States spent their quality funds on a variety of improvements, including child care resource and referral services (20 percent of states), enhanced licensing inspections (14 percent), meeting state standards (13 percent), caregiver compensation (12 percent), off-site caregiver training (11 percent), incentives for accreditation (8 percent), on-site caregiver training (2 percent), and other activities (12 percent) (states could report spending in more than one area).[6]

Third, as discussed above, CCDF gives states a great deal of latitude to set payment rates. To the extent that higher quality care is more costly to provide, states can, through their payment rates for providers, affect the quality mix that is purchased with their CCDF funds. At the same time, to the extent that high copayments would discourage families from participating in the program or from using more expensive forms of care that might be of higher quality, states can also affect the quality mix through the rules they set for copayments. (Copayments may be set as a percentage of family income, in which case high copayments may discourage families from participating; copayments may also be set as a percentage of the cost of care, in which case high copayments may also discourage parents from using higher priced care).

---

[6]The extent to which these quality improvements are improving child outcomes is unclear. While many of the state initiatives are targeting reforms that have been found in other research to be associated with better child outcomes, the GAO study concluded that few of the state studies had sufficient evidence to draw conclusions about child outcomes. Therefore, the study recommended that DHHS include selected state quality improvement initiatives as part of a larger impact evaluation of state child care subsidy approaches (U.S. General Accounting Office, 2002).

Social Services Block Grant Child Care

Starting with Title XX in 1974 and continuing as the Social Services Block Grant of 1981 (SSBG), states have received federal funds to assist them in delivering social services for adults and children. States have discretion in how they use these funds within a broad set of guidelines, and many states have used a substantial portion to fund child care for low-income families.

In 1999, the total SSBG block grant was about $3 billion, of which at least $400 million (13 percent) was spent on child care services. The $3 billion total includes a TANF transfer of $1.17 billion (discussed below). Whether the SSBG should be considered a growing or diminishing source of child care funding is unclear. Data from 23 states in 1990 indicated that they spent 16 percent of their SSBG funds on child care (U.S. House of Representatives, Committee on Ways and Means, 1994). At the time, child care advocates raised concerns that states significantly reduced their SSBG funds for child care when federal funds under the Family Support Act and the Child Care and Development Block Grant began flowing. Certainly, current child care spending under the SSBG is not nearly as high as it was during the mid- to late 1970s, when over $700 million was spent annually on child care (U.S. Department of Health, Education, and Welfare, 1978). However, recent SSBG reports indicate that child care spending may be on the rise again since at least 1998, thanks largely to TANF transfers (U.S. Department of Health and Human Services, Administration for Children and Families, 1999, 2000a, 2001a).

Data on SSBG usage has always been sparse. No data are available on who uses services—their income, work status, race/ethnicity, or education. Neither is there research on the impact of SSBG expenditures on children and families.

TANF Child Care and Transfers

TANF has grown to become a significant source of child care funding. In 1999, $604 million of TANF money was spent directly on child care for families receiving welfare payments. These funds were subjected to all the TANF restrictions.

Under law, portions of TANF money can also be transferred to the CCDF or the SSBG, transfers that then have to be spent under CCDF or SSBG rules. In 1999, $2.43 billion was transferred from TANF to the CCDF, and $1.17 billion was transferred from TANF to the SSBG. In 2001, $1.88 billion was transferred to the CCDF, making TANF a very large source of child care funding. TANF transfers accounted for 27 percent of all CCDF child care subsidies in 1999. For the SSBG funds, it is not clear what percentage of the transfer went to child care services, but dollars transferred from TANF accounted for 38 percent of overall expenditures under SSBG in 1999.

TANF funding of child care is important (and perhaps a concern) for those who receive services in several important ways. First, if the child care is provided directly under TANF, the CCDF rules for regulation and quality do not necessarily apply. Second, even for transfers to the CCDF or the SSBG, availability of care may be jeopardized down the road as demands on TANF funding grow. Furthermore, uncertainty about future federal TANF funding levels can make it difficult to conduct long-run state child care policy planning (Schumacher et al., 2001a).

Child and Adult Care Food Program

The Child and Adult Care Food Program (CACFP) is an open-ended, federal subsidy for meals, snacks, and nutrition education in licensed child care centers (including Head Start), family and group day care homes. The program resembles the school meals program in being administered by the U.S. Department of Agriculture (USDA) and reimbursing meals according to a flat fee. In 1999, the program served about 2 million children at a cost of $1.4 billion (U.S. Department of Agriculture, 2002a).

The primary target of the program is children whose income falls below 185 percent of the federal poverty level. However, subsidies for meals served in qualifying family home day care settings are not conditioned by the income levels of the children's families. In contrast, full subsides are paid in child care centers only for meals served to children from families with incomes 130 percent or less of the poverty level, at reduced prices for those at 130-185 percent of the poverty level, and with the smallest subsidies paid for meals served to children whose families earn over 185 percent of the federal poverty line.

Comprehensive information about CACFP comes from a national sample survey conducted in 1995 (Glantz et al., 1997). Of the average daily 2.3 million children served meals in FY 1995, two-fifths were in family home day care, and the remainder were enrolled in Head Start or day care centers.

Summer Food Service Program

The Summer Food Service Program (SFSP) was created to ensure that children in lower-income areas could continue to receive nutritious meals when they do not have access to the National School Lunch or School Breakfast program. About 2 million children receive the free meals provided during the summer months, at a cost of $238 million in 1999. Approximately 14 percent of the children who receive reduced-price or free school lunches participate in the SFSP (U.S. Department of Agriculture, 2002b).

Program sponsors receive payments for serving meals and snacks to children and teenagers, 18 years and younger, at approved sites in low-income areas. Schools, public agencies, and private nonprofit organizations may apply to sponsor the program. Potential sponsors must demonstrate that meal sites will meet either geographic or enrollment criteria. A site is geographically eligible if it is located in an area in which 50 percent of the children qualify for a free or reduced-price school meal. A site is enrollment eligible if 50 percent of the children enrolled can be documented to qualify for a free or reduced-price school meal (family income up to 185 percent of poverty). In addition, anyone attending a school program for people with disabilities, regardless of age, may also participate. Meals are served free to anyone at a site.

State Funding for Child Care Programs

As noted above, the various federal child care programs give states a great deal of latitude on how they spend federal child care funds. Another important source of variation across states is state funding for child care programs. States choose not only how to spend federal dollars but also how much to invest in state dollars. The 1990s saw an expansion of state funding initiatives in this area (Meyers et al., 2002a; Adams and Rohacek, 2002). However, with contracting state budgets, these expansions may not continue. Indeed, several states are currently projecting that they will cut back their funding in this area (see, for example, Goodnough, 2003).

STATE CHILD CARE REGULATIONS AND MONITORING

Another important aspect of child care policy involves child care regulatory and monitoring activity by the states. States play a potentially important role in the child care arena by establishing regulations for child care settings and by monitoring the extent to which child care providers comply with those regulations. States vary a good deal in which settings are subject to state regulation and in the tightness of those regulations; states also vary a good deal in the intensity with which they monitor providers' compliance with those regulations (for useful discussions, see Blau, 2001; Gormley, 1999). It is also important to note that the goal of state licensing is to ensure basic health and safety protections, not to ensure quality. States vary in the level of these protections. For example, only two states regulate all the provider types, and many states monitor programs once a year or less (U.S. General Accounting Office, 2000a).

It is not clear how much impact this state regulatory and monitoring activity has on the child care market. There is some evidence that regulations do have an effect on the type and quality of child care that is offered. For instance, a recent study by the Early Child Care Research Network of the National Institute of Child Health and Human Development (2002c) found that regulations regarding staff training and staff-child ratios affect process quality in child care settings and ultimately child outcomes. However, there is also evidence that, in many settings, child care regulations are not binding (Blau, 2001). There is also widespread agreement that any consideration of the role of regulations must take monitoring activity into account, since regulations that are on the books but not enforced will have little impact (Gormley, 1995).

Recently, there has been increased interest in more nuanced monitoring systems that would allow states to differentiate between providers that just meet minimal standards and those that meet higher quality standards (Blau, 2001; Gormley, 2000). At the same time, however, concerns have been raised that tighter regulations will raise costs at the same time as quality and thus may price lower income families out of the child care market (see, for instance, Currie and Hotz, 2001) unless additional funds are forthcoming.

MILITARY CHILD CARE

In 1989 the Military Child Care Act was passed to address issues of quality, program oversight, affordability, and availability of child care for families in the military. The act increased the amount of appropriated funds and increased inspections, regulations, training, and pay for child care staff. In the ensuing decade, the U.S. Department of Defense put energy, skill, and resources into creating a high-quality employer-supported child care system. A comprehensive system of child care options was established, with key components to ensure accountability and oversight and mandates for accreditation, training and professional development, wage enhancements for staff, and parent involvement.

The Department of Defense is recognized today as a model for the nation in terms of its high-quality child care system. It has established over 800 child development centers for military personnel in over 300 locations worldwide, and 98 percent of these programs are accredited. Each day, the Department of Defense cares for over 200,000 children in centers, family child care homes, and school-age programs.

EUROPEAN POLICIES TO SUPPORT WORKING FAMILIES

While the policies from other countries may not be fully replicable in the United States, Europe's family and work policies provide a useful comparison of the extent to which working families are supported. Public policies in the United States provide less public support for the care of children than in other countries, relying more heavily on family members, nonpublic child care centers, and employers and less heavily on direct public provision. In the area of family leave, for instance, the United States mandates that certain employers provide leave, rather than publicly funding leave, as is the case in most European countries. In the area of child care policy, the United States supports child care mainly through subsidies to parents or private market providers, rather than through public or publicly subsidized child care programs.

A second point of difference is that programs in the United States tend to be more narrowly targeted to low-income families, rather than provided universally to all families with children. In the area of child care policy, for instance, the United States mainly targets assistance to the very lowest income families, but it does not reach all such families with its programs. Relying on family members, private child care providers, and employers may have advantages, particularly with regard to parental choice and flexibility, but it also creates challenges in terms of ensuring equality of access and the quality of supports provided. Targeting resources to the lowest income families also has advantages in terms of efficiency, but it creates challenges in terms of ensuring the quality of programs in which children are placed and ensuring equal access to high-quality care. These challenges are particularly acute in the areas of family leave and child care.

In the area of family leave, because small firms are generally exempted from leave legislation and because the laws typically provide only unpaid leave, the United States has a system in which some new mothers lack the right to a job-protected maternity leave, and many face the loss of a substantial portion of their income if they take a leave. Those who lack leave tend to be the most disadvantaged; less educated and low-income workers are significantly less likely to be covered by the FMLA than other workers (see Table 8-4). Perhaps as a result of the limited leaves available, new mothers in the United States return to work much more quickly than do new mothers in other countries. Such early returns may pose risks for child health and development, particularly if the mother works full time (Ruhm, 2000a; Waldfogel et al., 2002). Accordingly, many analysts in the United States have called for expanding maternity (and paternity) leave coverage, extending the duration of leave allowed, and making some provision for income replacement during leave (see, for

TABLE 8-6   Share of Children in Publicly Supported Child Care,
Selected Peer Countries

Country	Share of Children in Publicly Supported Care		Share of Costs Covered by Government	
	Children Ages 0-2	Children Ages 3-6	Children Ages 0-2	Children Ages 3-6
United States	5	54	25-30	25-30
CaN/Ada	5	53	N/A	N/A
Denmark	48	82	70-80	70-80
Finland	21	53	85	85
Norway	20	63	68	68
Sweden	33	72	82-87	82-87
Austria	3	80	N/A	N/A
France	23	99	72-77	100
Germany	2	78	N/A	N/A
Italy	6	91	N/A	N/A
United Kingdom	2	60	N/A	N/A

N/A= not available.

SOURCE: Waldfogel (2001a).

example, Kamerman, 2000; Waldfogel, 2001b). Analysts have also called for expanded family and medical leave (see, for instance, Asher and Lenhoff, 2001; Heymann, 2000) and for more opportunities for mothers of young children to return to work part time (National Research Council and Institute of Medicine, 2000; Brooks-Gunn, Han, and Waldfogel, 2002).

In the area of child care, the United States has a system in which parents must pay directly for most types of care and in which low-income families are not guaranteed assistance with the cost of care. Many European countries, in contrast, guarantee a public or publicly subsidized child care place for any child whose parent wishes one from the age of 3, and several countries are now lowering the age at which child care is guaranteed to 1 or 2. Table 8-6 presents rates of enrollment in publicly supported child care in various countries. Even in Britain, which has had a strong tradition of exclusive maternal care until school entry at age 5, public opinion has shifted in favor of preschool experience beginning at age 3, and the government has made a commitment to guarantee at least a part-time child care place to each 3- and 4-year-old whose parent wishes them to have one (Hills and Waldfogel, 2002). It is likely that these European countries provide more equitable care than the United States, where affluent families can purchase high-quality care for their children, some low-income families may be fortunate enough to gain a subsidized place in high-quality care, but children from other low-income and middle-income families tend to experience lower quality care (Phillips et al., 1994).

SUMMARY

The public sector has responded to the challenges faced by working families in caring for their children by providing greater resources for them. Many important new public programs for children and adolescents have developed in the past 25 to 30 years in response to the increasing movement of mothers into the labor force. There has also been an expansion of social welfare programs to cover such services as early childhood education and medical care for low-income children.

There is a growing recognition in the United States that early childhood care and education can confer advantages in terms of children's school readiness. Several groups have recently called for a move to universal prekindergarten (see, for instance, Committee on Economic Development, 2002).

However, many of these programs are still not specifically designed to enhance the cognitive, social, and behavioral development of children. Those that do are not available to all children and adolescents.

Furthermore, only 45 percent of parents working in the private sector have guaranteed unpaid parental leave through the FMLA. Less than 5 percent have access to paid parental leave. Many parents do not have the right to the more than 12 weeks of leave mandated by the FMLA.

Fundamentally, policies and programs for working families and their children often focus on only one half of this equation—the employment of the parent or the well being of the child—without taking into consideration the simultaneous and interactive needs of both. There is a need for both policies and research that consider the needs of both parents and the children and adolescents in working families.

Our review of the evidence on the role of public policies suggests two other priorities in the area of child care policy. One is the importance of guaranteeing funding for subsidies for low-income families with employed parents. The other is the need for efforts to raise the quality of child care that children in the United States experience, although analysts continue to debate the most effective means of doing so. In terms of research priorities, it is striking that for the majority of policies discussed in this chapter, very limited data are available on the effects on children. While this lack of data is being addressed in some areas with new evaluations under way, there clearly is a need for further data that would allow researchers to learn how the U.S. choice of public policies to support working families is affecting outcomes for their children.

9

Findings and Next Steps

his report describes employment trends and trends in the care of
children and adolescents in the United States, discusses implications of these trends for child and adolescent development, and
characterizes the availability of public supports for parents as they attempt
to balance family and work. This final chapter presents the findings, conclusions, and policy options that are warranted, in the committee's view, by
these trends and research evidence.

Our primary focus is the area of overlap among four spheres of
interest (illustrated in Figure 1-1): the work patterns and experiences
of working parents; (2) the developmental needs of children and adolescents; (3) the support available to families; and (4) the roles of
parents and caregivers. Our foremost priority is to understand the
implications of work on the well-being of children and adolescents in
working families.

We also reviewed information on the ways in which supports for families have been integrated into the employment policies of private-sector
companies. The data that exist suggest that access to corporate policies and
benefits is uneven, with lower-income workers less likely to be covered.
However, overall, we found that the scientific data in this area are limited
and do not provide a comprehensive understanding of who these policies
affect and the extent to which they support the well-being of children in
working families. Our findings and array of policy options are therefore
focused on public policies.

FINDINGS

Employment Trends

- **More children have employed parents.**

Among the many transformations that have occurred in the American family over the past 30 years, few are as dramatic as the increased rates of paid employment and the changing patterns of work among mothers with children. From 1970 to 2000, overall maternal labor force participation rates of mothers rose from 38 to 68 percent (while employment of fathers remained high and stable); for mothers with the youngest children, birth to age 3, this rate rose from 24 to 57 percent. This trend has held for mothers in a wide variety of circumstances—first-time mothers and never-married mothers, for example—and for all groups, regardless of family income, education, race and ethnicity, or place of residence. The result of this labor force change is that a larger fraction of children live in families in which all available parents are in the labor force—either they live with a single parent who is employed or they live with two parents, both of whom work at least some hours for pay each week.

These changes in maternal labor force participation are in part a result of the fact that programs that provide income support to low-income families with children have increasingly emphasized and required parental employment. This trend is particularly striking for low-income families with a single parent, in which 55.5 percent of low-income children resided in 2000. Aid to Families with Dependent Children (AFDC) was originally intended to provide cash assistance to low-income single mothers to allow them to remain at home and take care of their children. In 1997 AFDC was replaced with Temporary Assistance for Needy Families (TANF), a program that requires mothers to work or seek employment or training or both as a condition for receiving cash assistance. Under AFDC, mothers with a child under the age of one were exempt from work requirements. Under TANF, states may impose work requirements on mothers with newborns. In almost half of the states, the employment/training requirement extends to mothers with children under 1 year of age, and in some states, mothers with children 3 months old or younger are required to work.

- **Access to parental leave is limited.**

Only 45 percent of parents working in the private sector have guaranteed unpaid parental leave through the 1993 Family and Medical Leave Act (FMLA). According to data from recent employee benefit surveys, less than

5 percent have access to paid parental leave. Many parents do not have the right to more than the 12 weeks of leave mandated by the FMLA.

The United States currently has what is essentially a three-tier system of family leave. One group of employees works for firms that offer paid leave for family or medical reasons. Currently no national or state laws or policies require firms to offer paid family leave, although five states—California, Hawaii, New Jersey, New York, and Rhode Island—have temporary disability insurance programs that typically cover six to eight weeks of paid leave for maternity disability for qualifying workers. California has recently extended its program to cover individuals who take time off work to care for a new child (or to care for a sick or injured family member).

The second group of employees works for firms that offer 12 (or more) weeks of unpaid leave for family or medical reasons. Under the FMLA, firms that employ 50 or more workers must provide 12 weeks of unpaid job-protected leave for qualifying workers who need to take leave to care for a newborn or for other family or medical reasons specified in the law. Also, various state parental leave laws require certain firms to offer unpaid leave for new parents who meet qualifying conditions. And some firms not covered by the FMLA or comparable state laws voluntarily offer 12 (or more) weeks of unpaid leave.

The third group of employees has access to less than 12 weeks of unpaid family or medical leave. Over half (55 percent) of all private-sector workers do not qualify for leave under the FMLA because they do not work for large enough firms or because they have not worked the requisite number of hours in the previous year. Some of them have access to some period of unpaid leave for family or medical reasons, while others have no leave rights at all and could be fired if they took time off for family or medical reasons.

Child and Adolescent Care

• **Children and adolescents spend significant time in nonparental care.**

Children and adolescents are spending many hours in the care of someone other than their parents. Among the 12.2 million children ages 5 and younger with employed mothers in 1999, 80 percent were in a child care arrangement with someone other than a parent. These 9.8 million children cared for by someone other than a parent spent an average of 40 hours per week in child care. The 22 million children ages 6 to 14 with an employed mother spent an average of 22 hours per week in the care of someone other than their parents before and after school.

- Opportunities for care for adolescents are limited.

Opportunities are limited for school-age children and adolescents, particularly those from low-income families, to engage in meaningful and enriching activities during the nonschool hours. The existing range of after-school programs and activities does not serve many young persons. For example, it is estimated that as little as 20 percent of the potential demand for programs is met in urban areas.

Since the workdays of most parents often do not fully coincide with the schooldays of older children and adolescents, many adolescents—as many as 40 percent of 14-year-olds—care for themselves without adult supervision during nonschool hours. Furthermore, many after-school programs are not presently able to provide services during nonschool days (i.e., weekends, holidays, summertime) or for parents working nonstandard hours (e.g., in the early morning hours and evenings).

- Quality of care matters for children and adolescents.

Children

The quality of child care has implications for children's development, but the relation between participation in child care and children's development depends on such variables as the activities they experience in care, the quality of their interactions with their caregivers, the type of setting (i.e., day care center, family day care home, relative care), and the amount of time in care. Some evidence also suggests bigger effects of high-quality child care for the most disadvantaged children.

The best evidence of these effects comes from a set of studies in which samples of low-income children were randomly assigned either to a treatment group receiving high-quality child care and other social services or to a control group that did not receive any special services. Long-term follow-ups of the children revealed statistically significant and large effects of the treatment in reducing crime, welfare, teen childbearing, education, employment, and earnings. In nonexperimental studies that follow children over time, high-quality child care is associated with better developmental outcomes. Some evidence also suggests bigger effects of high-quality child care for the most disadvantaged children. It remains uncertain to what extent these are causal impacts; however, child care quality appears to remain a significant determinant of children's development.

Adolescents

The quality of care does not matter only in early childhood. The characteristics of care and activities for school age children and adolescents are also linked with developmental outcomes. For example, structured, supervised, and skill-focused activities for adolescents tend to show favorable outcomes, while unstructured programs may not only fail to offer benefits, they may also amplify existing problems or encourage the development of new problems. Rigorous evaluations of programs serving adolescents are quite limited; however, results from a few well-designed evaluations indicate that engagement in structured, adult-supervised after-school programs that focus on prevention of problem behaviors and enhancement of psychosocial competence may prevent onset of a variety of problems during adolescence and promote engagement in school and community and aspirations for the future.

- **Much child care is not of high quality or developmentally beneficial.**

There is a wide range in the quality of care that is available for young children in the United States, but the evidence indicates that much of the care in the United States is mediocre or worse, and children in lower-income families often receive lower quality care than children in higher income families. The best available data (from the National Institute of Child Health and Human Development's Study of Early Child Care) on a diverse sample of children of varying ages in different types of arrangements (centers, child care homes, in-home nannies, grandparents) observed that very poor quality and very high quality are relatively uncommon, with the mode being care that was categorized as "fair" and in which positive caregiving was "somewhat uncharacteristic."

Despite the growth in public supports, many publicly funded early care and education programs which are intended to provide developmentally beneficial nonparental care for young children, such as Head Start and Early Head Start, also do not reach all eligible children. Funding for the major existing child care programs is insufficient to allow services to be provided for all eligible children. For example, Head Start serves about 40 percent of eligible children ages 3 to 4 years, and the Child Care and Development Fund (CCDF) and TANF programs together serve about 15 percent of eligible children. Furthermore, Head Start eligibility rules require that 90 percent of children enrolled are from families with income below the poverty line, thereby excluding additional children in families with income above the poverty line who could benefit from Head Start.

Several public programs do provide significant funding for child care services for low-income families in the United States (i.e., CCDF, TANF, the Child Care and Adult Food Program, Head Start, Title I, and state prekindergarten programs); however, these programs do not ensure care that is both of high quality and meets the needs of working families.

The CCDF and TANF provide funding primarily in the form of subsidies distributed through vouchers that can be used to purchase child care services from any provider that meets state regulatory standards or is legally exempt from the standards. Regulatory standards are often not set to ensure that child care is of high developmental quality, and many caregivers are exempt from regulations. Thus, subsidies from these two programs can be used to purchase child care services of low or mediocre quality.

In contrast, Head Start, Title I, and state prekindergarten programs must meet standards intended to ensure that the services provided are of high developmental quality. These programs provide child care services as a byproduct of their main function, which is to enhance the development of children who are at risk of developmental delay as a result of low income. The parents of children enrolled in these programs are not required to work, and the services are often provided for only part of the day or part of the year. Hence, these programs are likely to provide services to children of high developmental quality, but they may not be compatible with full-time employment of their parents, unless additional child care services are available from other sources.

Implications of Work and Care Trends

In some circumstances, employment of both parents in a two-parent family or employment of the only resident parent in a single-parent family can be beneficial for children. Work can result in additional income, provide a positive role model for children, and expose children to stimulating and supportive care environments—if the child is being cared for in a quality setting—and, for adolescents, result in increased autonomy and responsibility.

If a consequence of employment is the use of poor-quality child care, lack of supervision of children and adolescents before and after school, or increased parental stress because of time demands or a stressful or low-paying job, then the implications for children and adolescents can be negative.

Some young children are particularly affected by maternal employment. For newborns, outcomes for mothers and children are better when mothers are able to take longer periods of leave. Outcomes for children may be better when mothers are able to return to work part time or to delay returning to work full time until after the first year. Workers who do not have any family or medical leave rights may be forced to choose between putting their job at risk by taking care of their children or putting their children at risk by staying on the job. Furthermore, some workers eligible only for unpaid leave either do not take as much time as they need or face financial hardship to do so. As a result, some employees who need leave for family reasons do not take leave or cut their leave short. Others take leave but then turn to public assistance, draw down their savings, or go into debt to make ends meet while they are on leave.

Adolescents whose parents work and who do not have an adult-supervised arrangement after school may experience social and academic problems as a result of time spent in self-care. Adolescents who spend large amounts of time in out-of-home self-care that features frequent and unstructured socialization with peers have the potential to develop antisocial behaviors and related adjustment problems. The quality of available after-school programs is also highly variable, and there is evidence that program quality is related to child academic performance and emotional well-being. The content of many after-school programs is limited, and many programs focus on providing a safe environment or providing academic assistance (homework time, tutoring, and preparation for mandated standardized tests) at the expense of promoting other aspects of the developing child, such as physical health and fitness, interpersonal competence, creativity, and motivation.

In summary, while data are not available to establish that the average well-being of children has declined, the situation of some children and adolescents is clearly not good. Many children are spending many hours in nonparental care, and much of it is of mediocre quality or worse. Evidence shows that high-quality out-of-home care has the potential to improve the social and cognitive skills of children and adolescents, but this quality of care is not available to all children and adolescents in working families.

Current Public Policy Response

The public sector has responded to the challenges facing working families in caring for their children by providing them with greater resources. Many important new public programs for children and adolescents have developed in the past 25 to 30 years, and social welfare programs to cover such services as early childhood education and medical care for low-income children have been expanded. However, many of these programs are still not specifically designed to enhance the cognitive, social, and behavioral development of children. Those that do are not available to all children and adolescents. Fundamentally, policies and programs for working families and their children often focus on only half of the equation—either the employment of the parent or the well-being of the child—without taking into consideration the simultaneous and interactive needs of both.

POLICY OPTIONS

A primary goal for public policy should be to improve the quality of care for children and adolescents in working families.

The committee identified *policy options* in the areas of child and adolescent care and family leave that could assist in meeting the goal of improving the care of children and adolescents. The committee also suggests further consideration of new research primarily intended to strengthen the empirical base on which future policies can rest. The committee is sensitive to the reality that additional funds will be required to improve care for children and that budgets are constrained and therefore, whenever possible, the committee developed rough cost estimates of these policy options, as well as some of the likely benefits. The information needed for a complete cost-benefit analysis of all of the policies discussed here is not available. The policy options presented have implications for state and federal decision making. The recent devolution of much public responsibility for child and family well-being from the federal government to the states presents opportunities to develop innovative strategies that respond to local employment and demographic conditions.

Child and Adolescent Care

In the committee's view, the key problem of working families with children and adolescents is a lack of care that both supports child and adolescent development and meets the needs of working parents.

The most plausible explanation for the low quality of care in the United States is lack of demand for better care due to its high cost and lack of awareness by parents of how to assess child care quality. One justification for public support of high-quality child care is its benefits to society beyond the benefits that accrue directly to children and their parents. A second justification is its potential to enhance equality of opportunity. Public support for high-quality care for poor children may be justified on the grounds that, even if benefits accrue only to the poor children who receive the better care, this society believes that these children should have opportunities enjoyed by others that would otherwise not be available to them. The evidence on the external benefits of high-quality child care is limited, but the evidence available (from evaluations of programs such as the Perry Preschool Project, Abecedarian, Early Head Start National Evaluation) indicates that substantial external benefits are achievable.

Increased funding for subsidies for low-income families is critical to sustain the employment and income gains made by low-income families in the 1990s. However, funding increases alone do nothing to address the problem of low-quality care. Increased subsidies not tied to the use of high-quality care will not result in a significant improvement in the quality of child care available.

Cost information for the child care policy options is summarized in Box 9-1 and discussed in more detail below. Fully implemented, these policy options could cost as much as an extra $25.2 billion for Head Start and Early Head Start, as much as $35 billion for prekindergarten and early education, or as much as $54 billion for quality vouchers. Costs could be reduced through partial implementation of these options. The implementation of one or more options could also make the expansion of the other options unnecessary, given the overlap in the populations they serve.

Policy Option: Expand and increase access to Head Start and Early Head Start.

Expand the hours of Head Start, increase access to serve more children who are currently not eligible, including children under age 3, or provide full-day year-round care in order to help address the problem of insufficient availability of high-quality child care for young children. Head Start and Early Head Start are currently limited to children whose families have incomes below the poverty line (or whose child has a disability). Head Start targets children ages 3 and 4; Early Head Start targets children under age 3. The results of the Early Head Start Evaluation, as well as the National Head Start Impact Study currently under way, will provide guidance for program improvement, as the program expands to serve more children from birth to age 5 for more hours and ensures that the program meets the full-day, year-round needs of working families.

Cost estimate: The costs in addition to the current budget of $6.67 billion (appropriation for FY 2003) to expand or enhance services would vary. To illustrate the cost of these options, we estimate that extending part-day, part-year Head Start services to all eligible children ages 3 to 4 years not currently served would cost $2.9 billion (2001 dollars); extending full-day, full-year services to all children ages 3 to 4 years currently served only part-day, part-year would cost $2.5 billion; extending full-day, full-year services to all eligible children ages 3 to 4 years who currently are not served at all or are served only part-day, part-year would cost an additional $7.8 billion; and serving all eligible children ages birth to age 5 not currently served would cost an additional $14.0 billion for part-day, part-year services and an additional $25.2 billion for full-day, full-year services.[1]   It

---

[1]Currie (2001: 221) reports that in 1998 the cost of part-day Head Start services for 34 weeks per year was $5,021 per child, and the cost of full-day, year-round service was $9,030. Adjusted to 2001 dollars, these figures become $5,455 and $9,811, respectively. In FY 2002, the Head Start Bureau estimates that 24.6 percent of children served were in full-day, year-round programs. There were 3.93 million children in poverty in calendar year 2000, and we assume one-third (1.31 million) were age 3 to 4. Of these 1.31 million poor 3- to 4-year-old children, 0.536 million were not served by Head Start, and 0.774 million were served by Head Start, 0.584 million part-day, part-year, and 0.190 million full-day, year-round. We

should be noted that some of the eligible children not currently served by Head Start might be enrolled in similar programs funded by Title I-A or by state prekindergarten initiatives. Thus, these figures may overestimate the cost of expanding Head Start, but insufficient information is available to estimate by how much.

Policy Option: Expand prekindergarten and other early education programs delivered in community-based child care programs.

Over the past decade, there has been an increased interest in providing prekindergarten programs to children under age 5. In the past, such programs were often funded for a half-day and delivered primarily in public schools. However, in more recent years, several states, including Georgia, New Jersey, New York, and others, are providing state prekindergarten dollars directly in full-day (full school-day) community-based child care programs. And in other states, such as North Carolina (i.e. the Smart Start Program), early education funding is being made available for children from birth to 5.

Providing state prekindergarten funding directly to full-day community-based child care programs and tying prekindergarten funding to higher standards, teacher qualifications, and curriculum requirements has the potential to improve the overall quality of community-based child care. These approaches would allow parents to choose providers that meet their full-day needs, but also allow programs to improve quality.

Cost estimate: States are currently spending a little over $2 billion on prekindergarten initiatives for children at risk of school failure (Blank and Mitchell, 2001); at the federal level, $500 million is spent on prekindergarten through Title I (the education program for disadvantaged students); $6.67 billion is spent on the federal Head Start program (appropriation for FY 2003). These expenditures do not take into account the amount spent on child care and prekindergarten by private paying parents with children ages 3 and 4.

The Committee for Economic Development (2002) considered the likely costs of universal prekindergarten. The estimated costs for a part-day, part-year program are $4,000 to $5,000 per child. There are approximately 8.3 million children ages 3 to 5 not yet enrolled in prekindergarten. If all these children were enrolled in publicly funded prekindergarten, the

---

assume that three-quarters of 5-year-old children are in kindergarten and therefore not eligible for Head Start. Finally, we estimate that 0.870 million children in total were served by Head Start in calendar year 2000.

BOX 9-1
Cost Estimates for Child Care Policy Options

Policy Option: Expand and increase access to Head Start and Early Head Start.

Per child cost estimate (in 2001)
Part-day, part-year Head Start: approximately $5,021 per child.
Full-day, full-year Head Start: approximately $9,811 per child.

Current spending
$6.67 billion

Cost estimate for this policy option
The costs in addition to the current budget to expand or enhance services would vary depending upon who is served and by what level of services:

- Full-day, full-year services provided to all eligible children ages birth to age 5 not currently served: $25.2 billion.
- Part-day, part-year services provided to all eligible children ages birth to age 5 not currently served: $14.0 billion.
- Year-round, full-day services extended to all children ages 3 to 4 years currently served only part-day, part-year: $2.5 billion.
- Year-round, full-day services extended to all eligible children ages 3 to 4 years who currently are not served at all or are served only part-day, part-year: $7.8 billion.

It should be noted that some of the eligible children not currently served by Head Start might be enrolled in similar programs funded by Title I-A or by state prekindergarten initiatives. Thus, these figures may overestimate the cost of expanding Head Start, but insufficient information is available to estimate by how much.

Policy Option: Expand prekindergarten and other early education programs delivered in community-based child care programs.

Per child cost estimate
Part-day, part-year prekindergarten program: $4,000 to $5,000 per child.

Current spending
States are currently spending a little over $2 billion on prekindergarten initiatives for children at risk of school failure; at the federal level, $500 million is spent on prekindergarten through Title I (the education program for disadvantaged students); $6.67 billion is spent on the federal Head Start program. These expenditures do not take into account the amount spent on child care and prekindergarten by private paying parents with children ages 3 and 4.

(continued)

BOX 9-1 Continued

Cost estimate for this policy option
It is estimated that publicly funded prekindergarten for all would cost an additional $25 to $35 billion annually.

Policy Option: Expand child care subsidies through quality-related vouchers.

Per child cost estimate
The estimated cost of a voucher for full-day year round high-quality child care for a child aged 0-5 in a family with income below the poverty line is $6,000, with lower estimates for older children, lower-quality care, and children in higher-income families.

Current spending
Approximately $21 billion

Cost estimate for this policy option
It is estimated that the program would cost an additional $54 billion.

---

cost would be $33.2 to $41.5 billion annually. Head Start and state-funded prekindergarten programs already meet some of these costs, and therefore it is estimated that publicly funded prekindergarten for all would cost an additional $25 to $35 billion annually.

Policy Option: Expand child care subsidies through quality-related vouchers.

A relatively new concept in child care policy would provide vouchers with a reimbursement rate that increases with the developmental quality of child care purchased from accredited child care centers or family day care homes for children from birth to 12. Quality would be defined by process measures, such as the Early Childhood Environmental Rating Scale (ECERS) rather than (or in addition to) structural features and would be certified by an independent accreditation organization, such as the National Association for the Education of Young Children (NAEYC). Quality-related vouchers would give parents an incentive to seek child care of high quality and the purchasing power to afford it. This in turn would give providers an incentive to improve quality in order to attract consumers with the greater purchasing power. The value of the voucher would have to be high enough to cover the cost of high-quality care and relatively low (perhaps zero) if used for low-quality care. This approach would give parents an incentive to be employed *and* to seek high-quality child care, unlike existing programs, which encourage one or the other but not both. This approach could be implemented with a new program, or through transformation of existing programs, such as CCDF and TANF.

Cost estimate: Blau (2001) estimated the cost of a quality-related voucher. His proposal would reimburse families in poverty for up to $6,000 per year for high-quality child care for preschool age children, $4,000 for mediocre to good-quality care, and $2,000 for lower quality care. The value of the voucher would be reduced by one-sixth for families with income between one and two times the poverty line, reduced by half for families with income between two and four times the poverty line, and would not provide any reimbursement for families with income over four times the poverty line. High-quality care defined as care with an ECERS score of 5.5 or greater would cost roughly $6,000. Mediocre to good-quality care (ECERS score of 3.50 to 5.49) would cost roughly $5,000, of which 80 percent is the subsidy value of $4,000, while $2,000 is about half the cost of low-quality care (ECERS less than 3.5). These differential reimbursement rates by quality provide an incentive for consumers to purchase high-quality care.

Approximately $21 billion is currently spent on child care and early education subsidies (Blau, 2001). Using estimates of the number of children in the relevant age ranges and assuming take-up rates of 65 percent for high-quality care, 15 percent for good-quality care, 10 percent for low-quality care, and with 10 percent of families assumed not to take up the voucher at all, the estimated annual cost is $75 billion (in 1999 dollars). After accounting for savings from eliminating other child care subsidy programs, the net cost is $54 billion. The cost could be reduced by making the vouchers less generous, thereby reducing take-up rates, and by restricting eligibility.

Policy Option: Increase the availability, hours, and quality of after-school programs.

After-school programs and activities are a critical source of child care and offer opportunities for preventing problems and promoting competencies during childhood and adolescence. The benefits are most apparent for young persons residing in high-risk and disadvantaged areas. These programs have rapidly expanded during the past decade. However, opportunities for participation in after-school programs and activities are still both costly, and for many, inaccessible, particularly for children and adolescents from families with low incomes. Expanding opportunities for participation in quality after-school programs and activities could be supported through expanding opportunities for participation in quality after-school programs and activities in multiple settings, such as schools, faith-based organizations, and community centers.

One possibility would be to increase funding for the 21st Century Community Learning Centers Programs (CCLC). Increased funding for CCLCs would (1) increase the number of available after-school programs, particularly for children and adolescents in economically disadvantaged areas; (2) offer stable support to established programs that demonstrate quality programming and benefits to participants; and (3) increase the quality of existing and developing programs, including a greater emphasis on enrichment activities other than academic remediation.

In the 2000 competition for CCLC funding, 2,252 communities sought funds to establish or expand after-school programs. Funds were available to support only 310 grantees (13.7 percent of the total applicants), even though over 1,000 of the applicants who did not receive funds were regarded as high-quality applicants. Accordingly, the disparity of available funding to grantee applications is substantial. In addition, the stability of funding from CCLC is also a consideration. CCLC grants typically provide funding for three years, with an option to extend the use of funds (but not the amount of funding) to five years. Because after-school programs rely heavily on cash grants for development and maintenance, and because developing high-quality programs requires a substantial time commitment and program continuity, the funding support from CCLC should allow for the possibility for previous grantees to apply for continuation of funds.

Cost estimate: To fund all grantees in 2000 that submitted high-quality applications (at the amount of funds requested), the CCLC budget would need to expand to approximately $600 million. To fund all grantees regardless of the application quality (at the amount of funding requested), an expanded budget of approximately $900 million would be required.

Family Leave

- **Policy Option: Improve parents' ability to take leave after the birth of a child, especially among low-income parents.**

There is evidence that taking family leave benefits parents and children, and that the right to do so is available to some but not others. Unless there is some provision for earnings replacement while on leave, many low-income workers will likely forgo the opportunity to take unpaid leave.

Options for public financing of income replacement include: (1) allowing the use of unemployment insurance (UI) funds to provide pay to workers at home caring for a newborn, (2) extending the temporary disability insurance (TDI) programs currently in place in five states to cover family or medical leave, (3) developing a new social insurance program to cover the costs of replacing at least a portion of parents' incomes while they are out on family or medical leave, or (4) developing a new cash benefit program to offset the costs associated with caring for a young child.

Proposals to allow the use of UI funds to provide pay for parental leave are under consideration in many states. In 2000, the U.S. Department of Labor issued new regulations, the Birth and Adoption Unemployment Compensation regulations, which would allow states to use unemployment benefits to pay for a period of parental leave. This "Baby UI" option has been considered by about half the states but has not been enacted by any to date, and in December 2002 the Labor Department proposed rescinding the regulations that would allow this option.

Estimates of the costs of such a program vary. Currently, the UI program pays out about $20 billion a year nationwide. The Labor Department, in issuing the regulations, estimated that the new program might increase these overall UI costs by roughly $1.2 to $1.8 billion—an increase of 6 to 9 percent. However, the Employment Policy Foundation (2000) estimated that UI costs would increase by $14.4 billion—an increase of 70 percent. The discrepancy between these estimates reflects different views of how many new parents would take up the benefit and how long they would stay out on leave. A subsequent analysis conducted at the Urban Institute (Vroman, 2001) considers both these issues and projects that expansion of the UI program to cover births or adoptions or both would raise costs by 6 to 7 percent relative to the overall cost of the program. There would also be some cost savings, due to reductions in the numbers of new parents receiving payments through TDI or public assistance programs and in the numbers receiving child care subsidies.

Another way to provide paid leave is via extensions of existing TDI programs. As discussed earlier, five states currently have TDI programs that provide paid leave for maternity disability, along with other types of leave for disability. Because these are large states, together these programs cover over 20 percent of all American workers. One of the five TDI states, California, recently enacted legislation to extend its program to provide paid leave for up to six weeks for parents with a newborn or for employees with an ill family member. Funding for leave provided under the new law will come from an increase in the payroll tax rate on employees of 0.08 percent per year in 2004 and 2005 to cover the initial costs of the program; this amounts to about $22 per year in additional payroll taxes per employee in the state. The law requires employees to use up to two weeks of accrued vacation time before claiming pay from TDI. TDI programs pay benefits as a percentage of usual weekly earnings and tend to be more generous than

UI programs. Employees on TDI leave in California will be paid about 55 percent of their salary, with a maximum benefit of $728 per week.[2]

A third type of proposal is to establish a new social insurance program. An example of this approach is a proposal by Walker (1996) for a parental leave account (PLA), which he envisions as a savings account combined with a line of credit from the federal government, which parents could use to cover the costs associated with a leave of up to one year following the birth or adoption of a child. The PLA would be financed by an additional payroll tax of 3.5 percent, deducted from an individual's paycheck and credited to his or her PLA. Families could draw on their accounts to finance one parent to stay at home with a new child for up to one year. If a family did not have enough funds in its PLA, the federal government would extend a loan, which would be repaid from subsequent payroll taxes over the remaining working lifetime of the parents. Upon retirement, positive balances in a PLA would be transferred to the social security system and would lead to an increased retirement benefit, while negative balances would lead to lower benefits. Thus, a family that did not take advantage of the PLA would receive a "return" on their extra payroll tax payments upon retirement.

A fourth option that has been proposed is the development of a cash benefit to offset the costs to parents of caring for a young child, in particular in the first year of life. Such a benefit could be instituted on a means-tested or universal basis. With regard to means-tested benefits, two states— Minnesota and Montana—currently have at-home infant child care programs, which provide cash benefits to low-income parents with a child under the age of 1. These programs differ from welfare in that, while means-tested, they are limited to families with a child under the age of 1 (and they do not involve work or other activity requirements). They differ from child care in that the funds are used to support the parents in caring for the child themselves, rather than purchasing nonparental child care. In Minnesota, the first state to enact such a program, payment comes from the state's child care funds and is limited to 90 percent of what would have been paid for care for that child. Thus, the program results in cost savings for each family that result from the shift from using paid child care to using parental care. With regard to universal programs, Waldfogel (2001c) has proposed an early childhood benefit system, which, modeled on programs in Finland and Norway, would provide cash benefits to parents with chil-

---

[2] For more information on California's new program, see Broder (2002). See also Vroman (2001) for a discussion of the California and other TDI programs. For cost-benefit analyses of paid family leave in California, see Dube and Kaplan (2002) and the Employment Development Department (2000).

dren under age 3. Parents could choose to use the benefit to cover the costs of a leave from work, the costs of child care, or a combination of the two. Another European example comes from the United Kingdom's baby tax credit, which doubles the value of the child tax credit for families with infants.

Policy Option: Discourage the practice of requiring mothers on welfare to return to work at 12 weeks following a birth.

There is some evidence of a negative effect of early and extensive maternal employment on children's outcomes in some groups of families. TANF rules currently allow states to require mothers to return to work as soon as their child is born; this would not change under pending reauthorization proposals. Under current rules, single-parent families with children under age 6 are able to meet federal participation requirements by engaging in 20 hours a week of work-related activity. The reauthorization proposal currently being considered seeks to modify this provision so that such families would need to engage in 40 hours a week of work-related activity in order to fully count toward participation requirements. Policies that would allow new mothers to delay returning to full-time employment until after the first three months of a child's life, and possibly until after the first birthday, deserve attention.

Cost estimate: There is little evidence available on the potential costs or benefits of such policies. Two states that have experimented with such policies—Minnesota and Montana—are using child care funds (in place of TANF funds) to cover cash grants to mothers in this situation. If all the families supported through these programs received child care funding, the cost of these programs is essentially zero, since they use funds that would have been spent on child care. However, to the extent that take-up of the cash grant is higher than the take-up of child care would have been, the cost of providing the cash benefits would be higher.

Policy Option: Expand coverage of the Family and Medical Leave Act.

The Family and Medical Leave Act could be expanded to cover activities and individuals not currently eligible (for example, attending meetings at children's schools, taking children to routine medical or dental visits), to provide options for working part time or with flexible hours, and to cover other family members (such as grandparents).

The committee did not explore the details of specific policies in this area but did hear evidence that the lack of such policies is a growing concern to working families. We therefore have not identified options for specific polices to be pursued; rather, we flag these issues as an area of concern and suggest them as the topic of further research and analysis. Such analysis should make use of survey and other data to identify the numbers of families who might benefit from particular policy expansions and the likely costs of such policies. Further research should also examine the relative advantages and disadvantages of policies that require employers to provide such benefits compared with policies that provide such benefits through social insurance mechanisms.

RESEARCH

The committee notes throughout the report areas in need of further research. Here we highlight priorities.

Child and Adolescent Care

The most recent nationally representative data on the structural measures (group sizes, caregiver-to-child ratios, provider education and training, provider turnover rates) are from 1990, and no nationally representative data are available on the process measures (the experiences that children have with their caregivers, with other children, and with age-appropriate activities and materials). In the committee's view, the highest priority should therefore be the collection of national data on process quality through the institution of a new nationally representative survey of child care arrangements with a focus on the quality of care. The survey should include all types of child care arrangements used by children of preschool, primary, and secondary school age. The survey should include a household module or be linked to a major household survey so that detailed information on family socioeconomic characteristics and child care quality can be linked. Ideally, such data would be longitudinal and would include assessments of child health and development, in order to develop a better understanding of the effects of child care quality on children's development, school progress, and health. One model would be a telephone survey like the 1990 Profile of Child Care Settings to collect data on structural quality from a large representative sample of centers and family day care homes, supplemented by in-person interviews and observation of a subsample of the survey to measure process quality. The survey should also collect data on cost and fees.

Another high priority is a random-assignment child care experiment: the care provided must be above basic quality standards and include children in circumstances in which no subsidized care would be otherwise available, such as areas in which there are long waiting lists. The experiment should assign children to facilities of varying quality, give families subsidies that come with varying incentives or requirements regarding quality, and monitor their developmental progress. This should be done for children of both preschool and school age.

Research is needed on how young people spend their time during the summer months. Most of the available research on children and adolescents is collected during the school year, in part because of the convenience of the school setting for recruiting samples and collecting data. However, because school provides the dominant form of child care for most young people during the morning and early afternoon during weekdays, alternative arrangements and patterns of time use must occur during the summer. A report on child care for school-age children (ages 6 to 12) during the summer months using data from the 1999 National Survey of Families highlights marked differences in the use of structured enrichment activities and programs, hours spent in supervised care by relatives, and hours spent in self-care, as well as the use and cost of paid child care during the summer compared with the school year. The extent to which child care arrangements during the summer impact child adjustment, however, is not elucidated. More generally, how adolescents spend their time during the summer and how this use of time impacts adjustment represents a gap in the knowledge base.

The impact of sibling care—both for older siblings who provide care and for younger siblings who receive such care—is not well understood. Many families rely on older siblings to provide care and supervision for younger siblings while parents are working. Qualitative evidence makes clear the utility and necessity of such arrangements for working families. Theoretical perspectives on this issue are conflicting, and quantitative empirical evidence is limited and mixed. Whether care from older siblings is beneficial or detrimental to the recipient(s) depends on the individuals and family considered. Research on the possible effects of sibling care for the adolescents who provide the caregiving is nearly absent. Considerably more attention to this form of child care is needed.

The processes by which adolescent involvement in structured after-school endeavors (enrichment activities and employment) affect adjustment need to be clarified. The empirical knowledge base on how structured after-school endeavors relate to short- and long-term adjustment has expanded greatly in recent decades. Enrichment activities and paid employment are both normative for adolescents and represent a form of supervision while parents are working. However, research on why and how engagement in these structured activities affects adolescent functioning is only beginning to emerge. Longitudinal investigations of structured activities that are theory-driven, account for possible selection biases, assess putative mediators, and consider individual differences and activity experiences are particularly scarce.

Family Leave

A systematic effort to evaluate the impact of access to leave on child and family outcomes should be undertaken. One option is to treat the recent passage of a paid leave law in California as a natural experiment, in which before-after differences in outcomes are compared with those in other states in which the policy did not change. Another more costly, but probably more informative, approach would be a random assignment experiment in which families are assigned to different leave policies beyond those that would otherwise have been available.

Income Support

Although many studies have examined the role of income on child cognitive and socioemotional development, a variety of questions remain. First, the causal role of income on child development and the size of income effects continue to be debated. We now have data from several experiments that manipulated income for low-income families inside and outside the welfare system in the 1990s. However, these experiments were limited to a few areas of the country and were conducted during an economic boom. A new generation of experiments should be conducted, both inside and outside welfare systems, to examine how experimentally manipulated income influences child and youth development. These should be conducted in a variety of state and local settings and should include sufficient numbers of populations that have been underrepresented in studies to date (e.g., very young children, families with children with disabilities, immigrants).

Second, the question of threshold effects of income has not been sufficiently explored. How much income change is required to produce not just statistically but developmentally and societally important effects? How might such income thresholds differ, depending on previous education, income, employment, and child characteristics? Such questions can be addressed through large-scale nonexperimental research or through carefully designed experimental studies. Answers would be critical in helping to inform future changes in income support policies.

Finally, data on the effects of particular income support policy approaches on children and youth are needed. For example, there has been no research documenting the effects on children of variation in earned income credit policies (at the state level, for example, where there is some variation). There have been no experiments testing particular policy options, such as making the dependent care tax credit refundable. Experiments that altered levels of income support within the welfare system, through earnings disregards, have been conducted, but only in a few localities. These and other efforts to examine the impacts of income support policies should be encouraged through federal and state evaluation initiatives.

Work Benefits and Policies

New research and collection of data on private sector policies and benefits for employees with children would further enhance our understanding of the current patterns of support for working families. This research could build on existing surveys being conducted by government agencies and private organizations with the aim of providing more detail about who is covered and how well the policies support the well-being of the children and adolescents in these families.

CLOSING THOUGHTS

This report has identified some important opportunities that have the potential to improve the quality of child and adolescent development in this country through new or expanded public policies. Children are spending vast numbers of hours in child care that fails to add as much to their social and cognitive skills as we know can be provided. Recent research has convinced the committee that the nation is not doing nearly enough to help families, particularly low-income families, with the difficult task of providing for the material and developmental needs of their children. The committee has identified some promising policy options for action by policy makers. These policies should receive serious consideration.

References

Aber, J.L., Brooks-Gunn, J., and Maynard, R. (1995). Effects of welfare reform on teenage parents and their children. *The Future of Children: Critical Issues for Children and Youth, 5*(2), 53-71.

Abt Associates, Inc. (2000). *National study of child care for low-income families: State and community substudy interim report.* Cambridge, MA: Author.

Achatz, M., and MacAllum, C. (1994). *Young unwed fathers: Report from the field.* Philadelphia: Public/Private Ventures.

Achenbach, T.M. (1991). *Manual for the child behavior checklist/4-18 and 1991 profile.* Burlington, VT: University of Vermont.

Adams, G., and Rohacek, M. (2002). More than a work support? Issues around integrating child development goals into the child care subsidy system. *Early Childhood Research Quarterly, 17,* 418-440.

Adams, G., and Sandfort, J. (1994). *First steps, promising futures: State pre-kindergarten initiatives in the early 1990's.* Washington, DC: Children's Defense Fund.

Adams, G., and Snyder, K. (2003). *Child care subsidies and practices: Implications for child care providers.* (Series A, No. A-57, Assessing the New Federalism Project). Washington, DC: Urban Institute.

Adams, G., Snyder, K., and Sandfort, J.R. (2002a). *Getting and retaining child care assistance: How policy and practice influence parents' experiences.* (Report No. 55). Washington, DC: Urban Institute.

Adams, G., Snyder, K., and Sandfort, J.R. (2002b). *Navigating the child care subsidy system: policies and practices that affect access and retention.* (Series A, No. 50, Assessing the New Federalism Project). Washington, DC: Urban Institute.

Adams, G., Snyder, K., and Sandfort, J.R. (2003). *Essential but often ignored: Child care providers in the subsidy system.* (Occasional paper No. 63, Assessing the New Federalism Project). Washington, DC: Urban Institute.

Administration for Children and Families. (1998). *Compilation of the Head Start Act.* Available: http://www.acf.hhs.gov/programs/hsb/budget/headstartact.htm. [Accessed 2002].

Administration for Children and Families. (1999). *Access to child care for low-income families.* Washington, DC: Author.

Administration for Children and Families. (2000). *New statistics show only small percentage of eligible families receive child care help.* Available: http://www.acf.dhhs.gov/news/ccstudy2.htm. [Accessed July 2002].

Administration for Children and Families. (2002). *Head Start: Promoting early childhood development.* Washington, DC: Author.

Afterschool Alliance. (2002). *Afterschool alert, poll report* Available: www.afterschoolalliance.org. [Accessed July 2002].

Ahituv, A., Tienda, M., and Tsay, A. (1998). *Early employment activity and school continuation decisions of young white, black, and Hispanic women.* Revised paper presented at the 1996 annual meeting of the Population Association of America.

Ahluwalia, S.K., McGroder, S.M., Zaslow, M.J., and Hair, E.C. (2001). *Symptoms of depression among welfare recipients: A concern for two generations.* (Child Trends Research Brief). Washington, DC: Child Trends.

Ainsworth, M.D.S., Blehar, M.D., Waters, E., and Wall, S. (1978). *Patterns of attachment: A psychological study of the strange situation.* Hillsdale, NJ: Erlbaum.

Aizer, A. (2001). *Home alone: Maternal employment, child care, and adolescent behavior.* (Working paper No. 807). Los Angeles: University of California.

Albano, A.M., Chorpita, B.F., and Barlow, D.H. (1996). Childhood anxiety disorders. In E.J. Mash, and R.A. Barkley (Eds.), *Child psychopathology* (pp. 196-241). New York: Guilford Press.

Allen, J.P., Philliber, S., Herrling, S., and Gabriel, K.P. (1997). Preventing teen pregnancy and academic failure. *Child Development, 64,* 729-742.

Amstutz, E. (2002). The role of health care in work and welfare. In T. Lengyel, and D. Campbell (Eds.), *Faces of change: Welfare policy through the lens of personal experience* (pp. 63-82). Milwaukee, WI: Alliance for Children and Families.

Anderson, E. (1999). *Code of the street.* New York: Norton.

Armistead, L., Wierson, M., and Forehand, R. (1990). Adolescents and maternal employment: Is it harmful for a young adolescent to have an employed mother? *Journal of Early Adolescence, 10*(3), 260-278.

Arnett, J. (1989). Caregivers in day-care centers: Does training matter? *Journal of Applied Developmental Psychology, 10,* 541-552.

Aronson, S.R., and Huston, A.C. (2001). *Maternal employment, mother's time with infants, and the mother-infant relationship.* Paper presented at the meetings of the Society for Research in Child Development.

Asher, L., and Lenhoff, D. (2001). Family and medical leave: Making time for family is everyone's business. *The Future of Children: Caring for Infants and Toddlers, 11*(1), 113-121.

Bachman, J.G., and Schunlenberg, J. (1993). *How part-time work intensity relates to drug use, time use, and satisfaction among high school seniors: Are these consequences, or mere correlates?* Ann Arbor, MI: Institute for Social Research, Survey Research Center.

Bachman, J.G., Johnson, L.S., and O'Malley, P.M. (1987). *Monitoring the future: Questionnaire responses from the nation's high school seniors.* Ann Arbor, MI: Institute for Social Research, Survey Research Center.

Bailyn, L., Drago, R., and Kochan, T.A. (2001). *Integrating work and family life: A holistic approach.* Chestnut Hill, MA: Sloan Work-Family Policy Network.

Bainbridge, J., Meyers, M., and Waldfogel, J. (in press). Child care reform and employment of lone mothers. *Social Science Quarterly.*

Barnett, R.C., and Baruch, G.K. (1987). Determinants of fathers' participation in family work. *Journal of Marriage and the Family, 49,* 29-40.

Barnett, W.S. (1993). New wine in old bottles: Increasing coherence in early childhood care and education policy. *Early Childhood Research Quarterly, 8*(4), 519-538.

Barnett, W.S. (1995). Long-term effects of early childhood programs on cognitive and school outcomes. *The Future of Children: Long-Term Outcomes of Early Childhood Programs, 5*(3), 25-50.

Barnett, W.S. (1996). *Lives in the balance: Age-27 benefit-cost analysis of the High/Scopes Perry Preschool Program.* (Monographs of the High/Scope Educational Research Foundation, 11). Ypsilanti, MI: High/Scope Press.

Baron, R.M., and Kenny, D.A. (1986). The moderator-mediator variable distinction in social psychological research: Conceptual, strategic, and statistical considerations. *Journal of Personality and Social Psychology, 51,* 1173-1182.

Bates, J., Marvinney, D., Kelly, T., Dodge, K., Bennett, R., and Pettit, G. (1994). Child-care history and kindergarten adjustment. *Developmental Psychology, 30,* 690-700.

Baydar, N., and Brooks-Gunn, J. (1991). Effects of maternal employment and child-care arrangements on pre-schoolers' cognitive and behavioral outcomes: Evidence from the children of the National Longitudinal Survey of Youth. *Developmental Psychology, 27,* 918-945.

Bayley, N. (1969). *Bayley scales of infant development.* New York: Psychological Corporation.

Bayley, N. (1993). *Bayley scales for infant development, second edition.* San Antonio, TX: Psychological Corporation.

Beck, E.L. (1999). Prevention and intervention programming: Lessons from an after-school program. *The Urban Review, 31*(1), 107-124.

Becker, P.E., and Moen, P. (1999). Scaling back: Dual-career couples' work-family strategies. *Journal of Marriage and the Family, 61,* 995-1007.

Beers, T.M. (2000). Flexible schedules and shift work: Replacing the "9-to-5" workday? *Monthly Labor Review,* 33-40.

Belle, D. (1997). Varieties of self-care: A qualitative look at children's experiences in the after-school hours. *Merrill-Palmer Quarterly, 43*(3), 478-496.

Belsky, J. (1984). Two waves of day care research: Developmental effects and conditions of quality. In R. Ainslie (Ed.), *The child and the day care setting* (pp. 1-34). New York: Prager.

Belsky, J. (1986). Infant day care: A cause for concern? *Zero to Three, 6,* 1-9.

Belsky, J. (1988). The "effects" of infant day care reconsidered. *Early Childhood Research Quarterly, 3,* 235-272.

Belsky, J. (1999). Quantity of nonmaternal care and boys' problem behavior/adjustment at ages 3 and 5: Exploring the mediating role of parenting. *Psychiatry, 62,* 1-20.

Belsky, J. (2001). Developmental risk (still) associated with early child care. *Journal of Child Psychology and Psychiatry, 42,* 845-860.

Belsky, J. (2002) Quantity counts: Amount of child care and children's socioemotional development. *Developmental and Behavioral Pediatrics, 23*(3), 167-170.

Belsky, J., and Eggebeen, D. (1991). Early and extensive maternal employment/child care and 4-6 year olds socioemotional development: Children of the National Longitudinal Survey of Youth. *Journal of Marriage and the Family, 53,* 1083-1099.

Belsky, J., and Steinberg, L. (1978). The effects of day care: A critical review. *Child Development, 49,* 929-949.

Bennett, N.G., and Lu, H. (2001). *Untapped potential.* New York: Columbia University, National Center for Children in Poverty.

Berger, L., Hill, J., and Waldfogel, J. (in press). Family leave policies, maternal employment, and child well-being. *Journal of Population Economics.*

Berger, L., and Waldfogel, J. (2002). *Maternity leave and employment of new mothers in the United States.* Unpublished paper, Columbia University, New York.

Berger, M., and Black, D. (1992). Child care subsidies, quality of care, and the labor supply of low-income single mothers. *Review of Economics and Statistics, 74*(4), 635-642.

Bergmann, B.R. (1999). *Subsidizing child care by mothers at home.* New York: Foundation for Child Development.

Bergmann, B.R., and Helburn, S.W. (2002a). Policy recommendations. In B.R. Bergmann, and S.W. Helburn (Eds.), *America's child care problem: The way out* (pp. 223-228). Hampshire, UK: Palgrave Macmillan

Bergmann, B.R., and Helburn, S.W. (2002b). The design: What should a new child care system look like? In B.R. Bergmann, and S.W. Helburn (Eds.), *America's child care problem: The way out* (pp. 33-54). Hampshire, UK: Palgrave Macmillan.

Berk, L. (1985). Relationship of caregiver education to child-oriented attitudes, job satisfaction, and behaviors toward children. *Child Care Quarterly, 14*(2), 103-129.

Berlin, L.J. (1998). Opening the black box: What makes early child and family development programs work? *Zero to Three, 18*(4), 1-40.

Berndt, T. (1982). The features and effects of friendship in early adolescence. *Child Development, 53,* 1447-1460.

Bernheimer, C., Weisner, T., and Lowe, E. (in press). Impacts of children with troubles on working poor families. *Children and Youth Services Review.*

Besharov, D.J. (Ed.). (2002). *Family well-being after welfare reform.* Committee to Review Welfare Reform Research. College Park, MD: Maryland School of Public Affairs, Welfare Reform Academy.

Besharov, D.J., and Samari, N. (2001). Child care after welfare reform. In R.M. Blank, and R. Haskins (Eds.), *The new world of welfare* (pp. 461-481). Washington, DC: Brookings Institution.

Bianchi, S.M. (2000a). Maternal employment and time with children: Dramatic change or surprising continuity? *Demography, 37*(4), 401-414.

Bianchi, S.M. (2000b). Setting the stage: Work and family lives of Americans. In E. Appelbaum (Ed.), *Balancing acts* (pp. 13-24). Washington, DC: Economic Policy Institute.

Bianchi, S.M., Milkie, M.A., Sayer, L.C., and Robinson, J.P. (2000). Is anyone doing the housework? Trends in the gender division of household labor. *Social Forces, 79,* 191-228.

Bianchi, S.M., Robinson, J.P., and Milkie, M.M. (in press). *Changing rhythms of American family life.* New York: Russell Sage.

Birmaher, B., Ryan, N.D., Williamson, D.E., Brent, D.A., Kaufman, J., Dahl, R.E., Perel, J., and Nelson, B. (1996). Childhood and adolescent depression: A review of the past 10 years: Part I. *Journal of the American Academy of Child and Adolescent Psychiatry, 35,* 1427-1439.

Bitler, M.P., Gelbach, J.B., Hoynes, H.W., and Zavodny, M. (2002). *The impact of welfare reform on marriage and divorce.* (Working paper). Atlanta: Federal Reserve Bank of Atlanta.

Blank, H., and Mitchell, A. (2001). *The status of preschool policy in the states.* Available: www.earlychildhoodfinance.org. [Accessed 2003].

Blank, R.M. (in press). Evaluating welfare reform in the United States. *Journal of Economic Literature.*

Blank, R.M. (2000). Strong employment, low inflation: How has the U.S. economy done so well? *Canadian Public Policy, 26*(Supplement), 75-86.

Blank, R.M. (2002). *Evaluating welfare reform in the United States.* (NBER Working Paper No. 8983). Cambridge, MA: National Bureau of Economic Research.

Blank, R.M., and Haskins, R. (Eds.). (2001). *The new world of welfare*. Washington, DC: Brookings Institution.

Blank, R.M., Card, D.E., and Robbins, P.K. (2000). Financial incentives for increasing work and income among low-income families. In D.E. Card, and R.M. Blank (Eds.), *Finding jobs: Work and welfare reform*. New York: Russell Sage.

Blau, D.M. (1997). The production of quality in child care centers. *Journal of Human Resources, 32*(3), 354-387.

Blau, D.M. (1999a). The effect of income on child development. *The Review of Economics and Statistics, 8*, 261-276.

Blau, D.M. (1999b). The effects of child care characteristics on child development. *Journal of Human Resources, 34*(4), 786-822.

Blau, D.M. (2000). The production of quality in child care centers: Another look. *Applied Developmental Science, 4*(3), 136-148.

Blau, D.M. (2001). *The child care problem: An economic analysis*. New York: Russell Sage.

Blau, D.M. (in press). Child care subsidy programs. In R. Moffitt (Ed.), *Means tested transfer programs in the United States*. Chicago: Chicago University.

Blau, D.M. (2003). Interpreting the association between maternal employment and child outcomes. Unpublished manuscript, Department of Economics, University of North Carolina, Chapel Hill.

Blau, D.M., and Hagy, A.P. (1998). The demand for quality in child care. *Journal of Political Economy, 106*(1), 104-146.

Blau, D.M., and Mocan, H.N. (2002). The supply of quality in child care centers. *The Review of Economics and Statistics, 84*(3), 483-496.

Blau, D., and Tekin, E. (2001). The determinants and consequences of child care subsidies for single mothers. (Discussion Paper No. 383). Department of Economics, University of North Carolina, Chapel Hill.

Blau, F.D., and Grossberg, A.J. (1992). Maternal labor supply and children's cognitive development. *Review of Economics and Statistics, 74*, 474-481.

Bloom, D., Kemple, J.J., Morris, P.A., Scrivener, S., Verma, N., and Hendra, R. (2000). *The family transition program: Final report on Florida's initial time-limited welfare program*. New York: Manpower Demonstration Research Corporation.

Bloom, D., Scrivener, S., Michalopoulos, C., Morris, P.A., Hendra, R., Adams-Ciardullo, D., Walter, J., and Vargas, W. (2002). *Jobs first: Final report on Connecticut's welfare reform initiative*. New York: Manpower Demonstration Research Corporation.

Bloom, D., Michalopoulos, C., Walter, J., and Auspos, P. (1998). *WRP: Implementation and early impacts of Vermont's welfare restructuring project*. New York: Manpower Demonstration Research Corporation.

Bloom, D., and Michalopoulos, C. (2001). *How welfare and work policies affect employment and income: A synthesis of research*. New York: Manpower Demonstration Research Corporation.

Bogen, K., and Joshi, P. (2002). *Bad work or good move: The relationship of part-time and nonstandard work schedules to parenting and child behavior in working poor families*. Paper presented at the Conference on Working Poor Families: Coping as Parents and Workers, NIH, Bethesda, MD, November 13-14.

Boggild, H., and Knutsson, A. (1999). Shift work, risk factors, and cardiovascular disease. *Scandinavian Journal of Work, Environment, and Health, 25*(2), 85-99.

Bogenschneider, K., and Steinberg, L. (1994). Maternal employment and adolescent academic achievement: A developmental analysis. *Sociology of Education, 67*, 60-77.

Bohle, P., and Tilley, A.J. (1998). Early experience of shiftwork: Influences on attitudes. *Journal of Occupational and Organizational Psychology, 71*, 61-79.

Booth, A., Johnson, D.R., White, L., and Edwards, J. (1984). Women, outside employment, and marital instability. *American Journal of Sociology, 90*, 567-583.

Booth, C.L., Clarke-Stewart, K.A., Vandell, D., McCartney, K., and Tresch, O.M. (2002). Child-care usage and mother-infant "quality time." *Journal of Marriage and Family, 64*, 16-26.

Bornstein, M.H., Gist, N.F., Hahn, C.S., Haynes, O.M., and Voigt, M.D. (2001). *Long-term cumulative effects of daycare experience on children's mental and socioemotional development.* Washington, DC: National Institute of Child Health and Human Development.

Bos, J., Huston, A., Granger, R., Duncan, G.J., Brock, T., and McLoyd, V. (1999). *New hope: Two-year results of a program to reduce poverty and reform welfare.* New York: Manpower Demonstration Research Corporation.

Bowlby, J. (1969). *Attachment and loss.* New York: Basic Books.

Bracken, B.A. (1984). *Bracken basic concept scales.* San Antonio, TX: Psychological Corporation.

Braddock, J.H., Royster, D.A., Winfield, L.F., and Hawkins, R. (1991). Bouncing back: Sports and academic resilience among African-American males. *Education and Urban Society, 24*, 113-131.

Bradley, R.H. (1995). Environment and parenting. In M.H. Bornstein (Ed.), *Handbook of parenting: Biology and ecology of parenting, volume 2* (pp. 235-261). New York: Erlbaum.

Bradley, R.H., and Caldwell, B.M. (1984a). The HOME inventory and family demographics. *Developmental Psychology, 55*, 803-809.

Bradley, R.H., and Caldwell, B.M. (1984b). The relation of infants' home environments to achievement test performance in first grade: A follow-up study. *Child Development, 55*, 803-809.

Bradley, R.H., Caldwell, B.M., and Rock, S.L. (1988). Home environment and school performance: A ten-year follow-up and examination of three models of environmental action. *Child Development, 59*, 852-867.

Bradley, R.H., Caldwell, B.M., Rock, S.L., Ramey, C.T., Barnard, K.E., Gary, C., Hammond, A., Mitchell, S., Gottfried, A.W., Siegel, L., and Johnson, D. (1989). Home environment and cognitive development in the first 3 years of life: A collaborative study involving six sites and three ethnic groups in North America. *Developmental Psychology, 25*(2), 217-235.

Brady-Smith, C., Brooks-Gunn, J., Waldfogel, J., and Fauth, R. (2001). Work or welfare? Assessing the impacts of recent employment and policy changes on very young children. *Evaluation and Program Planning, 24*, 409-425.

Brainbridge, J. (2002). *Who supports children in the U.S.?* Unpublished doctoral dissertation, Columbia University, New York.

Brandon, P.D. (1999). Determinants of self-care arrangements among school-age children. *Children and Youth Services Review, 21*(6), 497-520.

Brauner, S., and Loprest, P. (1999). *Where are they now? What states' studies of people on welfare tell us.* (Series A-32, Assessing the New Federalism Project). Washington, DC: Urban Institute.

Brayfield, A. (1995). Juggling jobs and kids: The impact of employment schedules on fathers caring for children. *Journal of Marriage and the Family, 57*, 321-333.

Brazelton, T. (1986). Issues for working parents. *American Journal of Orthopsychiatry, 56*, 14-25.

Brimhall, D.W., Reaney, L.M., and West, J. (1999). *Participation of kindergarteners through third graders in before- and after-school care.* (Report No. NCES, 1999-013). Washington, DC: U.S. Department of Education.

Broberg, A.G., Hwang, C.P., Lamb, M.E., and Bookstein, F.L. (1990). Factors related to verbal abilities in Swedish preschoolers. *British Journal of Developmental Psychology, 8*, 335-349.

Broberg, A.G., Wessels, H., Lamb, M.E., and Hwang, C.P. (1997). Effects of day care on the development of cognitive abilities in 8-year-olds: A longitudinal study. *Developmental Psychology, 33*, 62-69.

Broder, J. (2002 September). Family leave in California now includes pay benefit. *New York Times*, p. 20.

Bronfenbrenner, U. (1979). *The ecology of human development: Experiments by nature and design*. Cambridge, MA: Harvard University.

Bronfenbrenner, U. (1989). Ecological systems theory. In R. Vasta (Ed.), *Annals of child development* (pp. 187-249). Greenwich, CT: JAI Press.

Bronfenbrenner, U., and Crouter, N. (1982). Work and family through time and space. In S. Kammerman, and C. Hayes (Eds.). *Families that work: Children in a changing world*. Committee Panel on Work, Family and Community, Committee on Child Development Research and Public Policy, Commission on Behavioral and Social Sciences and Education Washington, DC: National Academy Press.

Bronfenbrenner, U., and Morris, P.A. (1998). The ecology of developmental processes. In W. Damon (Ed.), *Handbook of child psychology, 5th edition, volume 1* (pp. 993-1028). New York: Wiley.

Brooks, J.L., Hair, E.C., and Zalsow, M.J. (2001). *Welfare reform's impacts on adolescents: Early warning signs*. (Child Trends Research Brief). Washington, DC: Child Trends.

Brooks-Gunn, J., and Duncan, G.J. (1997). The effects of poverty on children. *Future of children: Children and poverty, 7*(2), 55-71.

Brooks-Gunn, J., Berlin, L.J., and Fuligni, A.S. (2000). Early childhood intervention programs: What about the family? In J.P. Shonkoff, and S.J. Meisels (Eds.), *Handbook of early childhood intervention, 2nd edition* (pp. 549-588). New York: Cambridge.

Brooks-Gunn, J., Gross, R., Kraemer, H., Spiker, D., and Shapiro, S. (1992). Enhancing the cognitive outcomes of low birthweight, premature infants: For whom is the intervention most effective? *Pediatrics, 89*, 1209-1215.

Brooks-Gunn, J., Han, W., and Waldfogel, J. (2002). Maternal employment and child cognitive outcomes in the first three years of life: The NICHD study of early child care. *Child Development, 73*, 1052-1072.

Brooks-Gunn, J., Klebanov, P.K., and Duncan, G.J. (1996). Ethnic differences in children's intelligence test scores: Role of economic deprivation, home environment, and maternal characteristics. *Child Development, 67*, 396-408.

Brooks-Gunn, J., McCarton, C., Casey, P., McCormick, M., Bauer, C., Bernbaum, J., Tysons, J., Swanson, M., Bennett, F.C., Scott, D., Tonascia, J., and Meinert, C. (1994). Early intervention in low birth-weight premature infants. *Journal of the American Medical Association, 272*, 1257-1262.

Brown, B.B. (1990). Peer groups and peer cultures. In S.S. Feldman, and G.R. Elliot (Eds), *At the threshold: The developing adolescent* (pp. 171-196). Cambridge, MA: Harvard University.

Brown, B.B., Clasen, D., and Eicher, S. (1986). Perceptions of peer pressure, peer conformity dispositions, and self-reported behavior among adolescents. *Developmental Psychology, 22*, 521-530.

Brown-Lyons, M., Robertson, A., and Layzer, J. (2001). *Kith and kin: Informal care highlights from recent research*. New York: National Center for Children in Poverty.

Bryant, D.M., and Maxwell, K. (1997). The effectiveness of early intervention for the disadvantaged children. In M. Guralnick (Ed.), *The effectiveness of early intervention* (pp. 23-46). Baltimore: Paul Brookes.

Budig, M. J., and England, P. (2001). The wage penalty for motherhood. *American Sociological Review, 66,* 204-205.

Burchinal, M.R., Ramey, S.L., Reid, M.K., and Jaccard, J. (1995). Early child care experiences and their association with family and child characteristics during middle school. *Early Childhood Research Quarterly, 10,* 33-61.

Burchinal, M., Roberts, J., Nabors, L., and Bryant, D. (1996). Quality of center child care and infant cognitive and language development. *Child Development, 67,* 606-620.

Burchinal, M.R., Campbell, F.A., and Bryant, D.M. (1997). Early intervention and mediating processes in cognitive performance of children of low-income African-American families. *Child Development, 68,* 935-954.

Burchinal, M.R., Howes, C. and Kontos, S. (1999). *Structural predictors of child care quality in child care homes.* Paper presented at the SEED Conference, Bethesda, MD.

Burchinal, M.R., Peisner-Feinberg, E., Bryant, D.M., and Clifford, R. (2000). Children's social and cognitive development and child-care quality: Testing for differential associations related to poverty, gender, or ethnicity. *Applied Developmental Science, 4,* 149-165.

Burchinal, M.R., Cryer, D., Clifford, R.M., and Howes, C. (2002). Caregiver training and classroom quality in child care centers. *Applied Developmental Science, 6,* 2-11.

Burden, D.S., and Googins, B.K. (1986). *Boston University balancing job and homelife study.* Boston: Boston University School of Social Work.

Bureau of Labor Statistics. (1997). *Employment characteristics of families in 1996.* Available: http://www.bls.gov. [Accessed June 16, 1997].

Bureau of Labor Statistics. (2000). *Report on the youth labor force.* Available: http://www.bls.gov/opub/rylf/rylfhome.htm. [Accessed January 2003].

Bureau of Labor Statistics. (2001). *Employee benefits in private industry, 1999.* Available: http://www.bls.gov/ncs/ebs/home.htm. [Accessed May 20, 2002].

Bureau of Labor Statistics. (2002). *Employment characteristics of families in 2001.* Available: http://www.bls.gov/cps. [Accessed December 2002].

Bureau of Labor Statistics. (2003). *Occupational outlook handbook.* Available: http://www.bls.gov/oco/ocos069.htm. [Accessed August 1, 2003].

Burton, L. (1991). Caring for children. *The American Enterprise, 2,* 34-37.

Burton, L., Tubbs, C., Odoms, A.M., Oh, H.J., Mello, Z., and Cherlin, A. (2002). *Welfare reform, poverty, and health: Low-income families' health status and health insurance.* Menlo Park, CA: Henry J. Kaiser Family Foundation.

Burton, L.M., Allison, K.W., and Obeidallah, D. (1995). Social context and adolescence: Perspectives on development among inner-city African-American teens. In L.J. Crockett, and A.C. Crouter (Eds.), *Pathways through adolescence* (pp. 119-138). Hillsdale, NJ: Erlbaum.

Burton, L.M., and Jarrett, R.L. (2000). In the mix, yet on the margins: The place of families in urban neighborhood and child development research. *Journal of Marriage and the Family, 62,* 444-465.

Cairns, R.B. (1979). *Social development: The origins and plasticity of interchanges.* San Francisco: W.H. Freeman.

Cairns, R.B., and Cairns, B.D. (1994). *Lifelines and risks: Pathways of youth in our time.* New York: Cambridge University Press.

Cambell, D., and Parisi, M. (2001). *Individual income tax returns, 1999.* (Statistics of Income Bulletin, fall). Washington, DC: Internal Revenue Service.

Campbell, F.A., and Ramey, C. (1995). Cognitive and school outcomes for high risk African American students at middle adolescence: Positive effects of early intervention. *American Educational Research Journal, 32,* 743-772.

Campbell, J.L., Lamb, M., and Hwang, C. (2000a). Early child-care experiences and children's social competence between 1 1/2 and 15 years of age. *Applied Developmental Science, 4,* 166-175.

Campbell, N.D., Appelbaum, J.C., Martinson, K., and Martin, E. (2000b). *Be all that we can be: Lessons from the military for improving our nation's child care system.* Washington, DC: National Women's Law Center.

Cancian, M., Haveman, R., Meyer, D., and Wolfe, B. (1999). *Before and after TANF: The economic well-being of women leaving welfare.* Madison, WI: Institute for Research on Poverty.

Cancian, M., Haveman, R., Meyer, D. and Wolfe, B. (2002). The economic well-being of women leaving welfare. *La Follette Policy Report, 13*(1), 11-17.

Cantor, D., Waldfogel, J., Kerwin, J., McKinley-Wright, M., Levin, K., Rauch, J., Hagerty, T., and Stapleton-Kudela, M. (2001). *Balancing the needs of families and employers: Family and medical leave surveys.* Rockville, MD: Westat.

Capizzano, J., and Adams, G. (2000). *The hours that children under five spend in child care: Variations across states.* Washington, DC: Urban Institute.

Capizzano, J., Adams, G., and Sonenstein, F. (2000a). *Child care arrangements for children under five: Variation across states.* (Assessing the New Federalism Project). Washington, DC: Urban Institute.

Capizzano, J., Tout, K., and Adams, G. (2000b). *Child care patterns of school-age children with employed mothers.* Washington, DC: Urban Institute.

Capizzano, J., Adelman, S., and Stagner, M. (2002). *What happens when the school year is over? The use and costs of child care for school-age children during the summer months.* (Assessing the New Federalism, Occasional paper no. 58). Washington, DC: Urban Institute.

Carr, R.V., Wright, J.D., and Brody, C.J. (1996). Effects of high school work experience a decade later: Evidence from the National Longitudinal Survey. *Sociology of Education, 69,* 66-81.

Casper, L.M. (1997). *My daddy takes care of me! Fathers as care providers.* (Current Population Reports) Washington, DC: U.S. Department of Commerce.

Casper, L.M., and Bianchi, S.M. (2002). *Continuity and change in the American family.* Thousand Oaks, CA: Russell Sage.

Casper, L.M., and O'Connell, M. (1998). Work, income, the economy, and married fathers as child-care providers. *Demography, 35,* 243-250.

Castellino, D.R., Lerner, J.V., Lerner, R.M., and von Eye, A. (1998). Maternal employment and education: Predictors of young adolescent career trajectories. *Applied Developmental Science, 2*(3), 114-126.

Cauthen, N. (2002). *Earned income tax credits.* New York: National Center for Children in Poverty.

Center for the Child Care Workforce and Human Services Policy Center. (2002). *Estimating the size and components of the U.S. child care workforce and caregiving population: Key findings from the child care workforce estimate.* Washington, DC: Author.

Center on Budget and Policy Priority. (1999). *Poverty and income trends.* Washington, DC: Author.

Centers for Disease Control and Prevention. (2000). *Youth risk behavior surveillance—United States, 1999.* Available: http://www.cdc.gov. [Accessed July 2002].

Centers for Disease Control and Prevention. (2002a). *Overweight high school students: The burden of chronic diseases and their risk factors: National and state perspectives, 2002.* Available: http://www.cdc.gov/nccdphp/burdenbook2002/03_overhs.htm. [Accessed December 2002].

Centers for Disease Control and Prevention. (2002b). Trends in sexual risk behaviors among high school students: United States, 1991-2001. *Morbidity and Mortality Weekly Report, 51*(38), 856-859.

Chang, Y.E., Huston, A.C., Crosby, D.A., and Gennetian, L.A. (2002). *The effects of welfare and employment programs on children's participation in Head Start.* (Working paper No. 10, Next Generation Research Consortium). New York: Manpower Demonstration Research Corporation.

Chaplin, D., and Hannaway, J. (1996). *High school employment: Meaningful connections for at-risk youth.* Washington, DC: Urban Institute.

Chaplin, D.D., Robins, P.K., Hofferth, S.L., Wissoker, D.A., and Fronstin, P. (1999). *The price elasticity of child care demand: A sensitivity analysis.* (Working paper). Washington, DC: Urban Institute.

Chase-Lansdale, P.L., Coley, R.L., Lohman, B.J., and Pittman, L.D. (2001). *Welfare reform, what about the children? Welfare children and families: A three-city study.* (Policy Brief 02-1). Baltimore: Johns Hopkins University.

Chase-Lansdale, P.L., Moffitt, R.A., Lohman, B.J., Cherlin, A.J., Coley, R.L., Pittman, L.D., Roff, J., and Votruba-Drzal, E. (2003). Mothers' transitions from welfare to work and the well-being of preschoolers and adolescents. *Science, 299,* 1548-1552.

Chase-Lansdale, P.L., and Pittman, L.D. (2002). Welfare reform and parenting: Reasonable expectations. *The Future of Children: Children and Welfare Reform, 12*(1), 167-185.

Cherlin, A.J., and Fomby, P. (2002). *A closer look at changes in children's living arrangements in low-income families. Welfare children and families: A three-city study.* (Policy Brief 02-3). Baltimore: Johns Hopkins University.

Child Care Bureau. (2000). *Child Care and Development Fund (CCDF) report to Congress—fiscal year 2001.* Available: http://www.acf.hhs.gov/programs/ccb/policy1/congress report/2001CCDFreport.doc. [Accessed August 2003].

Children's Foundation. (2002). *Family child care licensing study: Summary data.* Available: http://www.childrensfoundation.net/centerssum.htm and http://www.childrens foundation.net/summaryfcc.htm. [Accessed March 2003].

Chin-Quee, D.S., and Scarr, S. (1994). Lack of early child care effects on school-age children's social competence and academic achievement. *Early Development and Parenting, 3,* 103-112.

Clark, R. (1983). *Family life and school achievement.* Chicago: University of Chicago Press.

Clark, R., Hyde, J.S., Essex, M.J., and Klein, M.H. (1997). Length of maternity leave and quality of mother-infant interaction. *Child Development, 68,* 364-383.

Clarke-Stewart, K. (1989). Infant day care: Maligned or malignant. *American Psychologist, 44,* 266-273.

Clarke-Stewart, K.A., Gruber, C.P., and Fitzgerald, L.M. (1994). *Children at home and in day care.* Hillsdale, NJ: Erlbaum.

Clarke-Stewart, K.A., Vandell, D.L., Burchinal, M., O'Brien, M., and McCartney, K. (2000). Do features of child care homes affect children's development. *Early Childhood Research Quarterly, 17*(1), 52-86.

Clarke-Stewart, K.A., Vandell, D.L., Burchinal, M., O'Brien, M., and McCartney, K. (2002). Do regulable features of child homes affect children's development. *Early Childhood Research Quarterly, 17,* 52-86.

Cohen, P., and Bianchi, S. (1999). Marriage, children, and women's employment: What do we know? *Monthly Labor Review, 122,* 22-30.

Coley, R.L., Chase-Lansdale, L. (2000). Welfare receipt, financial strain, and African-American adolescent functioning. *Social Service Review, 74,* 380-404.

Collins, A., Layzer, J., Kraeder, L., Werner, A., and Glantz, F. (2000). *National study of child care for low-income families: State and community sub-study interim report.* Cambridge, MA: Abt Associates.

Collins, W.A. (in press). Presidential address. *Society for Research in Adolescence.*

Colwell, M.J., Pettit, G.S., Meece, D., Bates, J.E., and Dodge, K. (2001). Cumulative risk and continuity in nonparental care from infancy to early adolescence. *Merrill-Palmer Quarterly, 47,* 207-234.

Commission on Family and Medical Leave Act. (1996). *A workable balance: Report to the Congress on family and medical leave policies.* Washington, DC: U.S. Department of Labor, Women's Bureau.

Committee on Economic Development. (2002). *Preschool for all: Investing in a productive and just society.* Available: http://www.ced.org/projects/educ.htm. [Accessed May 20, 2002].

Conger, K., Conger, R., and Elder, G.H. (1994). Sibling relationships during hard times. In R. Conger, and G.H. Elder (Eds.), *Families in troubled times: Adapting to change in rural America* (pp. 235-252). New York: Aldine de Gruyter.

Conger, R.D., Conger, K.J., and Elder, G.E. (1997). Family economic hardship and adolescent adjustment: Mediating and moderating processes. In G. Duncan, and J. Brooks-Gunn (Eds.), *Consequences of growing up poor* (chapter 10). New York: Russell Sage.

Conger, R.D., and Elder, G.H. (1994). *Families in troubled times: Adapting to change in rural America.* New York: Aldine de Gruyter.

Congressional Budget Office. (2001). *Historical effective tax rates, 1979-1997.* Washington, DC: Author.

Cook, D., and Fine, M. (1995). Motherwit: Childrearing lessons from African-American mothers of low income. In B. Swadener, and S. Lubeck (Eds.), *Children and families "at promise": Deconstructing the discourse of risk* (pp. 118-142). New York: SUNY Press.

Coolson, P., Seligson, M., and Garbarino, J. (1985). *When school's out and nobody's home.* Chicago, IL: National Committee for the Prevention of Child Abuse.

Coontz, S., and Folbre, N. (2002). *Marriage, poverty, and public policy.* Prepared for the Fifth Annual CCF Conference.

Cosden, M., Morrison, G., Albanese, A.L., and Macias, S. (2001). When homework is not home work: After-school programs for homework assistance. *Educational Psychologist, 36*(3), 211-221.

Council of Economic Advisors. (1998). *Expansions in the Earned Income Tax Credit and the minimum wage.* Washington, DC. Author.

Coverman, S., and Sheley, J.F. (1986). Change in men's housework and child-care time, 1965-1975. *Journal of Marriage and the Family, 48,* 413-322.

Crispell, D. (1994). Child-care choices don't match mom's wishes. *American Demographics, 16,* 11-13.

Crittendon, A. (2001). *The price of motherhood: Why the most important job in the world is still the least valued.* New York: Metropolitan Books.

Crosby, D.A., Gennetian, L.A., and Huston, A.C. (2001). *Does child care assistance matter? The effects of welfare and employment programs on child care for preschool and young school-aged children.* New York: Manpower Demonstration Research Corporation.

Crouter, A.C., MacDermid, S.M., McHale, S.M., and Perry-Jenkins, M. (1990). Parental monitoring and perceptions of children's school performance and conduct in dual- and single-earner families. *Developmental Psychology, 26*(4), 649-657.

Crouter, A.C., Maquire, M.C., Helms-Erikson, H., and McHale, S.M. (1999). Parental work in middle childhood: Links between employment and the division of housework, parent-child activities, and parental modeling. In R. Hodson (Series Ed.), *Research in the sociology of work.* Stamford, CT: JAI Press.

Cryer, D., Peisner-Feinberg, E.S., Culkin, M.L., Phillipsen, L., and Rustici, J. (1995). Design of study. In S.W. Helburn (Ed.), *Cost, quality, and child outcomes in child care centers, technical report*. Denver, CO: University of Colorado, Department of Economics, Center for Research in Economic and Social Policy.

Csikszentmihalyi, M., Rathunde, K., and Whalen, S. (1993). *Talented teenagers: The roots of success and failure*. Cambridge: Cambridge University.

Csikszentmihalyi, M., and Schneider, B. (2000). *Becoming adult: How teenagers prepare for the world of work*. New York: Basic Books.

Currie, J. (2001). Early childhood intervention programs. *Journal of Economic Perspectives, 15*(2), 213-238.

Currie, J., and Hotz, J. (2001). *Accidents will happen? Unintentional injury, maternal employment, and child care policy*. (NBER Working paper 8090). Cambridge, MA: National Bureau of Economic Research.

Currie, J., and Thomas, D. (1995). Does Head Start make a difference? *American Economic Review, 85*(3), 341-364.

Currie, J., and Thomas, D. (1999). Does Head Start help Hispanic children? *Journal of Public Economics, 74*(2), 235-262.

Currie, J., and Thomas, D. (2000). School quality and the long-term effects of Head Start. *Journal of Human Resources, 34*(4), 755-774.

Danziger, S. (2001). Commentary. In R. Blank, and R. Haskins (Eds.), *The new world of welfare*. Washington, DC: Brookings Institution.

Danziger, S., Corcoran, M., Danziger, S., and Heflin, C.M. (2000a). Work, income, and material hardship after welfare reform. *Journal of Consumer Affairs, 34*(1), 6-30.

Danziger, S., Kalil, A., and Anderson, N. (2000b). Human capital, health, and mental health characteristics of welfare recipients: Co-occurrence and correlates. *Journal of Social Issues, 56*, 635-654.

Danziger, S.K., Corcoran, M., Danziger, S., Heflin, C., Kalil, A., Levine, J., Rosen, D., Seefeldt, K., Siefert, K., and Tolman, R. (2000c). Barriers to the employment of welfare recipients. In R. Cherry, and W.M. Rodgers (Eds.), *Prosperity for all? The economic boom and African Americans*. New York: Russell Sage.

Danziger, S., Heflin, C., Corcoran, M., Oltmans, E., and Wang, H.C. (2002). Does it pay to move from welfare to work? *Journal of Policy Analysis and Management, 21*(4).

Dearing, E., McCartney, K., and Taylor, B.A. (2001). Change in family income-to-needs matters more for children with less. *Child Development, 72*, 1779-1793.

Deater-Deckard, K., Pinkerton, R., and Scarr, S. (1996). Child care quality and children's behavioral adjustment: A four-year longitudinal study. *Journal of Child Psychology, 37*, 937-948.

DeMarco, D., and Mills, G. (2000). *The New York state child assistance program: Five-year impacts, costs and benefits*. Cambridge, MA: Abt Associates.

Desai, S., Chase-Lansdale, P.L., and Michael, R.T. (1989). Mother or market? Effects of maternal employment on the intellectual ability of four-year-old children. *Demography, 26*, 545-561.

Dettling, A., Gunnar, M., and Donzella, B. (1999). Cortisol levels of young children in full-day childcare centers. *Psychoneuroendocrinology, 24*, 519-536.

Deutsch, F.M. (1999). *Halving it all: How equally shared parenting works*. Cambridge, MA: Harvard University.

DeVaus, D., and Millward, C. (1998). Home alone before or after school. *Family Matters, 49*, 34-37.

Dishion, T.J., Capaldi, D., Spacklen, K.M., and Li, F. (1995). Peer ecology of male adolescent drug use: Developmental processes in peer relations and psychopathology. *Developmental and Psychopathology, 7*, 803-824.

Dishion, T.J., McCord, J., and Poulin, F. (1999). When interventions harm: Peer groups and problem behavior. *American Psychologist, 54,* 755-764.

Dishion, T.J., and McMahon, R.J. (1998). Parental monitoring and the prevention of child and adolescent problem behavior: A conceptual and empirical formulation. *Family Psychology Review, 1,* 61-75.

Dodson, L., Manuel, T., and Bravo, E. (2002). *Keeping jobs and raising families in low-income America: It just doesn't work.* Cambridge, MA: Radcliffe Institute for Advanced Study.

Donahoe, D., and Tienda, M. (2000). The transition from school to work: Is there a crisis? What can be done? In S.D. Danziger, and J. Waldfogel (Eds.), *Securing the future: Investing in children from birth to college* (pp. 231-262). New York: Russell Sage.

Downey, G., and Coyne, J.C. (1990). Children of depressed parents: An integrative review. *Psychological Bulletin, 108*(1), 50-76.

Dube, A., and Kaplan, E. (2002). *Paid family leave in California: An analysis of the costs and benefits.* Chicago, IL and Berkeley: University of Chicago and University of California, Berkeley.

Duckett, E., and Maryse, R. (1995). Maternal employment and the quality of daily experience for young adolescents of single mothers. *Journal of Family Psychology, 9*(4), 418-432.

Duncan, G.J., and Brooks-Gunn, J. (1997). Income effects across the life span: Integration and interpretation. In G.J. Duncan, and J. Brooks-Gunn (Eds.), *Consequences of growing up poor* (pp. 596-610). New York: Russell Sage.

Duncan, G.J., and Brooks-Gunn, J. (2000). Family poverty, welfare reform, and child development. *Child Development, 71,* 188-196.

Duncan, G.J., and Gibson, C. (2000). *Selection and attrition in the NICHD Child Care Study's analysis of the impacts of child care quality on child outcomes.* Unpublished paper, Northwestern University, Evanston, IL.

Duncan, G.J., and Magnuson, K.A. (in press). Policies to promote the healthy development of infants and preschoolers. Washington, DC: Brookings Institution.

Duncan, G.J., Brooks-Gunn, J., and Klebanov, P.K. (1994). Economic deprivation and early childhood development. *Child Development, 65,* 296-318.

Duncan, G.J., Brooks-Gunn, J., Yeung, J., and Smith, J. (1998). How much does childhood poverty affect the life chances of children? *American Sociological Review, 63,* 406-423.

Dunn, L. (1993). Proximal and distal features of day care quality and children's development. *Early Childhood Research Quarterly, 8,* 16-192.

Dunn, L., Beach, S.A., and Kontos, S. (1994). Quality of the literacy environment in day care and children's development. *Journal of Research in Childhood Education, 9,* 24-34.

Dupree, A., and Primus, W. (2001). *Declining share of children living with single mothers in the late 1990s.* Washington, DC: Center on Budget and Policy Priorities.

Dworkin, J.B., Larson, R., and Hansen, D. (in press). Adolescents' accounts of growth experiences in youth activities. *Journal of Youth and Adolescence.*

DYG, Inc. (2002). *What grown-ups understand about child development: A national benchmark survey.* Available: http://www.zerotothree.org/parent_poll.html. [Accessed 2002].

Early Head Start Research Consortium. (2001). *Building their futures: How early Head Start programs are enhancing the lives of infants and toddlers in low-income families. Summary report.* Washington, DC: U.S. Department of Health and Human Services, Administration for Children and Families.

Eccles, J.S., Midgley, C., Wigfield, A., Buchanon, C.M., Reuman, D., Flanagan, C., and MacIver, D. (1993). Development during adolescence. *American Psychologist, 48,* 90-101.

Eder, D., Evans, C., and Parker, S. (1995). *School talk: Gender and adolescent culture.* New Jersey: Rutgers University.

Eder, D., and Kinney, D.A. (1995). The effects of middle school extracurricular activities on adolescents' popularity and peer status. *Youth and Society, 26,* 298-324.

Eder, D., and Parker, S. (1987). The cultural production and reproduction of gender: The effect of extracurricular activities on peer-group culture. *Sociology of Education, 60,* 200-214.

Edin, K., and Lein, L. (1997). *Making ends meet.* New York: Russell Sage.

Edin, K., Lein, L., and Nelson, T. (2002). Taking care of business: The economic survival strategies of low-income, noncustodial fathers. In F. Munger (Ed.), *Laboring below the poverty line: The new ethnography of poverty, low-wage work, and survival in the global economy* (pp. 125-147). New York: Russell Sage.

Education Week. (2001). *State policy updates: Sources.* Available: http://www.edweek.org/sreports/qc01/articles/qc01story.cfm?slug=17updates.h20andkeywords=pre%2Dk. [Accessed 2003].

Egeland, B., and Heister, M. (1995). The long-term consequences of infant day-care and mother-infant attachment. *Child Development, 66,* 74-85.

Ehrenreich, B. (2001). *Nickel and dimed: On (not) getting by in America.* New York: Henry Holt.

Elder, G.H. (1997). The effects of parents' working conditions and family economic hardship on parenting behaviors and children's self-efficacy. *Social Psychology Quarterly, 60*(4), 291-303.

Elder, G.H., Eccles, J.S., Ardelt, M., and Lord, S. (1995). Inner-city parents under economic pressure: Perspectives on the strategies of parenting. *Journal of Marriage and the Family, 57*(3), 771-784.

Elder, G.H., Modell, J., and Parke, R.D. (Eds.). (1993). *Children in time and place: Developmental and historical insights.* New York: Cambridge University.

Elicker, J., Fortner-Wood, C., and Noppe, I.C. (1999). The context of infant attachment in family child care. *Journal of Applied Developmental Psychology, 20*(2), 319-336.

Ellwood, D. (1988). *Poor support: Poverty and the American family.* New York: Basic Books.

Ellwood, D. (1999). *The plight of the working poor.* (Children's Roundtable Number 2). Washington, DC: Brookings Institution.

Ellwood, D. (2001). The impact of the Earned Income Tax Credit and social policy reforms on work, marriage, and living arrangements. *National Tax Journal, 53,* 1063-1106.

Emlen, A.C., and Koren, P.E. (1984). *Hard to find and difficult to manage: The effects of child care on the workplace services.* Oregon: Portland State University, Regional Research Institute for Human Services.

Employment Development Department. (2000). *The fiscal impact on the Disability Insurance Fund of extending disability benefits to individuals granted family leave.* Sacramento: State of California.

Employment Policy Foundation. (1999). *Paid parental leave: A $14 billion to $128 billion entitlement.* Available: http://www.epf.org. [Accessed June 23, 2000].

Employment Policy Foundation. (2000). *Paid family leave: At what cost?* Washington, DC : Author.

Erikson, E.H. (1968). *Identity, youth and crisis.* New York: W.W. Norton.

Evans, C., and Eder, D. (1993). "No exit": Processes of social isolation in the middle school. *Journal of Contemporary Ethnography, 22,* 139-170.

Fenwick, R., and Tausig, M. (2001). Family and health outcomes of shift work and schedules control. *American Behavioral Scientist, 44*(7), 1179-1198.

Fernandez, J. (1986). *Child care and productivity: Resolving family/work conflicts.* Lexington, MA: Lexington Books.

Field, T.M. (1991). Quality infant day-care and grade school behavior and performance. *Child Development, 62,* 863-870.

Finn-Stevenson, M., and Zigler, E. (1999). *Schools of the twenty first century: Linking child care and education.* Boulder, CO: Westview.

Florian, J.E., Schweinhart, L.J., and Epstein, A.S. (1997). *Early returns: First-year report of the Michigan school-readiness program evaluation.* Ypsilanti, MI: High/Scope Educational Reasearch Foundation.

Folk, K.F., and Yi, Y. (1994). Piecing together childcare with multiple arrangements: Crazy quilt or preferred pattern for employed parents of preschool children. *Journal of Marriage and the Family, 56,* 669-680.

Fordham, S. (1996). *Blacked out: Dilemmas of race, identity, and success at Capital High.* Chicago: University of Chicago.

Fraker, T.M., Ross, C.M., Staplonis, R.A., Olsen, R.B., Kovac, M.D., Dion, M.R., and Rangarajan, A. (2002). *The evaluation of welfare reform in Iowa: Final impact report.* Princeton, NJ: Mathematica Policy Research.

Fremstad, S., and Parrott, S. (2002). *The Senate finance committee's "tri-partisan" TANF reauthorization.* Washington, DC: Center on Budget and Policy Priorities.

Friedlander, D., and Burtless, G. (1995). *Five years after: The long-term effects of welfare-to-work programs.* New York: Russell Sage.

Friedman, D.E. (1989). *Linking work-family issues to the bottom line.* (Report No. 962). New York: The Conference Board.

Friedman, D.E., and Galinsky, E. (1992). Work and family issues: A legitimate business concern. In S. Zedeck (Ed.), *Work, families, and organizations* (pp. 168-207). New York: Jossey-Bass.

Fuller, B., and Kagan, S.L. (2002). *New lives for poor families? Mothers and young children move through welfare reform.* Berkeley, CA and New York: University of California, Berkeley and Columbia University.

Fuller, B., Caspary, G., Kagan, S.L. et al. (2001). *Does maternal employment influence poor children's social development?* (Working paper). Berkeley: University of California.

Fursteberg, F., Cook, T., Eccles, J., Elder, G., and Sameroff, A. (1999). *Managing to make it: Urban families and adolescent success.* Chicago: University of Chicago.

Fusaro, J. (1997). The effect of full-day kindergarten on student achievement: A meta-analysis. *Child Study Journal, 27*(4), 269-277.

Galambos, N.L., and Maggs, J.L. (1991). Out-of-school care of young adolescents and self-reported behavior. *Developmental Psychology, 27*(4), 644-655.

Galambos, N.L., and Sears, H.A. (1998). Adolescents' perceptions of parents' work and adolescents' work values in two-earner families. *Journal of Early Adolescence, 18*(4), 397-420.

Galinsky, E. (1998). *Child care and productivity.* New York: Families and Work Institute.

Galinsky, E. (1999). *Ask the children: What America's children really think about working parents.* New York: William Morrow.

Galinsky, E., and Bond, J.T. (1998). *The 1998 business work-life study: A sourcebook.* New York: Families and Work Institute.

Galinsky, E., and Bond, J.T. (2000). Supporting families as primary caregivers: The role of workplace. In D. Cryer, and T. Harms (Eds.), *Infants and toddlers in out-of-home care* (p. 321). Baltimore: National Center for Early Development and Learning.

Galinsky, E., and Friedman, D.E. (1993). *Education before school: Investing in quality child care.* New York: Scholastic.

Galinsky, E., Friedman, D.E., and Hernandez, C.A. (1992). *The corporate reference guide to work-family programs.* New York: Families and Work Institute.

Galley, M. (2001). Early years. *Education Week, 21*(9).

Gantz, F., Rodda, D., Cutler, M.J., Rhodes, W., and Wrobel, M. (1997). *Early childhood and child care study: Profile of participants in the CACFP.* Alexandria, VA: U.S. Department of Agriculture, Food and Consumer Service.

Garasky, S., and Meyer, D.R. (1996). Reconsidering the increase in father-only families. *Demography, 33,* 385-393.

Garces, E., Thomas, D., and Currie, J. (2000). Longer term effects of Head Start. *American Economic Review, 85*(3), 341-364.

Garey, A.I. (1999). *Weaving work and motherhood.* Philadelphia: Temple University Press.

Gassman-Pines, A. (2002). *The effects of welfare and employment policies on child care use of low-income young mothers.* (Working paper, Next Generation Research Consortium). New York: Manpower Demonstration Research Corporation.

Gelbach, J. (2002). Public schooling for young children and maternal labor supply. *American Economic Review, 92*(1), 307-323.

Gennetian, L.A., Crosby, D.A., and Huston, A.C. (2001). *Does child care assistance matter? The effects of welfare and employment programs on child care for very young children.* New York: Manpower Demonstration Research Corporation.

Gennetian, L.A., Crosby, D.A., Huston, A.C., and Lowe, E.D. (2002a). *How child care assistance in welfare and employment programs can support the employment of low-income families.* New York: Manpower Demonstration Research Corporation.

Gennetian, L.A., Duncan, G.J., Knox, V., Vargas, W., Clark-Kauffman, E., and London, A.S. (2002b). *How welfare and work policies for parents affect adolescents: A synthesis of research.* New York: Manpower Demonstration Research Corporation.

Gennetian, L.A., and Miller, C. (2000). *Reforming welfare and rewarding work: Final report on the Minnesota Family Investment Program, vol. 2: Effects on children.* New York: Manpower Demonstration Research Corporation.

Gennetian, L.A., and Miller, C. (2002). Children and welfare reform: A view from an experimental welfare program in Minnesota. *Child Development, 73,* 601-620.

Gentry, W., and Hagy, A. (1995). *The distributional effects of the tax treatment of child care expenses.* (NBER Working Paper, No. 5088). Cambridge, MA: National Bureau of Economic Research.

Gibson, C., and Weisner, T.S. (2002). "Rational" and ecocultural circumstances of program take-up among low-income working parents. *Human Organization: Journal of the Society for Applied Anthropology, 61,* 154-166.

Gilliam, W.S., and Zigler, E.F. (2000). A critical meta-analysis of all evaluations of state-funded preschool from 1977 to 1998: Implications for policy, service delivery and program evaluation. *Early Childhood Research Quarterly, 15,* 441-473.

Gish, M., and Harper, S. (2002). *Child Care: State Programs Under the Child Care and Development Fund.* Congressional Research Service. Available: http://www.financeprojectinfo.org/win/childcareandwelfare.asp. [Accessed 2003].

Gladden, T., and Taber, C. (2000). Wage progression among less skilled workers. In D. Card, and R. Blank (Eds.), *Finding jobs: Work and welfare reform.* New York: Russell Sage.

Glantz, F.B., Rodda, D.T., Cutler, M.J., Rhodes, W., and Wrobel, M. (1997). *Early childhood and child care study: Profile of participants in the CACFP, final report volume I.* Alexandria, VA: USDA-Food and Consumer Service.

Glass, J., and Riley, L. (1998). Family responsive policies and employee retention following childbirth. *Social Forces, 76*(4), 1401-1435.

Goelman, H. (1988). The relationship between structure and process variables in home day care settings on children's language development. In A. Pence, and H. Goelman (Eds.), *The practice of ecological research: From concepts to methodology.* New York: Teachers College Press.

Gold, D.R., Rogaca, S., Bock, N., Tosteson, T.D., Baum, T., Speizer, F.E., and Czeisler, C.A. (1992). Rotating shift work, sleep, and accidents related to sleepiness in hospital nurses. *American Journal of Public Health, 82,* 1011-1014.

Goldberg, B. (2002). The most important story you ever saw. In *Bias: A CBS insider exposes how the media distorts the news* (pp. 163-178). Washington, DC: Regnery.

Gomby, D.S., Cuross, P.L., and Behrman, R.E. (1999). Home visiting: Analysis and recommendations. *The Future of Children: Home Visiting: Recent Program Evaluations, 9*(1), 4-26.

Goodman, S.H., and Brumley, H.E. (1990). Schizophrenic and depressed mothers: Relational deficits in parenting. *Developmental Psychology, 26,* 31-39.

Goodnough, A. (2003). Pataki's budget would cut city's prekindergarten programs. *New York Times,* February 5.

Googins, B.K. (1997). Shared responsibility for managing work and family relationships: A community perspective. In S. Parasuraman, and J. H. Greenhaus (Eds.), *Integrating work and family: Challenges and choices for a changing world* (pp. 220-231). Westport, CT: Praeger.

Gordon, N.P., Cleary, P.D., Parker, C.E., and Czelsler, C.A. (1986). The prevalence and health impact of shiftwork. *American Journal of Public Health, 76,* 1225-1228.

Gormley, W.T. (1995). Reinventing child care. In W. Gormley (Ed.), *Everybody's children: Child care as a public problem* (pp. 166-191). Washington, DC: Brookings Institution.

Gormley, W.T. (1999). Regulating child care quality. *The Annals of the American Academy of Political and Social Science, 563,* 116-129.

Gormley, W.T. (2000). Early childhood education and care regulation: A comparative perspective. *International Journal of Educational Research, 33,* 55-74.

Gottfried, A.E., Gottfried, A.W., and Bathurst, K. (1995). Maternal and dual-earner employment status and parenting. In M. Bornstein (Ed.), *Handbook of parenting* (vol. 2, pp. 139-160). Mahwah, NJ: Erlbaum.

Greenberger, E., and Steinberg, L. (1986). *When teenagers work: The psychological and social costs of adolescent employment.* New York: Basic Books.

Greenstein, R., and Shapiro, I. (1998). *New research findings on the effects of the Earned Income Tax Credit.* Washington, DC: Center on Budget and Policy Priorities.

Grogger, J. (2000). *Time limits and welfare use.* (NBER Working Paper 7709). Cambridge, MA: National Bureau of Economic Research.

Grogger, J. (2001). *The effects of time limits and other policy changes on welfare use, work, and income among female-headed families.* (NBER Working Paper 8153). Cambridge, MA: National Bureau of Economic Research.

Grogger, J., Karoly, L.A., and Klerman, J.A. (2002). *Consequences of welfare reform: A research synthesis.* Santa Monica, CA: Rand Corporation. Available: http://www.acf. dhhs.gov/programs/opre/welfare_reform/reform_ch10.html. [Accessed 2003].

Grossman, J.B., Price, M.L., Fellerath, V., Jucovy, L.Z., Kotloff, L.J., Raley, R., and Walker, K.E. (2002). *Multiple choices after school: Findings from the extended-service schools initiative.* Public/Private Ventures.

Grossman, J.B., and Tierney, J.P. (1998). Does mentoring work? An impact study of the Big Brothers Big Sisters program. *Evaluation Review, 22,* 403-426.

Grosswald, B. (1999). *"I raised my kids on the bus": Transit shift workers' coping strategies for parenting.* Berkeley: University of California, Center for Working Families.

Grych, J.H., and Clark, R. (1999). Maternal employment and development of the father-infant relationship in the first year. *Developmental Psychology, 35,* 893-903.

Gueron, J., and Pauly, E. (1991). *From welfare to work.* New York: Russell Sage.

Gullo, D., Bersani, C.U., Clements, D.H., and Bayless, K.M. (1986). A comparative study of "all-day", "alternate-day", and "half-day" kindergarten schedules: Effects on achievement and classroom social behaviors. *Journal of Research in Childhood Education, 1*(2), 87-94.

Gullo, D., and Clements, D. (1984). The effects of kindergarten schedule on achievement, classroom behavior, and attendance. *Journal of Educational Research, 78*(1), 31-36.

Gustafsson, S., Wetzels, C., Vlasblom, J.D., and Dex, S. (1996). Women's labor force transitions in connection with childbirth: A panel data comparison between Germany, Sweden, and Great Britain. *Journal of Population Economics, 9,* 223-246.

Gutman, L.M., and Eccles, J. (1999). Financial strain, parenting behaviors and adolescents' achievement: Testing model equivalence between African Americans and European American single and two-parent families. *Child Development, 70*(6), 1464-1474.

Hahn, A., Leavitt, T., and Aaron, P. (1994). *Evaluation of the Quantum Opportunity Program (QOP): Did the program work?* Waltham, MA: Brandeis University, Heller Graduate School.

Hair, E.C., McGroder, S.M., Zaslow, M.J., Ahluwalia, S.K., and Moore, K.A. (2002). How do maternal risk factors affect children in low-income families? Further evidence of two-generational implications. *Journal of Prevention and Intervention in the Community, 23*(12), 65-94.

Halpern, R. (2002). *A different kind of child development institution: The history of after-school programs for low-income children.* Chicago: Erikson Institute for Graduate Study in Child Development, University of Chicago.

Hamer, J. (2001). *What it means to be daddy.* New York: Columbia University Press.

Hamilton, G., Freedman, S., Gennetian, L., Michalopoulos, C., Walter, J., Adams-Ciardullo, D., Gassman-Pines, A., McGroder, S., Zaslow, M., Brooks, J., and Ahluwalia, D. (2001). *How effective are different welfare-to-work approaches? Five-year adult and child impacts for eleven programs.* Washington, DC: U.S. Department of Health and Human Services Administration for Children and Families and Office of the Assistant Secretary for Planning and Evaluation; and U.S. Department of Education, Office of the Deputy Secretary, Planning and Evaluation Service and Office of Vocational and Adult Education.

Han, W. (2002a). *Nonstandard work schedules and child care choices: Evidence from the NICHD study of early child care.* New York: Columbia University.

Han, W. (2002b). *Who is working nonstandard hours during the early years of a child's life? What are the likely consequences for mothers?* New York: Columbia University.

Han, W.J., and Waldfogel, J. (2002). *Parental leave-taking and the FMLA.* New York: Columbia University.

Han, W., Waldfogel, J., and Brooks-Gunn, J. (2001). The effects of early maternal employment on later cognitive and behavioral outcomes. *Journal of Marriage and the Family, 63,* 336-354.

Han, W., Waldfogel, J., and Brooks-Gunn, J. (2002). *Early maternal employment and child behavior outcomes: What do we know? Evidence from two longitudinal studies.* Paper presented at the Annual Meeting of the Population Association of America.

Harms, T., and Clifford, R. (1980). *Early childhood environment rating scale.* New York: Teachers College Press.

Harms, T., and Clifford, R. (1989). *Family day care rating scale.* New York: Teachers College Press.

Harms, T., Cryer, D., and Clifford, R.M. (1990). *Infant/toddler environment rating scale.* New York: Teachers College Press.

Harnish, J.D., Dodge, K.A., and Valente, E. (1995) Mother-child interaction quality as a partial mediator of the roles of maternal depressive symptomatology and socioeconomic status in the development of child behavior problems. *Child Development, 66*(3), 739-753.

Harris, J., and Lengyel, T. (2002). Ends that don't meet: Employment under welfare reform. In T. Lengyel, and D. Campbell (Eds.), *Faces of change: Welfare policy through the lens of personal experience* (pp. 9-28). Milwaukee, WI: Alliance for Children and Families.

Harvey, E. (1999). Short-term and long-term effects of early paternal employment on children of the National Longitudinal Survey of Youth. *Developmental Psychology, 35,* 445-459.

Haskins, R. (1985). Public school aggression among children with varying day-care experience. *Child Development, 56,* 689-703.

Haskins, R. (2001). Effects of welfare reform at four years. In G.J. Duncan, and P.L. Chase-Lansdale (Eds.), *For better and for worse* (pp. 264-289). New York: Russell Sage.

Hattery, A.J. (2001). Tag-team parents: Costs and benefits of utilizing nonoverlapping shift work in families with young children. *Families in Society: The Journal of Contemporary Human Services, 82*(4), 419-427.

Hausfather, A., Toharia, A., LaRoche, C., and Engelsmann, F. (1997). Effects of age of entry, day-care quality, and family characteristis on preschool behavior. *Journal of Child Psychology and Psychiatry and Allied Disciplines, 38,* 441-448.

Heckman, J. (2000). *Policies to foster human capital.* (Joint Center for Poverty Research Policy Brief). Chicago, IL: Northwestern University/University of Chicago.

Helburn, S.W. (1995). *Cost, quality and child outcomes in child care centers: Technical report.* Denver: University of Colorado, Department of Economics, Center for Research in Economic and Social Policy.

Helburn, S.W., and Bergmann, B.R. (2002). *America's child care problem: The way out.* New York: Pelgrave for St. Martin's Press.

Hembry, K. (1988). *Repeat childbearing among black, never-married, adolescent mothers.* Unpublished doctoral dissertation, University of California, Berkeley.

Hestenes, L.L., Kontos, S., and Bryan, Y. (1993). Children's emotional expression in child care centers varying in quality. *Early Childhood Research Quarterly, 8,* 295-307.

Heymann, J. (2000). *The widening gap: Why America's working families are in jeopardy and what can be done about it.* New York: Basic Books.

Heymann S.J., Toomey S., and Furstenberg F. (1999). Working parents: What factors are involved in their ability to take time off from work when their children are sick? *Pediatric Adolescent Medicine, 153*(8), 870-874.

Hicks-Barlett, S. (2000). Between a rock and a hard place: The labyrinth of working and parenting in a poor community. In S. Danziger, and A. Lin (Eds.), *Coping with poverty: The social contexts of neighborhood, work, and family in the African American community* (pp. 27-51). Ann Arbor, MI: University of Michigan.

Hill, C.J., Hotz, J., Mullin, C.H., and Scholz, J.K. (1999). *EITC eligibility, participation, and compliance rates for AFDC households: Evidence from the California caseload.* Los Angeles: University of California, Economics Department.

Hill, J., Waldfogel, J., and Brooks-Gunn, J. (2003). Differential effects of high-quality child care. *Journal of Policy Analysis and Management, 21*(4), 601-627.

Hill, J., Waldfogel, J., Brooks-Gunn, J., and Han, W. (2001). *Towards a better estimate of casual links in child policy: The case of maternal employment and child outcomes.* New York: Columbia University.

Hillman, S.B., and Sawilowsky, S. (1991). Maternal employment and early adolescent substance abuse. *Adolescence, 26,* 829-837.

Hillman, S.B., Sawilowsky, S.S., and Becker, M.J. (1993). Effects of maternal employment patterns on adolescents' substance abuse and other risk-taking behavior. *Journal of Child and Family Studies, 2*(3), 203-219.

Hills, J., and Waldfogel, J. (2002) *Welfare reform in the UK: Are there lessons for the U.S.?* London: London School of Economics.

Hofferth, S. (1996). Effects of public and private policies on working after childbirth. *Work and Occupations, 23*(4), 378-404.

Hofferth, S. (2002). *Biology versus marriage as the basis for investment in children.* Paper presented at the Maryland Population Research Center Seminar.

Hofferth, S.L. (2000). Effects of public and private policies on working after childbirth. In T. L. Parcell, and D.B. Cornfield (Eds.), *Work and family: Research informing policy* (pp. 131-159). Thousand Oaks, CA: Russell Sage.

Hofferth, S.L., Brayfield, A., Deich, S., and Holcomb, P. (1991). *National childcare survey, 1990.* (Report No. 91-5). Washington, DC: Urban Institute.

Hofferth, S.L., Jankuniene, Z., and Brandon, P.D. (2000). *Self-care among school-age children.* Paper presented at the biennial meeting of the Society for Research on Adolescence, Minneapolis, MN.

Hofferth, S.L., Pleck, J., Stueve, J.L., Bianchi, S., and Sayer, L. (2002). The demography of fathers: What fathers do. In C.S. Tamis-LeMonda, and N. Cabrera (Eds.), *Handbook of father involvement* (pp. 63-92). Mahwah, NJ: Erlbaum.

Hofferth, S.L., Shauman, K.A., Henke, R.R., and West, J. (1998). *Characteristics of children's early care and education programs: Data from the 1995 National Household Education Survey.* (Report No. 98-128). Washington, DC: U.S. Department of Education, National Center for Education Statistics.

Hoffman, L. (1974). Effects of maternal employment on the child: A review of the research. *Developmental Psychology, 10,* 204-228.

Hoffman, L. (1989). Effects of maternal employment in the two-parent family. *American Psychologist, 44,* 283-292.

Hoffman, L., Youngblade, L.M., Coley, R.L., Fuligni, A.S., and Kovacs, D.D. (1999). *Mothers at work: Effects on children's well being.* New York: Cambridge University Press.

Hoffman, L.W. (1979). Maternal employment. *American Psychologist, 34,* 859-865.

Hoffman, L.W. (1984). Maternal employment and the young child. In M. Permutter (Ed.), *Minnesota symposium in child psychology* (vol. 17, pp. 101-128). Hillsdale, NJ: Erlbaum.

Holloway, S.D., and Reichhart-Erickson, M. (1988). The relationship of day care quality to children's free play behavior and social problem-solving skills. *Early Childhood Research Quarterly, 3,* 39-53.

Hotz, V.J., Imbens, G., and Klerman, J. (2000). *The long-term gains from GAIN: A reanalysis of the impacts of the California GAIN program.* (NBER Working Paper 8007). Cambridge, MA: National Bureau of Economic Research.

Hotz, V.J., Mullin, C.H., and Scholz, J.K. (2001). *The Earned Income Tax Credit and labor market participation of families on welfare.* Chicago: Northwestern University and the University of Chicago, Joint Center for Poverty Research.

Hotz, V.J., Xu, L.C., Tienda, M., and Ahituv, A. (in press). Are there returns to the wages of young men from working while in school? *Review of Economics and Statistics.*

Howard, D.R., and Madrigal, R. (1990). Who makes the decision: The parent or the child? The perceived influence of parents and children on the purchase of recreation services. *Journal of Leisure Research, 22,* 244-258.

Howes, C. (1983). Caregiver behavior in center and family day care. *Journal of Applied Developmental Psychology, 4,* 99-107.

Howes, C. (1988). Relations between early child care and schooling. *Developmental Psychology, 24,* 53-57.

Howes, C. (1990). Can the age of entry into child care and the quality of child care predict adjustment in kindergarten? *Developmental Psychology, 26*(2), 292-303.

Howes, C. (1997). Children's experience in center-based child care as a function of teacher background and adult:child ratio. *Merrill-Palmer Quarterly, 43,* 404-425.

Howes, C. (2000). *Social-emotional classroom climate in child care, child-teacher relationships and children's second grade peer relations.* Malden, MA: Blackwell.

Howes, C., and Olenick, M. (1986). Family and child care influences on toddlers' compliance. *Child Development, 57,* 202-216.

Howes, C., Phillips, D., and Whitebrook, M. (1992). Thresholds of quality: Implications for the social develoment of children in center-based care. *Child Development, 63,* 449-460.

Howes, C., and Rubenstein, J. (1985). Determinants of toddlers' experiences in day care: Age of entry and quality of setting. *Child Care Quarterly, 14,* 140-151.

Howes, C., and Smith, E. (1995). Relations among child care quality, teacher behavior, children's play activities, emotional security, and cognitive activity in child care. *Early Childhood Research Quarterly, 10,* 381-404.

Howes, C., and Stewart, P. (1987). Child's play with adults, toys, and peers: An examination of family and child care influences. *Developmental Psychology, 23,* 423-530.

Huang, C.-C., Garkinel, I., and Waldfogel, J. (2002a). *Child support and welfare caseloads.* New York: Columbia University.

Huang, C.-C., Kunz, J., and Garkinel, I. (2002b). The effect of child support on welfare exits and re-entries. *Journal of Policy Analysis and Management, 21*(4), 557-576.

Hultzman, W.Z. (1992). Constraints to activity participation in early adolescence. *Journal of Early Adolescence, 12,* 280-299.

Huston, A.C. (2002). Reforms and child development. *The Future of Children: Children and Welfare Reform, 12*(1), 59-77.

Huston, A.C., Duncan, G.J., Granger, R., Bos, J., McLoyd, V., Mistry, R., Crosby, D., Gibson, C., Magnuson, K., Romich, J., and Ventura, A. (2001). Work-based anti-poverty programs for parents can enhance the school performance and social behavior of children. *Child Development, 72,* 318-336.

Hyde, J.S., Essex, M.J., Clark, R., Klein, M.H., and Byrd, J.E. (1996). Parental leave: Policy and research. *Journal of Social Issues, 52*(3), 91-109.

Internal Revenue Service. (2002). *Tax topics—general information: Topic 302—Highlights of tax changes.* Available: http://www.irs.gov. [Accessed May 20, 2002].

International Archive of Educational Data. (2001). *National Education Longitudinal Study, 1988 series.* Available: http://www.icpsr.umich.edu:8080/IAED-SERIES/00107.xml. [Accessed July 2002].

Iutcovich, J., Fiene, R., Johnson, J., Koppel, and Langan, J. (1997). *Investing in our children's future: The path to quality child care through the Pennsylvania child care/early childhood development training system.* Erie, PA: Keystone University Research Corporation.

Iversen, R. (2002). *Moving up is a steep climb: Parents' work and children's welfare in the Annie E. Casey Foundation's jobs initiative.* Baltimore: Annie E. Casey Foundation.

Jackson, E.L., and Rucks, J.C. (1995). Negotiation of leisure constraints by junior-high and high-school students: An explorative study. *Journal of Leisure Research, 27,* 85-105.

Jacobs, E.V., and White, D.R. (1994). The relationship of child-care quality and play to social behavior in the kindergarten. In H. Goelman, and E.V. Jacobs (Eds.), *Children's play in child care settings.* Albany, NY: State University of New York Press.

Jacobs, J.A., and Gerson, K. (2001). Overworked individuals or overworked families? Explaining trends in work, leisure, and family time. *Work and Family Occupations, 28*(1), 40-63.

Jacobs, L.C., and Chase, C.I. (1989). Student participation in and attitudes toward high school activities: Findings from a national study. *The High School Journal,* April/May, 175-181.

Jacobson, K., and Crockett, L.J. (2000). Parental Monitoring and Adolescent Adjustment: An Ecological Perspective. *Journal of Research on Adolescence, 10,* 65-97.

Jamieson, A., Curry, A., and Martinez, G. (2001). *School enrollment in the United States: Social and economic characteristics of students, October 1999.* (Report No. P20-533, Current Population Report). Washington, DC: U.S. Census Bureau.

Jarrett, R.L. (1990). *A comparative examination of socialization patterns among low-income African American, Chicano, Puerto Rican, and White families: A review of the ethnographic literature.* (Social Science Research Council Working Paper).

Jarrett, R.L. (1992). A family case study: An examination of the underclass debate. In J. Gilgun, G. Handel, and K. Daley (Eds.), *Qualitative methods in family research* (pp. 172-197). New York: Russell Sage.

Jarrett, R.L. (1994). Living poor: Family life among single parent, African American women. *Social Problems, 41,* 30-49.

Jarrett, R.L. (1995). Growing up poor: The family experiences of socially mobile youth in low-income African American neighborhoods. *Journal of Adolescent Research, 10,* 111-135.

Jarrett, R.L. (1996). Welfare stigma among low-income, African American single mothers. *Family Relations, 45,* 368-374.

Jarrett, R.L. (1997a). African American family and parenting strategies in impoverished neighborhoods. *Qualitative Sociology, 20,* 275-288.

Jarrett, R.L. (1997b). Bringing families back in: Neighborhood effects on child development. In J. Brooks-Gunn, G. Duncan, and J.L. Aber (Eds.), *Neighborhood poverty: Context and consequences for children* (vol. 2, pp. 104-138). Thousand Oaks: Russell Sage.

Jarrett, R.L. (1997c). Resilience among low-income African American youth: An ethnographic perspective. *ETHOS, 25*(2), 218-229.

Jarrett, R.L. (1998a). African American children, families, and neighborhoods: Qualitative contributions to understanding developmental pathways. *Applied Developmental Science, 2,* 2-16.

Jarrett, R.L. (1998b). African American mothers and grandmothers in poverty: An adaptational perspective. *Journal of Comparative Family Studies, 29,* 388-396.

Jarrett, R.L. (1998c). *Indicators of family strengths and resilience that influence positive child-youth outcomes in urban neighborhoods: A review of quantitative and ethnographic studies.* Background paper prepared for the Neighborhood Transformation and Family Development Initiative of the Annie E. Casey Foundation.

Jarrett, R.L. (1999). Making a way: Successful parenting in high-risk neighborhoods. *The Future of Children: When School Is Out, 9*(1), 45-50.

Jarrett, R.L. (2000a). Neighborhood effects models: A view from the neighborhood. *Research in Community Sociology, 10,* 305-323.

Jarrett, R.L. (2000b). Voices from below: The use of ethnographic research for informing public policy. In J.M. Mercier, S. Garasky, and M.C. Shelley II (Eds.), *Redefining family policy: Implications for the 21st century* (pp. 67-84). Ames: Iowa State University.

Jarrett, R.L. (2002). *To marry or not to marry? Evidence for marriage promotion policies under welfare reform.* Baltimore: Annie E. Casey Foundation.

Jarrett, R.L. (in press). A good mother got to fight for her kids: Maternal management strategies in a housing project. *Journal of Children and Poverty.*

Jarrett, R.L., and Burton, L.M. (1999). Dynamic dimensions of family structure in low-income African American families: Emergent themes in qualitative research. *Journal of Comparative Family Studies, 30,* 177-188.

Jarrett, R.L., Roy, K., and Burton, L. (2002). Fathers in the "hood": Insights from qualitative research on low-income African-American men. In C.T. LeMonda, and N. Cabrera (Eds.), *Handbook on fatherhood: Interdisciplinary perspectives* (pp. 211-248). Hillsdale, NJ: Erlbaum.

Jencks, C. (1997). The hidden paradox of welfare reform. *The American Prospect, 8*(3).

Jencks, C., and Swingle, J. (2000). Without a net. *The American Prospect, 11*(4).

Jessor, R. (1993). Successful adolescent development among youth in high-risk settings. *American Psychologist, 48,* 117-126.

Joesch, J. (1997). Paid leave and the timing of women's employment before and after birth. *Journal of Marriage and the Family, 59,* 1008-1021.

Johnson, C.M., and Gais, T.L. (2001). Welfare reform, management systems, and policy theories of child well-being. In G.J. Duncan, and P.L. Chase-Lansdale (Eds.), *For better and for worse: Welfare reform and the well-being of children and families* (pp. 37-52). New York: Sage.

Johnson, D.S., and Lino, M. (2000). Teenagers: Employment and contributions to family spending. *Monthly Labor Review,* September.

Johnson, E., and Doolittle, F. (1996). *Low income parents and the parents' fair share demonstration.* New York: Manpower Demonstration Research Corporation.

Johnson, J. (2002). *Getting by on the minimum: The lives of working-class women.* New York: Routledge.

Johnson, N. (2001). *A hand up: How state earned income tax credits help working families escape poverty in 2001.* Washington, DC: Center on Budget and Policy Priorities.

Johnson, W. (2000). Work preparation and labor market experiences among urban, poor, non-resident fathers. In S. Danziger, and A. Lin (Eds.), *Coping with poverty: The social contexts of neighborhood, work and family in the African American community* (pp. 24-261). Ann Arbor, MI: University of Michigan Press.

Johnston, L.D., O'Malley, P.M., and Bachman, J.G. (2002). *The monitoring the future national survey results on adolescent drug use: Overview of key findings, 2001.* Available: www.monitoringthefuture.org. [Accessed 2002].

Joint Center for Poverty Research. (2000). Effects of welfare reform on children. *Poverty Research News, 4*(4).

Juhn, C., and Murphy, K.M. (1997). Wage inequality and family labor supply. *Journal of Labor Economics,* 72-97.

Juster, T. (1985). The validity and quality of time use: Estimates obtained from recall diaries. In F.T. Juster, and F.P. Stafford (Eds.), *Time, goods, and well-being* (pp. 63-91). Ann Arbor: University of Michigan, Survey Research Center, Institute for Social Research.

Kachur, S.P., Potter, L.B., James, S.P., and Powell, K.E. (1995). *Suicide in the United States, 1980-1992.* Atlanta, GA: Centers for Disease Control and Prevention, National Center for Injury Prevention.

Kagan, S.L., and Cohen, N.E. (1996). A vision for a quality early care and education system. In S.L. Kagan, and N.E. Cohen (Eds.), *Reinventing early care and education: A vision for a quality system* (pp. 309-332). San Francisco: Jossey-Bass.

Kalil, A., Schweingruber, H., and Seefeldt, K. (2001). Correlates of employment among welfare recipients: Do psychological characteristics and attitudes matter? *American Journal of Community Psychology, 29,* 701-723.

Kamerman, S. (2000). Parental leave policies: An essential ingredient in early childhood education and care policies. *Social Policy Report, 14*(2), 3-15.

Kamerman, S., and Kahn, A. (1995). Getting started on starting right. In S. Kamerman, and A. Kahn (Eds.), *Starting right: How America neglects its youngest children and what we can do about it* (pp. 181-213). Oxford: Oxford University.

Karoly, L., Greenwood, P., Everingham, S., Hoube, J., Kilburn, R., Rydell, P., Sanders, M., and Chiesa, J. (1998). *Investing in our children: What we know and don't know about the costs and benefits of early childhood interventions.* Santa Monica: RAND.

Karoly, L.A., Kilburn, M.R., Bigelow, J.H., Caulkins, J.P., Cannon, J.S., and Chiesa, J.R. (2001). Benefit-cost findings for early childhood intervention programs. In *Assessing costs and benefits of early childhood intervention programs: Overview and application to the starting early starting smart program* (pp. 49-138). New York: RAND.

Kaushal, N., and Kaestner, R. (2001). From welfare to work: Has welfare reform worked? *Journal of Policy Analysis and Management, 20(4)*, 699-719.

Kearney, M.S. (2002). *Is there an effect of incremental welfare benefits on fertility behavior? A look at the family cap.* (NBER Working paper #9093). Washington, DC: National Bureau of Economic Research.

W.K. Kellogg Foundation. (2002) *Devolution initiative: Child care and early education: Supporting children and families.* Available: http://www.wkkf.org/pubs/devolution/pub673. pdf. [Accessed 2002].

Kessler, R., and McRae, J. (1982). The effects of wives' employment on the mental health of married men and women. *American Sociological Review, 47*, 216-227.

Kinney, D.A. (1993). From nerds to normals: The recovery of identity among adolescents from middle school to high school. *Sociology of Education, 66*, 21-40.

Kisker, E., Hofferth, S.L., Phillips, D.A., and Farquhar, E. (1991). *A profile of child care settings: Early education and care in 1990.* Princeton, NJ: Mathematica Policy Research.

Kisker, E.E., Rangarajan, A., and Boller, K. (1998). *Moving into adulthood: Were the impacts of mandatory programs for welfare-dependent teenage parents sustained after the programs ended?* Princeton, NJ: Mathematica Policy Research.

Klebanov, P.K., Brooks-Gunn, J., McCarton, C., and McCormick, M.C. (1998). The contribution of neighborhood and family income to developmental test scores over the first three years of life. *Child Development, 69*, 1420-1436.

Klerman, J., and Haider, S. (2001). *A stock flow analysis of the welfare caseload: Insights from California economic conditions.* Santa Monica, CA: RAND.

Klerman, J., Leibowitz, A., and Leibowitz, A. (1990). Child care and women's return to work after childbirth. *AEA Papers and Proceedings, 80(2)*, 284-288.

Klerman, J., Leibowitz, A., and Leibowitz, A. (1994). The work-employment distinction among new mothers. *Journal of Human Resources, 21(2)*, 277-303.

Klerman, J., Leibowitz, A., and Leibowitz, A. (1998a). *FMLA and the labor supply of new mothers: Evidence from the June CPS.* Santa Monica, CA: RAND.

Klerman, J., Leibowitz, A., and Leibowitz, A. (1998b). Labor supply effects of state maternity leave legislation. In F. Blau, and R. Ehrenberg (Eds.), *Gender and family issues in the workplace* (pp. 65-91). New York: .

Klerman, J., Leibowitz, A., and Leibowitz, A. (1999). Job continuity among new mothers. *Demography, 36(2)*, 143-155.

Knox, V., Miller, C., and Gennetian, L. (2000). *Reforming welfare and rewarding work: A summary of the final report on the Minnesota Family Investment Program.* New York: Manpower Demonstration Research Corporation.

Kohn, M.L., and Schooler, C. (with Miller, J., Miller, K.A., Schoenbach, C., and Schoenberg, R.). (1983). *Work and personality: An inquiry into the impact of social stratification.* Norwood, NJ: Ablex.

Kontos, S., Howes, C., and Galinsky, E. (1997). Does training make a difference to quality in family child care. *Early Childhood Research Quarterly, 11*, 427-445.

Kontos, S., and Wilcox-Herzog, A. (1997). Influences on children's competence in early childhood classrooms. *Early Childhood Research Quarterly, 12*, 247-262.

Kontos, S., Howes, C., Shinn, M., and Galinsky, E. (1995). *Quality in family child care and relative care.* New York: Teachers College Press.

Kontos, S.J. (1991). Child care quality, family background, and children's development. *Early Childhood Research Quarterly, 6*, 249-262.

Koopmans, M. (1991). *A study of longitudinal effects of all-day kindergarten attendance on achievement.* Newark, NJ: Newark Board of Education, Office of Research, Testing, and Evaluation.

Korfmacher, J., Kitzman, H., and Olds, D. (1998). Intervention processes as predictors of outcomes in a preventive home-visitation program. *Journal of Community Psychology, 26*, 49-64.

Laird, R.D., Pettit, G.S., Dodge, K.A., and Bates, J. (1998). The social ecology of school-age child care. *Journal of Applied Developmental Psychology, 19*, 341-360.

Lake Snell Perry and Associates. (2002). *Public views on welfare reform and children in the current economy.* Available: http://www.futureofchildren.org/usr_doc/lsp_welfare_survey.pdf. [Accessed July 2002].

Lamb, M.E. (1998). Nonparental child care: Context, quality, correlates, and consequences. In W. Damon (Ed.), *Handbook of child psychology, 5th edition, volume 4: Child psychology in practice* (pp. 73-133). New York: John Wiley and Sons.

Larner, M.B., Zippiroli, L., Behrman, R.E. (1999). When school is out: Analysis and recommendations. *The Future of Children: When School Is Out, 9*(2), 4-20.

Larson, J. (1994). Violence Prevention in the Schools: A review of selected programs and procedures. *School Psychology Review, 23*(2), 151-164.

Larson, R.W. (2000). Toward a psychology of positive youth development. *American Psychologist, 55*, 170-183.

Larson, R.W. (2001). How U.S. children and adolescents spend time: What it does (and doesn't) tell us about their development. *Current Directions in Psychological Science, 10*, 160-164.

Laursen, B., Coy, K.C., and Collins, W.A. (1998). Reconsidering changes in parent-child conflict across adolescence: A meta-analysis. *Child Development, 69*, 817-832.

Lazar, I., and Darlington, R. (1982). Lasting effects of early education: A report from the Consortium for Longitudinal Studies. *Monographs of the Society for Research in Child Development, 47*(2-3, Serial No. 195).

Lehrer, E.L. (1989). Preschoolers with working mothers: An analysis of the determinants of child care arrangements. *Journal of Population Economics, 1*, 251-268.

Lehrer, E.L., and Kawasaki, S. (1985). Child care arrangements and fertility: An analysis of two earner households. *Demography, 22*, 499-513.

Lein, L., Benjamin, A.F., McManus, M., and Roy, K. (2002). *Economic roulette: When is a job not a job?* Paper presented at the annual meeting of the American Sociological Association.

Lengyel, T.E., and Campbell, D. (2002). *Faces of change: Welfare policy through the lens of personal experience.* Milwaukee, WI: Alliance for Children and Families.

Lerman, R.I. (1996). *Helping disconnected youth by improving linkages between high schools and careers.* Washington, DC: Urban Institute.

Lerman, R.I. (2000). *Are teens in low-income and welfare families working too much?* (Report no. B-25). Available: http://newfederalism.urban.org/html/series_b/anf_b25.html. [Accessed September 2002].

Lerner, J.V., and Noh, E.R. (2000). Maternal employment influences on early adolescent development: A contextual view. In R.D. Taylor, and M.C. Wang (Eds.), *Resilience across contexts: Family, work, culture, and community* (pp. 121-145). Mahwah, NJ: Erlbaum.

Levesque, R. (1993). The romantic experience of adolescents in satisfying love relationships. *Journal of Youth and Adolescence, 22*, 219-251.

Lindsay, P. (1984). High school size, participation in activities, and young adult social partici-pation: some enduring effects of schooling. *Educational Evaluation and Policy Analysis,* 73-83.

Loeb, S., and Corcoran, M. (2001). Welfare, work experience and economic self-sufficiency. *Journal of Policy Analysis and Management, 20*(1), 1-20.

Lombardi, J. (2003). *Time to care: Redesigning child care to promote education, support families, and build communities.* Philadelphia, PA: Temple University.

London, A.S., Scott, E.K., Edin, K., and Hunter, V. (2000). *Ethnographic perspectives on welfare to work transitions, work-family tradeoffs, and children's well-being.* Paper presented at the 22nd Annual Research Conference of the Association for Public Policy Analysis and Management.

London, A.S., Scott, E.K., Edin, K., and Hunter, V. (2001). *Juggling low-wage work and family life: What mothers say about their children's well-being in the context of welfare reform.* New York: Manpower Demonstration Research Corporation.

London, A.S., Scott, E.K., Edin, K., and Hunter, V. (in press). Health-related carework for children in the context of welfare reform. In F. Cancian, D. Kurz, A.S. London, R. Reviere, and M. Tuominen (Eds.), *Child care and inequality: Re-thinking carework for children and youth.* New York: Routledge.

Loprest, P. (2001). *How are families that left welfare doing? A comparison of early and recent welfare leavers.* (Series B, No. B-36). Washington, DC: Urban Institute.

Love, J., Lougue, M.E., Trudeau, J.V., and Thayer, K. (1992). *Transitions to kindergarten in American schools: Final report of the National Transition Study.* Portsmouth, NH: RMC Research Corporation.

Love, J.M., Eliason-Kisker, E.E., Ross, C.M., Schochet, P.Z., Brooks-Gunn, J., and Paulsell, D. (2002). *Making a difference in the lives of infants and toddlers and their families: The impacts of early Head Start.* Washington, DC: U.S. Department of Health and Human Services, Commissioners Office of Research and Evaluation, Administration for Children Youth and Families.

Love, J.M., Schochet, P.Z., and Meckstroth, A. (1996). *Are they are in any real danger? What research does—and doesn't—tell us about child care quality and children's well-being.* Princeton, NJ: Mathematica Policy Research.

Lowe, E.D., and Weisner, T.S. (2001) *Situating child care and child care subsidy use in the daily routines of lower income families.* (Next Generation working paper). New York: Manpower Demonstration Research Corporation.

Lowe, E.D., and Weisner, T.S. (in press). "You have to push it—who's gonna raise your kids?" Situating child care and child care subsidy use in the daily routines of lower-income families. *Children and Youth Services Review.*

Lundberg, S.J., Pollak, R.A., Wales, R.J. (1997). Do husbands and wives pool their resources? Evidence from the United Kingdom child benefit. *Journal of Human Resources, 32*(3), 463-480.

Luthar, S., and Cicchetti, D. (2000). The construct of resilience: Implications for interventions and social policies. *Development and Psychopathology, 12,* 857-885.

Luthar, S.S., Cicchetti, D., and Becker, B. (1971). The construct of resilience: A critical evalua-tion and guidelines for future work. *Child Development,* 543-562.

Magnusson, D., and Stattin, H. (1998). Person-context interaction theories. In W. Damon, and R.M. Lerner (Eds.), *Handbook of child psychology, volume 1: Theoretical models of human development, fifth edition* (pp. 685-760). New York: Wiley.

Mahoney, J.L. (2000). Participation in school extracurricular activities as a moderator in the development of antisocial patterns. *Child Development, 71,* 502-516.

Mahoney, J.L. (2002). Are American youth ready to work? *Contemporary Psychology,* Octo-ber.

Mahoney, J.L., and Bergman, L.R. (2002). Conceptual and methodological issues in a developmental approach to positive adaptation. *Applied Developmental Psychology, 23,* 195-217.

Mahoney, J., and Cairns, R. (1997). Do extracurricular activities protect against early school dropout? *Developmental Psychology, 33*(2), 241-253.

Mahoney, J.L., Eccles, J.S., and Larson, R. (in pressa). Organized activities as developmental contexts for children and adolescents. In J.L. Mahoney, R. Larson, and J. Eccles (Eds.), *Organized activities as developmental contexts: Extracurricular activities, after-school and community programs.* Mahwah, NJ: Erlbaum.

Mahoney, J.L., Koutakis, N., and Stattin, H. (in pressb). *Unstructured leisure and the development of antisocial behavior: A contemporary longitudinal study of the Swedish youth recreation centers.*

Mahoney, J.L., Schweder, A.E., and Stattin, H. (in pressc). Structured after-school activities as moderator of depressed mode for adolescents with detached relations to their parents. *Journal of Community Psychology.*

Mahoney, J.L., and Magnusson, D. (2001). Parent community engagement and the persistence of criminality. *Development and Psychopathology, 13*(1), 125-141.

Mahoney, J.L., Stattin, H., and Magnusson, D. (2001). Youth Recreation Centre participation and criminal offending: A 20-year longitudinal study of Swedish boys. *International Journal of Behavioral Development, 25*(6), 509-530.

Manning, W.D. (1990). Parenting employed teenagers. *Youth and Society, 22,* 184-200.

Marsh, H.W. (1991). Employment during high school: Character building or a subversion of academic goals. *Sociology of Education, 64,* 172-189.

Marshall, N.L., Coll, C.J, Marx, F., McCartney, K., Keefe, N., and Ruh, J. (1997). After-school time and children's behavioral adjustment. *Merrill-Palmer Quarterly, 43*(3), 497-514.

Maryse, R.H., and Duckett, E. (1994). The relationship of maternal employment to early adolescent daily experience with and without parents. *Child Development, 65*(1), 255-236.

Masten, A.S., and Coatsworth, J.D. (1998). The development of competence in favorable and unfavorable environments. *American Psychologist, 53,* 205-220.

Mayer, S.E. (1997). *What money can't buy.* Cambridge, MA: Harvard University Press.

McCall, R.B. (1983). A conceptual approach to early mental development. In M. Lewis (Ed.), *Origins of intelligence: Infancy and early childhood* (2nd ed., pp. 107-133). New York: Plenum.

McCartney, K. (1984). Effect of quality of day-care environment on children's language development. *Developmental Psychology, 20,* 244-260.

McCartney, K., Scarr, S., Phillips, D., and Grajek, S. (1985). Day care as intervention: Comparison of varying quality programs. *Journal of Applied Developmental Psychology, 6,* 247-260.

McCartney, K., Scarr, S., Rocheleau, A., Phillips, D., Abbott-Shim, M., and Eisenberg, M. (1997). Teacher-child interaction and child-care auspices as predictors of social outcomes in infants, toddlers, and preschoolers. *Merrill-Palmer Quarterly, 43,* 426-450.

McCarton, C., Brooks-Gunn, J., Wallace, I., Bauer, C., Bennett, F., and Bernbaum, J. (1997). Results at age 8 years of early intervention for low-birth-weight premature infants. *Journal of the American Medical Association, 277,* 126-132.

McCord, J. (1978). A 30-year follow-up of treatment effects. *American Psychologist, 33,* 284-289.

McCormick, M.C., McCarton, C.M., Tonascia, C., and Brooks-Gunn, J. (1993). Early educational intervention for very low birth weight infants: Results from the infant health and development program, *Journal of Pediatrics, 123,* 527-533.

McGroder, S.M., Zaslow, M.J., Moore, K.A., Hair, E.C., and Ahluwalia, S.K. (2002). The role of parenting in shaping the impacts of welfare-to-work programs on children. In J.G. Borkowski, S.L. Ramey, and M. Bristol-Power (Eds.), *Parenting and the child's world: Influences on academic, intellectual, and social-emotional development* (pp. 283-310). Mahwah, NJ: Erlbaum.

McGroder, S.M., Zaslow, M.J., Moore, K.A., and LeMenestrel, S. (2000). *The national evaluation of welfare-to-work strategies: Impacts on young children and their families two years after enrollment: Findings from the Child Outcomes Study.* Washington, DC: U.S. Department of Health and Human Services and U.S. Department of Education.

McHale, S.M., Crouter, A.C., and Tucker, C.J. (2001). Free-time activities in middle childhood: Links with adjustment in early adolescence. *Child Development, 72*(6), 1764-1778.

McLanahan, S.S., and Carlson, M.J. (2002). Welfare reform, fertility, and father involvement. *The Future of Children: Children and Welfare Reform, 12*(1), 147-165.

McLaughlin, M., Irby, M., and Langman, J. (1994). *Urban sanctuaries: Neighborhood organizations in the lives and futures of inner-city youth.* San Francisco: Jossey-Bass.

McLoyd, V.C. (1990). The impact of economic hardship on black families and children: Psychological distress, parenting, and socioemotional development. *Child Development, 61,* 311-346.

McLoyd, V.C., Jayaratne, T.B., Ceballo, R., and Borquez, J. (1994). Unemployment and work interruption among African American single mothers: Effects on parenting and adolescent socioemotional functioning. *Child Development, 65*(2), 562-584.

McNeal, R.B. (1998). High school extracurricular activities: Closed structures and stratifying patterns of participation. *The Journal of Educational Research, 91,* 183-191.

Menaghan, E.G., and Parcel, T.L. (1995). Social sources of change in children's home environments: The effects of parental occupational experiences and family conditions. *Journal of Marriage and the Family, 57,* 69-84.

Mensing, J., French, D., Fuller, B., and Kagan, S. (in press). Childcare selection under welfare reform: How mothers balance work requirements and parenting. *Early Education Development.*

Meyer, B., and Rosenbaum, D.T. (2001). Welfare, the Earned Income Tax Credit, and labor supply of single mothers. *Quarterly Journal of Economics, 116*(3), 1063-1114.

Meyer, B., and Sullivan, J.X. (2001). *The effects of welfare and tax reform: The material well-being of single mothers in the 1980s and 1990s.* (NBER working paper no. 8298). Washington, DC: National Bureau of Economic Research.

Meyers, M., Heintze, T., and Wolf, D. (2002a). Child care subsidies and the employment of welfare recipients. *Demography, 39*(1), 165-179.

Meyers, M., Rosenbaum, D., Ruhm, C., Waldfogel, J. (2002b). *Inequality in early childhood education and care: What do we know?* New York: Columbia University.

Mezey, J., Schumacher, R., Greenburg, M., Lombardi, J., and Hutchins, J. (2002). *Unfinished agenda: Child care for low-income families since 1996: Implications for federal and state policy.* Washington, DC: Center for Law and Social Policy.

Michalopoulos, C., and Berlin, G. (2002). Financial work incentives for low-income families. In R. Blank, and R. Haskins (Eds.), *The new world of welfare* (part III). Washington, DC: Brookings Institution Press.

Michalopoulos, C., Card, D., Gennetian, L.A., Harknett, K., and Robbins, P.K. (2000). *The self-sufficiency project at six months: Effects of a financial work incentive on employment and income.* Ottawa, Canada: Social Research and Demonstration Group.

Michalopoulos, C., and Schwartz, C. (2001). *What works best for whom: Impacts of 20 welfare-to-work programs for subgroups.* Washington, DC: U.S. Department of Health and Human Services and U.S. Department of Education.

Mihalic, S.W., and Elliot, D. (1997). Short and long term consequences of adolescent work. *Youth and Society, 28,* 464-498.

Miller, B.M., and Marx, F. (1990). *Aftershool arrangements in middle childhood: A review of the literature.* (Action research paper #2). Available: http://www.wellesley.edu/WCW/ CRW/SAC/publications.html. [Accessed July 2002].

Miller, B.M., O'Connor, S., Siriganano, S.W., and Joshi, P. (1997). *I wish the kids didn't watch so much TV: Out-of-school time in three low-income communities.* Wellesley, MA: Wellesley College, Center for Research on Women, National Institute on Out-of-School Time.

Miller, C., Knox, V., and Gennetian, L.A. (2000). *Reforming welfare and rewarding work: Final report on the Minnesota family investment program, vol 1: Effects on adults.* New York: Manpower Demonstration Research Corporation.

Mitchell, A. (2001). *Education for all children: The role of states and the federal government in promoting prekindergarten and kindergarten.* New York: Foundation for Child Development.

Mitchell, A., Ripple, C., and Chanana, N. (1998). *Prekindergarten programs funded by the states: Essential elements for policy makers.* New York: Families and Work Institute.

Mitchell, A., Stoney, L., and Dichter, H. (2001). *Financing child care in the United States: An expanded catalog of current strategies.* Kansas City, MO: Ewing Marion Kauffman Foundation.

Mocan, H.N., Burchinal, M., Morris, J.R., and Helburn, S.W. (1995). Models of quality in center child care. In S.W. Helburn (Ed.), *Cost, quality, and child outcomes in child care centers, technical report.* Denver, CO: University of Colorado at Denver, Department of Economics, Center for Research in Economic and Social Policy.

Moffitt, R. (1999). Effects of pre-PRWORA waivers on welfare caseloads and female earnings, income and labor force behavior. In S.H. Danziger (Ed.), *Economic conditions and welfare reform.* Kalamazoo, MI: Upjohn Institute.

Moffitt, R. (1992). Incentive effects of the U.S. welfare system. *Journal of Economic Literature, 30*(1), 1-61.

Moffitt, R. (2002). Welfare programs and labor supply. (NBER working paper no. 9168). Washington, DC: National Bureau of Economic Research.

Moffitt, R. (in press). The Temporary Assistance for Needy Families program. In R. Moffit (Ed.), *Means tested transfer programs in the United States.* Chicago: Chicago University.

Moffitt, R.A., and Roff, J. (2000). *The diversity of welfare leavers, welfare children and families: A three-city study.* (Policy Brief 00-02). Baltimore: Johns Hopkins University.

Monetmayor, R. (1984). Maternal employment and adolescents' relations with parents, siblings, and peers. *Journal of Youth and Adolescence, 13,* 543-557.

Moore, K.A. (2001). How do state policymakers think about family processes and child development in low-income families? In G.J. Duncan, and P.L. Chase-Lansdale (Eds.), *For better or for worse: Welfare reform and the well-being of children and families* (pp. 53-62). New York: Russell Sage.

Moore, W. (1969). *The vertical ghetto.* New York: Random House.

Morris, P., Knox, V., and Gennetian, L.A. (2002). *Welfare policies matter for children and youth: Lessons for TANF reauthorization.* Available: http://www.mdrc.org/Reports2002/ NG_PolicyBrief/NG_PolicyBrief.htm. [Accessed 2002].

Morris, P.A. (2001). The effects of welfare reform policies on children. *Social Policy Report, 16*(1), 4-19.

Morris, P.A., and Gennetian, L.A. (2001). *Identifying effects of income on children's development: Integrating an instrumental variables analytic method with an experimental design.* New York: Manpower Demonstration Research Corporation.

Morris, P.A., Huston, A.C., Duncan, G.J., Crosby, D., and Bos, J.M. (2001a). *A synthesis of effects of welfare-to-work programs on children.* New York: Manpower Demonstration Research Corporation.

Morris, P.A., Huston, A.C., Duncan, G.J., Crosby, D., and Bos, J.M. (2001b). *How welfare and work policies affect children: A synthesis of research.* New York: Manpower Demonstration Research Corporation.

Morris, P.A., and Michalopoulos, C. (2000). *The self-sufficiency project at 36 months: Effects on children of a program that increased parental employment and income.* Ottawa, Ontario: Social Research and Demonstration Corporation.

Morse, J.R. (2001). *Love and economics: Why the laissez-fair family doesn't work.* Dallas, TX: Spence.

Mortenson, E.L., Michaelson, K.F., Sanders, S.A., and Reinisch, J.M. (2002). The association between duration of breastfeeding and adult intelligence. *Journal of the American Medical Association, 287*(18), 2365-2371.

Mortimer, J.T., Finch, M., Shanahan, M., and Ryu, S. (1992). Work experience, mental health, and behavioral adjustment in adolescence. *Journal of Research on Adolescence, 2,* 25-57.

Mortimer, J.T., Finch, M.D., Ryu, S., Shanahan, M.J., and Call, K.T. (1996). The effects of work intensity on adolescent mental health, achievement, and behavioral adjustment: New evidence from a prospective study. *Child Development, 67,* 1243-1261.

Mortimer, J.T., and Shanahan, M. (1994). Adolescent work experiences and family relations. *Work and Occupations, 21,* 369-384.

Mortimer, J.T., Shanahan, M., and Ryu, S. (1993). The effects of adolescent employment on school related orientations and behavior. In R.K. Silbereisen, and E. Todt (Eds.), *Adolescence in context: The interplay of family, school, peers, and work in adjustment.* New York: Springer-Verlag.

Munger, F. (2002). *Laboring below the line: The new ethnography of poverty, low-wage work, and survival in the global economy.* New York: Russell Sage.

National Center for Education Statistics. (2001). *Dropout rates in the United States: 2000.* Washington, DC: U.S. Department of Education, Office of Educational Research and Improvement. Available: http://nces.ed.gov/pubs2002/droppub_2001. [Accessed 2002].

National Conference of State Legislatures. (2002). *States and new 21st century funds.* Available: http://www.ncsl.org/programs/cyf/aspubs.htm. [Accessed March 2003].

National Institute of Child Health and Human Development Early Child Care Research Network. (1994). Child care and child development: The NICHD study of early child care. In S.L. Friedman, and H.C. Haywood (Eds.), *Developmental follow-up: Concepts, domains, and methods.* New York: Academic Press.

National Institute of Child Health and Human Development Early Child Care Research Network. (1996). Characteristics of infant child care: Factors contributing to positive caregiving. *Early Childhood Research Quarterly, 11,* 269-306.

National Institute of Child Health and Human Development Early Child Care Research Network. (1997a). Child care in the first year of life. *Merrill-Palmer Quarterly, 43,* 340-360.

National Institute of Child Health and Human Development Early Child Care Research Network. (1997b). The effects of infant child care on infant-mother attachment security: Results of the NICHD study of early child care. *Child Development, 68*(5), 860-879.

National Institute of Child Health and Human Development Early Child Care Research Network. (1997c). Familial factors associated with characteristics of nonmaternal care for infants. *Journal of Marriage and the Family, 59,* 389-408.

National Institute of Child Health and Human Development Early Child Care Research Network. (1998). Early child care and self-control, compliance, and problem behavior at 24 and 36 months. *Child Development, 69*(4), 1145-1170.

National Institute of Child Health and Human Development Early Child Care Research Network. (1999a). Child Care and Mother-Child Interaction in the First 3 Years of Life. *Developmental Psychology, 35*(6), 1399-1413.

National Institute of Child Health and Human Development Early Child Care Research Network. (1999b). Child outcomes when child care center classes meet recommended standards of quality. *American Journal of Public Health, 89*(7), 1072-1077.

National Institute of Child Health and Human Development Early Child Care Research Network. (1999c). Chronicity of maternal depressive symptoms, maternal sensitivity, and child functioning at 36 months. *Developmental Psychology, 35*, 1297-1310.

National Institute of Child Health and Human Development Early Child Care Research Network. (2000a). Characteristics and quality of child care for toddlers and preschoolers. *Applied Developmental Science, 4*(3), 116-135.

National Institute of Child Health and Human Development Early Child Care Research Network. (2000b). The relation of child care to cognitive and language development. *Child Development, 71*(4), 958-978.

National Institute of Child Health and Human Development Early Child Care Research Network. (2000c). Factors associated with fathers' caregiving activities and sensitivity with young children. *Journal of Family Psychology, 14*(2), 200-219.

National Institute of Child Health and Human Development Early Child Care Research Network. (2001a). Child care and children's peer interaction at 24 and 36 months: The NICHD Study of Early Child Care. *Child Development, 72*(5), 1478-1500.

National Institute of Child Health and Human Development Early Child Care Research Network. (2001b). *Does amount of time spent in child care predict socioemotional adjustment during the transition to kindergarten?* Paper presented at the biennial meetings of the Society for Research in Child Development.

National Institute of Child Health and Human Development Early Child Care Research Network. (2001c). Nonmaternal care and family factors in early development: An overview of NICHD Study of Early Child Care. *Applied Developmental Psychology, 22*, 457-492.

National Institute of Child Health and Human Development Early Child Care Research Network. (2001d). Child care and common communicable illnesses. *Archives of Pediatrics and Adolescent Medicine, 155*, 481-488.

National Institute of Child Health and Human Development Early Child Care Research Network. (2002a). Child care and children's peer interaction at 24 and 36 months. *Child Development, 72*, 1478-1500.

National Institute of Child Health and Human Development Early Child Care Research Network. (2002b). Child care and children's development prior to school entry. *American Education Research Journal, 39*(1), 133-164.

National Institute of Child Health and Human Development Early Child Care Research Network. (2002c). Child care structure to process to outcome: Direct and indirect effects of child-care quality on young children's development. *Psychological Science, 13*(3), 199-206.

National Institute of Child Health and Human Development Early Child Care Research Network. (in pressa). Are child developmental outcomes related to before- and after-school care arrangements? *Child Development.*

National Institute of Child Health and Human Development Early Child Care Research Network. (in pressb). Child-care structure, process, outcome: Direct and indirect effects of child-care quality on young children's development. *Psychological Science.*

National Institute of Child Health and Human Development Early Child Care Research Network. (in pressc). Early child care and children's development prior to school entry: Results from the NICHD study of early child care. *American Education Research Journal.*

National Institute of Child Health and Human Development Early Child Care Research Network. (in pressd). Does quality of child care affect child outcomes at age 4¹/₂? *Developmental Psychology.*

National Institute of Child Health and Development Early Child Care Research Network and Duncan, G.J. (2003). Modeling the impacts of child care quality on children's preschool cognitive development. *Child Development,* September/October.

National Partnership for Women and Families. (2000). *Overestimating the costs of parental leave: Fundamental flaws in the Employment Policy Foundation's cost assessments of birth and adoption unemployment compensation programs* Available: http://www.nationalpartnership.org. [Accessed 2000].

National Research Council. (1982). *Families that work: Children in a changing world.* Kamerman, S.B., and Hayes, C.D. (Eds.). Panel on Work, Family, and Community and Committee on Child Development Research and Public Policy. Commission on Behavioral and Social Sciences and Education. Washington, DC: National Academy Press.

National Research Council. (1990). *Who cares for America's children? Child care policy for the 1990's.* C.D. Hayes, J.L. Palmer, and M.L. Zaslow (Eds.). Panel on Child Care Policy. Washington, DC: National Academy Press.

National Research Council. (1991). *Work and family: Policies for a changing workforce.* M.A. Ferber, B. O'Farrell, and L. Allen (Eds.). Panel on Employer Policies and Working Families. Committee on Women's Employment and Related Social Issues. Commission on Behavioral and Social Sciences and Education. Washington, DC: National Academy Press.

National Research Council. (1998). *Welfare, the family, and reproductive behavior: Research perspectives.* R. Moffit (Ed.). Committee on Population. Commission on Behavioral and Social Sciences and Education. Washington, DC: National Academy Press.

National Research Council. (2000a). *Eager to learn: Educating our preschoolers.* B.T. Bowman, M.S. Donovan, and M.S. Burns (Eds.). Committee on Early Childhood Pedagogy. Commission on Behavioral and Social Sciences and Education. Washington, DC: National Academy Press.

National Research Council. (2000b). *How people learn: Brain, mind, experience, and school: Expanded edition.* J.D. Bransford, A.L. Brown, and R.R. Cocking (Eds.). Committee on Developments in the Science of Learning and Committee on Learning Research and Educational Practice. Commission on Behavioral and Social Sciences and Education. Washington, DC: National Academy Press.

National Research Council and Institute of Medicine. (1999). *Risks and opportunities: Synthesis of studies on adolescence.* Board on Children, Youth, and Families. Division of Behavioral and Social Sciences and Education. Washington, DC: National Academy Press.

National Research Council and Institute of Medicine. (2000). *From neurons to neighborhoods: The science of early childhood development.* J.P. Shonkoff, and D.A. Phillips (Eds.). Committee on the Science of Early Childhood Development. Board on Children, Youth, and Families. Division of Behavioral and Social Sciences and Education. Washington, DC: National Academy Press.

National Research Council and Institute of Medicine. (2002). *Community programs to promote youth development.* J. Eccles, and J.A. Gootman (Eds.). Committee on Community-Level Programs to Promote Youth Development. Board on Children, Youth, and Families. Division of Behavioral and Social Sciences and Education. Washington, DC: National Academy Press.

National Survey of America's Families. (1997). *1997 NSAF benchmarking measures of child and family well-being: NSAF methodological reports.* (Report No. 6). Washington, DC: Urban Institute.

Nelson, C., and Keith, J. (1990). Comparisons of female and male early adolescent sex role attitude and behavior development. *Adolescent, 25,* 246-259.

Newman, K. (1999). *No shame in my game.* New York: Knopf and Russell Sage.

Nicolas, G., and Baptiste, V. (2001). Experiences of women on public assistance. *Journal of Social Issues, 57,* 299-309.

O'Connell, M. (1993). *Where's papa? Father's role in child care.* (Population trends and public policy report #20). Washington, DC: Population Reference Bureau.

O'Connell, M. (2002). Child bearing. In L.M. Casper, and S.M. Bianchi (Eds.), *Continuity and change in the American family* (pp. 67-94). Thousand Oaks, CA: Russell Sage.

O'Conner, M., Ross-Phillips, K., and Smeeding, T.M. (2000). The EITC: Expectation, knowledge, use, and economic and social mobility. *National Tax Journal, LIII,* 4(2), 1187-1209.

O'Connor, C. (2000). Dreamkeeping in the inner city: Diminishing the divide between aspirations and expectations. In S. Danziger, and A. Lin (Eds.), *Coping with poverty: The social contexts of neighborhood, work and family in the African American community* (pp. 105-140). Ann Arbor: University of Michigan.

Office of Technological Assessment. (1991). *Biological rhythms: Implications for the worker.* Washington, DC: Author.

Oliker, S. (1992). The proximate contexts of workfare and work: A framework for studying poor women's economic choices. *Sociological Quarterly, 36,* 251-272.

Oliker, S.J. (1995). Work commitment and constraints among mothers on welfare. *Journal of Contemporary Ethnography, 24,* 165-194.

Ondrich, J., Spiess, C.K., and Yang, Q. (1996). Barefoot and in a German kitchen: Federal parental leave and benefit policy and the return to work after childbirth in Germany. *Journal of Population Economics, 9,* 247-266.

Ondrich, J., Spiess, C.K.Y.Q., and Wagner, G.G. (1998). *The liberalization of maternity leave policy and the return to work after childbirth in Germany.* Bonn, Germany: Research Institute for the Future of Work.

Orthner, D.K. (1991). Parental work and early adolescence: Issues for research and practice. *Journal of Early Adolescence, 10,* 246-259.

Osgood, D.W., Wilson, J.K., O'Malley, P.M., Bachman, J.G., and Johnston, L.D. (1996). Routine activities and individual deviant behavior. *American Sociological Review, 61,* 635-655.

Parcel, T.L., and Menaghan, E.G. (1990). Maternal working conditions and child verbal facility: Studying the intergenerational transmission of inequality from mothers to young children. *Social Psychology Quarterly, 53,* 132-147.

Parcel, T.L., and Menaghan, E.G. (1994). Early parental work, family social capital, and early childhood outcomes. *American Journal of Sociology, 99,* 972-1009.

Paulson, S.E., Koman, J.J., and Hill, J.P. (1990). Maternal employment and parent-child relations in the families of 7th graders. *Journal of Early Adolescence, 10*(3), 279-295.

Pavetti, L. (1997). *Against the odds: Steady employment among low-skilled women. Report to the Annie E. Casey Foundation.* Washington, DC: Urban Institute.

Paxson, C., and Waldfogel, J. (in press). Work, welfare, and child maltreatment. *Journal of Labor Economics.*

Peisner-Feinberg, E.S., and Burchinal, M.R. (1997). Relations between preschool children's childcare experiences and concurrent development: The cost, quality, and outcomes study. *Merrill-Palmer Quarterly, 43*, 451-477.

Peisner-Feinberg, E.S., Burchinal, M.R., Clifford, R.M., Culkin, M., Howes, C., Kagan, S.L., Yazejian, N., Byler, P., and Rustici, J. (1999). *The children of the cost, quality, and outcomes study go to school*. Chapel Hill: University of North Carolina, Frank Porter Graham Child Development Center.

Peisner-Feinberg, E.S., Burchinal, M.R., Clifford, R.M., Culkin, M.L., Howes, C., Kagan, S.L., and Yazejian, N. (2001). The relation of preschool child-care quality to children's cognitive and social developmental trajectories through second grade. *Child Development, 72*, 1534-1553.

Perry-Jenkins, M., Repetti, R.L., and Crouter, A.C. (2000). Work and family in the 1990s. *Journal of Marriage and the Family, 62*, 981-998.

Pettit, G.S., Bates, J.E., Dodge, K.A., and Meece, D.W. (1999). The impact of after-school peer contact on early adolescent externalizing problems is moderated by parental monitoring, perceived neighborhood safety, and prior adjustment. *Child Development, 70*(3), 768-778.

Pettit, G.S., Laird, R.D., Bates, J.E., and Dodge, K.A. (1997). Patterns of after-school care in middle childhood: Risk factors and developmental outcomes. *Merrill-Palmer Quarterly, 43*(3), 525-538.

Phillips, D., and Adams, G. (2001). Child care and our youngest children. *The Future of Children: Caring for Infants and Toddlers, 11*(1), 35-51.

Phillips, D., McCartney, K., Scarr, S., and Howes, C. (1987a). Selective review of infant day care research: A cause for concern. *Zero to Three, 7*, 18-21.

Phillips, D.A., McCartney, K., and Scarr, S. (1987b). Child-care quality and children's social development. *Developmental Psychology, 23*, 537-544.

Phillips, D., Voran, M., Kisker, E., Howes, C., and Whitebrook, M. (1994). Child care for children in poverty: Opportunity or inequity? *Child Development, 65*(2), 472-492.

Phillips, K.R. (2002). *Parent work and child well-being in low-income families*. (Assessing the New Federalism occasional paper no. 56). Washington, DC: Urban Institute.

Phillipsen, L.C., Burchinal, M.R., Howes, C., and Cryer, D. (1997). The prediction of process quality from structural features of child care. *Early Childhood Research Quarterly, 12*, 281-303.

Pierce, K.M., Hamm, J.V., and Vandell, D.L. (1999). Experiences in after-school programs and children's adjustment in first grade classrooms. *Child Development, 70*(3), 756-767.

Pierrehumbert, B., Ramstein, T., Karmaniola, A., and Halfon, O. (1996). Child care in the preschool years: Attachment, behaviour problems and cognitive development. *European Journal of Psychology of Education, 11*, 201-214.

Pleck, J.H., and Staines, G.L. (1985). Work schedules and family life in two-earner couples. *Journal of Family Issues, 6*, 61-82.

Posner, J.K., and Vandell, D.L. (1994). Low-income children's after school care: Are there beneficial effects of after-school programs? *Child Development, 65*, 440-456.

Posner, J.K., and Vandell, D.L. (1999). After-school activities and the development of low-income urban children: A longitudinal study. *Developmental Psychology, 35*(3), 868-879.

Powell, D.R. (1987). *After-school child care: Research in review*. West Lafayette, IN: Purdue University.

Presser, H.B. (1984). Job characteristics of spouses and their work shifts. *Demography, 21*, 575-589.

Presser, H.B. (1986). Shift work among American women and child care. *Journal of Marriage and the Family, 48*, 551-563.

Presser, H.B. (1988). Shift work and child care among young dual-earner American parents. *Journal of Marriage and the Family, 50*, 133-148.

Presser, H.B. (1989). Can we make time for children? The economy, work schedules, and child care. *Demography, 26*, 523-543.

Presser, H.B. (1994). Employment schedules among dual-earner spouses and the division of household labor by gender. *American Sociological Review, 59*, 348-364.

Presser, H.B. (1995a). Are the interests of women inherently at odds with the interests of children or the family? In K.O. Mason, and A. Jensen (Eds.), *Gender and family change in industrialized countries* (pp. 297-319). Oxford: Oxford University Press.

Presser, H.B. (1995b). Job, family, and gender: Determinants of nonstandard work schedules among employed Americans in 1991. *Demography, 32*, 577-598.

Presser, H.B. (1998). Toward a 24-hour economy: The U.S. experience and implications for the family. In D. Vannoy, and P.J. Dubeck (Eds.), *Challenges for work and family in the 21st century*. Hawthorne, NY: Aldine de Gruyter.

Presser, H.B. (1999). Toward a 24-hour economy. *Science, 284*, 1778-1779.

Presser, H.B. (2000). Nonstandard work schedules and marital instability. *Journal of Marriage and the Family, 62*(1), 93-110.

Presser, H.B. (2001). Toward a 24-hour economy: Implications for the temporal structure and functioning of family life. In *The social contract in the face of demographic change: Proceedings* (pp. 115-129). 2nd Renontres Sauvy International Seminar, Montreal, Quebec.

Presser, H.B. (in press). *Working in a 24/7 hour economy: Challenges for American families*. New York: Russell Sage.

Presser, H.B., and Cox, A.G. (1997). The work schedules of low-educated American women and welfare reform. *Monthly Labor Review, 120*, 25-34.

Primus, W.E. (2002). *Child living arrangements by race and income: A supplementary analysis*. Washington, DC: Center on Budget and Policy Priorities.

Puntenney, D. (1999). The work of mothers: Strategies for survival in an inner-city neighborhood. *Journal of Poverty, 3*, 63-92.

Quinn, J. (1999). Where need meets opportunity: Youth development programs for early teens. *The Future of Children: When School Is Out, 9*(2), 96-116.

Quint, J., Bos, J., and Polit, D. (1997). *New chance: Final report on a comprehensive program for young mothers in poverty and their children*. New York: Manpower Demonstration Research Corporation.

Radloff, L. (1977). The CES-D scale: A self-report depression scale for research in the general population. *Journal of Applied Psychological Measurement, 1*, 385-401.

Rahman, A., and Pal, S. (1994). Subjective health and family life of rotating shift workers. *Bangladesh Journal of Psychology, 14*, 49-55.

Ramey, C.T., Campbell, F.A., and Blair, C. (1998). Enhancing the life-course for high-risk children: Results from the Abecedarian Project. In J. Crane (Ed.), *Social programs that really work*. New York: Russell Sage.

Ramey, C.T., Campbell, F.A., Burchinal, M., Skinner, M.L., Gardner, D.M., and Ramey, S.L. (in press). Persistent effects of early childhood education on high-risk children and their mothers. *Applied Developmental Science*.

Ramey, C.T., Campbell, F.A., Burchinal, M.R., Bryant, D.M., Wasik, B.H., Skinner, M.L., and Gardner, D.M. (1999). *Early learning, later success: The Abecedarian study*. Chapel Hill, NC: Frank Porter Graham Child Development Institute.

Rank, M. (1994). *Living on the edge*. New York: Columbia University.

Rayman, P. (2001). *Beyond the bottom line: The search for dignity at work*. New York: St. Martin's Press.

Reaves, A. (2000). Black male employment and self-sufficiency. In S. Danziger, and A. Lin (Eds.), *Coping with poverty: The social contexts of neighborhood, work, and family in the African American community* (pp. 172-197). Ann Arbor, MI: University of Michigan.

Reid, J.B., and Patterson, G.R. (1989). The development of antisocial behavior patterns in childhood and adolescence: Personality and aggression-special issue. *European Journal of Personality, 3*, 107-119.

Repetti, R., Matthews, K., and Waldron, I. (1989). Employment and women's health: Effects of paid employment on women's mental and physical health. *American Psychologist, 44*, 1394-1401.

Reynell, J. (1991). *Reynell developmental language scales, U.S. edition.* Los Angeles, CA: Western Psychological Service.

Reynolds, A.J. (1994). Effects of a preschool plus follow-on intervention for children at risk. *Developmental Psychology, 30*, 787-804.

Reynolds, A.J. (2000). *Success in early childhood intervention: The Chicago child-parent centers.* Lincoln, NE: University of Nebraska.

Reynolds, A.J., and Temple, J.A. (1998). Extended early childhood intervention and school achievement: Age thirteen findings from the Chicago Longitudinal Study. *Child Development, 69*, 231-246.

Reynolds, A.J., Temple, J.A., Robertson, D.L., and Mann, E.A. (2000). *Long-term benefits of participation in Title I Chicago child-parent centers.* Paper presented at the Biennial Meeting of the Society for Research on Adolescence.

Reynolds, A.J., Temple, J.A., Robertson, D.L., and Mann, E.A. (2001). Long-term effects of an early childhood intervention on educational achievement and juvenile Arrest: A 15-year follow-up of low-income children in public schools. *Journal of the American Medical Association, 285*(18), 2339-2346.

Rhodes, J.E. (1994). Older and wiser: Mentoring relationships in childhood and adolescence. *The Journal of Primary Prevention, 14*, 187-196.

Rhodes, J.E., Frossman, J.B., and Resch, N.L. (2000). Agents of change: Pathways through which mentoring relationships influence adolescents' academic adjustment. *Child Development, 71*, 1662-1671.

Richards, M.H., and Duckett, E. (1991). Maternal employment and adolescents. In V. Lerner, and N.L. Galambos (Eds.), *Employed mothers and their children* (pp. 75-130). New York: Garlands.

Richards, M.H., and Duckett, E. (1994). The relationship of maternal employment to early adolescent daily experience with and without parents. *Child Development, 65*, 225-236.

Richters, J., and Zahn-Waxler, C. (1990). The infant day care controversy: Current status and future directions. In N. Fox, and G. Fein (Eds.), *Infant day care: The current debate* (pp. 87-106). Norwood, NJ: Ablex.

Riley, L., and Glass, J. (2002). You can't always get what you want: Infant care preferences and use among employed mothers. *Journal of Marriage and Family, 64*, 2-15.

Ripple, C., Gilliam, W.S., Chanana, N., and Zigler, E. (1999). Will fifty cooks spoil the broth? The debate over entrusting Head Start to the states. *American Psychologist, 54*, 327-343.

Robinson, J.P., and Godbey, G. (1999). *Time for life, second edition.* University Park, PA: Pennsylvania State University.

Rodman, H., Pratto, D.J., and Nelson, R.S. (1985). Child care arrangements and children's functioning: A comparison of self-care and adult-care supervision. *Developmental Psychology, 21*, 413-418.

Rodman, H., Pratto, D.J., and Nelson, R.S. (1986). Toward a definition of self-care children: A commentary on Steinberg. *Developmental Psychology, 24*, 292-294.

Rogers, S.J., Parcel, T.L., and Menaghan, E.G. (1991). The effects of maternal working conditions and mastery on children's behavior problems: Studying the intergenerational transmission of social control. *Journal of Health and Social Behavior, 32*, 145-164.

Romero, D., Chavkin, W., Wise, P.H., Smith, L.A., and Wood, P.R. (2002). Welfare to work? Impact of maternal health on employment. *American Journal of Public Health, 92*, 1462-1468.

Romich, J.L., and Weisner, T.S. (2000). How families view and sue the EITC: Advance payment versus lump sum delivery. *National Tax Journal, 53*(4), 1245-1265.

Rones, P., Ilg, R., and Gardner, J. (1997). Trends in the hours of work since the mid-1970s. *Monthly Labor Review, 120*, 3-14.

Rosenthal, R., and Vandell, D.L. (1996) Quality of care at school-age child-care programs: Regulatable features: Observed experiences, child perspectives, and parent perspectives. *Child Development, 67*, 2434-2445.

Rosier, K. (2000). *Mothering inner-city children*. New Brunswick, NJ: Rutgers University Press.

Rosman, E.A., Yoshikawa, H., and Knitzer, J. (2002). Towards an understanding of the effects of welfare reform on children with disabilities and their families: A research policy agenda. *Social Policy Reports of the Society for Research in Child Development, 16*(4), 1-16.

Ross, K. (1998). *Labor pains: The effects of the Family and Medical Leave Act on recent mothers' returns to work after childbirth*. Paper presented at the Population Association of America Annual Meeting.

Ross Phillips, K. (2002a). *Parent work and child well-being in low-income families*. (Occasional paper, no. 56). Washington, DC: Urban Institute.

Ross Phillips, K. (2002b). *Who knows about the Earned Income Tax Credit?* (Assessing the New Federalism Project). Washington, DC: Urban Institute.

Rossi, P.H. (1998). *Feeding the poor*. Washington, DC: American Enterprise Institute Press.

Rothenberg, D. (1995). *Full-day kindergarten programs*. Champaign, IL: ERIC Digest.

Roy, K. (1999). *On the margins of family and work: Life course patterns of low-income single fathers in an African American Community*. Unpublished doctoral dissertation, Northwestern University.

Ruhm, C. (2000a). *Parental employment and child cognitive development*. Greensboro: University of North Carolina.

Ruhm, C. (2000b). Parental leave and child health. *Journal of Health Economics, 19*(6), 931-960.

Ruhm, C.J. (1997). Is high school employment consumption or investment? *Journal of Labor Economics, 15*, 735-776.

Ruopp, R., Travers, J., Glantz, F., and Coelen, C. (1979). *Children at the center: Final report of the National Day Care Study*. Cambridge, MA: Abt Associates.

Ryu, S., and Mortimer, J.T. (1996). The "occupational linkage hypothesis" applied to occupational value formation in adolescence. In J.T. Morhmer, and M.D. Finch (Eds.), *Adolescents, work and family: An intergenerational developmental analysis* (pp. 167-190). Thousand Oaks, CA: Russell Sage.

Sandberg, J.F., and Hofferth, S.L. (2001). Changes in parental time with children. *Demography, 38*, 423-436.

Sandstrom, M.J., and Coie, J.D. (1999). A developmental perspective on peer rejection: Mechanisms of stability and change. *Child Development, 70*, 955-966.

Sawhill, I., and Thomas, A. (2001). *A tax proposal for working families with children*. (Welfare Reform and Beyond brief no. 3). Washington, DC: Brookings Institution.

Sayer, L.C., Bianchi, S.M., and Robinson, J.P. (2002). *Are parents investing less in children? Trends in mothers' and fathers' time with children*. (Working paper). College Park, University of Maryland.

Scarr, S., Eisenberg, M., and Deater-Deckard, K. (1994). Measurement of quality in child care centers. *Early Childhood Research Quarterly, 9,* 131-151.

Scarr, S., and McCartney, K. (1983). How people make their own environments. *Child Development, 54,* 424-435.

Schaefer, S.A. (2001). *Welfare to work: Does it work for kids? Research on work and income welfare experiments.* Washington, DC: National Association of Child Advocates.

Schernhammer E.S., Laden F., Speizer, F.E., Willett, W.C., Hunter D.J., Kawachi, I., and Colditz, G.A. (2001). Rotating night shifts and risk of breast cancer in women participating in the nurses' health study. *Journal of the National Cancer Institute, 93,* 1563-1568.

Schliecker, E., White, D.R., and Jacobs, E. (1991). The role of day care quality in the prediction of children's vocabulary. *Canadian Journal of Behavioural Science, 23,* 12-24.

Schoenhals, M., Tienda, M., and Schneider, B. (1998). The educational and personal consequences of adolescent employment. *Social Forces, 77,* 723-762.

Schoeni, R.F., and Blank, R.M. (2000). *What has welfare reform accomplished? Impacts on welfare participation, employment, income, poverty, and family structure. (NBER working paper #7627).* Washington, DC: National Bureau of Economic Research.

Schor, J.B. (1992). *The overworked American: The unexpected decline of leisure.* New York: Basic Books.

Schulman, K., Blank, H., and Ewen, D. (1999). *Seed of success: State pre-kindergarten initiatives 1998-1999.* Washington, DC: Children's Defense Fund.

Schumacher, R., and Greenberg. M. (1999). *Child care after leaving welfare: Early evidence from state studies.* Washington, DC: Center for Law and Social Policy.

Schumacher, R., Greenberg, M., and Duffy, J. (2001a). *The impact of TANF funding on state child care subsidy programs* (September ed.). Washington, DC: Center for Law and Social Policy.

Schumacher, R., Greenburg, M., and Lombardi, J. (2001b). *State initiatives to promote early learning: Next steps in coordinating subsidized child care, Head Start, and state prekindergarten.* Washington, DC: Center for Law and Social Policy.

Schweinhart, L.J., Barnes, H.V., and Weikart, D.P. (1993). *Significant benefits: The High/Scope Perry preschool study through age 27.* Ypsilanti, MI: High/Scope Press.

Scott, E.K., Edin, K., London, A.S., and Kissane, R.J. (2001). *Unstable work, unstable income: Implications for family well-being in the era of time-limited welfare.* New York: Manpower Demonstration Research Corporation.

Seecombe, K. (1999). *So you think I drive a Cadillac? Welfare recipients' perspectives on the system and its reform.* Boston: Allyn and Bacon.

Seitz, V. (1990). Intervention programs for impoverished children: A comparison of educational and family support models. In R. Vasta (Ed.), *Annals of child development: A research annual, volume 7* (pp. 73-103). London: Jessica Kingsley.

Seppanen, P., Love, J., deVries, D., Berstein, L., Seligson, M., Marx, F., and Kisker, E. (1993). *National study of before- and after-school programs. Final report.* Washington, DC: U.S. Department of Education, Office of Policy and Planning.

Shook, K. (1999). Does the loss of welfare income increase the risk of involvement with the child welfare system. *Children and Youth Services Review, 21,* 781-814.

Simon, B.L. (1990). Impact of shift work on individuals and families. *Families in Society: The Journal of Contemporary Human Services, 71*(16), 342-348.

Singer, J.D., Fuller, B., Keiley, M.K., and Wolf, A. (1998). Early child-care selection: Variation by geographic location, maternal characteristics, and family structure. *Developmental Psychology, 34*(5), 1129-1144.

Skinner, M.L., Elder, G.H., and Conger, R.D. (1992). Linking economic hardship to adolescent aggression. *Journal of Youth and Adolescence, 21*(3), 259-276.

Smeeding, T.M., Ross Phillips, K., and O'Connor, M. (2000). *The EITC: Expectation, knowledge, use, and economic and social mobility.* (JCPR working paper #139). Chicago: Joint Center for Poverty Research.

Smith, K. (2000). *Who's minding the kids? Child care arrangements, fall 1995.* (Report no. P70-70). Washington, DC: U.S. Department of Commerce, U.S. Census Bureau.

Smith, K. (2002). *Who's minding the kids? Child care arrangements.* (Current Population Reports no. P70-86). Washington, DC: U.S. Department of Commerce, U.S. Census Bureau.

Smith, K., and Bachu, A. (1999). *Women's labor force attachment patterns and maternity leave: A review of the literature.* Washington, DC: U.S. Department of Commerce, U.S. Census Bureau.

Smith, S. (1995). *Two generation programs for families in poverty: A new intervention strategy.* Norwood, NJ: Ablex.

Stack, C. (2002). In exile on main street. In F. Munger (Ed.), *Laboring below the poverty line: The new ethnography of poverty, low-wage work, and survival in the global economy* (pp. 29-44). New York: Russell Sage.

Staines, G.L., and Pleck, J.H. (1983). *The impact of work schedules on the family.* Ann Arbor, MI: University of Michigan.

Stallings, J., and Porter, A. (1980). *National day care home study: Observation component, final report, volume III.* Washington, DC: Administration for Children, Youth, and Families, Department of Health and Human Services, SRI Project No. 6903.

Stattin, H., and Magnusson, D. (1989). Social transition in adolescence: A biosocial perspective. In A. de Ribaupierre (Ed.), *Transition mechanisms in child development: The longitudinal perspective* (pp. 147-190). Cambridge: Cambridge University Press.

Stattin, M.L., and Kerr, M. (2000). Parental monitoring: A reinterpretation. *Child Development, 71,* 1072-1085.

Steinberg, L. (1986). Latchkey children and susceptibility to peer pressure: An ecological analysis. *Developmental Psychology, 22,* 433-439.

Steinberg, L. (1987). Single parents, stepparents, and the susceptibility of adolescents to antisocial peer pressure. *Child Development, 58,* 269-275.

Steinberg, L., and Cauffman, E. (1995). The impact of employment on adolescent development. In R. Vasta (Ed.), *Annals of child development, volume 11.* London: Jessica Kingsley.

Steinberg, L., and Dornbusch, S. (1991). Negative correlates of part-time work in adolescence: Replication and elaboration. *Developmental Psychology, 17,* 304-313.

Steinberg, L., Fegley, S., and Dornbusch, S. (1993). Authoritative parenting, psychological maturity, and academic success among adolescents. *Child Development, 29,* 179-180.

Stern, D., Finkelstein, N., Urquiola, M., and Cagampang, H. (1997). What difference does it make if school and work are connected? Evidence on cooperative education in the United States. *Economics of Educational Review, 16,* 213-229.

Stewart, R. (2001). Adolescent self-care: Reviewing the risks. *Families in Society, 82,* 119-126.

Stith, S.M., and Davis, A.J. (1984). Employed mothers and family day-care substitute caregivers: A comparative analysis of infant day care. *Child Development, 55,* 1340-1348.

Stone III, J.R., and Mortimer, J.T. (1998). The effect of adolescent employment on vocational development: Public and educational policy implications. *Journal of Vocational Behavior, 53,* 184-214.

Stone III, J.R., Stern, D., Hopkins, C., and McMillan, M. (1990). Adolescents' perceptions of their work: School-supervised and non-school-supervised. *Journal of Vocational Education Research, 15,* 31-53.

Stoney, L. (1998). *Looking into new mirrors: Lessons for early childhood finance and system building*. Boston: Horizon Institute.

St. Pierre, R.G., Swartz, J.P., Gamse, B., Murray, S., Deck, D., and Nickel, P. (1995). *National evaluation of even start family literacy program: Final report*. Cambridge, MA: Abt Associates.

Strawn, J., Greenberg, M., and Savner, S. (2001). From welfare-to-work to workforce development. In R. Blank, and R. Haskins (Eds.), *The new world of welfare*. Washington, DC: Brookings Institution.

Stuckey, M.F., McGhee, P.E., and Bell, N.J. (1982). Parent-child interaction: The influence of maternal employment. *Developmental Psychology, 18*, 635-644.

Sullivan, M. (1989). *Getting paid: Youth crime and work in the inner city*. Ithaca, NY: Cornell University Press.

Sullivan, M. (1992). Non-custodial fathers' attitudes and behaviors. In F. Furstenberg, K. Sherwood, and M. Sullivan (Eds.), *Caring and paying: What mothers and fathers say about child support* (pp. 6-33). New York: Manpower Demonstration Research Corporation.

Tapp, W.N., and Holloway, F.A. (1981). Phase shifting and circadian rhythms produces retrograde amnesia. *Science, 211*, 1056-1058.

Teti, D.M., Gelfand, D.M., Messinger, D.H., and Isabella, R. (1995). Maternal depression and the quality of early attachment: An examination of infants, preschoolers, and their mothers. *Developmental Psychology, 31*, 364-376.

The David and Lucile Packard Foundation. (2002). *New poll shows public concerned about effects of welfare reform on children*. Available: http://www.futureofchildren.org/newsletter2861/newsletter_show.htm?doc_id=102827. [Accessed February 20, 2002].

Thomas, D. (1990). Intra-household resource allocation: An inferential approach. *Journal of Human Resources, 25*(4), 635-664.

Thomlinson, E., and Burrows, R. (2002). The critical role of transportation. In T. Lengyel, and D. Campbell (Eds.), *Faces of change: Welfare policy through the lens of personal experience* (pp. 83-96). Milwaukee, WI: Alliance for Children and Families.

Thompson, R. (1988). The effects of infant day care through the prism of attachment theory. *Early Childhood Research Quarterly, 3*, 273-282.

Tienda, M., and Ahituv, A. (1996). Ethnic differences in school departure: Does youth employment promote or undermine educational attainment? In G. Mangum, and S. Mangum (Eds.), *Of heart and mind: Social policy essays in honor of Sar A. Levitan* (pp. 93-110). Kalamazoo, MI: W.E. Upjohn Institute for Employment Research.

Tierney, J.P., Grossman, J.B., and Resch, N.L. (1995). *Making a difference: An impact study of Big Brothers/Big Sisters*. Philadelphia, PA: Public/Private Ventures.

Tout, K., Scarpa, J., and Zaslow, M.J. (2002). *Children of current and former welfare recipients: Similarly at risk*. Washington, DC: Child Trends.

U.S. Census Bureau. (2000). *Poverty in the United States 2000*. (P60-214). Washington, DC: Author.

U.S. Census Bureau. (2001). *Maternity leave and employment patterns: 1961-1995*. Washington, DC: Household Economic Studies.

U.S. Census Bureau. (2002a). *1997 economic census*. Available: http://www.census.gov/epcd/www/ec97stat.htm. [Accessed May 2003].

U.S. Census Bureau. (2002b). *Who's minding the kids? Child care arrangements: Spring, 1997*. Available: http://www.census.gov/population/www/socdemo/childcare.html. [Accessed 2002].

U.S. Department of Agriculture. (2002a). *USDA child and adult care food program data*. Available: http://www.fns.usda.gov/pd/cccash.htm. [Accessed 2002].

U.S. Department of Agriculture. (2002b). *USDA summer food service program data.* Available: http://www.fns.usda.gov/pd/sfsummar.htm. [Accessed 2002].

U.S. Department of Education (1965). *Title I—amendments to the Elementary and Secondary Education Act of 1965.* Available: http://ed.gov/legislation/ESEA/sec1001.html. [Accessed 2003].

U.S. Department of Education. (1999). *Twenty-first annual report to Congress on the implementation of the Individuals with Disabilities Education Act, 1999.* Available: http://www.ed.gov/offices/OSERS/OSEP/Research/OSEP99AnlRpt/. [Accessed 2002].

U.S. Department of Education. (2002). *21st century community learning centers* Available: http://www.ed.gov/21stcclc. [Accessed May 20, 2002].

U.S. Department of Education. (2003). *When schools stay open late: The National Evaluation of the 21st-Century Community Learning Centers Program.* Available: http://www.ed.gov/pubs/21cent/firstyear/. [Accessed March 5, 2003].

U.S. Department of Health and Human Services. (2002). *Head Start: Promoting early childhood development.* Available: http://www.hhs.gov/news/press/2002pres/headstart.html. [Accessed May 16, 2002].

U.S. Department of Health and Human Services, Administration for Children and Families. (1999). *Social services block grant program: Analysis of expenditure and recipient data 1995-1997.* Washington, DC: U.S. Government Printing Office.

U.S. Department of Health and Human Services, Administration for Children and Families, and Office of Community Services. (2000a). *Social services block grant program: Annual report of expenditures and recipients 1998.* Washington, DC: U.S. Government Printing Office.

U.S. Department of Health and Human Services, Administration for Children and Families, and Office of Community Services. (2000b). *TANF Program: Third annual report to Congress.* Washington, DC: U.S. Government Printing Office.

U.S. Department of Health and Human Services, Administration for Children and Families, and Office of Community Services. (2001a). *Social Services Block Grant Program: Annual report of expenditures and recipients, 1999.* Washington, DC: U.S. Government Printing Office.

U.S. Department of Health and Human Services, Administration for Children and Families, and Office of Community Services. (2001b). FACES findings: New research on Head Start Program quality and outcomes. Available: http://www.acf.hhs.gov/programs/core/ongoing_research/faces/pamphlet/facefindings.pdf. [Accessed February 2003].

U.S. Department of Health, Education, and Welfare. (1978). *The appropriateness of the federal interagency day care requirements: Report findings and recommendations.* Washington, DC: U.S. Government Printing Office.

U.S. Department of Justice. (2001). *Crime in the United States 2000.* Washington, DC: Federal Bureau of Investigation.

U.S. Department of Labor. (1995). *Care around the clock: Developing child care resources before nine and after five.* (Women's Bureau Special Reports). Washington, DC: Author.

U.S. Department of Labor. (2000). *Report on the youth labor force.* Available: http://www.bls.gov/opub/rylf/rylfhome.htm. [Accessed 2002].

U.S. General Accounting Office. (1997). *Head Start: Research provides little information on impact of current program.* (GAO/HEHS-97-59). Washington, DC: Author.

U.S. General Accounting Office. (1998). *Head Start: Challenges in monitoring program quality and demonstrating results.* (GAO/T-HEHS-98-186). Washington, DC: Author.

U.S. General Accounting Office. (2000a). *Preschool education: Federal investment for low-income children significant but effectiveness unclear.* (GAO/T-HEHS-00-83). Washington, DC: Author.

U.S. General Accounting Office. (2000b). *Title I preschool education: More children served by gauging effect on school readiness difficult.* (GAO/HEHS-00-171). Washington, DC: Author.

U.S. General Accounting Office. (2001). *Child care: States increased spending on low-income families.* (GAO-01-293). Washington, DC: Author.

U.S. General Accounting Office. (2002). *Child care: States exercise flexibility in setting reimbursement rates and providing access for low-income children.* (GAO-02-894). Washington, DC: Author. Available: http://www.gao.gov/new.items/d02894.pdf. [Accessed February 2003].

U.S. House of Representatives. (2000). *2000 green book: Background material and data on programs within the jurisdiction of the Committee on Ways and Means, table 7-25.* Washington, DC: U.S. Government Printing Office.

U.S. House of Representatives, Committee on Ways and Means. (1994). *1994 green book: Background material and data on programs within the jurisdiction of the Committee on Ways and Means.* Washington, DC: U.S. Government Printing Office.

U.S. Office of Management and Budget. (2003). *Budget of the United States government: Fiscal year 2003, analytical perspectives.* Washington, DC: U.S. Government Printing Office.

Uttal, L. (1999). Using kin for childcare: Embedment in the socioeconomic networks of extended families. *Journal of Marriage and the Family, 61,* 845-857.

Vandell, D. (1979). Effects of a playgroup experience on mother-son and father-son interaction. *Developmental Psychology, 15,* 379-385.

Vandell, D.L., and Corasaniti, M.A. (1988). The relation between third graders' after-school care and social, academic, and emotional functioning. *Child Development, 59,* 868-875.

Vandell, D.L., and Corasaniti, M.A. (1990). Child care and the family: Complex contributors to child development. *New Directions for Child Development, 49,* 23-37.

Vandell, D.L., Henderson, V.K., and Wilson, K.S. (1988). A longitudinal study of children with day-care experiences of varying quality. *Child Development, 59,* 1286-1292.

Vandell, D.L., and Hsiu-chih, S. (1999). Childcare and school-age children. *Young Children,* 62-71.

Vandell, D.L., Hyde, J.S., Plant, E.A., and Essex, M.J. (1997). Fathers and others as infant care providers: Predictors of parents' emotional well being and marital satisfaction. *Merrill Palmer Quarterly, 43*(3), 361-385.

Vandell, D.L., and Pierce, K.M. (1999). *Can after-school programs benefit children who live in high crime time? The next generation of research.* Poster symposium conducted at the meeting for the Society for Research in Child Development, Albuquerque, NM, April 14-18.

Vandell, D.L., and Pierce, K.M. (2001). *Experiences in after-school programs and children's well-being.* Paper presented at the Biennial Meeting of the Society for Research in Child Development, Minneapolis, MN, April.

Vandell, D.L., and Pierce, K.M. (in press). Child care quality and children's success at school. In A. Reynolds, and M. Wang (Eds.), *Early childhood learning: Programs for a new age.* New York: Child Welfare League.

Vandell, D.L., Posner, J., Shumow, L., and Kang, K. (1995). *Concurrent, short-term, and long-term effects of self-care.* Paper presented at the biennial meetings of the Society for Research in Child Development, Indianapolis, IN, March.

Vandell, D.L., and Posner, J.K. (1999). Conceptualization and measurement of children's after-school environments. In S.L. Friedman, and T. Wachs (Eds.), *Measuring environments across the lifespan: Emerging methods and concepts.* Washington, DC: American Psychological Association.

Vandell, D.L., and Powers, C.P. (1983). Day care quality and children's free play activities. *American Journal of Orthopsychiatry, 53*, 493-500.

Vandell, D.L., and Ramanan, J. (1992). Effects of early and recent maternal employment on children from low-income families. *Child Development, 63*, 938-949.

Vandell, D.L., and Shumow, L. (1999). After-school child care programs. *Future of Children: When School Is Out, 9*(2), 64-80.

Vandell, D.L., and Su, H.-C. (1999). Child care and school-aged children. *Young Children, 54*, 62-71.

Vandell, D.L., and Wolfe, B. (2000). *Child care quality: Does it matter and does it need to be improved?* Office of the Assistant Secretary for Planning and Evaluation, U.S. Department of Health and Human Services. Available: http://aspe.hhs.gov/hsp/ccquality00/index.htm. [Accessed 2002].

Vander Ven, T.M., Cullen, F.T., Carrozza, M.A., and Wright, J.P. (2001). Home alone: The impact of maternal employment on delinquency. *Social Problems, 48*, 236-257.

Vast, T. (1998). *Learning between systems: Higher education as a model for financing early care and education.* Minneapolis: The Minnesota Early Care and Education Financing Partnership.

Venkatesh, S. (2000). *American project: The rise and fall of a modern ghetto.* Cambridge: Harvard University Press.

Vernon-Feagans, L., Emanuel, D.C., and Blood, I. (1997). The effect of Otitis Media and quality daycare on children's language development. *Journal of Applied Developmental Psychology, 18*, 395-409.

Volling, B.L., and Feagans, L.V. (1995). Infant day care and children's social competence. *Infant Behavior and Development, 18*, 177-188.

Vroman, W. (2001). *Compensating American families for births and adoptions.* Washington, DC: Urban Institute.

Waldfogel, J. (1999a). Family leave coverage in the 1990's. *Monthly Labor Review*, October, 13-21.

Waldfogel, J. (1999b). The impact of the Family and Medical Leave Act. *Journal of Policy Analysis and Management, 18*(2), 281-302.

Waldfogel, J. (2001a). Family and medical leave: Evidence from the 2000 surveys. *Monthly Labor Review*, September, 17-23.

Waldfogel, J. (2001b). Family-friendly policies for families with young children. *Employee Rights and Employment Policy Journal, 5*(1), 273-296.

Waldfogel, J. (2001c). International policies toward parental leave and child care. *The Future of Children: Caring for Infants and Toddlers, 11*(1), 99-111.

Waldfogel, J., Danziger, S., Danziger, S., and Seefeldt, K. (2001). Welfare reform and lone mothers' employment in the U.S. In J. Millar, and K. Rowlingson (Eds.), *Lone parents, employment and social policy: Cross-national comparisons.* Bristol: Policy Press.

Waldfogel, J., Han, W.-J., and Brooks-Gunn, J. (2002). The effects of early maternal employment on child cognitive development. *Demography, 39*(2), 369-392.

Walker, J. (1996). Funding child rearing: Child allowance and parental leave. *The Future of Children: Financing Child Care, 6*(2), 122-126.

Warr, P., and Parry, G. (1982). Depressed mood in working class mothers with and without paid employment. *Sociology of Psychiatry, 17*, 161-165.

Waters, E., and Sroufe, L.A. (1983). Social competence as a developmental construct. *Developmental Review, 3*, 79-97.

Watamura, S.E., Donzella, B., Alwin, J., and Gunnar, M.R. (in press). *Morning to afternoon increases in cortisol concentrations for infants and toddlers at child care: Age differences and behavioral correlates. Child Development.*

Webster-Stratton, C., Reid, M.J., and Hammond, M. (2001). Preventing conduct problems, promoting social competence: A parent and teacher training partnership in Head Start. *Journal of Clinical Child Psychology, 30*, 283-302.

Wedderburn, A. (2000). *Shiftwork and health.* (Bulletin of European Studies on Time). Dublin, Ireland: European Foundation for the Improvement of Living and Working Conditions.

Welsh, M.E., Russell, C.A., Williams, I., Reisner, E., and White, R.N. (2002). *Promoting learning and school attendance through after-school programs: Student level changes in educational performance across TASC's first three years.* Washington, DC: Policy Studies Associates.

Werner, E.E. (1993). Risk, Resilience, and Recovery: Perspectives from the Kauai longitudinal study. *Development and Psychopathology, 5*, 503-515.

Werner, E.E., and Smith, R. (1992). *Overcoming the odds: High-risk children from birth to adulthood.* New York: Cornell University.

West, J., Denton, K., and Germino-Hausken, E. (2000). *America's kindergarteners.* Washington, DC: National Center for Education Statistics.

Westinghouse Learning Corporation. (1969). *The impact of Head Start: An evaluation of the effects of Head Start on children's cognitive and affective development.* (Report No. ED 036 321). Washington, DC: Clearinghouse for Federal and Technical Information.

Whitbeck, L.B., Simons, R.L., Conger, R.D., Wickrama, K.A., Ackley, K.A., and Elder, G.H. (1997a). The effects of parents' working conditions and family economic hardship on parenting behaviors and children's self-efficacy. *Social Psychology Quarterly, 60*, 291-303.

Whitbeck, L.B., Simons, R.L., Conger, R.D., Wickrama, K.A., Ackley, K.A., Youniss, J., and Yates, M. (1997b). *Community service and social responsibility in youth.* Chicago: University of Chicago.

White, L., and Keith, B. (1990). The effect of shift work on the quality and stability of marital relations. *Journal of Marriage and the Family, 52*, 453-462.

White, R.N., Reisner, E.R., Welsh, M., and Russel, C. (2001). *Patterns of student-level change linked to TASC participation based on TASC projects in year 2.* Washington, DC: Policy Studies Associates.

Whitebook, M., Howes, C., and Phillips, D. (1989). *Who cares? Child care teachers and the quality of care in America. Final report of the National Care Staffing Study.* Oakland, CA: Child Care Employee Project.

Whitebook, M., Howes, C., and Phillips, D. (1998). *Worthy work, unlivable wages: The national child care staffing study, 1988-97.* Washington, DC: Center for the Child Care Workforce.

Whitebook, M., Sakai, L., Gerber, E., and Howes, C. (2001). *Then and now: Changes in child care staffing, 1994-2000.* [Technical report]. Washington, DC: Center for the Child Care Workforce.

Williams, T., and Kornblum, W. (1985). *Growing up poor.* Lexington, MA: Lexington.

Williams, T., and Kornblum, W. (1994). *The uptown kids: Struggle and hope in the projects.* New York: G.P. Putnam.

Wilson, W. (1987). *The truly disadvantaged: The inner city, the underclass, and public policy.* Chicago: University of Chicago.

Wilson, W. (1996). *When work disappears: The world of the new urban poor.* New York: Knopf.

Winkler, A.E. (1998). Earnings of husbands and wives in dual-earner families. *Monthly Labor Review, 121*(4), 42-49.

Wolfe, B., and Vandell, D.L. (2002). Child care for low-income working families. *Focus, 22*(1), 106-111.

Woods, M.B. (1972). The unsupervised child of the working mother. *Developmental Psychology, 6*(1), 14-25.

Wright, D.W., Peterson, L.R., and Barners, H.L. (1990). The relation of parental employment and contextual variables with sexual permissiveness and gender role attitudes of rural early adolescents. *Journal of Early Adolescence, 10,* 382-398.

Wright, J.D., and Carr, R. (1995). *Effects of high school work experience a decade later: Evidence from the National Longitudinal Survey.* Washington, DC: Employment Policies Institute Foundation.

Yarrow, L.J., Rubenstein, J.C., and Pedersen, F.A. (1975). Review of infant and environment: Early cognitive and motivational development. *Psychological Record, 25,* 451-452.

Yoshikawa, H. (1995). Long-term effects of early childhood programs on social outcomes and delinquency. *The Future of Children: Long-Term Outcomes of Early Childhood Programs, 5*(3), 51-75.

Yoshikawa, H. (1999). Welfare dynamics, support services, mother's earnings, and child cognitive development: Implications for contemporary welfare reform. *Child Development, 70,* 779-801.

Yoshikawa, H., and Hsueh, J. (2001). Child development and public policy: Toward a dynamic systems perspective. *Child Development, 72*(6), 1887-1903.

Yoshikawa, H., Magnuson, K.A., Bos, J., and Hsueh, J. (in press). Effects of earnings supplement policies on adult economic and middle-childhood outcomes differ for the "hardest to employ." *Child Development.*

Yoshikawa, H., and Seidman, E. (2000). Competence among urban adolescents in poverty: Multiple forms, contexts, and developmental processes. In R. Montemayor, G.R. Adams, and T.P. Gullota (Eds.), *Advances in adolescent development, volume 10: Adolescent diversity in ethnic, economic, and cultural contexts* (pp. 9-42). Thousand Oaks, CA: Russell Sage.

Yoshikawa, H., and Seidman, E. (2001). Multi-dimensional profiles of welfare to work dynamics: Development, validation, and relationship to child cognitive and mental health outcomes. *American Journal of Community Psychology, 29,* 907-936.

Young, A. (2000). On the outside looking in: Low-income men's conception of work opportunities and the good job. In S. Danziger, and A. Lin (Eds.), *Coping with poverty: The social contexts of neighborhood, work, and family in the African American community* (pp. 141-171). Ann Arbor, MI: University of Michigan.

Youniss, J., and Yates, M. (1997). *Community service and social responsibility in youth.* Chicago: University of Chicago Press.

Zaslaw, M.J., Dion, M.R., Morrison, D.R., Weinfield, N., Ogawa, J., and Tabors, P. (1999). Protective factors in the development of preschool-age children of young mothers receiving welfare. In E.M. Hetherington (Ed.), *Coping with divorce, single parenting, and remarriage: A risk and resiliency perspective* (pp. 193-223). Mahwah, NJ: Erlbaum.

Zaslow, M.J., and Eldred, C.A. (1998). *Parenting behavior in a sample of young mothers in poverty: Results of the New Chance observational study.* New York: Manpower Demonstration Research Corporation.

Zaslow, M.J., and Emig, C. (1997). When low-income mothers go to work: Implications for children. *Future of Children: Welfare to Work, 7*(1), 110-115.

Zaslow, M., McGroder, S., Cave, G., and Mariner, C. (1999). Maternal employment and measures of children's health and development among families with some history of welfare receipt. In R. Hodson (Ed.), *Research in the sociology of work, volume 7* (pp. 233-259). Stamford, CT: JAI Press.

Zaslow, M., Moore, K., Morrison, D.R., and Coiro, M.J. (1995). The Family Support Act and children: Potential pathways of influence. *Children and Youth Services Review, 17,* 231-249.

Zaslow, M.J., Moore, K.A., Brooks, J.L., Tout, K., Redd, Z.A., and Emig, C.A. (2002). Experimental studies of welfare reform and children. *Future of Children: Children and Welfare Reform, 12*(1), 79-98.

Zaslow, M.J., Oldham, E., Moore, K.A., and Magenheim, E. (1998). Welfare families' use of early childhood care and education programs, and implications for their children's development. *Early Childhood Research Quarterly, 13*, 535-563.

Zaslow, M.J., Rabinovich, B.A., and Suwalsky, J.T.D. (1991). From maternal employment to child outcomes: Pre-existing group differences and moderating variables. In J.V. Lerner, and N.L. Galambos (Eds.), *Employed mothers and their children* (pp. 237-282). New York: Garland.

Zaslow, M.J., and Tout, K. (2002). Child care quality matters. *The American Prospect, 13*(7), 49.

Zedlewski, S.R. (2002). Family economic resources in the post-reform era. *The Future of Children: Children and Welfare Reform, 12*(1), 123-147.

Zigler, E., and Styfco, S. (1993). *Head Start and beyond: A national plan for extended early childhood intervention.* New Haven, CT: Yale University.

Zill N., Moore K., Smith E., Stief T., and Coiro M. (1995). The life circumstances and development of children in welfare families: A profile based on national survey data. In P.L. Chase-Lansdale, and J. Brooks-Gunn (Eds.), *Escape from poverty: What makes a difference for children?* (pp. 38-59). New York: Cambridge University Press.

Zill, N., Resnick, G., McKey, R.H., Clark, C., Connell, D., and Swartz, J. (1998). *Head Start program performance measures: Second progress report.* Washington, DC: Research, Demonstration and Evaluation Branch and Head Start Bureau, Administration.

Zukow-Goldring, P. (1995). Sibling caregiving. In M.H. Bornstein (Ed.), *Handbook of parenting, vol. 3: Status and social conditions of parenting* (pp. 177-208). Hillsdale, NJ: Erlbaum.

Biographical Sketches

Eugene Smolensky (*Chair*) is an economist and current professor of public policy at the University of California, Berkeley. Smolensky studies welfare policy and the impact of political, economic and demographic changes on the distribution of income among various social groups. He is a member of the National Academy of Public Administration and the National Academy of Social Insurance, and serves on the Board of Trustees of the Russell Sage Foundation. He is past editor of the *Journal of Human Resources* and has served as chair of the Department of Economics and director of the Institute for Research on Poverty at the University of Wisconsin-Madison. He served as dean of the Graduate School of Public Policy at Berkeley, from 1988 to 1997. He has been a member of three NAS committees, including the Committee on Child Development Research and Public Policy. His research interests and areas of expertise include public policy, income distribution, poverty policy, public finance, and welfare reform. He has a Ph.D. in economics from the University of Pennsylvania.

Suzanne Bianchi is professor of sociology and currently directs the Maryland Population Research Center at the University of Maryland. She was formerly Assistant Chief for Social and Demographic Statistics in the Population Division of the U.S. Census Bureau. She served as president of the Population Association of America in 2000. She currently serves on the National Institute of Child Health and Human Development's (NICHD) Population Research Subcommittee. She is a past chair of both the Family and the Population Sections, and currently a council member of the Children and Youth Section, of the American Sociological Association. Bianchi is a family demographer with research interests in maternal employment, children and parents' time use, and child poverty and inequality. She has a Ph.D. in sociology from the University of Michigan.

David Blau is professor of economics and fellow of the Carolina Population Center at the University of North Carolina at Chapel Hill. He is a labor and population economist with research interests in aging and child care. His aging research focuses on the dynamics of employment behavior of individuals and couples at older ages. His recent research examines links between saving and retirement decisions. He is the director of the Demography and Economics of Aging research program at the Carolina Population Center at UNC. His child care research has examined the impact of the cost of child care on women's labor force participation, mode of care, and fertility. More recently he has analyzed the determinants and consequences of the quality of child care, and the impact of child care subsidies on employment and welfare participation. His book, *The Child Care Problem: An Economic Analysis*, was recently published by the Russell Sage Foundation. He is a past co-editor of the *Journal of Human Resources*, a past deputy editor of *Demography*, and a past member of the NIH Social Sciences and Population Study Section. He has a Ph.D. in economics from the University of Wisconsin at Madison.

Amy Gawad (*Research Associate*) is a staff member with the Board on Children, Youth, and Families of the National Research Council/Institutes of Medicine. As well as working on this project, she oversees the Academy's W.T. Grant Youth Development Prize Committee. She recently served as research associate on the National Academy of Sciences report *Community Programs to Promote Youth Development*. Prior to her work on youth development at NAS, she had responsibility at the board for the dissemination of *From Neurons to Neighborhoods*, a report on the science of early childhood development, and for supporting members of the Forum on Adolescence. She has an M.P.H. from the George Washington University School of Public Health.

Jennifer Appleton Gootman (*Study Director*) is a staff member with the Board on Children, Youth, and Families of the National Research Council/ Institutes of Medicine. Most recently she served as study director and co-editor of a National Academy of Sciences report *Community Programs to Promote Youth Development*. Prior to her work at NAS, she served as a social science analyst for the Office of Planning and Evaluation in the U.S. Department of Health and Human Services. Her work has focused on child and family policy for low-income families, including welfare reform, child care, child health, youth development, and teen pregnancy prevention issues. She has directed a number of community youth programs in Los Angeles and New York City, involving young people in leadership development, job preparedness, and community service. She has an M.A. in public policy from the New School for Social Research.

Francine Jacobs is an associate professor with a joint appointment in the Departments of Child Development and Urban and Environmental Policy and Planning (UEP) at Tufts University, and is currently the chairperson of UEP. She has been a program evaluation consultant to numerous community-based child and family programs, and is currently co-directing a statewide home visiting program evaluation. She is an editorial board member for the journal *Applied Developmental Science*. She was the former director of the National Child Welfare Research Center, Center for the Study of Social Policy in Washington, D.C. Her research interests include child and family policy, including child welfare and child care policy, family development, family preservation and support programs, program evaluation, and public policy analysis. She has an Ed.D. from Harvard University.

Robin L. Jarrett is associate professor of family studies in the Department of Human and Community Development, University of Illinois at Urbana-Champaign. She has been a member of key groups that focus on neighborhood processes and family and child-youth development including the Social Science Research Council's Working Group on Communities and Neighborhoods, Family Processes and Individual Development; the MacArthur Foundation Task Force on Successful Pathways through Middle Childhood; The National Council on Family Relations Study Group on Financial Decision Making Processes; and the Family Research Consortium III. Jarrett also serves on several editorial boards including the *Journal of Research on Adolescence* and the *Encyclopedia of Community*. She uses ethnographic field methods (participant observation, intensive interviewing) to examine family coping strategies among inner-city families with children and adolescents. A particular focus is how demographic, social, and ecological aspects of neighborhoods influence specific parenting practices and child-youth developmental processes and trajectories. She has conducted research that examined how welfare reform affected family coping strategies among diverse ethnic families living in inner-city neighborhoods. Currently, she is collaborating on a project that examines how extracurricular and community-based youth activities promote adolescent development. Recent publications reflect her interests in families and neighborhoods. She has a Ph.D. in sociology from the University of Chicago.

Donna Klein is vice president of diversity and workplace effectiveness at Marriott International, Inc. In 1999 she assumed responsibility for Marriott's worldwide diversity strategy that included an increased focus on the development and retention of minority and women talent. She is co-chair of The Conference Board's Work Life Leadership Council, a member of The Conference Board's Diversity Council, Boston College's Solutions, and The Urban Institute. She is also a founder and current co-chair of The Employer Group, a partnership of employers engaged in identifying quality of life solutions for hourly workers. She has been the catalyst for many employer-based collaborative projects addressing the complex needs of low-income workers. She has a B.A. in psychology from the University of Akron.

Sanders Korenman is a professor of public affairs at the City University of New York at Baruch College and a research associate of the National Bureau of Economic Research. Since 1998, he has been a member of the Board on Children, Youth, and Families. In 1997-1998, he served as senior economist for labor, welfare, and education for President Clinton's Council of Economic Advisers. His expertise is in labor economics and demography. He has a Ph.D. in economics from Harvard University.

Joan Lombardi is a child and family policy specialist, serving as an advisor to a number of national organizations and foundation across the county on early care and education issues. She served as the deputy assistant secretary for external affairs in the Administration for Children and Families, U.S. Department of Health and Human Services. Prior to this appointment, she served as the first associate commissioner of the Child Care Bureau and as the staff director of the Secretary's Advisory Committee on Head Start Quality and Expansion. Her recent book, *Time to Care: Redesigning Child Care to Promote Education, Support Families and Build Communities,* was published by Temple University Press. She has a Ph.D. in human development education from the Institute for Child Study at the University of Maryland.

Meredith Madden (*senior project assistant, until June 2002*) was a staff member with the Board on Children, Youth, and Families of the National Research Council/Institutes of Medicine. As well as working on this project, she worked on activities related to motivation and engagement in secondary schools. Before joining the board she worked at the Home for Little Wanderers. She has an M.A. in public policy from the George Washington University.

Joseph L. Mahoney is assistant professor in the department of psychology at Yale University. His research interests focus on social adjustment during the school years, and he has written extensively on adolescent participation in after-school activities. At Yale, he directs the Social Policy and Intervention Laboratory and the Yale Study of Children's After-School Time. He is a faculty member of the Yale Bush Center for Social Policy and Child Development, a member of the National Board of Directors for the Horizons National summer enrichment program, and is affiliated with the Yale Child Study Center. He has a Ph.D. in developmental psychology from the Center for Developmental Science at the University of North Carolina at Chapel Hill.

Harriet Presser is distinguished university professor in the department of sociology at the University of Maryland at College Park. She was the founding director of the University's Center on Population, Gender, and Social Inequality from 1988-2001. Recently elected a fellow of the American Association for the Advancement of Science, she is past president of the Population Association of American and has been a council member-at-large of the American Sociological Association. She has held residential fellowships at the Center for Advanced Study in the Behavioral Sciences, the Netherlands Institute for Advanced Study in the Humanities and Social Science, the Russell Sage Foundation, and the Rockefeller Foundation's Bellagio Study and Conference Center. She has been a member of two NAS Committees: the Panel on Child Care Policy and the Committee on Youth Employment Programs. Her research expertise is in the area of social demography, focusing on the intersections of gender, work, and family, and she has a book forthcoming on the movement toward a 24-hour economy and its impact on families. Additionally, she studies population and family policy issues from a national and international perspective. She has a Ph.D. from the University of California at Berkeley.

Gary Sandefur is a professor of sociology at the University of Wisconsin-Madison. He began his career at the University of Oklahoma and has been on the faculty at the University of Wisconsin since 1984. Sandefur's work focuses on issues at the intersection of social demography and public policy, including work on families and racial and ethnic inequality. He is the co-author with Sara McLanahan of *Growing Up with a Single Parent: What Hurts? What Helps?*, published by Harvard University Press in 1994, and co-editor with Barney Cohen and Ronald Rindfuss of *Changing Numbers, Changing Needs: American Indian Demography and Public Health,* published by the National Academy Press in 1996. He is currently a funded PI in the National Institute for Child Health and Human Development's Family and Child Well-Being Research Network. He is also working on a project funded by Russell Sage to examine trends in family inequality over time and the implications of this for child well-being. He has a Ph.D. in sociology from Stanford University.

Elizabeth Townsend (*senior project assistant, from June* 2002) is a staff member with the Board on Children, Youth, and Families of the National Research Council/Institutes of Medicine. As well as working on this project, she is working on a report related to motivation and engagement among high school students. Before joining the National Academies, she worked as an instructor for public schools in Orange County, California, and Fairfax, Virginia. She has a B.S. in leisure studies management from the Radford University.

Deborah Vandell is a professor in the department of educational psychology at the University of Wisconsin at Madison. She holds joint appointments in the Department of Psychology and the School of Human Ecology. She is a member of the Maternal and Child Health review panel at the National Institute of Child Health and Human Development (NICHD). She has served as an Associate Editor for Child Development and on the editorial boards for *Contemporary Psychology, Developmental Psychology,* and the *Journal of Family Issues.* She is a principal investigator with the NICHD Study of Child Care and Youth Development, a multi-site collaborative study of the effects of child care, schools, and families on children's developmental outcomes through middle childhood. Her research interests include examining relations among children's peer, sibling, and parent relationships over time. She has a Ph.D. from Boston University.

Jane Waldfogel is professor of social work and public affairs at Columbia University School of Social Work. She is also a research associate at the Centre for Analysis of Social Exclusion at the London School of Economics. She has written extensively on the impact of public policies on child and family well-being. She is the author of *The Future of Child Protection: How to Break the Cycle of Abuse and Neglect* (Harvard University Press, 1998) and co-editor (with Sheldon Danziger) of *Securing the Future: Investing in Children from Birth to Adulthood* (Russell Sage Foundation, 2000). Her current research includes studies of family leave and parental care for children, child care policies, inequality in early childhood care and education, and child abuse and neglect. She has a Ph.D. in public policy from Harvard University.

Hirokazu Yoshikawa is assistant professor of psychology at New York University, in community psychology. He has conducted research on effects of early childhood care and education programs, public policies, and prevention programs on the development of children and adolescents in poverty in the United States. He is presently conducting research on effects of experimental welfare reform and anti-poverty policy demonstrations on children and families, as an investigator in the Next Generation, a consortium of researchers from the Manpower Demonstration Research Corporation (MDRC) and research universities. He is also carrying out research on the prevention of HIV infection among Asian/Pacific Islander immigrant communities in the United States. In 1999 he served on the U.S. Department of Health and Human Services Advisory Committee on Head Start Research and Evaluation, a panel appointed to help design the national impact evaluation of Head Start. In 2001 he was awarded the Louise Kidder Early Career Award of the Society for the Psychological Study of Social Issues, the American Psychological Association Minority Fellowship Early Career Award, and the William T. Grant Foundation Faculty Scholars Award. He has a Ph.D. in clinical psychology from New York University.

Martha Zaslow is a senior scholar at Child Trends in Washington, D.C. Her work focuses on the implications of welfare policies for families and children, the development of children in poverty, maternal employment, child care, and improving survey measures of parenting and of children's development. Her research interests and areas of expertise include implications of welfare policies for families and children, development of children in poverty, maternal employment, child care, and survey measures. She has a Ph.D. in developmental psychology from Harvard University.

Index

A

Academic achievement
  see also Educational attainment
  adolescents, 80, 180-181, 188, 189, 190,
    192-195, 197-198, 220, 224,
    225, 226, 266
  after-school programs, 128, 129-130
  aspirations, 68, 76, 180
  child care homes, 122
  early childhood education, 176
  family income, 68, 74
  maternal employment, 68, 88, 92, 127
  paternal involvement, 91
  self-care, 127, 266
  welfare reform, 215, 220, 224, 225, 226
Adolescents
  see also After-school programs
  academic achievement, 80, 180-181, 188,
    189, 190, 192-195, 197-198, 220,
    224, 225, 226, 266
  after-school programs, 7, 18, 128, 129-
    130, 131, 132, 187, 189-190,
    247, 272-273
  alcohol/substance abuse, 180, 192
  behavioral development, 80, 180, 181,
    184-185, 187, 188-189
  child care by, 81, 183-184
  child care for, 1, 4, 7, 263-264

cognitive development, 179
community-based care, 17, 187, 188
costs of care, family expenditures,
  189-190
defined, 178
delinquency, 80, 82, 117, 118, 180
depression, 181, 184
developmental factors, 16, 17, 65,
  79-82, 98, 178-181, 197
employment of adolescents, 81, 180,
  187, 190-198
family functioning, 16, 17, 65, 79-82,
  98, 178, 180, 185, 187, 195-197
funding of programs for, 131, 188, 246,
  273
gender factors, 191, 198, 225
health status, 17, 180, 181, 184, 192,
  193, 217
income, family, 195
maternal employment, 4, 79-82
mothers, adolescent, 219-220, 222, 223
National Longitudinal Survey of Youth
  (NLSY), 82, 83, 87, 122, 125,
  186, 190-191, 235, 237
outcome assessments, 79-82, 188-189,
  192-198, 263-264
parental employment, 65, 178-198
parenting of, 79-82, 98, 179, 181-198,
  266

peer influences, 129, 179, 183, 185, 190, 192
policy options, 7, 272-273
pregnancy, 181
quality of care, 187-188, 263-264
racial/ethnic factors, 191
research recommendations, 81-82, 277-278
self-care, 48, 49-50, 88, 126-128, 135, 181-186, 266
sexual activity, 179-180, 181
social development, 17, 178-179, 180, 185, 189, 190, 192-193, 266
structured voluntary activities, 132-133, 135, 187, 188
substance abuse, 180, 192
welfare reform, 79-82, 219-220, 222, 223-226
AFDC, see Aid to Families with Dependent Children
African Americans, see Black persons
The After-School Corporation programs, 130-131, 247
After-school programs, 2, 7, 18, 81, 125-126, 128-132, 135, 180, 186-190, 246-247, 263
academic achievement and, 128, 129-130
behavioral development, 129-130, 131, 187
cost factors, 189-190, 247, 273
disabled persons, 128
faith-based, 7, 273
language development, 129
maternal parenting, 76, 77
process quality measures, 106, 130
research recommendations, 11, 189-190
rural areas, 128, 246
structured voluntary activities, 132-133, 135, 187, 188
21st Century Community Learning Centers (CCLC), 7, 128-129, 131, 246, 273
Age factors
see also Adolescents; Developmental factors; Early childhood care/education; Infants; Preschool children; School-aged children
childbearing, 24
leave from work, policies, 230, 234
maternal employment, 26-27, 29-31

quality of child care, 56-63 (passim), 110, 113-114
school-age children, child care, 47-50, 125-133, 134-135
self-care, 126, 181, 182
Aid to Families with Dependent Children (AFDC), 199-200, 203, 220, 221, 261
see also Temporary Assistance for Needy Families
child care development block grant, 248, 265
marital status, impacts on, 216
research methodology, 201-202, 216, 220, 221
single mothers, employment, 204, 206
Alcohol abuse, 192
American Indians, 243, 245
American Public Health Association, 114-115
APECP, see Assessment Profile for Early Childhood Programs
Armed forces, see Military personnel, children of
Arnett Scale, 101
Asians, 243, 245
Assessment Profile for Early Childhood Programs (APECP), 147
Attachment Q-Set, 141
Attitudes and motivation
academic aspirations, 68, 76, 180
caregiver satisfaction, 141, 145
toward child care, 11
childrearing attitudes, 86-87, 92, 137
employment aspirations, 69, 76, 193
father's parenting role, 90
gender role attitudes, 68
maternal employment impacts, 68, 69, 76, 87, 221
toward self-care, 126, 127
welfare reform, 221
toward work, 69, 221

B

Before-school programs, 106, 125
Behavioral development, 115, 120-121, 163, 225
see also Social development
adolescent, 80, 180, 181, 184-185, 187, 188-189

caregiver characteristics, 106, 111, 112,
   113, 118
classroom, 76
delinquency, 80, 82, 117, 118, 180
family income, 74-75, 79, 86
father's role, 89-90
Head Start, 117
maternal depression, 92
mother/infant interaction, 86, 87
parental absence, 16, 38, 127
parental intervention programs, 5, 79,
   95
self-care, 126-127, 183, 184-185
sexual activity, 179-180, 181
substance abuse, 180, 192
time spent in care, 124
Big Brothers Big Sisters, 187, 188
Black persons
adolescent employment, 191
after-school programs, 129
child care arrangements, 43, 48
child care expenditures, 51, 53
Head Start, 243
infant development, 83
maternal psychological well-being, 92
parental discipline, 86-87
self-care, 126
single mothers, 86-87, 206, 215
Title I preschool program, 245
Block grants,
child care development, 247-252, 265,
   272
Social Services Block Grant, 253
vouchers, 7, 9, 248-249, 265, 268,
   271-272
welfare reform, 200, 250-254, 265, 272

C

CACFP, see Child and Adult Care Food
   Program
Canada, welfare reform, 214-215
Caregiver Interaction Scale (CIS), 107, 137
Caregivers, nonparental, 42-49 (passim),
   56-60 (passim), 101, 102, 180,
   260
see also Grandparents; Relatives, other
   than parents; Teachers
adolescent caregiver characteristics, 106,
   111, 112, 113, 118
adolescents, care by, 81, 183-184

after-school programs, 130
attitudes of, 141, 145
committee study at hand, methodology,
   2
developmental impacts, 108-110,
   114-115
education and training, 10, 57-59, 101,
   109, 110, 114, 133, 136-145,
   150-151, 256
group size (children), 56, 57, 58, 110,
   114, 121, 136-150 (passim),
   162-163, 166-167, 170-171
mentors, 187, 188
neighbors and friends, 42
process measures, 10, 101, 109-115
qualifications, 6-7, 59, 101, 114-115,
   136-145, 150-151, 256
quality of, general, 4, 10, 12, 17,
   108-110, 114-115, 130, 137-151
ratio of caregivers to children, 10, 56,
   57, 58, 109, 115, 117, 121, 130,
   136-150 (passim), 162-171, 256
supply of, 54-56
structural caregiver characteristics,
   general, 108-110, 114-115, 130,
   133
table of research findings, 136-149
wages, 110, 144-145, 164
Carolina Abecedarian Project, 117-118
CCDF, see Child Care Development Fund
CC-HOME Scale, 107, 121, 150-151
CCLC, see 21st Century Community
   Learning Centers
Census data
see also Current Population Survey
Study of Early Child Care vs, 100
Census of Services, 55
Center-based intervention programs,
   116-122
see also Early Head Start; Head Start
process quality measures, 105-149
   (passim)
Center for the Child Care Workforce, 55-56
Centers for Disease Control and Prevention,
   181
CF, see Children's Foundation
Charles Stewart Mott Foundation, 131
Chicago Parent-Child Centers, 117
Child and Adult Care Food Program
   (CACFP), 254

Child care, general, 1-2, 3-4, 6-7, 12-13,
    17-18, 42-64, 99-177
  see also Caregivers, nonparental; Child
    care centers; Child care homes;
    Community-based child care;
    Early childhood care/education;
    Family day care centers;
    Home-based care; Leave policies;
    Quality of care; Relatives, other
    than parents; Self-care
  adolescents, 1, 4, 7, 263-264
  arrangements, 47-50 (passim)
  block grants for development, 247-252,
    264-265, 272
  cognitive development, 1-2, 99, 102
  committee policy options, 267-273
  developmental outcomes, 99-177
  ecological systems theory, 102-103,
    183-184
  expenditures on child care by families,
    18, 42, 46, 50-54, 56, 63,
    189-190
  family leave from work, 235, 236,
    257-258, 275-276
  historical perspectives, 1-2, 11, 23-24,
    40, 42-64 (passim), 99, 103
  immigrants, 44, 45, 48, 129
  income and, 2, 5, 47, 48-50, 53, 63,
    100, 107
  international policy comparisons,
    258-259
  military personnel, children of, 256
  parental time spent, 23-24, 31, 32-36
  racial/ethnic factors, 43-45, 48
  regional factors, 44, 46, 48
  supply, 54-56
  tax credits, 238-239, 240
  vouchers, 7, 9, 248-249, 265, 268,
    271-272
Child care centers, 42, 44, 45-46, 48-49, 77
  see also Family day care centers
  after-school programs, 128
  caregiver/children ratios, 10, 56, 57, 58,
    109, 115, 117, 121, 130,
    136-150 (passim), 162-171, 256
  center-based intervention programs,
    116-122, 176-177
  developmental outcomes, 99, 102
  ecological systems theory, 102, 183-184
  employment, 54-56, 57-59
  group size, 56, 57, 58, 110, 114, 121,
    136-150 (passim)

  maternal employment, use of, 43-44, 77
  military personnel, children of, 256
  process quality measures, 105-135
    (passim)
  quality assessment, general, 56-63
    (passim), 99-102, 103-104, 106
  racial/ethnic factors, 43-45, 48, 125
  time spent in, 103-104
  welfare reforms, 223, 226
Child Care Development Block Grant, 248
Child Care Development Fund (CCDF),
    247-252
Child care homes, 42, 107, 121-122
  see also Family day care centers
  academic achievement and, 122
  quality of care, 107, 109-110, 121-122,
    138-139, 144-145, 175-176
  welfare reforms, 223
Child Care Staffing Study, see National
    Child Care Staffing Study
Child Outcomes Study, 74, 87
Children's Foundation (CF), 55
CIS, see Caregiver Interaction Scale
Cities, see Urban areas
Citizenship status, 44, 45, 48
Cognitive development, 16
  see also Academic achievement;
    Language development
  adolescents, 179
  caregiver characteristics, 108-109,
    114-115
  child care, general, 1-2, 99, 102
  early child care, 99, 100-101, 105,
    108-122 (passim)
  Early Head Start, 120
  family functioning and management, 76,
    78
  maternal employment, 1-2, 73, 76, 78,
    83, 87, 125, 217
  process quality measures, 106, 108-109,
    111-112, 113, 125
  self-care, 127
  tabulated research results, 150-151
  welfare reform, 216, 217, 219, 222, 279
Community-based child care, 6-7, 18
  adolescents, general, 17, 187, 188
  after-school programs, 7, 18, 128, 187
  self-care, 126, 127
Community Programs to Promote Youth
    Development, 17
Consumer Expenditure Survey, 191
Cortisol, 124

Cost and cost-benefit factors
adolescents, expenditures on care, 51
child care policy options, 7, 8-9, 63-64,
267-277
committee study methodology, 6
econometrics, 72, 110, 195, 209, 210,
216-217
family expenditures on child care, 18,
42, 46, 50-54, 56, 63, 189-190
family leave, employer/public costs,
274-275
health care, 15
welfare reform, family economics, 74,
75, 272
Cost, Quality, and Outcome Study (CQO),
59-61, 100-101, 112-113, 143
CPS, *see* Current Population Survey
CQO, *see* Cost, Quality, and Outcome
Study
Cultural factors
see also Attitudes and motivation;
International perspectives; Race/
ethnicity
child care, low-income families, 77
committee study methodology, 2, 13, 14
faith-based after-school programs, 7,
273
welfare-to-work, 69, 221, 224, 225
Current Population Survey (CPS)
adolescent employment, 191, 192
adolescent mothers, child abuse, 222
nonstandard work schedules, 36, 37, 39

D

David and Lucile Packard Foundation, 2
DCAP, *see* Dependent Care Assistance
Program
Definitional issues
adolescence, 178
low-income, 97
process quality, 105-106
research terms, 72
self-care, 126
shift work schedules, 37
Delinquency, 80, 82, 117, 118, 180
Demographic factors, *see* Educational
attainment; Income; Marital
status; Race/ethnicity; Regional
factors; Rural areas;
Socioeconomic status; State-level
factors; Urban areas

Department of Agriculture, 254
Department of Defense, 256
Department of Education
21st Century Community Learning
Centers (CCLC), 7, 128-129,
131, 246, 273
Department of Health and Human Services
Centers for Disease Control and
Prevention, 181
child care block grants, 249, 251
Study of Early Child Care, 61, 83, 84,
90, 100, 106-108, 112, 113,
123-125
U.S. Child Care Workforce and
Caregiving Population, 55-56
Department of Labor, 274
Dependent Care Assistance Program
(DCAP), 238
Depression
adolescents, 181, 184
children, 128, 133
maternal, 78-79, 84, 88, 91-93,
102-103, 113, 133, 214,
219-220, 224
paternal, 102-103
Developmental factors, 16, 99-177, 260,
263-264
see also Age factors; Attitudes and
motivation; Behavioral
development; Cognitive
development; Educational
attainment; Social development
adolescents, 16, 17, 65, 79-82, 98,
178-198, 264, 266
after-school programs, 128-132
caregiver characteristics and outcomes,
108-110, 114-115
child care centers, 99, 102
committee methodology, 2, 13
discipline, 76
early child care, 99-135 (passim), 263
ecological systems theory, 102, 183-184
family functioning, 65, 67, 68-70,
75-91, 100, 101, 108
income, family, 74-75, 131, 151-155,
159, 163, 165, 217, 279-280
infants, 82-84, 95-96, 113-114,
117-118, 120-124, 150-151
maternal employment, 1-2, 67-98, 125,
217, 231, 265
quality of care, 2, 4, 56, 61-62, 64, 65,
67, 99-102, 104, 105

self-care, 126-127, 183, 184-185
socioeconomic status, general, 74, 131,
    151-155, 159, 163, 165, 277
Study of Early Child Care, 61, 83, 84,
    90, 100, 106-108, 112, 113,
    123-125
tabular results, 136-171
welfare reform, 216-226
Diet, *see* Nutrition
Disabled persons
adolescent caregivers, 183-184
after-school programs, 128
child care supply, 56
Education of the Handicapped Act, 245
Head Start, 243-244
Individuals with Disabilities Act, 245
infants, public educational policies, 245
leave from work, temporary disabilities,
    2, 231, 262, 273-275
Pregnancy Disability Act, 231
special education, 118, 224
welfare reform, 25, 118, 224
Diseases, disorders, and illness
see also Disabled persons; Health
    insurance; Health status
children, leave policies, 15, 230
medical leave, 230, 231
psychological, *see* Depression
public education policy, 245
welfare reform, 217, 218, 225
Divorced persons, 23, 28, 29
child care arrangements, 44, 48
child care expenditures, 51
nonstandard work schedules, 39
Dropouts, 180-181, 188, 189, 192-193, 224
Drug abuse, *see* Substance abuse

E

Early Child Care Research Network, 61,
    106-107, 109, 114, 122, 256
Early childhood care/education, 2, 4, 6-9,
    11, 16-17, 25, 26, 56-60, 101,
    116-119
see also Caregivers, nonparental; Family
    day care centers; Preschool
    children; Teachers
academic achievement later, 176
childhood-to-adulthood studies,
    118-119, 176

cognitive development, 99, 100-101,
    105, 108-122 (passim)
Cost, Quality, and Outcome Study
    (CQO), 59-61, 100-101,
    112-113, 143
developmental impacts, 99-135 (passim),
    263
Early Head Start, 4, 6, 120, 121, 244,
    268-269, 270
Family and Relative Care Study, 101
family functioning, 101-103, 113
funding, 4, 6-7, 8-9, 247-252, 268-271
Head Start, 4, 6, 7, 8, 16, 55, 117, 118,
    119, 120, 223, 242-244,
    268-269, 270
multiplicity of arrangements, 104
National Child Care Staffing Study, 59,
    60, 101, 108, 110
National Day Care Study, 101
parental emotional impact, 102-103
parent-focused programs, 116, 117-118,
    119-121
placement considerations, 104-105
quality assessment, 2, 4, 6-7, 16-17, 57,
    58, 100-101, 105-125, 263, 264,
    267-272
self-care, 127
social development, 99, 105, 106, 109,
    111, 112-113, 114, 120, 121,
    122
standards, 6-7, 101, 256
Study of Early Child Care, 61, 83, 84,
    90, 100, 106-108, 112, 113,
    123-125
tabular research results, 136-161
Three-State Study, 101
time spent in, by age, 25, 26
Early Childhood Environmental Rating
    Scale (ECERS), 59, 60, 101, 106,
    109, 112, 119, 137-147,
    150-158, 162-167, 271, 272
Early Childhood Observation Instrument
    (ECOI), 141
Early Head Start, 4, 6, 120, 121, 244,
    268-269, 270
cost factors, 7, 8
Earned income tax credit (EITC), 12, 18,
    73, 199, 202, 203, 206, 207-208,
    212, 220, 239-240
ECERS, *see* Early Childhood Environment
    Rating Scale

ECOI, *see* Early Childhood Observation Instrument
Ecological systems theory, 102-103, 183-184
Econometrics, 72, 110, 195, 209, 210, 216-217
Economic factors
  see also Cost and cost-benefit factors; Funding; Income; Poverty; Socioeconomic status; Tax policies; Welfare; Welfare reform
  committee study methodology, 2
  husband's earnings, wife's employment, 29
  maternal employment, family economics, 73-78
  welfare-to-work, 209
    economic cycles, 204, 208, 210, 212
    incentives, 70, 77, 78, 97, 98, 203, 214-215
  wives as primary earners, 31-32, 40-41
Education and training, professional
  child care providers/teachers, 10, 57-59, 101, 109, 110, 114, 133, 136-145, 150-151, 162-164
  job training, adolescents, 187, 188, 191, 194
  teachers, 10, 57-59, 101, 114, 162-163
Education of the Handicapped Act, 245
Educational attainment
  see also Academic achievement
  adolescents, 80, 180-181, 188, 189, 190
  aspirations, 68, 76
  dropouts, 180-181, 188, 189, 192-193, 224
  hours of work, 29
  leave from work, eligibility, 233, 234, 235, 237
  maternal, 113
  parental, general, 116, 119-121, 137, 222
  welfare reform, 76, 119, 203
EITC, *see* Earned income tax credit
Elementary and Secondary Education Act, 245
Employment, general, 260, 280
  see also Household work; Income; International perspectives; Leave policies; Maternal employment; Part-time employment; Wages and salaries; Welfare reform
  adolescents, 81, 180, 187, 190-198

aspirations of children, 69, 76, 193
attitudes toward, general, 69, 221
caregiver satisfaction, 141, 145
child care centers, 54-56, 57-59
child care tax assistance, 238
committee findings, 261-266
educational attainment, adolescent, 191
educational attainment, maternal, 1, 29, 78, 95, 119, 120
hours of work, 15, 24, 29-31, 36-40, 44, 48, 49, 70, 83, 125
job training, adolescents, 187, 188, 191, 194
shift work, 36, 37, 45, 48, 49, 52, 182
single mothers, 1, 3, 4, 23, 26-28, 31, 40, 204-206, 210-212
temporary employment, 15
unemployment insurance as leave pay substitute, 273, 274
welfare-to-work reforms, *see* Welfare reform
work schedules, 15, 24, 36-40, 41, 45, 56
Europe, 257-259
  family leave from work, 235, 236, 275
Extended Services School Initiative, 129-130

F

Faith-based organizations, after-school programs, 7, 273
Family and Medical Leave Act (FMLA), 2, 3, 9, 12, 17, 231, 232-235, 237, 261, 262, 276-277
Family and Relative Care Study, 101
Family day care centers
  caregiver/children ratio, 56, 57, 58, 136-149 (passim)
  ecological systems theory, 102
  group sizes, 56, 57, 58, 114, 136-149 (passim)
  Head Start, 119
  licensing requirements, 54-55, 58, 101
  process quality, 101, 106, 107, 136-149 (passim)
  quality assessment, 56-63 (passim), 103, 121
  supply, 54-56
  use, demographics, 44, 45
Family Day Care Rating Scale (FDCRS), 101, 106, 137, 150

Family functioning and management, 18,
  65, 67, 68-98, 260
  see also Depression; Home-based care;
    Household work; Marital status
  adolescents, 16, 17, 65, 79-82, 98, 178,
    180, 185, 187, 195-197
  childrearing attitudes, 86-87, 92, 137
  cognitive stimulation, 76, 78
  control and discipline, 76, 78, 81,
    86-87, 92
  developmental outcomes, 65, 67, 68-70,
    75-91, 100, 101, 108
  early child care, 101-103, 113
  ecological systems theory, 102-103,
    183-184
  emotional support, 76, 77-78, 102-103
  gatekeeping, 76, 77
  maternal employment, 65, 67, 68-98
  adaptation to, 69, 93-94
  maternal psychological well-being, 70,
    71, 73, 75, 86, 87, 88, 91-93, 95,
    96, 102-103, 113, 133, 214, 218,
    219-220, 224
  modeling, 76
  National Day Care Study, 101
  nonstandard work schedules, 36-40, 41,
    70, 88-89, 97-98
  routines and traditions, 76
  self-care, 126, 127, 181-185
  Study of Early Child Care, 100
  welfare reforms, 69, 70, 71, 74-82
    (passim), 92-93, 95, 96-98,
    217-219, 220, 221-222
  child abuse/domestic violence,
    222-223
  wives as primary earners, 31-32, 40-41
Family leave, *see* Leave policies
Family members, other than parents, *see*
    Relatives, other than parents
Family size, 73, 219, 250
Family structure
  see also Fathers; Grandparents; Marital
    status; Maternal employment;
    Relatives, other than parents;
    Single mothers
  after-school programs, 129-130
  child care expenditures, 51-52
  outcome measures, 108, 162-171,
    174-175
  self-care, 126, 127
  welfare reform, 217, 218-219, 221-222

Family Support Act, 199, 220
Fathers
  attitudes toward parenting, 90
  behavioral development, 89-90
  child care, 70, 89-91
  educational, 90
  quality assessment, 62, 90, 120,
    172-173
  time spent, 32, 34-36, 40, 41, 46
  depression, 102-103
  employment, 29, 41, 46, 89
  household work, time spent, 33, 40
  single, 89
  wives as primary earners, 31-32, 40-41
FDCRS, *see* Family Day Care Rating Scale
Federal government, 6
  see also Legislation; Policy issues; State
    government; *specific departments
    and agencies*
  devolution of responsibilities to states, 6,
    11-12, 200, 202-203
Fertility, 24
  family size, 73, 219, 222, 250
  welfare reform, 200, 215-216, 219, 222
FMLA, *see* Family and Medical Leave Act
Food and nutrition, *see* Nutrition
Food stamps, 45, 49, 75, 220
Ford Foundation, 2
Foreign countries, *see* Immigrants;
    International perspectives
Foundation for Child Development, 2
From Neurons to Neighborhoods, 17
Funding, 6, 259, 264
  see also Block grants; Cost and
    cost-benefit factors; Welfare
  adolescent programs, 131, 188, 246,
    273
  after-school programs, 131, 246-247,
    273
  Child Care Development Fund, 247-252,
    264
  committee study methodology, 2, 6
  early childhood education, 4, 6-7, 8-9,
    247-252, 268-271
  Military Child Care Act, 256
  public education, 241
  state prekindergarten programs, 119,
    269, 270-271
  Summer Food Service Program, 254
  21st Century Community Learning
    Centers (CCLC), 131, 246, 273

U.S. Child Care Workforce and Caregiving Population, 55-56
vouchers, 7, 9, 248-249, 265, 268, 271-272

G

Gender factors
see also Fathers; Fertility; Marital status; Maternal employment; Single mothers
adolescent academic achievement, 225
adolescent employment, 191, 198
after-school programs, 76, 130
attitudes toward gender roles, 68
corporate work place policies, access to, 230
household work time, 23-24, 32, 33, 38, 39, 40
leave from work, policies, 230, 234
maternal psychological well-being, 70, 71, 73, 75, 86, 87, 88, 91-93, 95, 96
maternity leave, 9, 83-84, 231-233, 235-237, 274, 276
parental child care, 32-36
parenting, 76-93
paternity leave, 231, 232, 233, 236
General Accounting Office, 128-129
Government, *see* Federal government; Legislation; Policy issues; Regulations; State government; Tax policies; Welfare; Welfare reform
Grandparents, 44, 47, 48-49, 62, 121, 122, 144-145, 173-174
ecological systems theory, 102

H

Handicapped persons, *see* Disabled persons
Head Start, 4, 6, 16, 117, 118, 119, 120, 242-244, 268-269, 270
see also Early Head Start
cost factors, 7, 8
supply, 55
welfare reforms, 223
Health insurance, 230
disability, wage coverage, 2, 231, 262, 273-275
low-wage/part-time employment, 15

Medicaid, 15, 75, 208
Health status
see also Disabled persons; Diseases, disorders, and illness; Fertility; Nutrition
adolescents, 17, 180, 181, 184, 192, 193, 217
child safety, 15-16, 38, 73, 248-249, 252, 266
costs of health care, 15
nonstandard work schedules, 37-38, 40
psychological, *see* Depression
Title I preschool program, 245
welfare reform, 224-225
Hispanics
adolescent employment, 191
after-school programs, 129
child care arrangements, 43, 44, 48
child care expenditures, 51, 53
dropouts, 180-181
Head Start, 243
infant development, 83
self-care, 126, 182
single mothers, 206
Title I preschool program, 245
Historical perspectives, 1-2, 3, 16, 23
after-school programs, 128
child care, general, 1-2, 11, 23-24, 40, 42-64 (passim), 99, 103
childbearing age, 24
family expenditures, 50
leave from work, 229-240
maternal employment, 1, 3, 11, 14, 23, 24-32, 34-35, 40, 99, 204-206
nonstandard work schedules, 36
parental, 32-36
public policy, 5, 6, 11-12, 16-17, 266
education, 241-247
single parents, 1, 3, 4, 14, 23, 26-29, 31, 40-41, 204-206
welfare reform, 2, 12, 199-201, 202, 204-207, 209-226 (passim)
Home-based care, 23, 31, 42, 62, 77
see also Child care homes; Family day care centers; Family functioning and management; Grandparents; Relatives, other than parents; Self-care
grandparents, 44, 47, 48-49, 62, 102, 121, 122, 144-145, 173-174
parental time spent, 23-24, 31, 32-36

process quality, 142-145, 148-149
Hours of work, 15, 24, 29-31, 36-40, 44,
    48, 49, 70, 83, 125
    see also Part-time work; Time factors
    adolescent employment, 81, 192-193,
        197-198
    fathers, 90
    infant development, 83
    welfare beneficiaries, work
        requirements, 200, 203, 210,
        214-215
    welfare leavers, 206-207, 211
Household work
    adolescents, 81, 193
    maternal time spent, 23-24, 32, 33, 38,
        39
    paternal time spent, 33, 40

I

Illness, *see* Diseases, disorders, and illness
Immigrants
    see also Hispanics
    adolescent employment, 192, 193
    after-school programs, 129
    child care arrangements, 44, 45, 48
    welfare reforms, 200
Income, family, 5
    see also Poverty; Socioeconomic status;
        Wages and salaries; Welfare;
        Welfare reform
    academic achievement, 68, 74
    adolescents, 195
    behavioral development, 74-75, 79, 86
    child care expenditures, 52, 53, 63
    child care quality, 100, 107
    developmental outcomes, 74-75, 131,
        151-155, 159, 163, 165, 217,
        279-280
    earned income tax credit (EITC), 12, 18,
        73, 199, 202, 203, 206, 207-208,
        212, 220, 239-240
    husband's earnings, wife's employment,
        29
    leave from work, 7, 17, 230, 234, 273-
        276
    maternal employment, 1, 4, 5, 29,
        48-50, 52, 53, 265
    school-age children, child care, 47,
        48-50, 52
    self-care, 126, 127, 182

structured voluntary activities, 132-133
Study of Early Child Care, 100
welfare reform impacts, 203, 206-208,
    211, 212-215, 220, 221
wives as primary earners, 31-32, 40-41
Individuals with Disabilities Act, 245
Infant Health and Development Program,
    120
Infant Toddler Environmental Rating Scale
    (ITERS), 59, 60, 61, 101, 106,
    137-139, 143-147, 150-151, 154-
    157, 162-165
Infants, 105
    see also Early Head Start
    birth weight, 120
    caregiver characteristics, 113-114,
        150-151
    developmental outcomes, 82-84, 95-96,
        113-114, 117-118, 120-124, 150-
        151
    disabled, public educational policies, 245
    father's parenting role, 90
    grandparental care, 122
    maternal employment, 24-25, 82-84,
        122, 231, 261
    parental leave, 6, 7, 9, 13, 18, 229-237,
        261-262, 265-266, 279
    quality of care, 57-61 (passim), 113-114,
        117-118, 120-121, 123-124
    single mothers, 205
    welfare reforms, 83, 205
In-home care, *see* Home-based care
Inner-city environments, *see* Urban areas
Insurance, *see* Health insurance
International perspectives
    Canadian welfare reform, 214-215
    Europe, 235, 236, 257-259, 275-276
    family leave from work, 235, 236,
        257-258, 275-276
    immigrants, child care arrangement, 44,
        45, 48
ITERS, *see* Infant Toddler Environmental
    Rating Scale

J

Job training
    adolescents, 187, 188, 191, 194
    welfare reform, 74, 78, 95, 116, 119-
        121, 220, 248
JOBS programs, 74, 78, 95, 248

L

Language development, 106
   after-school programs, second-language
      speakers, 129
   Carolina Abecedarian Project, 117
   center-based care, 120, 122
   Early Head Start, 120
   process quality, 111-115 (passim),
      150-151, 163
Latchkey care, see Self-care
Leave policies
   age factors, 230, 234
   disabilities, 2, 231, 262, 273-275
   Family and Medical Leave Act (FMLA),
      2, 3, 9, 12, 17, 231, 232-235,
      237, 261, 262, 276-277
   income level and, 7, 17, 230, 234,
      273-276
   medical leave, 230, 231, 237
   parental leave, 6, 7, 9, 13, 18, 229-237,
      261-262, 265-266, 279
   part-time employment, 231, 232, 233
   time factors, 2, 9, 83-84, 230, 235-237,
      276
   wages and salaries, 230, 232, 233,
      235-237, 265-266
Legislation
   see also Policy issues; Regulations
   after-school programs, 247
   Education of the Handicapped Act, 245
   Elementary and Secondary Education
      Act, 245
   Family and Medical Leave Act (FMLA),
      2, 3, 9, 12, 17, 231, 232-235,
      237, 261, 262, 276-277
   Family Support Act, 199, 220
   Individuals with Disabilities Act, 245
   Military Child Care Act, 256
   Omnibus Budget Reconciliation Acts,
      240
   Personal Responsibility and Work
      Opportunities Act (PRWOA,
      1996 Act), 2, 12, 64, 199, 200,
      203, 216-217
   Pregnancy Disability Act, 231
   wages, 14
   Younger Americans Act, 188
Longitudinal studies
   child care, general, 103, 104
   childhood-to-adulthood studies, 118-119
   Cost, Quality, and Outcome Study
      (CQO), 59-61, 100-101,
         112-113, 143
   National Education Longitudinal Survey
      (NELS), 187(n.3)
   National Longitudinal Survey of Youth
      (NLSY), 82, 83, 87, 122, 125,
         186, 190-191, 235, 237
   quality of care, general, 61, 64
   self-care, 183
   Study of Early Child Care, 61, 83, 84,
         90, 100, 106-108, 112, 113,
         123-125
Low-income families, see Poverty; Welfare;
      Welfare reform

M

Marital status
   see also Single mothers
   child care expenditures, 51, 53
   child care use, 44, 47, 48
   corporate work place policies, access to,
      230
   divorced persons, 23, 28, 29, 39, 44, 48,
      51
   leave from work, policies, 234
   never married mothers, 28, 29, 44, 48,
      51, 204, 234
   nonstandard work schedules, marital
      quality, 38, 39, 41
   parental child care, 32-36
   welfare reform, 200, 205, 212, 215-216,
      218-219
   widowed persons, 28, 29, 235
Maternal employment, 1, 2, 5, 18, 99
   academic achievement of children, 68,
      88, 92, 127
   adolescents, 4, 79-82
   age factors, 26-27, 29-31
   attitudes and motivation, 68, 69, 76, 87,
      221
   child care, time spent, 32, 34-35
   child care arrangements, 43-45, 48
   child care center use, 43-44, 77
   child care expenditures, 50-54, 63
   child development, 65, 67, 68, 74, 99
   children's age, 1, 24-27, 29-30, 31,
      42-53 (passim), 67, 68, 88, 204,
      205, 212
   cognitive development, 1-2, 73, 76, 78,
      83, 87, 125, 217

committee findings, 261
developmental impacts, 1-2, 67-98, 125,
    217, 231, 265
earned income tax credit, 12, 18, 73,
    199
economic factors, family, 73-78
    child outcomes, 73-78
educational attainment, 1, 29, 78, 95,
    119, 120
expenditures on child care, 18, 42, 46,
    50-54, 56, 63
family functioning, general, 65, 67,
    68-98
historical perspectives, 1, 3, 11, 14, 23,
    24-32, 34-35, 40, 99, 204-206
hours of work, 29-31, 70, 83, 88
household work, 32, 33, 38, 39
income, family, 1, 4, 5, 29, 48-50, 52,
    53, 265
infants, 24-25, 82-84, 122, 231, 261
labor force participation, 1, 3, 11, 23,
    25, 28, 42, 204, 205, 211-212,
    216, 261
part-time, 40-41, 96
poverty, general, 84-86, 199
preschool children, 42-46, 67, 205, 231
psychological well-being of mother, 70,
    71, 73, 75, 86, 87, 88, 91-93, 95,
    96
race/ethnicity, 1, 43-45, 48, 51, 83
school-aged children, child care, 47-50
social development, 1-2, 68, 73, 231,
    265
welfare reforms, 14, 38, 64, 65, 69, 199,
    200, 203
welfare-to-work reimbursements/
    incentives, 77, 78, 97, 98, 203,
    214
Medicaid, 15, 75, 208
Men, *see* Fathers; Gender factors
Mentors, 187, 188
MFIP, *see* Minnesota Family Investment
    Program
Military Child Care Act, 256
Military personnel, children of, 256
Minnesota Family Investment Program
    (MFIP), 214, 218, 221, 222
Minority groups, *see* Race/ethnicity; *specific*
    groups

N

NAEYC, *see* National Association for the
    Education of Young Children
National Association for the Education of
    Young Children (NAEYC), 271
National Child Care Staffing Study, 59, 60,
    101, 108, 110
National Child Care Survey (NCCS), 54-55,
    104, 132
National Day Care Study, 101
National Education Longitudinal Survey
    (NELS), 187(n.3)
National Evaluation of Welfare-to-Work
    Strategies, 74, 87, 222-223
National Head Start Impact Study, 6
National Household Education Survey, 104
National Institute of Child Health and
    Human Development (NICHD)
    Early Child Care Research Network, 61,
        106-107, 109, 114, 122, 256
    Observational Record of the Caregiving
        Environment, 61, 106-107,
        108-109, 112, 113-114, 145,
        150-151
    Study of Early Child Care, 61, 83, 84,
        90, 100, 106-108, 112, 113,
        123-125
National Longitudinal Survey of Youth
    (NLSY), 82, 83, 87, 122, 125,
    186, 190-191, 235, 237
National Survey of America's Families
    (NSAF), 187
Native Americans, *see* American Indians
NCCS, *see* National Child Care Survey
NELS, *see* National Education Longitudinal
    Survey
NICHD, *see* National Institute of Child
    Health and Human Development
NLSY, *see* National Longitudinal Survey of
    Youth
NSAF, *see* National Survey of America's
    Families
Nutrition
    Child and Adult Care Food Program,
        254
    food stamps, 45, 49, 75, 220
    Head Start, 254
    Summer Food Service Program, 254-255
    Title I preschool program, 245

O

Observational Record of the Caregiving Environment (ORCE), 61, 106-107, 108-109, 112, 113-114, 145, 150-151
Omnibus Budget Reconciliation Acts, 240
ORCE, *see* Observational Record of the Caregiving Environment
Outcome assessments, 56, 64, 65, 265
  see also Developmental factors
  adolescents, 79-82, 188-189, 192-198, 263-264
  early child care, 99, 102, 263-264
  Head Start, 244
  process quality, 111-114
  welfare reform, 201-226
The Overworked American, 31

P

Parental employment, 65, 178-198
Parental leave, 6, 7, 9, 13, 18, 229-237, 261-262, 265-266, 279
  to arrange child care, 211
  costs to employer/public, 274-275
  maternity leave, 9, 83-84, 95-96, 231-233, 274, 275-276
  parental leave accounts, 275
  paternity leave, 231, 232, 233, 236
  public policy, general, 6, 13, 18, 229, 273-277
Parent-focused programs, 116, 117-118, 119-121
Parenting behavior, *see* Family functioning and management
Part-time employment, 14-15
  child care arrangements, 44, 45-46, 48, 49
  child care expenditures, 52, 53-54
  health insurance, 15
  leave policies, 231, 232, 233
  maternal, 40-41, 94, 96
  temporary employment, 15
  welfare beneficiaries or leavers, 206-207, 214
PCS, *see* Profile of Child Care Settings
Peer influences
  adolescents, 129, 179, 183, 185, 190, 192
  after-school programs, 129
  care by peers, 126, 183
  social skills, 92, 102, 111, 112, 122, 124, 129, 190
  time spent with, 128
Personal Responsibility and Work Opportunities Act (PRWOA), 2, 12, 199, 200, 203, 216-217
  see also Temporary Assistance for Needy Families
Child Care Development Fund (CCDF), 247-252
Policy issues, general, 3, 5-12, 63, 227-259, 272-273
  see also Federal government; International perspectives; Legislation; Regulations; Standards; State government; Tax policies; Welfare reform
  access to corporate work place policies, table, 230
  committee methodology, 2, 3, 12-13
  committee recommendations, 7, 8-9, 266-277
  costs, 7, 8-9, 63-64, 267-277
Poverty, 10, 14-16
  see also Welfare; Welfare reform
  adolescent employment, 191
  after-school programs, 129, 131, 190, 263
  child care expenditures, 52, 53, 63
  child development, 68, 70, 83, 84-85, 217
  committee study methodology, 2, 14
  early child care/education, 2, 16-17, 102, 104, 107, 263
  earned income tax credit (EITC), 12, 18, 73, 199, 202, 203, 206, 207-208, 212, 220, 239-240
  family adaptation, 69
  infant development, 83
  international policy comparisons, 257-259
  kindergarten/prekindergarten, 241-242, 269, 270-271
  maternal employment, 84-86, 199
  nonstandard work schedules, 38
  parental leave, 7, 17, 230, 234, 273-276
  physical labor, 15
  private sector employee policies, 3
  quality of care, 2, 4, 101, 102, 104, 107, 129, 131, 172-177

self-care, 127, 182
single mothers, 14, 199, 206, 207
unskilled work, 14-15, 38
Pregnancy
    adolescents, 181
    employment during, 24-25, 40
    Head Start, 244
    maternity leave, 83-84
    mothers, 219-220, 222
    Pregnancy Disability Act, 231
    sexual activity, 179-180, 181
Pregnancy Disability Act, 231
Preschool children
    see also Child care centers; Early
        childhood care/education; Family
        day care centers; Infants
    adolescents, child care provided by, 81
    arrangements for care, 42-47, 54-56, 57,
        58
        impacts, 105, 110, 113-114
    corporate work place policies, access to,
        230
    Cost, Quality, and Outcome Study
        (CQO), 59-61, 100-101
    disabled children, public education
        policy, 245
    expenditures for care, 50, 51, 56
    international policy comparisons,
        258-259
    maternal employment, 42-46, 67, 205,
        231
    National Child Care Staffing Study, 59,
        60, 101, 108, 110
    providers of care, 54-56, 57-63, 101
    public policy, 241-245
    quality of care, 57-63, 101, 108-125
    supply of care, general, 54-56
    welfare reform, 219, 223, 245
Private sector, 3
    see also Leave policies
Process quality, 56, 57, 105-115, 256
    after-school programs, 106, 130
    before-school programs, 106
    caregivers, nonparental, 10, 101,
        109-115
    child-case centers, 105-135 (passim)
    cognitive development, 106, 108-109,
        111-112, 113, 125
    defined, 105-106
    developmental factors, general, 70-71,
        106-115, 136-177

family day care centers, 101, 106, 107,
    136-149 (passim)
home-based care, 142-145, 148-149
Infant Toddler Environmental Rating
    Scale (ITERS), 59, 60, 61, 101,
    106
language development, 111-115
    (passim), 150-151, 163
measures, 70-71, 106-115, 136-177
outcome assessments and, 111-114
School-Aged Environment Rating Scale,
    106
socioeconomic status, 176-177
statistical analyses, 136-149
structural caregiver characteristics,
    general, 108-110, 114-115, 130,
    133
table of research findings, 136-149
time factors, 25, 26, 32-36, 99, 103,
    120-121, 123-125
Professional education, see Education and
    training, professional
Profile of Child Care Settings (PCS), 54, 57,
    277
PRWOA, see Personal Responsibility and
    Work Opportunities Act
Psychometrics, 105, 107, 111, 133
    defined, 72

Q

Quality of care, 2, 4, 5, 6-7, 56-63,
    100-177, 263
    see also Outcome assessments; Process
        quality; Regulations; Standards
    adolescents, 187-188, 263-264
    after-school programs, 7, 130-132,
        272-273
    age factors, 56-63 (passim), 110,
        113-114
    caregivers, nonparental
        client group size (children), 56, 57,
            58, 110, 114, 121, 136-150
            (passim), 162-163, 166-167,
            170-171
        general, 4, 10, 12, 17, 108-110,
            114-115, 130, 137-151
        ratio of caregivers to children, 10, 56,
            57, 58, 109, 115, 117, 121, 130,
            136-150 (passim), 162-171, 256

child care centers, 56-63 (passim),
99-102, 103-104, 106
child care homes, 107, 109-110,
121-122, 138-139, 144-145,
175-176
Cost, Quality, and Outcome Study
(CQO), 59-61, 100-101
developmental outcomes, 2, 4, 56,
61-62, 64, 65, 67, 99-102, 104,
105
early child care, 2, 4, 6-7, 16-17, 57, 58,
100-101, 105-125, 263, 264,
267-272
family day care centers, 56-63 (passim),
103, 121
Head Start, 118, 119
home-based care, 142-145, 148-149
preschool children, 57-63, 101, 108-125
public policy, general, 6, 16-17,
266-267, 272-273
research recommendations, 10, 277-278
school-aged children, 125-133, 134-135
socioeconomic status, 1, 4, 6-7, 14, 74,
131, 151-155, 159, 163, 165,
263
state prekindergarten programs, 119,
269, 270-271
Study of Early Child Care, 61, 83, 84,
90, 100, 106-108, 112, 113,
123-125
tabular research results, 150-171
Three-State Study, 101
vouchers, 7, 9, 248-249, 265, 268,
271-272
welfare reforms, 223
Quantum Opportunities Program, 187-188

R

Race/ethnicity
see also Black persons; Cultural factors;
Hispanics; Immigrants
adolescent employment, 191
after-school programs, 129
American Indians, 243, 245
Asians, 243, 245
child care center arrangements, 43-45,
48, 125
child care expenditures, 51, 53
child development, 125, 223

dropouts, 180-181
Head Start, 243
immigrants, 44, 45, 48
leave from work, policies, 234
maternal employment, 1, 43-45, 48, 51,
83
National Day Care Study, 101
self-care, 126, 182
structured voluntary activities, 132
Study of Early Child Care, 100, 113
Title I preschool program, 245
Regional factors
see also Rural areas; State-level factors;
Urban areas
child care arrangements, 44, 46, 48
Regulations
see also Standards
child care, 255-256
day care center providers, licensing,
54-55, 58, 101
military personnel, child care, 256
Relatives, other than parents, 1, 42-49
(passim), 101, 102, 105, 180
see also Self-care
adolescent caregivers, 81, 183-184
child care, general, 1, 42, 43, 121,
144-145
ecological systems theory, 102, 183-184
Religious influences, see Faith-based
organizations
Research recommendations, 10, 277-280
adolescent development, 81-82, 277-278
after-school programs, 11, 189-190
child care arrangements, 104, 277-278
time factors in child care, 124-125
National Head Start Impact Study, 6
quality assessment, 64, 104, 124,
277-278
relatives, nonparental, 122
terminology, 72
welfare reform, 201-202, 279-280
Rural areas
adolescents as caregivers, 183
after-school programs, 128, 246
self-care, 126

S

Safety considerations, 15-16, 38, 73,
248-249, 252, 266

School-aged children, 125-133, 134-135,
220, 225
see also Adolescents; After-school
programs; Self-care; Structured
voluntary activities
before-school programs, 106
child care, general, 47-50, 125-133,
134-135
family income and child care, 47, 48-50,
52
maternal employment, 47-50
public policy, 241-247
School-Aged Environment Rating Scale, 106
Self-care, 48, 49-50, 88, 126-128, 135,
181-186, 266
academic achievement, 127, 266
age factors, 126, 181, 182
attitudes toward, 126, 127
behavioral development, 126-127, 183,
184-185
cognitive development, 127
defined, 126
income, family, 126, 127, 182
social development, 127, 185, 266
Self Sufficiency Project (SSP), Canada,
214-215
Sexual activity, 179-180, 181
see also Pregnancy
SFPS, see Summer Food Service Program
Single mothers, 1, 3, 4, 14, 23, 26-29, 261
see also Aid to Families with Dependent
Children; Divorced persons;
Widowed persons
black persons, 86-87, 206, 215
child care expenditures, 51, 53
child care use, 44, 47
cohabiting partners, 28, 36
employment, general, 1, 3, 4, 23, 26-28,
31, 40, 204-206, 210-212
family economic well-being, 75
Hispanic, 206
historical perspectives, 1, 3, 4, 14, 23,
26-29, 31, 40-41, 204-206
maternal psychological well-being, 92
never married, 28, 29, 44, 48, 51, 204
poverty, 14, 199, 206, 207
welfare reform, 75, 199-200, 204-206,
210-212, 213, 215-216, 219
SIPP, see Survey of Income and Program
Participation
Small businesses, leave policies, 231, 232

Socioeconomic status, 277
see also Educational attainment;
Employment; Income; Poverty;
Race/ethnicity; Socioeconomic
status
after-school programs, 131, 189-190
age factors, 151-155, 159, 163, 165,
172-177
child care arrangements, 44, 46, 48
developmental outcomes, 74, 131,
151-155, 159, 163, 165, 277
maternal employment, developmental
outcomes, 85, 86-89
quality of child care, 1, 4, 6-7, 14, 74,
131, 151-155, 159, 163, 165,
263
Social development, 16
see also Attitudes and motivation;
Behavioral development;
Educational attainment; Language
development; Peer influences
academic aspirations, 68
adolescents, 17, 178-179, 180, 185, 189,
190, 192-194, 266
after-school programs, 129
caregiver characteristics, 109, 114-115
child care, 1-2, 99, 102
delinquency, 80, 82, 117, 118, 180
early child care, 99, 105, 106, 109, 111,
112-113, 114, 120, 121, 122
Early Head Start, 120
gender role attitudes, 68
maternal employment, 1-2, 68, 73, 231,
235
self-care, 127, 185, 266
structured voluntary activities, 132-133
welfare reform, 216, 279-280
Social Services Block Grant (SSBG), 253
Special education, 118, 224
Sports and athletics, 47, 125, 132, 133,
135, 186, 187
SSBG, see Social Services Block Grant
SSP, see Self Sufficiency Project
Standards
see also Regulations
American Public Health Association,
114-115
caregiver/teacher qualifications, 6-7, 59,
101, 114-115, 136-145, 150-151,
256
early childhood care, 6-7, 101, 256

State government, 6
    after-school programs, 247
    child care development, 247-252, 255
    employer family leave policies, 262, 275,
        279
    federal devolution of responsibilities to
        states, 6, 11-12, 200, 202-203
    Head Start, 242-243
    Medicaid, 15
    prekindergarten programs, 119, 242,
        269, 270-271
    public education policy, 241-247
    regulations, child care, 54-55, 58, 101,
        255-256
    Social Services Block Grant, 253
    21st Century Community Learning
        Centers (CCLC), 7, 128-129,
        131, 246, 273
    vouchers, child care, 7, 9, 248-249, 265,
        268, 271-272
    welfare reform, 200, 202-203, 208-209
        evaluation research methodology, 202
        family caps, 219, 222
State-level factors
    Cost, Quality, and Outcome Study
        (CQO), 59-61, 100-101,
        112-113, 143
    Family and Relative Care Study, 101
    Three-State Study, 101, 110
Statistical analyses
    econometrics, 72, 110, 195, 209, 210,
        216-217
    maternal employment and child
        outcomes, 71
    maternal leave and depression, 84, 93
    structural caregiver characteristics and
        process quality, 136-149
    unobserved factors, bias, 104
    welfare reform, 201-202, 207, 208-209,
        210-213, 216-217
Structured voluntary activities, 132-133,
    135, 187, 188
    sports and athletics, 47, 125, 132, 133,
        135, 186, 187
Study of Early Child Care, 61, 83, 84, 90,
    100, 106-108, 112, 113, 123-125
Substance abuse, 180, 192
Suicide, adolescents, 181
Summer Food Service Program (SFPS),
    254-255
Survey of Income and Program Participation
    (SIPP), 42-54, 181-182

T

TANF, *see* Temporary Assistance for Needy
    Families
Tax policies, 12, 18, 73
    child tax credits, 238-239, 240
    earned income tax credit (EITC), 12, 18,
        73, 199, 202, 203, 206, 207-208,
        212, 220, 239-240
    family leave wages, temporary disability
        insurance (TDI) taxes, 231, 262,
        273-275
Teachers
    early childhood, quality of, 10, 56-60
        (passim), 101, 107, 110, 112-113
    educational attainment, 10, 57-59, 101,
        114, 162-163
    qualifications, standards, 6-7, 101
    wages, 110
Teen Outreach Program, 187, 188
Teenage Parent Demonstration, 222
Temporary Assistance for Needy Families
    (TANF), 12, 14, 79, 199-226,
        250-254, 261, 264, 276
    see also Welfare reform
    key provisions, 200
Temporary employment, 15
Three-State Study, 101, 110
Time factors
    see also Leave policies; Longitudinal
        studies
    adolescent crime, time of day, 180
    adolescents, 81, 126-128 (passim), 181-
        182, 192-193, 197-198
    after-school programs, 7, 125-126, 128,
        129-130, 272-273
    child care, general, 99, 103, 134, 262,
        280
    child care centers, time spent in,
        103-104
    child care observation, 101-102, 105,
        106
    early child care, 25, 26, 32-36, 99, 103,
        120-121, 123-125
    Early Head Start, 8, 270
    Head Start, 6, 8, 265, 270
    hours of work, 15, 24, 29-31, 36-40, 44,
        48, 49, 70, 83, 125
    household work, 23-24, 32, 33, 38, 39,
        40, 81, 193
    infant development and care time,
        120-121, 123-124

leave from work, 2, 9, 83-84, 230, 235-237, 276
leisure time, 31
maternal parenting, 93-94
maternal wage penalty, experience/ seniority, 31-32
non-parental child care, general, 1, 2, 3-4, 10, 45, 46, 48, 67, 99
parental child care, 32-36, 221
peers, time spent with, 128
process quality, 25, 26, 32-36, 99, 103, 120-121, 123-125
self-care, 126-128 (passim), 181-182
shift workers, 36, 37, 45, 48, 49, 52, 182
structured voluntary activities, 132-133
time diaries, 31, 32-36
welfare, benefit time limits, 199, 200, 203, 209, 210-211, 214
work schedules, 15, 24, 36-40, 41, 45, 56
Training, see Education and training, professional
Transportation costs, 15
adolescents, 189-190
costs, welfare-to-work, 14, 203
21st Century Community Learning Centers (CCLC), 7, 128-129, 131, 246, 273

U

Unskilled workers, 14-15, 38
Urban areas
after-school programs, 128, 129
Chicago Parent-Child Centers, 117
child care arrangements, general, 45, 49
Family and Relative Care Study, 101
National Child Care Staffing Study, 59, 60, 101, 108, 110
National Day Care Study, 101
self-care, 126
shift work, 38
Study of Early Child Care, 61, 83, 84, 90, 100, 106-108
welfare reform, impacts on children, 219, 224
U.S. Child Care Workforce and Caregiving Population, 55-56

V

Vacation and holidays, 230
see also Leave policies
Voluntary activities, see Structured voluntary activities
Vouchers, 7, 9, 248-249, 265, 268, 271-272

W

Wages and salaries
adolescent employment, future wages, 194
caregiver, 110, 144-145, 164
earned income tax credit (EITC), 12, 18, 73, 199, 202, 203, 206, 207-208, 212, 220, 239-240
health insurance, low-wage employment, 15
husband's earnings, wife's employment, 29
leave policies, 230, 232, 233, 235-237, 265-266
low-income, 14-15
maternal penalty, 31-32
minimum wage, 202
teachers, 110
temporary disability insurance (TDI), 231, 262, 273-275
unemployment insurance as pay substitute, 273, 274
welfare reform and, 203, 206-208, 211
wives as primary earners, 31-32, 40-41
Welfare
see also Aid to Families with Dependent Children; Early Head Start; Head Start; Poverty; Welfare reform
adolescent employment, 191
Child and Adult Care Food Program, 254
child care arrangements of recipients, 44, 48
early childhood education as program participation, 118
Head Start, 254
historical perspectives, 2, 5, 12, 14, 199-201
housing, 208, 220
Medicaid, 15, 75, 208

nutrition, food stamps, 45, 49, 75, 220
part-time employment, 206-207, 214
Summer Food Service Program, 254
Survey of Income and Program
Participation (SIPP), 42-54, 181-182
Title I preschool program, 245
Welfare reform, 9, 14, 38, 64, 65, 69, 70, 71, 95, 96-97, 199-226
see also Personal Responsibility and Work Opportunities Act; Temporary Assistance for Needy Families
academic achievement, 215, 220, 224, 225, 226
adolescents, 79-82, 219-220, 222, 223-226
attitudes toward, 221
block grants, 200, 250-254, 265, 272
Canada, work requirements, 214-215
caseloads, 200, 202, 203, 204-206, 209-211
child care centers, 223, 226
child care costs/benefits, 200, 203, 207, 221-226, 272
child care homes, 223
child well-being, 216-226
cognitive development of child, 216, 217, 219, 222, 279
disabled persons, 25, 118, 224
earned income tax credit (EITC), 12, 18, 73, 199, 202, 203, 206, 207-208, 212, 220, 239-240
econometrics, 209, 210, 216-217
economic factors, general, 209
economic cycles, 204, 208, 210, 212
incentives, 70, 77, 78, 97, 98, 203, 214-215
educational attainment, 76, 119, 203
exemptions, 200
family economics, 74, 75, 272
family functioning, 69, 70, 71, 74-82 (passim), 92-93, 95, 96-98, 217-219, 220, 221-222
Family Support Act, 199, 220
fertility, 200, 215-216, 219, 222
Head Start, 119
health status of affected, general, 224-225

historical perspectives, 2, 12, 199-201, 202, 204-207, 209-226 (passim)
hours-of-work requirements, 200, 214-215
immigrants, 200
income family, impact on, 203, 206-208, 211, 212-215, 220, 221
infants, 83, 205
job training, 116, 119-121, 220
leaver studies, 202, 206, 209, 211-212, 213, 216-217
maternal employment, general, 14, 38, 64, 65, 69, 199, 200, 203
maternal parenting, 76-80 (passim), 87
marital status, impact on, 200, 205, 212, 215-216, 218-219
National Evaluation of Welfare-to-Work Strategies, 74, 87, 222-223
parenting, adolescents, 79-82
part-time employment, 206-207, 214
research methodology, 201-202, 279-280
single mothers, 75, 199-200, 204-206, 210-212, 213, 215-216, 219
social development, 216, 279-280
state-level variations, 202-203
statistical analyses, 201-202, 207, 208-209, 210-213, 216-217
time limits for benefits, 199, 200, 203, 209, 210-211, 214, 215, 220, 221
transportation assistance, 203
urban areas, impacts on children, 219, 224
waiver programs, 74(n.2), 199, 200, 213-214
work incentives, financial, 200, 203, 207, 210, 214-215, 219, 220, 221, 225
work search requirements/benefits, 203, 209, 214-215, 218, 220, 221, 222
Who Cares for America's Children, 16, 99, 111
Widowed persons, 28, 29, 235
child care arrangements, 44, 48
child care expenditures, 51
Wisconsin Family and Work Project, 102
Women, *see* Gender factors; Maternal employment; Single mothers

Work and Family: Policies for a Changing Work Force, 16
Work schedules, 15, 24, 36-40, 41, 45, 56
  see also Leave policies
  child care arrangements, 44, 48, 49, 52, 53-54
  child care expenditures, 52
  flextime, 230
  leave policies, 2, 9, 83-84, 230, 235-237

nonstandard, 24, 36-40, 41, 56, 70, 88-89, 128, 182
shift work, 36, 37, 45, 48, 49, 52, 182

Y

Young children, *see also* Early childhood care/education; Preschool children
Younger Americans Act, 188
Youth, *see* Adolescents